Religions of Asia

THIRD EDITION

John Y. Fenton
EMORY UNIVERSITY

Norvin Hein
YALE UNIVERSITY

Frank E. Reynolds
UNIVERSITY OF CHICAGO

Alan L. Miller
MIAMI UNIVERSITY

Niels C. Nielsen, Jr.
RICE UNIVERSITY

Grace G. Burford
SHEPHERD COLLEGE

Robert K. C. Forman
GENERAL EDITOR
HUNTER COLLEGE, CUNY

RELIGIONS OF ASIA

THIRD EDITION

ST. MARTIN'S PRESS, NEW YORK

Senior editor: Don Reisman
Manager, publishing services: Emily Berleth
Production supervisor: Alan Fischer
Text design: Gene Crofts
Maps: Jeane E. Norton
Photo research: Gene Crofts
Cover design: Ed Butler/Butler Udell
Cover photo: Elisa Daggs

Library of Congress Catalog Card Number: 92-50026

Manufactured in the United States of America.

7 6 5
f e d c

For information write:
St. Martin's Press, Inc.
175 Fifth Avenue
New York, NY 10010

ISBN: 0-312-05753-9

PART OPENER PHOTOS

Pages 80–81—*background photo and panel photo:* Reuters/Bettmann
Pages 162–163—*background photo and panel photo:* Shashinka Photo
Pages 220–221—*background and panel photo:* Bruno J. Zehnder

ACKNOWLEDGMENTS

Excerpt reprinted with the permission of Macmillan Publishing Company and Macmillan Publishers, Ltd. from *Gitanjali* by Rabindranath Tagore. Copyright (New York: Collier Books/ Macmillan, 1971).

From Peter Koroche, *Once the Buddha Was a Monkey* (Chicago: University of Chicago Press, 1989). Reprinted by permission of the University of Chicago Press.

Preface

The study of Asian religions is a subject of enormous scope and depth, covering the full range of history and reaching from the most mundane aspects of people's lives to their most sublime thoughts and aspirations. This volume, which is substantially revised from the previous edition, describes in clear terms the principal doctrines, issues, and motifs of each religion and shows how the traditions have responded to their social, cultural, and geographic contexts.

We have been very pleased with the reception students and faculty gave to the first two editions of *Religions of Asia.* This third edition retains the authoritative scholarship of its predecessors. In addition, the text has been significantly improved in response to readers' criticisms and to changes in the field. While retaining strong coverage of history and doctrine, this edition contains additional material on significant teachings, rituals, and the lives of believers. Though attention is still given to primary theological doctrines, this is now balanced with more discussions of the effects of beliefs, myths, and rituals on believers' attitudes and daily lives.

As a result, the book has a broader perspective on religious belief and practice. We believe that even though the stories and concerns of the few—the emperors and other rulers—have played an important role in the development of the traditions, far more important for the history of religions have been the broad cultural changes affecting adherents' lives—events such as foreign conquests, large-scale emigration from rural to urban settings, or the spread of literacy. This new edition highlights such broad changes and shows how religions have responded to them. Without being reductionistic, we now give more attention to the underlying *social, economic,* and *political* context of the believers and to the ways in which their traditions have adapted. Also, with the introduction of more material on social history as it relates to religion, each chapter now offers more information on the role of women and the conception of gender roles within each tradition.

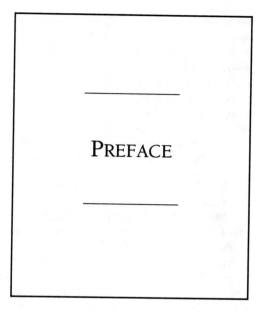

We believe that the study of religion is an inherently fascinating endeavor. However, to make the content of this new edition more accessible, the presentation has been streamlined. The writing has been given greater unity in style and approach; we hope it is accessible to a wider array of today's college students. We have included more useful maps and time lines. New maps now highlight both cross-cultural developments, such as trade routes and migration routes, and internal links, such as the relationship between sociopolitical factors and religion. More complete time lines show both specific developments and long eras and transformations. A new feature, the comparative box, compares and contrasts features of different religions. These boxes should encourage students to note similarities and differences among traditions in even broader ways. New pictures are more clearly related to the book's content. Pronunciation guides have been provided. We have added a glossary at the back of the book; each glossary term is boldfaced at its first appearance in the text.

Other changes, we believe, make the experience of teaching and studying from this book even more appealing and more valuable.

A new **introductory chapter** focuses on the relationship between the needs a religion articulates and the means whereby religion addresses those needs.

Part One presents five chapters on Hinduism, from its origins to the modern period and its role in the developing nationalism. One theme of this part is that Hinduism addresses its believers' changing needs and anxieties. Chapter 6 now places Jainism and Sikhism more logically, adjacent to other Indian religions, and offers a more balanced picture of these traditions.

Part Two, on Buddhism, focuses on the rise and character of early Buddhist doctrine and then shows how Buddhism spread to become a world religion. Its chapters are organized around three concerns that inform the tradition—the varying understandings of the Buddha, the Dharma (teaching), and the Saṅgha (community)—and shows how they changed to reflect historical and cultural circumstances.

Part Three focuses on the religions of China and Japan, showing how the traditions of Confucianism, Daoism, and Chinese Buddhism all respond differently in different contexts to common underlying issues of harmony and balance. Chapter 13 shows how the fundamental nature of Shintō becomes the guiding theme of Japanese religion.

Throughout the text, complex and unfamiliar traditions have been made easier for students to grasp. Though the book remains rich in history, we have tried to ensure that important themes are not lost in a sea of detail. Because much can be learned about religions from their manifestations in everyday life and from the works of art they have inspired, this edition, like its predecessors, offers an abundance of photographs and illustrations. Boxes set off descriptions of special rites and ceremonies, excerpts from primary source materials, and the comparisons mentioned earlier. Annotated bibliographies, updated to reflect the latest scholarship, appear at the end of the volume. These suggest both primary and secondary sources for students who wish to do additional research.

An expanded **Instructor's Manual** is available containing test questions, chapter outlines, lists of learning objectives, and suggestions for primary-source readings, films, and videos that can be used in the classroom. For more information, write St. Martin's Press, Inc., College Desk, 175 Fifth Avenue, New York, NY 10010; or contact your local St. Martin's sales representative.

Many people contributed to this third edition of *Religions of Asia*. Robert K. C. Forman was the new general editor of the book. John Y. Fenton wrote the introductory chapter. The chapters on Hinduism were written by Norvin Hein. Niels C. Nielsen, Jr., was responsible for the material on Jainism and Sikhism. Frank E. Reynolds was the principal author of the chapters on Buddhism. Alan L. Miller provided the chapters on the religions of China and Japan in Part Three. Grace G. Burford provided material on women and religion.

We are deeply indebted to reviewers and users of the second edition, whose criticism, suggestions, and encouragements were indispensable. They include Paul J. Griffiths, University of Chicago; Thomas M. Johnson, Riverside Community College; Walter O. Kaelber, Wagner College; Robert D. Maldonado, California State University—Fresno; R. Blake Michael, Ohio Wesleyan University; Lynda Sexson, Montana State University; Herman Tull, Princeton University; James Waltz, Eastern Michigan University; and Kenneth Zysk, New York University. Scott Lowe of the University of North Dakota reviewed the transliterations of Chinese terms.

Finally, we wish to thank the people at St. Martin's Press. We are especially grateful to Don Reisman, Frances Jones, Bruce Emmer, Richard Steins, Emily Berleth, and Gene Crofts.

Contents

CHAPTER 5

MODERN HINDUISM 81

CHAPTER 6

JAINISM AND SIKHISM 89

PART TWO

BUDDHISM

CHAPTER 7

THE RISE OF BUDDHISM 103

CHAPTER 8

THE DEVELOPMENT OF BUDDHISM IN INDIA 115

CHAPTER 9

BUDDHISM AS A WORLD RELIGION 132

PART THREE

RELIGIONS OF CHINA AND JAPAN

CHAPTER 10

ROOTS OF RELIGION IN CHINA 161

CHAPTER 11

THREE VISIONS OF HARMONY: CONFUCIAN, DAOIST, BUDDHIST 176

CHAPTER 12

NEO-CONFUCIANISM: FROM THE CLASSICAL ERA TO MODERN TIMES 184

MAPS AND TIME LINES

RELIGIONS OF ASIA

THIRD EDITION

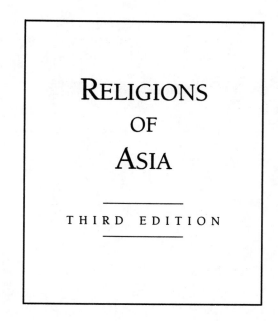

Introduction

Religion and Religions of Asia

Understanding Religion in the Context of Pluralism

With modern news coverage, international business contacts, and immigration to the United States from many parts of the world, the world's religious traditions have become part of our daily experience. As these cross-cultural contacts have multiplied, the need to understand religions other than our own has also increased.

How can we understand these other traditions? It is not helpful to project from one's own religion to others or to adopt vague simplicities about what religion is or is not. When, for example, someone from another religion insists that my scriptures are corrupted but his or her scriptures are the pure Word of God, it becomes very difficult to carry on any meaningful dialogue. Yet it is equally difficult to carry on dialogue with a person who insists that all religions are the same or that my tradition is just like every other.

What kinds of categories, then, should we use to understand other peoples' religions? During the past two centuries, Europeans and Americans developed categories for understanding other peoples' religions that have—probably unconsciously—served colonialist and racist interests. They suggested that other traditions are primitive, pagan, natural, or premonotheistic. Such categories tended either to provide justification for colonial expansion or to idealize the other as romantic or exotic. But both are misleading. Not only were they demeaning to non-Western cultures, but such categories have also led to profoundly inaccurate pictures of them.

Some scholars have suggested that we sidestep the problem of developing a general characterization of religion by focusing solely on the meaning each religion has for its adherents. This is the so-called insider's meaning of a religion, a description of that tradition by its adherents using indigenous language and categories. Focusing on the insider's view does have the advantage of stopping someone from one culture from projecting that culture's categories onto someone else's religious life. The interpretive concepts would at least be indigenous, not foreign.

However, when we use only this approach, other problems arise. First, there is no unequivocal meaning for *religion,* even within a single religious tradition. Second, if people from different religions use the word *religion* in incompatible ways, interreligious communication breaks down. Finally, if we used only insider approaches, how could we begin to make cross-cultural comparisons?

The insider's point of view should be complemented, then, with cross-cultural approaches. Indeed, the two should correct each other. Many investigators have used cross-cultural interpretive categories from a variety of scholarly disciplines. The insider's view narrows the investigation to fit a particular context, whereas cross-cultural categories broaden the base of the interpretation. Historians of religion, who study religions cross-culturally, use categories like "sacred," "deity," "ritual," "myth," "priest," and "symbol" as organizing principles to describe phenomena that are similar in many religions. Using such cross-cultural categories enables investigators to generalize about the significance of a local study and to use what they discover about one religious tradition to clarify another. Our understanding of religion must be formulated so that its cross-cultural description and its insider's meaning will be complementary. Even persons interested only in their own religious tradition can understand it better when they compare it to other religious traditions. Taken together, we believe, these two perspectives can best illuminate the phenomenon of religion.

We need a cross-cultural definition of *religion,* then, for at least three reasons: we need to use the word unequivocally so that we can apply it to the full array of religious traditions without imposing value judgments; it will allow us to carry out valid cross-cultural comparisons and thus identify underlying common structures; and it will help us to compare the traditions side by side, allowing us to see the uniqueness of each religious tradition more clearly.

Developing a Cross-Cultural Model of Religion: Religious Needs and Satisfactions

There is a relationship between the kinds of needs an endeavor addresses and the ways it satisfies those needs. Medicine, for example, is concerned with a type of need, disease, and addresses it with medical treatment. Psychology grapples with emotional needs and, in many cases, psychotherapeutic solutions. A need like hunger is satisfied with food. Religion, too, involves needs and satisfactions: religions are concerned with basic human needs and the satisfaction of those needs.

What are those needs and their solutions, and what is the relationship between them? There are no simple answers. Each religious tradition, responding to different human situations, articulates life's needs and its solutions differently. Furthermore, the relationship between needs and their satisfaction is different from tradition to tradition. We can say, however, that there is a polar relationship between the need and its satisfaction. They are binary opposites. Just as hot and cold, inside and outside, wet and dry, *define each other* (*dry* is defined as "not wet"), religious needs and their satisfaction also give each other meaning: religious safety is the answer to religious danger, religious pollution is answered by religious purification.

No sharp lines delineate religious needs and solutions from other kinds of problems and solutions. There are no uniquely religious emotions, for example, and religious rituals, forms of social organization, and concepts are not sharply different from nonreligious ones. But unlike the nonreligious, religious people seek satisfaction of their needs in ways that are in some sense extrahuman. Such people feel that our human life is not entirely self-sufficient and that we can reach our fullest development only when we find a proper relationship with some wider and deeper context than ordinary human life offers.

Only that wider context, such people feel, can give human life its fullest significance. People in some religious traditions, for example, regard newborn children as incomplete until their biological nature takes on a transhuman or "sacred" dimension. Through acts such as the giving of the sacred cotton threads *(upanāyana)* to male Hindu youths as a symbolic second birth *(dvija)* or the recitation of sacred words such as "There is no God but God, and Muḥammad is the Messenger of God" in Islam, religious people induct infants into that wider context. This indication also gives them an identity, an acknowledged place in society, and a sanctioned status in a religious community. Seeking satisfaction of human needs from these transhuman dimensions is peculiar to religion, and the relationship to these realities—often called "sacred realities" by scholars—is the unique element that sets religions apart from other relationships.

From the religious viewpoint, the development from child to adult is not merely a natural process of physical maturation but also a symbolic change that relates children positively to the sacred reality. This process transforms children into persons with a new significance and value whom their community recog-

These photos illustrate some of the diversity of religious expression that requires a cross-cultural approach to the study of religion. A Sikh pilgrim (above left) bathes in the Holy Lake surrounding the Golden Temple at Amritsar, India. A Japanese woman (above right) prays after placing a red slip of paper with a petition to the deities on a statue on the Tokaku-ji temple grounds near Tokyo. Jain pilgrims pray on Chandragiri Hill in Śravanabeḷgolā during a religious festival. (Raghu Rai/Magnum; Religious News Service; Alex Webb/Magnum)

nizes and accepts as adults. The transition is a symbolic rebirth that changes the children's social status, patterned after a sacred model of male or female adulthood. Now properly related to this symbolic order, the person is considered to be bound up with the transhuman reality.

The ancient Romans used the Latin word *religio* to refer to the binding quality of the relationship between human beings and the gods. In Roman culture, this relationship usually implied that the humans should perform the gods' rituals dependably. (The popular expression "doing something religiously" derives from this usage.) When the deities accepted gifts, the worshipers in turn expected the deities to return favors such as protection, sanction of the social order, economic or health benefits, or favorable weather. Thus Roman religion, like all religions, bound together needs and their sacred satisfactions.

In sum, religion offers sacred satisfaction of fundamental human needs.

The Structure of Religion

We will describe the cross-cultural structure of religion in a threefold way, exploring each of the following components in turn:

1 Relationships between human beings and sacred realities
2 Processes of transformation
3 Cultural traditions that incorporate systems of symbols

RELATIONSHIPS BETWEEN HUMAN BEINGS AND SACRED REALITIES

Describing Sacred Realities

Describing each religious tradition's views of sacred reality is a major concern of each section of this book. These views spread across a spectrum from an understanding that the sacred is plural (polytheism) to a belief that there is only one sacred reality (monotheism or monism). Some traditions hold that sacred reality cannot be numbered at all (nondualism). Some Native Americans, traditional Africans, and Australian Aborigines, for example, also hold that sacred reality is sometimes best apprehended as personal beings and at other times as nonpersonal forces. Some Hindus understand the many sacred realities or deities to be facets of the one great God or impersonal, eternal Being; other Hindus are monotheists, believing in one God; and still others maintain that personal gods are just preliminary symbols for a nondual, all-encompassing, infinite Being.

Most Christians believe that the one God is triune—that the same God is Father, Son, and Holy Spirit. Jews and Muslims stress the unity of God, excluding any possibility of plurality. Chinese Daoists relate religiously to the Dao (Tao), or Way, which they regard as the source of things while not being separate from things.

We need to find a common denominator among this diversity. Clearly, we cannot assume that the way one tradition uses a concept like "god" or "ultimate reality" will automatically be equivalent to (or better than) the way another tradition uses it. We will use the term *sacred reality* to label this cross-culturally occurring common denominator.

Some observers have identified the religious source as transcendence or the Transcendent. This term implies a real being or power that resides in another world beyond the limits of the natural world. But if we use it, we must recognize that religious people also want to be related to the immanent realities in this world and to find significance for human life here and now. Furthermore, though not wrong, the idea that something is beyond nature is a parochial notion that relies on Western ideas of nature and deity. People of other traditions may understand nature and what lies beyond it very differently.

We will also sometimes use the term *ultimate* for this common denominator. Some scholars have applied this to a metaphysical reality or transcendent being beyond the world. But we will intend by this term the point beyond which nothing can go, the last in a series. Or, seen from that end, *ultimate* can mean the first, fundamental, or primordial, the entity that is the basis for all things and for itself as well.

How does the sacred ultimate satisfy religious needs? In medieval Christian scholastic thought, the monotheistic (single) God was said to be *esse, verum,* and *bonum* (being, truth, and goodness). In Hindu Vedāntic thought, sacred ultimacy was *sat, cit,* and

Ānanda (being, consciousness, and bliss). In both traditions, the sacred was seen as the single foundation of all other truth, reality, and goodness.

In polytheistic traditions, sacred ultimacy may be seen as many gods and goddesses, each of which has only a local and limited form. It may be difficult for people reared in Western traditions to grasp the possibility of many ultimates, each of which is limited. Indeed, a limited ultimate may even sound contradictory. But although the idea that the sacred ultimate is universal is common to many traditions, it is only one variation. The sacred ultimate may be seen as universal in some religions but not in others.

Similarly, the sacred realities to which people turn are not always the most important thing in the world for them. For example, an individual might petition a deity for success in a risky business venture, which would in effect be a request for assistance. When he finishes the venture, the business and the petition might be of no further concern. In another example, some Hindus worship deities in hope of relief in times of affliction yet may ignore them when no one is ill.

Religious people often react to sacred realms with awe, fear, homage, and submission. Sacred realities are not under human control, and religious needs may or may not be satisfied. Sacred power can bring punishment and destruction. People typically treat sacred power with meticulous care, and they sometimes surround sacred objects with detailed rules of required or forbidden behavior (taboo).*

Yet these generalities are not universal. Divine beings sometimes have no close relationship with a religion's primary concerns. For example, the gods and goddesses of Theravāda Buddhism have little to do with a person's ultimate fate; in fact, Buddhists believe that these deities are themselves in need of salvation. Nonetheless, they may legitimize a believer's possession of a piece of land, control the weather, or help to heal a disease. Conversely, Theravādan Buddhists teach that the goal of religious striving is not godlike but impersonal. Further, the gods cannot aid humans; only one's own efforts on the prescribed Buddhist path can lead to ultimate liberation.

When individuals give voice to their religious needs, they generally do so in the context of their preexisting religious tradition, which defines for them both the character of the sacred reality and the kinds of prior relationships humans have had with that reality.

Individuals generally strive to meet their religious needs within the context of their religious tradition, which defines for them the character of the sacred reality and the kind of relationship humans might have with that reality. Here we see an elderly Hindu man who has left his home and family behind to become a sannyāsī and end his days as a spiritual seeker, living a wandering life with few possessions. (Kit Kittle)

**Taboo* or *tabu,* a Melanesian word, refers to the ritual prohibitions that many religious traditions prescribe for occasions when humans come into close contact with sacred powers. Respecting the taboo is believed both to safeguard sacred objects from pollution and to protect people from the sometimes dangerous sacred power.

Myths or sacred stories typically recount how humans and the sacred realities became involved with each other. They often depict an ideal relationship, account for the breakdown of that relationship, and provide ways to restore it. Such myths also provide individuals with models to emulate so that they may form interlocking relationships with sacred realities and with the rest of the world.

Creation stories have a common cross-cultural function: to exhibit the basic structure of the cosmos by giving an account of how the world came to be as it is. In many Hindu creation stories, for example, humans are separated neither from their world nor from the One Reality. They share the being of the One as fragments or parts. The world they inhabit relates to its source as part to whole, outside to inside. In this way, the myths depict the relationship of the individual to the source that may satisfy their needs.

Although our term *sacred reality* conveys a more general notion than a term like *god* in a particular religious tradition, specific religions are not mere accidental variations of a common religious core. Rather, the idea of a sacred reality is something like the fundamental human capacity to speak language that we had as infants, before we learned any particular language. That is, the capacity to speak a language and the basic structure of language appear to be innate and panhuman. This common linguistic structure accounts for the similarities among human languages and our ability to learn the languages of other cultures. Yet the existence of a deep structure does not make one language necessarily similar to any other. Some, like Spanish and Italian, are quite similar; others, like Chinese and German, are quite different. Analogously, Judaism and Islam are relatively similar, whereas Shintō and Christianity are sharply different.

We must emphasize that sacred reality cannot be defined, either by scholars of religion or by religious people themselves; it is mysterious, beyond definition. But religious people do characterize both the sacred realm and the human relationship to that realm. They do so through oral and written utterances, actions, institutional structures, and symbols. The task of religious scholars is to describe and interpret sacred-human relationships in the context of the various religious traditions. As religious scholars and students, we do not have to unravel the mystery of sacred realms. Our task is to describe and interpret how religious people describe their relationship to that mystery.

Sacredness belongs to realms that remain "other," even as they penetrate the human realm. Sacred realities conceal what they reveal, but they reveal enough to tantalize. Religious language referring to the sacred realities conveys more than can be said, and people often use negative language to prevent comparing sacred reality to anything else.

This tension between the mysterious sacred and its overt characterization often makes it extremely difficult to interpret a religious tradition. The opening lines of the Daoist classic Dao De Jing (Tao-te Ching; "The Way and Its Power") articulate this tension: "The Tao [Dao, or Way] that can be told of is not the eternal Tao. . . . Nameless, it is the origin of Heaven and earth; Nameable, it is the mother of all things. . . . That they are the same is the mystery."[1] Sacred reality in itself (the Dao itself) cannot be described directly; what can be described is merely how sacred reality appears to us. That the unnameable is also nameable or that the transcendent reality becomes the origin of all things is the mystery intrinsic to sacred reality.

Most Buddhists deny all eternal realities and consider belief in them to be a prime cause of human suffering. Yet there is, for the Buddhist, something about ordinary experience that can truly satisfy religious needs. To find it, we must become transformed so that we no longer live asleep, unaware, or defensive. Sacred reality is before us in an ordinary way, but we, in our ignorance, cannot see it.

Thus religious language points beyond itself. Religious language reveals a sacred reality that remains a mystery even as it reveals itself. Thus the sacred realm is the source of our definition, but it cannot itself be defined. This is the central impasse, a source of creative tension, for interpreters of any religious tradition, be they insiders or outsiders.

In ordinary English we sometimes refer to books, buildings, or images as "sacred." Such usage is appropriate, but it employs the term *sacred* in a secondary sense as something associated with sacred realities. No one worships a book, a building, or an image. Religious people regard a sacred text, for example, as sacred not because they expect the book to satisfy religious needs but because it puts a sacred reality within reach. Sikhs regard their sacred text, the Guru Granth Sāhib, for example, as the "gateway" to God because its study and recitation lead to God (see Chapter 8). Similarly, Eastern Orthodox Christians and Roman Catholics may use a wooden icon for worship, but it is not the block of wood that matters to them but the God it reveals.

The Relationship between Religious Need and Religious Satisfaction

Each tradition articulates in its own way the relationship between the basic religious need and its satisfaction. For example, Christians regard the fundamental human problem as sin. Correspondingly, they deem the solution as salvation overcoming sin. This pair of opposites is uniquely Christian: sin presupposes a broken relationship with God; its solution comes through salvation in Jesus Christ. This expresses a specifically Christian assessment of what the world is all about. Neither sin nor its solution means the same thing in other religions such as Judaism. Nor does the Christian's "salvation from sin" translate naturally into the Buddhist's "enlightenment that overcomes ignorance." Buddhists see the fundamental problem as ignorance, not sin; its solution is rooting out that ignorance, not faith in a deity. Both the rendering of the need and its solution, as well as the relationship between the two, are very different in the two systems.

Similarly, religions often talk of pollution and purification. Again, these opposites define each other. Yet what constitutes pollution varies from one culture to another. In Hinduism and Shintō, the prime sources of pollution are bodily secretions and human and animal corpses. They are the result of inevitable physiological processes such as urination, sexual intercourse, and death. This sort of pollution is washed away by such efforts as cleansing, ritual purification, and fasting. Again, the needs and their solutions are related like mirror images.

Individuals pick up their understanding of their fundamental need from their religious culture. For example, one will *acquire* the idea that one is fundamentally sinful and hence needs salvation from sin from the Christian tradition. That is why, for example, Christian evangelists spend much of their initial efforts on what they call the "conviction of sin," getting individuals to adopt this notion as a true account of what their need really is. Similarly, Buddhist missionaries must convince people that the problem is ignorance. When one sees the problem in these terms, one may come to see the need as, respectively, salvation from sin or enlightenment from ignorance.

Just as the articulation of the fundamental need differs among religious traditions, so does its answer, religious satisfaction. In one part of the Hindu tradition, liberation involves merging one's individuality into the featureless ocean of the nondual reality called Brahman—the True Self of the self. In the Buddhist tradition, by contrast, there is no self and hence no ultimate reality like Brahman. Because, they believe, craving for eternal realities can cause suffering, Buddhists teach that liberation will occur only when such craving ceases. While the goals of these two traditions are similar, they are also profoundly different—and that difference relates to their accounts of the human problem.

All traditions affirm that they received satisfaction in the past and expect that it can again be gained. Even so, religious people cannot be certain that following their procedures will necessarily provide the solution they seek. Sacred realities are not within human control. Requests may be denied, forgiveness withheld.

How the gap between human need and sacred power can be bridged is the central problem of any religious tradition. But every religion tries to satisfy human needs as it understands them.

PROCESSES OF TRANSFORMATION

Religions satisfy fundamental human needs through a process of transformation. This process can generally be divided into four stages:

1 Diagnosis of disorder
2 Symbolic distancing
3 Liminality
4 Restoration or rebirth

Diagnosis of disorder People must first see themselves as having a religious need. They may remind themselves through ritual; for example, an Episcopal Christian service begins, "O Lord, we confess to you and to one another . . . that we have sinned." People may express this need regularly, following a yearly or monthly liturgical calendar, or irregularly, in crisis situations only. Some attempt to worship constantly, others infrequently. The diagnosis of disorder may make reference to the sacred realities; it may also mention the perceived loss of sacred sanction.

Symbolic distancing The next step is to distance oneself from one's normal status. Dramatically breaking off one's normal relationships expresses the fact that one has a religious need—"I must leave the old way." It announces that one cannot satisfy one's religious needs by oneself.

People distance themselves from normal life in many ways: withdrawing from usual forms of social intercourse, fasting, giving away their possessions. Even the entire community can be symbolically separated from its normal condition: borders may be closed, people may be told to maintain vigils, holidays may be decreed, and usual behavioral patterns may be reversed. At such times, the primary sacred symbols of the society may be concealed; for example, some Christian denominations cover the cross with dark cloths during the last two weeks of Lent as a sign of mourning for Christ's suffering. Symbolic distancing eases the transition into the next phase.

Liminality In the liminal phase (the term comes from the Latin *limen,* meaning "threshold" or "boundary"), symbolic distancing intensifies to the greatest degree possible. One is separated not only from normal cultural categories but also from all possible cultural categories. Symbolically, the whole world disappears; one has gone as far as one can go. One has arrived, so to speak, at (or beyond) the brink of the abyss. The liminal state is without structure.

The nature of liminality varies from one tradition to another. Frequently it is marked by death symbols or regression to a helpless condition. This helplessness seems fraught with danger. Demons may appear and destroy one's most secret forms of self-reliance.

Monastics, such as these Chinese Buddhist nuns (above) and monks (left), live in a liminal state by separating themselves from their former social roles and personal identities. (Boris Erwitt; Eastfoto)

In one of many Christian examples, the liminal phase corresponds to the mourning period between Jesus's death on Good Friday and his resurrection two days later on Easter. Several mystical traditions describe this in-between state as a vacant darkness, a timeless experience of pure consciousness without content. Liminality is thus a state of both "no longer" and "not yet."

Restoration or rebirth At the end of this transformative process, one emerges symbolically new, reborn. One has gained sacred satisfaction, however it is understood. One now has sanction, power, and new significance. Ritually we often see actions symbolizing rebirth, release from bondage, or transfiguration. People who were secluded in the forest or a cave during the liminal phase come forth to a new life or status in society. They may receive new names or new clothes. They may see themselves differently. Others may act differently toward them, ratifying their new status, for example, as peers. Feasting often puts the seal on the transformation.

Certain people may participate in transformation ritually, and the entire community may play a role. Some people—mystics, for example—may have intense encounters with the sacred introspectively, with no ritual markers; the transformation is initially experienced as a private affair.

Puberty Rites: The Hindu Sacred Thread Ceremony

The Hindu *upanāyana* (investiture with the sacred thread) ritually transforms primarily brāhman (upper-class) boys into young men (Chapter 2). Brāhman boys may be initiated between 8 and 16 years of age, but nowadays the ceremony is sometimes performed just before marriage.

Just before the sacred thread ritual begins, the boy takes his last meal from his mother as a child. Shaving the boy's head and giving him a bath traditionally mark symbolic distancing from childhood. Special clothes (girdle, deerskin, staff, and the sacred thread) then demarcate the liminal state. The teacher's taking the boy's "heart" into his own as symbolic father and mother ushers in a rebirth to student status. The transition from one life stage to the other is a symbolic gestation process in which the teacher becomes "pregnant" with the boy and by virtue of sacred sounds *(mantra)* gives him a second birth *(dvija)*.

The Eightfold Path as Transformation

The four stages in processes of symbolic transformation are clear in most rites of passage. The Buddhist transformative path from suffering to peace—the so-called Noble Eightfold Path—also manifests these four stages.

The Eightfold Path is a process of undoing and discarding false understanding, unrealistic behavior, and unaware and unwholesome attitudes. The movement away from ordinary understanding, behavior, and ignorance eventually results in a complete divorce from the old way of living. Yet it does not translate immediately into a new birth of enlightenment. The in-between period of the Buddhist seeker may last for a very long time, even many lifetimes. Yet if one successfully traverses the path, total nonreliance on all the old defense mechanisms brings about a fundamentally new way of life.

Calendar Rituals

Rituals observed on regular fixed days of the yearly calendar celebrate birthdays of religious founders, set off special days of recognition or remembrance for gods or goddesses or holy men and women, inaugurate the new year, mark seasonal changes, or celebrate central events in the religious history of a community such as the Exodus of the ancient Hebrews from bondage in Egypt or the enlightenment of the Buddha. People also engage in personal and communal worship, prayer, and meditation at regular intervals, ranging from several times each day to once weekly. The calendar fixes the time for these rituals (diagnosis). Preparation for the rituals regularly involves suspension of normal business and withdrawal into the special time of commemoration of past events as present experience, the offering of material and spiritual gifts (symbolic distancing), the end of the old period (liminal point), and the new birth of the new (restoration).

Jains celebrate the birth of Mahāvira, the sixth-century B.C.E. founder of their tradition, with a ritual bathing of his image in late summer or early fall. This in part reenacts major events in Mahāvira's development into a Jina, or conqueror of life's problems. Part of the emperor's role in the traditional Chinese Confucian ritual was his conduct of the sacrifice on the Altar of Heaven at the change of seasons.

Part of the emperor's role in the traditional Chinese Confucian ritual was his conduct of the sacrifice on the Altar of Heaven (seen at left) at the change of seasons. (Eastfoto)

Sacred Places

Dedication rites transform ordinary places into holy sites. The dedication of a temple puts that territory in a liminal position between ordinary human culture and sacred realms for a considerable period. To enter a sacred place means to leave the world behind and to enter a border area from which concourse with the sacred reality becomes easier. A sacred place is on the edge, in the "twilight zone" between ordinary experience and the sacred realities. Frequent worship in such a place renews its power of access.

Many Hindus believe that the formless God condescends to take on form for the benefit of devotees. God, who is everywhere, appears in particular places and particular forms, being physically present in images and in the houses of God, the temples. In traditional temple architecture, over the site of the divine image, a tower—symbolizing the infinity of Brahman, or ultimate reality—thrusts toward the sky. Beneath the tower is a small rectangular room that is both the seat of the divine image and the womb or egg from which the world was created. This room symbolizes the presence of Brahman in each living being. Thus the worshiper who contains God within comes to worship God in a temple, despite the fact that God is everywhere. The temple thus separates in space what is eternally together so that the worshiper can there bring it together again.

Similarly, although Muslims believe that God is everywhere and closer to us than we are to ourselves, Muslims congregate in special places (mosques or *masjids*) for prayer. Mosques are set aside permanently for worship; they cannot be used for other purposes. Yet permanent places of worship are not themselves sacred. Instead they are separate from the ordinary world so that worshipers can contact sacred realities more easily.

Religious Specialists

Just as a religious site may come permanently to occupy a place between the human and sacred realms, so may some mediating religious roles also become permanent. Initiation rites transform religious mediators to a liminal status, expressed in a distinctive life style. The Buddhist professional monk *(bhikku)* or nun *(bhikkuni)* has a formalized role withdrawn from normal life, even if not yet totally released from human suffering. Buddhist monks and nuns do not marry, nor do they belong to ordinary social groups or possess property. They remain apart from society. They do have restricted, role-determined relationships with lay Buddhists who support them, and their careers serve as inspiration for lay people. The saffron, red, or black robes and shaved heads of monks clearly proclaim that they have a special role on the boundary between those who are enmeshed in social cares and the ideal goal of *nirvāṇa* (liberation). But theirs is not an ordinary social role like tailor or parent.

Priests may temporarily observe similar restrictions in preparation for their roles as mediators between the human and the sacred. To purify themselves in preparation for offering worship to the deities, Japanese Shintō priests take special cleansing precautions and observe temporary restrictions.

Prophets and shamans (religious healers) often do not undergo formal installation rituals, but accounts of their being called to a spiritual role contain initiation stories that often exhibit the four-phase structure of symbolic transformation. However, since the gift of prophets and shamans is personal rather than institutional, they may eventually lose their power of mediation.

Some religious people, the men and women mystics of many traditions, hope to merge with the ultimate reality continuously. To do so, they remove their psychic attachments to the things and honors of the world to such an extent that they care only about the ultimate reality. They may move into a liminal state by separating themselves from the world temporarily in meditation or into a more permanent liminal state by separating themselves from their earlier identity. They then dwell in an unstructured, will-less state while waiting for a final merging with the ultimate. Some reenter the world as a new, utterly selfless agent, working for the betterment of others.

Followers interpret the founders of some Asian religions—the Buddha (Buddhism), Mahāvira (Jainism), or Nanak (Sikhism)—as intermediaries between the human and the sacred. Whereas according to Theravāda Buddhism, the Buddha based his authority on what he discovered in his mystical experience, the Mahāyāna branch of Buddhism usually views the Buddha much as many Hindus see Kṛishṇa, as an immediate godlike manifestation of sacred reality. The guru, or teacher, in Hindu tradition is a mediator who serves as a channel of liberating truth or of contact with sacred realities. Sikhs believe that their first guru, Nanak, and the nine gurus succeeding him were revealers of the Truth in ways that are parallel to that of many Hindu gurus. In the Sikh tradition, the succession of living human teachers ended with the tenth guru. The Truth they revealed is recorded in a text called the Guru Granth Sāhib.

Life after Death

Probably all religious traditions carry out funeral ceremonies, both to transform the deceased into their new status beyond life and to revitalize their survivors. In many cultures, such as those of traditional Africa, people's interest in after-death existence does not extend beyond the interaction of ancestors with the living survivors. Sometimes ancestors provide aid, but more often they bring misfortune if their living descendants do not ritually attend to them properly.

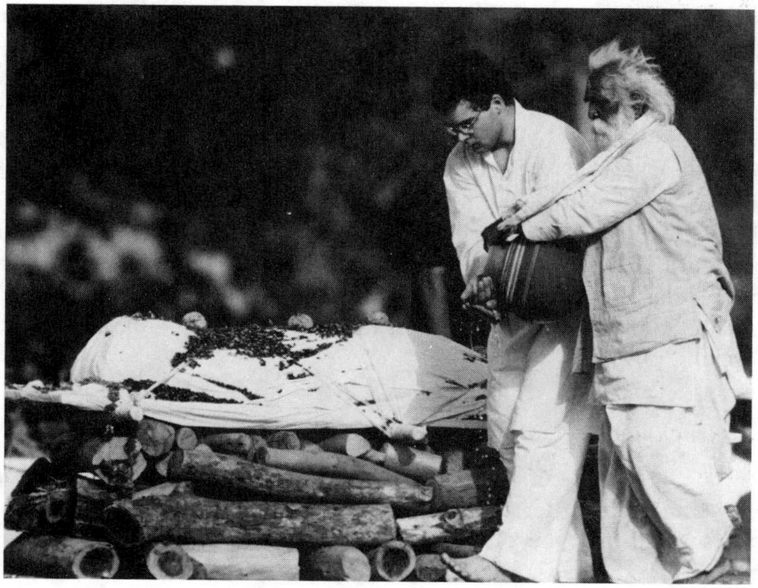

Religious traditions' attitudes toward death and their funeral ceremonies take many forms. An example is the Hindu custom of sprinkling water over the body before cremation. (Reuters/Bettmann)

The belief in some form of life after death is widespread. Some people believe that the individual's spirit is reborn. In some traditions (such as certain ones in Africa), the spirits of the dead become part of the life force of their descendants; in other traditions (for example, Hinduism and Buddhism), the dead may be reborn into any form of life, human or nonhuman.

Many Buddhists and Hindus share the conception of six realms (lokas) or spheres in which living spirits may be reborn. Besides the realms of human beings and animals, there are the realm of deities or devas, the realm of titans or ogres who continually fight with each other, the realm of the hungry ghosts, and the realm of various hells or "purgatories" that burn up the results of evil actions during life. Life in any of these locations, like life in the human realm, is always temporary. Without the insight that leads to release, even the life of a deity is really a form of suffering. But a fully enlightened person will no longer face rebirth.

In some religious traditions, such as Christianity, Islam, and the Hindu Śrivaishṇava tradition, people believe in a permanent heaven that offers eternal life. Passage to this realm often depends on the quality of the life the persons lived on earth. Temporary purgatories or eternal hells sometimes complement eternal heavens. Many Buddhists and Hindus seek not heaven but permanent liberation from the cyclical round of birth, death, and rebirth.

Life beyond death is not always merely an individual matter. The Western religions—Judaism, Zoroastrianism, Christianity, and Islam—teach that all creation will be fulfilled in a final, permanent transformation at the end of time. The transhistorical purpose of history will be materialized with the inauguration of a new heaven and a new earth. Then either the human world will ascend to the sacred realm, or the sacred world will descend to earth. In the Hindu and Buddhist traditions, history moves in long cycles, in which the beginning of a new cycle follows, after a totally dormant period, the end of time in a previous cycle.

Religion and Life in This World

The expectation of judgment after death is a powerful sanction for the behavior of the living, and for some people the central focus of religion is its other-worldly promise. But religious traditions are as much this-worldly as they are other-worldly. Although sometimes concern about life after death leads to largely other-worldly attitudes, the freedom and assurance that come from these attitudes often give shape and significance to life in this world and lead to active involvement in it.

Although the goal of the Hindu religious tradition is ultimate liberation from the round of rebirth, it also provides for meeting a wide range of more immediate religious needs. The Bhagavadgītā, besides teaching how liberation is possible, is very much concerned with one's work in the world as duty or vocation within society. The ritual forms of Hindu tradition give symbolic weight to the major transitions in the lives of individuals, to the cycles of agriculture, to the annual patterns of the lunar calendar, to the days of the week, and even to periods within a single day. In addition, Hindus seek material benefits from religious practice. At the beginning of a new year, for example, business people do *pūjā* for the goddess Lakshmi, for one's economic well-being is in the hands of this deity.

CULTURAL TRADITIONS THAT INCORPORATE SYSTEMS OF SYMBOLS

The certainty that adherents can satisfy their needs by interacting with sacred realities is the foundation for religious traditions. Adherents expect that sacred reality will renew them, justify their existence and their social identity, and provide values and attitudes that orient both themselves and their cultures.

Religions are social by nature. Their forms, ideas, and sanctions have an enormous impact on their societies. They provide a wider symbolic context that people can understand and to which they feel they belong. The relationship between humans and the sacred typically includes a notion of transformation that includes society and reconstitutes it as a religious community.

Most people learn the patterns of their community's religion from the previous generation, much as they learn a language. There are also special communication devices that transmit tradition. Sacred narratives and

A religious tradition is communicated in many ways such as through religious practices, behavioral patterns, artwork, and written and spoken teachings. Here a young Hare Kṛishṇa devotee hears recitations from the Bhagavadgītā. (Religious News Service)

myths convey a religion's concepts and understandings. So do systematized statements of beliefs such as creeds, stated or unstated behavioral norms, and systematic explanations (theologies). Most traditions are communicated orally, as when a leader explains something or relates a religious myth. But many also have written collections of their central stories and teachings, such as the Buddhist Tripiṭaka and Mahāyāna Sutras, the Hindu Vedas, and the Shintō Kojiki and Nihon Shoki.

Symbolic transformation is conveyed most directly in communal acts of worship. But in addition, the way members of a community live their lives and interact express and reinforce the religion's structures. Such practices and ways of acting teach norms and values as much as formal instruction, if not more.

A religion, like a language, offers a single overarching structure and vocabulary that makes community-wide communication possible. Yet few societies are completely homogeneous, and each of the many social subgroups—such as educated city dwellers or the peasantry—often have a sense of religious legitimacy that is different from that of the other subgroups or the "official" tradition. Rural people often have religious needs and interests different from those of urban people. A subgroup's religious patterns may reflect that group's special interests. For example, the priestly class may have an interest in enhancing the status of the rituals for which it is responsible.

Religious institutions can be almost any form of cultural association. Family and kinship groups are the most common: children tend to follow the religion of their parents. People in the same neighborhoods incline toward shared religious interests, as do members of a given occupational group or social class. In contemporary India, for example, relations among different castes with roughly the same social standing are fairly liberal, but great social and religious distance often separates castes with widely divergent status.

Religious communities often derive their social forms from nonreligious institutions. The Buddha organized his monasteries according to the principles that his ethnic group, the Śākyas, used to run their government. Architecturally, early Buddhist monasteries were patterned after the secular buildings of their respective lands.

Changes in Religions

Changes in a religion originate partly from the tradition's internal dynamics. Though traditions often view ultimate realities as ancient, eternal, and unchanging, their characterizations of sacredness are in history and thus are subject to change. The gap between inherited religious forms and the sacred realities they represent makes possible—even demands—the development of new understandings. Religions thus have a capacity for self-criticism and for new formulations of the transformation processes.

But changes are caused not only by internal dynamics but by other elements as well. One is a religion's interactions with other religious traditions. As we will see in Chapter 12, Chinese Confucianism emerged radically different after centuries of interaction with Buddhism.

Conservative countermovements sometimes develop to avoid the dangers of modernization. In twentieth-century Japan, an exodus from the farms to the cities, very rapid industrialization, and defeat in World War II provided the conditions for the so-called New Religions, which combine elements of traditional Buddhism, Shintō, and Confucianism into new forms. These religions have compensated in many ways for the loss of the traditional social structures on which Japanese life and religion once depended.

Among other things, this text will explore the main factors—internal, external, and sociocultural—that have led to the major changes in the world's religions and some of the effects of those changes on society.

Religious Traditions and Their Systems of Symbols

The systems of symbols developed by religious traditions vary dramatically. Meaning is a matter of internal interaction; that is, within each system, ideas or beliefs have meaning only in relation to one another. The parts of the system usually cannot be readily transferred to another system, and indeed, many religious systems are mutually incompatible.

The systemic nature of religious traditions can be conveniently illustrated by the Indian Jain tradition. The routine daily worship patterns of both householders and monastics in the Jain religious traditions include the composition of a design composed of uncooked rice particles in front of the worshiper as he or she meditates. This design represents the cosmos. The bottom figure in the design is a right-handed swastika (from Sanskrit *swa,* "self," and *asti,* "existing") surmounted by three dots in a horizontal row. Above the dots is a crescent opened upward (see Chapter 6). The rotating wheel of the swastika represents the world of birth, change, death, and rebirth into the same or even another life form. At the top of the design the upturned crescent represents release from all suffering and from the round of death and rebirth. Even though the realm above the crescent in the Jain cosmos corresponds structurally to Christianity's heaven, it is by no means the same. Furthermore, no personal god plays any role in securing the release of human beings from the round of rebirth; the whole responsibility falls on the individual. The sacred reality in the Jain tradition is systemically unique, as is its means of release or transformation.

A woman performs the Jain religious ritual of creating a rice design as she meditates. The design represents the cosmos. (Arthur Tress/Photo Researchers)

Religion and Society

Religions form cultural traditions to express and transmit symbolic systems. Religious traditions thus express religious needs at the cultural level and participate in the religious polarity of need and satisfaction. Yet the realization of sacred satisfaction is always partial and temporary. Religion is therefore distinguishable from culture but not separable from it.

Every religious tradition has to change to fit local conditions. Every religion indigenizes to some degree. Buddhist tradition accommodated to the cultures of Southeast Asia, China, and Japan. In each case, Buddhism appears to have become something in large measure new. Many paths (called "vehicles") developed in the northern (Mahāyāna) tradition, but many Buddhists contend that despite the appearance of plurality and even of inconsistency, all of the different paths are ultimately only one path to enlightenment.

Religious traditions clearly have political implications. Many religions have sanctioned existing political structures: Confucianism supported the imperial structures of China for 2,000 years, Protestantism sanctioned nationalism during the Reformation, and religious rhetoric is interjected into political campaigns and warfare even today. Christian missions were initially successful in sixteenth-century Japan because Franciscan and Jesuit missionaries aligned themselves with certain political forces. In another Japanese example, samurai warriors of the fifteenth to nineteenth centuries practiced meditation in the Rinzai Zen Buddhist style because, they felt, it made them better soldiers. Buddhism in many Asian countries endorsed the ruler as the supporter of truth and of Buddhist institutions.

A religion will also relate to other aspects of its context. It may be influenced by economic forces. In Parts One and Two we will see how Hinduism and Chinese religions were influenced by geographic and climactic factors. We will also see that gender issues are a major latent preoccupation of religion in nearly every culture.

Religious behavior may also be shaped by psychological factors. Some kinds of religious experience and behavior, such as possession by spirits, may appear to a Western psychologist as pathological or evidence of social maladjustment.

The contrast between the official view of a religion from inside (often called the *manifest meaning* by social scientists) and an outsider's view of the religion in concrete contexts that results from the application of social-scientific tools of interpretation (often called the *latent* or *hidden meaning*) sets up a potential conflict in interpretations of religions. Historians of religion tend to interpret religious traditions primarily in terms of the internal dynamics of the religion, whereas social scientists and psychologists tend to develop functional

Each statue of this row of nine represents the Amida Buddha, whose name was chanted regularly by Japanese Buddhists. Buddhist tradition accommodated to the cultures of Southeast Asia, China, and Japan, appearing to have become something in large measure new in each case. Buddhists contend that all of the paths are ultimately only one path to enlightenment. (Sekai Bunka Photo)

interpretations. The two approaches may result in very different accounts of a religious tradition.

The outsider's preoccupation with the latent functions of religions should be balanced with the insider's manifest meaning. Religions do not serve either latent or manifest functions exclusively. Indeed, both approaches can and should be combined, as we have tried to do in this book, for manifest and latent meanings clarify each other.

How to Read This Book

QUESTIONS TO ASK

The model of religion developed in this chapter will help you to understand the religions of Asia. As you read about each religious tradition, it will be helpful to keep this model in mind. We suggest that you employ the three parts of this model to ask questions during your reading.

For example, as you read about each tradition, look for the fundamental or characteristic relationship between human beings and the sacred reality around which the religion revolves. What is the sacred reality like to believers? How do their creation stories portray their view of the world? What is the status of human beings? What do they seem to need from sacred realities? How does life obtain its fundamental sanction, value, and significance for practitioners of this religion?

To answer these questions, pay attention to belief systems, cosmologies, myths, and the conceptualization of sacred realities. Ask yourself, what are these people's fears? What is thought to be wrong with human beings that needs to be set right? What provides believers with hope and assurance?

First, watch for the enduring elements of themes, issues, and structures. For example, Part Two focuses on three of the key elements of Buddhism—the Buddha, the Dharma (law and doctrine), and the Saṅgha (the monastic community)—and how they have changed over time.

Second, search as you read for the processes of religious transformation. Look for them in rituals, performances, individual and group meditation, development and growth patterns, changes from one life stage to another, and significant changes in the calendar year. How do believers come in contact with sacred power? How do they prepare themselves for this? Do they cleanse themselves? Do they make confessions? Do they seek absolution and forgiveness? Do they give offerings? Do individuals need help from religious specialists? What kind of devotion and prayer or meditation do people practice? Repeated symbolic transformations are typical of the rhythms of religious life.

Then hunt out the cultural patterns of the religious tradition, and map out how the tradition relates to its society. Note its primary social groups and institutions. Who are the religious leaders, and who are the followers? Which group wrote the texts? Are there assigned roles for men and for women? How does the religion shape behavioral patterns? With what economic and social groups are particular religious movements and ideas connected, and why? What meanings are hidden in the symbols people use?

Finally, what is unique about this religious tradition? What is comparable to other traditions? Throughout this text you will find boxes that highlight certain similarities and differences. Compare other features yourself. Even if some elements of the religious tradition seem similar to elements of others, how do these parts fit together in the religious system to which they belong?

USING MAPS AND TIME LINES

The maps included in the text will help to orient you geographically and, in some cases, historically. Many include information regarding the terrain of a region, often a factor in the development or movement of a religious tradition. Before modern methods of transportation, the ancient trade routes along rivers and through mountain passes were the primary means by which migration and trade took place and by which cultures and religions interacted.

The time lines provided in the text will help to orient you chronologically. The time lines present both temporally longer and more sweeping periods as well as pinpointing important events and individuals, thus helping you to see key developments in context. A complete listing of text maps and time lines appears at the end of the contents.

Because the primary time scheme in the West and much of the rest of the world, dated B.C. ("before Christ") and A.D. (*anno Domini,* "in the year of our Lord"), presupposes a specifically Christian theology, we have chosen to employ a more neutral era designation that is in increasing use. B.C.E. ("before the Common Era") replaces B.C., and C.E. ("Common Era") replaces A.D. The numbers for the years are the same in both systems.

We have boldfaced important terms. They are defined in the glossary at the back of the book.

NOTE

1 "Selections from the Lao Tzu (or Tao-te Ching)," in *Sources of Chinese Tradition,* comp. William Theodore de Bary, Wing-tsit Chan, and Burton Watson, vol. 1 (New York: Columbia University Press, 1960), p. 51.

PART ONE

Religions of India

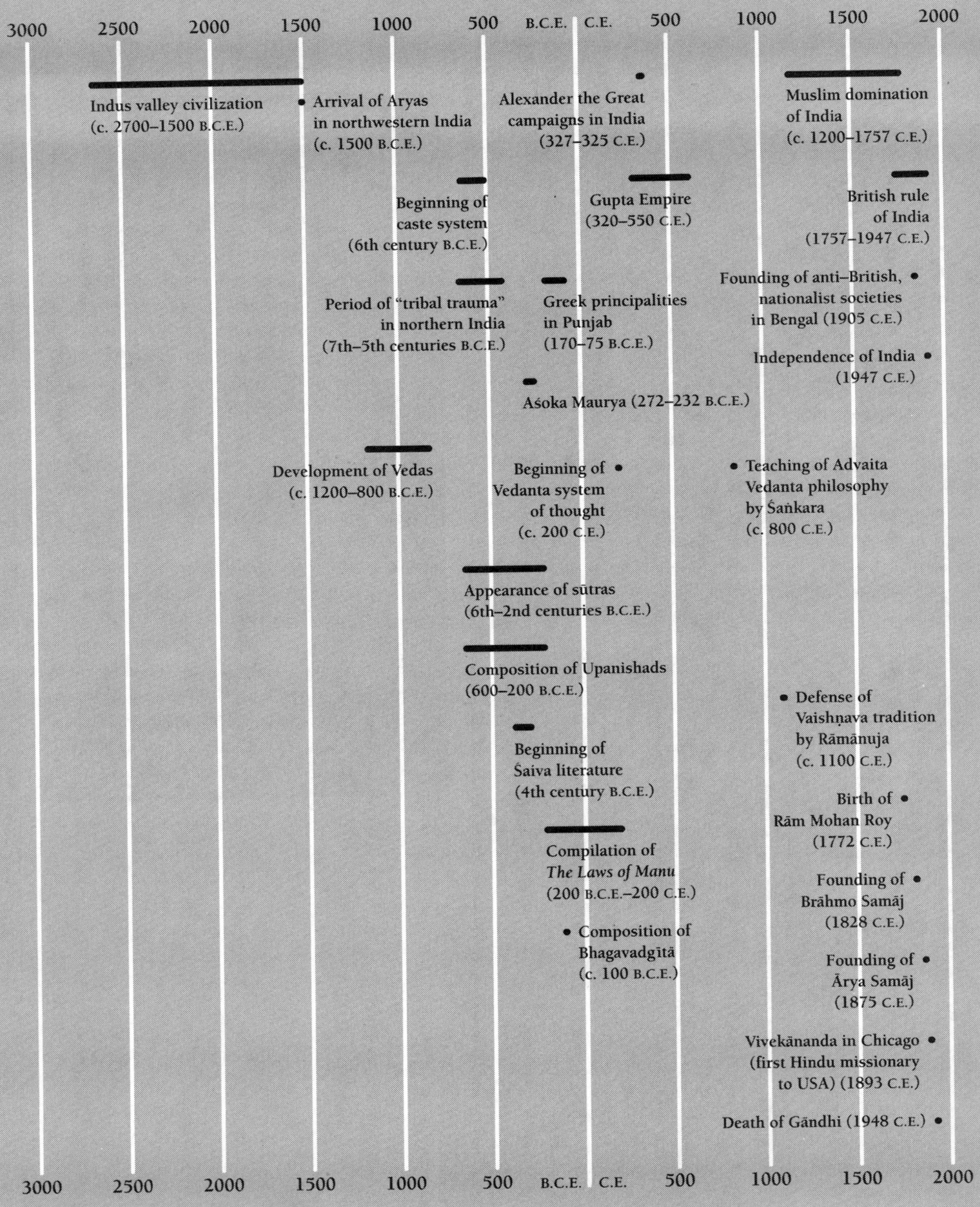
3000
2500
2000
1500
1000
500
B.C.E.
C.E.
500
1000
1500
2000
Indus valley civilization (c. 2700–1500 B.C.E.)
Arrival of Aryas in northwestern India (c. 1500 B.C.E.)
Alexander the Great campaigns in India (327–325 C.E.)
Muslim domination of India (c. 1200–1757 C.E.)
Beginning of caste system (6th century B.C.E.)
Gupta Empire (320–550 C.E.)
British rule of India (1757–1947 C.E.)
Period of "tribal trauma" in northern India (7th–5th centuries B.C.E.)
Greek principalities in Punjab (170–75 B.C.E.)
Founding of anti–British, nationalist societies in Bengal (1905 C.E.)
Independence of India (1947 C.E.)
Aśoka Maurya (272–232 B.C.E.)
Development of Vedas (c. 1200–800 B.C.E.)
Beginning of Vedanta system of thought (c. 200 C.E.)
Teaching of Advaita Vedanta philosophy by Śaṅkara (c. 800 C.E.)
Appearance of sūtras (6th–2nd centuries B.C.E.)
Composition of Upanishads (600–200 B.C.E.)
Defense of Vaishṇava tradition by Rāmānuja (c. 1100 C.E.)
Beginning of Śaiva literature (4th century B.C.E.)
Birth of Rām Mohan Roy (1772 C.E.)
Compilation of *The Laws of Manu* (200 B.C.E.–200 C.E.)
Founding of Brāhmo Samāj (1828 C.E.)
Composition of Bhagavadgītā (c. 100 B.C.E.)
Founding of Ārya Samāj (1875 C.E.)
Vivekānanda in Chicago (first Hindu missionary to USA) (1893 C.E.)
Death of Gāndhi (1948 C.E.)
3000
2500
2000
1500
1000
500
B.C.E.
C.E.
500
1000
1500
2000

HINDUISM TIME LINE

Religions of India

CHAPTER 1

The Earliest Forms of Hinduism

Hinduism, literally "the belief of the people of India," is the predominant faith of India and of no other nation. About 85 percent of all Indians declare themselves to be Hindu, along with a substantial minority in neighboring Bangladesh. In addition, conversions and migrations have given rise to small groups of Hindus in Sri Lanka, Indonesia, Africa, and Great Britain. There are half a million Hindus in the United States, as well. But like Confucianism in China and Shintō in Japan, Hinduism belongs primarily to the people of one country and has exceptionally strong ties to the national culture.

The term *Hindu* is of Persian origin. Muslims who conquered northern India in the twelfth century C.E. used it to describe persons belonging to the original population of Hind (India) and their religion. But India is also the birthplace of Jainism, Buddhism, and Sikhism; to distinguish Hinduism from these faiths we sometimes call it Brahmanism because it was taught by the ancient priestly class called **brāhmans.*** The authority of the brāhmans is one of the factors that sets Hinduism apart from these other beliefs.

Hinduism arose among a people who had no significant contact with the biblical religions. Hindu teaching does not consist of answers to the questions asked by Western faiths. For instance, Hinduism does not insist on any particular belief about God or gods. People reared in religions holding firmly to certain beliefs regarding God are often baffled by Hinduism's relaxed attitude in theology.

We must recognize that the special emphases of Hindu religion arose out of the problems that are especially acute in India and that Hindus' hopes are shaped by what seems desirable and possible under the special conditions of Indian life. Hindus, like others, seek superhuman resources to help to preserve life and to achieve its highest blessedness, but they perceive life's threats and promises as those posed by the Indian land and climate.

*This Hindu term can be confusing, for several related terms have developed over the centuries. *Brāhman* is the class or caste of priests. The brāhmans chanted the ancient scriptures (Vedas), and their sacred words came to be called *brahman*. The same term became associated with the world soul or divine absolute, the capitalized *Brahman* (not to be confused with a later creator deity, Brahmā). Certain religious texts were referred to as the *brāhmaṇas;* each of those texts has a name, for example, the *Aitareya Brāhmaṇa.*

Pronouncing Sanskrit
In transliterated Sanskrit, consonants and vowels, including those with accent marks on them, may generally be pronounced as in English—the differences are subtle and not readily apparent to people untrained in Indian languages. Observe the following: *ś* is pronounced "sh" as in *sure; c* is pronounced "ch" as in *chew;* and *th* and *ṭh* are pronounced not as in *the* or too*th* but as separate sounds, as in nu*th*atch or an*th*ill. Long vowels, with a bar over them, are held a little longer than their short counterparts: *a* is as in *maternal, ā* as in f*a*ther. We have used standard Monier Williams transliterations, with one exception, replacing that system's ṣ with *ś* (*Journal of the American Oriental Society* style).

GEOGRAPHIC SETTING

Two geographic factors have shaped many of Hinduism's themes and emphases: India is an agricultural land, and India is an isolated land.

India: A Land of Farmers

India was famed throughout the ancient world as a vast and fertile land of fabulous wealth. The rich soil of the northern river valleys, which extend about 2,000 miles from west to east, has supported a very large population for millennia. To a greater extent than any other major modern culture, India has been agrarian. And despite the recent growth of industrial cities, it remains overwhelmingly a land of farming villages.

The Hindu cosmology (view of the universe) is the creation of minds constantly aware of the natural cycles of plants and animals. Nature itself is seen as feminine, and female deities have a prominent place in classical Hindu mythology.

The persistent anxieties of India's farmers have had a dramatic impact on Hindu religion. India has always been both blessed and cursed by natural conditions, the most frightening of which is the matter of adequate water. As a rule, rainfall is plentiful, but several times each century the monsoon clouds fail to develop, rain does not fall, and crops do not grow. This persistent threat may account for the great attention paid to water in Hinduism's rituals. Scarcely any ritual is performed without preliminary bathings, sprinklings, sippings, libations, or other ceremonial uses of water. In Hindu mythology, Indra, the god of rain, is called king of the gods, and the mythology of many goddesses reflects an ever present concern with water.

Many goddess myths are also connected with the earth's fertility. The personalities of these deities reflect some of the forces controlling the agricultural world. In their worship of these goddesses, Hindus attempt to establish better relations with a generative force conceived as a mother who is usually generous but also moody and capable of violent anger. The ambivalence of this power is reflected in the goddess's different forms and dispositions; the divine mother may be the affectionate Ṣītā or Pārvatī or the dangerous Kālī, an irritable parent who sometimes destroys her children in inexplicable rages. The dual focus of worship symbolized the capricious pattern of abundant harvests and catastrophic droughts. And persistent anxiety about the food supply explains Hinduism's great tolerance for the pursuit of practical goals in worship.

India's Isolation and Stability

The second important geographic influence on Hinduism is the barrier of mountains and seas that has protected the subcontinent from invasions. On India's southern flanks the seas are wide, and powerful empires were far distant. India's north is shielded by the Himalayan mountains: no army approaching from China or Tibet has ever conquered India. Invaders have often used passes in the northwestern mountains, but to reach these they had to traverse wide deserts that limited the size of their armies. Only one early incursion—by the Aryas—has ever penetrated India so effectively as to transform Indian society.

In historical times Persians, Greeks, Scythians, Huns, Mongols, and others have invaded India in modest numbers and set up kingdoms on the northern plains. But they were always few in relation to the rest of the population, and they were able to rule successfully only by using local assistants, administrative institutions, and languages. The invaders soon intermarried with Indians and were given a traditional Indian social status. In the thirteenth century C.E. Muslims invaded and ruled most of India for 500 years, but the tide receded without leaving it an Islamic land. Even the British domination of the past two centuries did not radically transform the age-old Hindu social order. India's agricultural villages, the basic units of Hindu civilization, have always been too numerous and too remote to be forced into change.

THE QUEST FOR INNER PEACE AND HARMONY

India's cultural security has helped to determine Hinduism's prominent concerns. The Hindu scriptures are not preoccupied with the survival of a threatened tradition, nor is the Hindus' memory haunted, like the Jews', by recollections of past cultural traumas. India's natural defenses made the established order of Hinduism a secure cultural possession.

Yet the very cultural security that minimized one great problem created another: living with changeless-

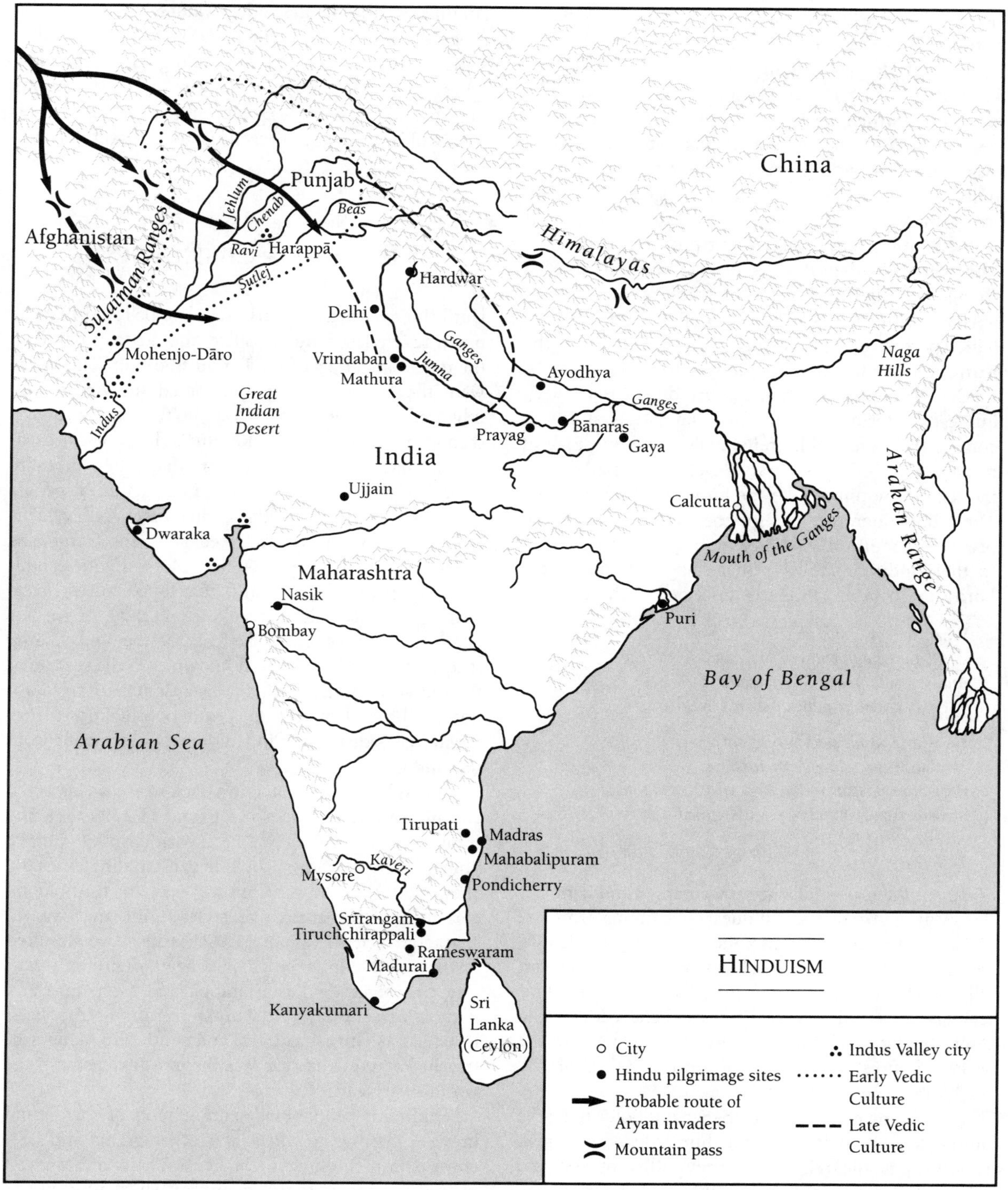
China
Himalayas
Afghanistan
Sulaiman Ranges
Punjab
Jehlum
Chenab
Beas
Ravi
Harappā
Sutlej
Hardwar
Delhi
Mohenjo-Dāro
Vrindaban
Mathura
Ganges
Jumna
Ayodhya
Ganges
Naga
Hills
Indus
Great
Indian
Desert
Prayag
Bānaras
Gaya
India
Arakan Range
Ujjain
Calcutta
Dwaraka
Mouth of the Ganges
Maharashtra
Nasik
Puri
Bombay
Bay of Bengal
Arabian Sea
Tirupati
Madras
Mahabalipuram
Kaveri
Mysore
Pondicherry
Srīrangam
Tiruchchirappali
Rameswaram
Madurai
Kanyakumari
Sri
Lanka
(Ceylon)
HINDUISM
City
Hindu pilgrimage sites
Probable route of Aryan invaders
Mountain pass
Indus Valley city
Early Vedic Culture
Late Vedic Culture

ness. India's traditional villages preserve even today a pattern of social relations that has not changed significantly for more than 2,000 years. Most Hindus have labored in an inherited occupation and died in the rank into which they were born. Hindu society's restraints on its members are severe and deeply felt, even if not resisted or even resented. The frustration of individual Hindus is experienced as a general sense of living in a bondage involving no external object of blame. Hindus rarely blame their problems on society or demand that their discontents be remedied by social changes. In Hinduism the responsibility for resolving tensions with the world lies squarely with the discontented person. One is to change oneself, not change the world. Inner adjustment is the way to tranquillity.

One distinguishing mark of Hinduism is its deep interest in techniques of self-examination and self-control that can enable individuals to attain peace of mind. At the most ordinary level these methods of inducing tranquillity take the form of moral teaching. The Hindu literature praises the saintly person who preserves emotional stability by mastery of impulses. In the Hindu classic, the Bhagavadgītā (Song of the Lord), the truly holy man is described in these terms:

When he sets aside desires
All that have entered his mind, O Pārtha,
And is contented in himself and through himself,
He is called a man of steady wisdom.

He whose mind stirs not in sorrows,
Who in joys longs not for joys,
He whose passion, fear, and wrath are gone,
That steady-minded man is called a sage.[1]

(Bhagavadgītā 2.55–56)

Beyond such moral encouragement, Hinduism has deeply introspective techniques for calming troubled minds. In meditational disciplines called **yoga**, Hindu teachers offer guidance in subjective processes that can still passions and replace the tedium of life with feelings of joyful release that are believed to be a foretaste of a blessed immortality. As a final resort, the seeker is urged to enter the separated life of the world-abandoning *sannyāsī*.

If a religion can be defined by what it holds to be the most blessed condition that humanity can know, Hinduism is the religion of tranquillity of self and society. Since it regards tranquillity as its highest goal, Hinduism subordinates other values, such as social progress, material well-being, and justice as we understand it in the West. In responding to this (or any other) religion, we must of course note the attainments that it holds in highest esteem and recognize that no faith will be effective in reaching goals that it does not seek.

THE INDUS CIVILIZATION

Until the twentieth century, scholars believed that the much-revered scriptures called the **Vedas** contained the oldest materials of the Hindu tradition. The Vedas were the hymns of a people called the **Aryas** who migrated into India from Iran in the middle of the second millennium B.C.E. Recent archaeological excavations have revealed, however, that 1,000 or more years before the Aryas arrived, an agricultural people had already settled in the Indus River valley. This **Indus civilization**, also referred to as the Harappans after the modern name of one of their cities, built carefully planned cities and developed a system of writing. Scholars now recognize a dual origin for Hinduism: the religious heritage of the Vedas, long studied and moderately well known, and the culture of the Indus civilization, which, because its writings have not yet been deciphered, is still poorly known. Yet much that is distinctive in Hinduism clearly came from this Indus source.

The Indus civilization dates back nearly as far as the cultures of Mesopotamia and Egypt. In 2700 B.C.E. the Indus valley was already dotted with farming villages. Shortly thereafter, the people began building cities. By about 2400 B.C.E. the culture was in full bloom, manifesting the distinctive style of life that was to characterize it for almost 1,000 years. Two hundred towns and five large cities have been identified so far. The two biggest cities, Harappā and Mohenjo-Dāro, both in present-day Pakistan, were true metropolises. Reaching as far east as Delhi and south into Maharashtra, the Indus civilization was the most extensive of the world's very early cultures.

The Indus people made simple tools of copper and bronze. They grew wheat and other grains and kept cows, sheep, pigs, and chickens. Their still undeciphered writing is found mainly in short inscriptions

The Indus people made tools of copper and bronze, as well as art. This bronze figure of a dancing girl from Mohenjo-Dāro dates from c. 2000 B.C.E. (The Granger Collection)

carved on soapstone seals that were used to mark trade shipments. On the face of the seals, plants and animals are carved with remarkable skill in a style that is one of the distinguishing marks of this civilization.

The crowning achievement of the Indus people was their city planning and sanitary engineering. In these aspects the Indus civilization had no rivals. Towns were laid out in a grid of wide, straight, intersecting thoroughfares. The houses, grouped into residential districts, were of a type still prevalent in India today, with plain walls facing the street and small rooms clustered around a central open-air courtyard. Carefully sleeved wells topped with broad masonry curbs were the source of household water. Each house had a bathroom with a latrine and large water pots from which the toilet could be flushed. Waste water ran into sewers buried under the street outside.

Many features suggest the presence of an effective ruling elite. A uniform measure of length used by builders and a precise system of merchants' weights suggest a system of official oversight, as does the regularity of the towns' layout. On a mound just beyond the western boundary of every Indus town we find a complex of facilities thought to be the administrative center. The mound at Mohenjo-Dāro features an assembly hall and a unique bathing pool, and both Mohenjo-Dāro and Harappā had large granaries. Archaeologists at first took these raised terraces to be citadels, but further excavations showed few barracks, weapons, or fortifications. From this we infer that methods of social control were most probably nonviolent—the presence of large granaries suggests that the early rulers were already using India's characteristic nonviolent method of controlling populations through the collective distribution of food. Another perennial method for ensuring conformity and order was also employed: the inculcation of reverence for established ways.

RELIGION IN THE INDUS CULTURE

Even the best scholarship cannot outline a religious system whose language is not understood. Our information on Indus religion is based only on what the spades of archaeologists have laid bare. Inferences from those findings continue to stir debate, but we shall present a few tentative conclusions.

Our first generalization is that the Indus people probably looked back on their ancestors with exceptional reverence. As archaeologists studied the development of city life from the earliest strata to the latest, they saw a scrupulous adherence to original patterns. For example, the city limits did not expand or contract, nor did the street layout change. When houses collapsed, they were rebuilt on the precise lines of the old foundations. For 1,000 years there was no change in the artistic style of the seals, tools, or weapons or in the alphabetic characters engraved on them. The Indus people probably looked on the ways of their ancestors as sacred and inviolable. Already, here in India's first civilization, something existed of the historic Hindu view that the hope of humanity lies not in the new but in the past, the sole source of holy truth.

Another aspect of Indus religion was an almost reverent regard for water. In the Indus cities water was carefully channeled in cleverly designed wells, drains, and toilets. The Mohenjo-Dāro bathing pool, elevated above the level of the city and surrounded by imposing arcades, suggests that bathing rites had a place in the solemn processes of government. Alas, archaeology cannot tell us the ideology behind these official lustrations. Their importance may rest on the fact that, especially in the area's arid climate, successful agriculture required much attention—and thus ritual attention—to water. Or we can speculate that here, as in later Hinduism, bathing was an essential preliminary to worship because it was believed to make "unclean" mortals fit to deal with the sacred realities. Or we can note that even today in rural India, wells, pools, and streams are held to be the residing places of superhuman beings and are often destinations of sacred pilgrimage. There may be a historical relationship here, for water has had a prominent place in both Indus and modern Hindu practice.

Goddess worship was widespread in Indus religion. In almost every house archaeologists have found small figurines, the most common of which was a broad-hipped and elaborately dressed female figure; some scholars hold that these figurines personified the earth. Near one such image, oil or incense had been burned in a cup, evidently in a home ritual. One well-preserved seal shows a female figure upside down, a bushy plant springing from her womb. Another shows what seems to be an animal sacrifice being offered to a goddess who is standing next to a large tree. This farming culture probably—and understandably—revered the earth, its source of plenty.

Seals like the ones mentioned earlier, hundreds of which bear inscriptions, will someday be a rich source of information on Harappan religious life. Though we cannot yet read the words, we can interpret the pictures. Some seals show interactions between beings with human characteristics but also superhuman traits. Tales about superhuman heroes and deities are no doubt being portrayed; some of the roots of Indian mythology probably lie here. Though we do not see the familiar divine forms of later Hinduism, some scholars feel that we are looking at their early representations. For instance, the male figure shown in lotus position on four of the seals is plausibly thought to prefigure the later god Śiva. Other observers point to his seated posture as evidence that yoga was already being practiced 4,000 years ago.

Goddess worship was widespread in the religion of the Indus civilization. This clay figurine was found in the ruins of the ancient Indus metropolis of Mohenjo-Dāro. (Borromeo/Art Resource)

In addition to such early god and goddess figures, impressive male powers are also often represented on the seals: great bulls, rhinoceroses, tigers, and elephants are carved with mighty horns and splendid musculature. Myths and perhaps even philosophical ideas probably circulated about interactions between these various male and female forces.

According to the scholar Marija Gimbutas and others, goddess worship and additional factors suggest that governance and organizational power in the Indus civilization may have been to a significant degree in the hands of women. At the very least, the social and religious values of this culture seem to reflect a very different orientation from the patriarchal and patrilinear Aryan civilization that was to follow it.

END OF THE INDUS CIVILIZATION

By 1900 B.C.E. Harappā and Mohenjo-Dāro were falling into disarray. Decay was staved off for a few centuries more in daughter cities of the Indus type that had been established far to the south. But by 1600 B.C.E. no Indus cities remained inhabited. The cause of their abandonment remains a mystery. A likely immediate cause was failure of the grain supply to the granaries of the cities. The deeper cause, some have proposed, was misuse of the soil, climatic change, or catastrophic floods. Other scholars believe that the cities ended bloodily—in massive attacks by the Indo-European people called the Aryas, who are known to have been on the move in Iran in the eighteenth century B.C.E. and to have occupied northern India by force by about 1600 B.C.E. The Aryas were indeed the next known people to have dominance in the Indus valley, and they could have seized control directly from the Indus rulers. But there was no wholesale slaughter of the Indus people or even of the population of their cities. Rather the cities and towns were abandoned one by one over several centuries through processes that left few signs of violence. The Aryas did not drive the population from the land as even some Vedic texts suggest, nor did they drastically change the agricultural life of the indigenous people.

What came to an end was city life, along with the high culture and skills that were distinctly urban. With the cities went urban planning, the sewers, the seals, the alphabet, and in time the pre-Aryan languages. The Aryan conquest caused the most radical linguistic displacement India has ever known. When 1,000 years later inscriptions were again written in India, they used entirely new alphabets expressing new languages belonging to the Indo-European family, and the dominant religion became that of the Aryan elite.

But quietly, among laborers and farmers, much of the pre-Aryan heritage in religion and custom would continue, to reappear centuries later in different form. After 500 B.C.E. many of the social and economic aspects of the old Indus life returned: intensive agriculture, great cities, and rulers exercising strict control. Elements of the old Indus religion, which had served populations under such conditions, became popular again. Mingling occurred, and the dominant religion became the blend that we now know as Hinduism.

THE RELIGION OF THE VEDAS

The Aryas are first noted in Mesopotamian records of 1800 to 1400 B.C.E., when they were probably migrating also into northwestern India. Those who settled in India first revealed themselves in a great body of oral literature composed and compiled by their priestly class between 1200 and 800 B.C.E. Whereas the religion of the Indus culture is known only from the discoveries of archaeologists, the outlook of the Aryas has been recovered from the Vedas, the oldest of the Hindu scriptures.

THE CULTURE OF THE EARLY ARYAS

In the Vedas we discern a people with a life style quite different from the Indus people's. These early Aryas built no cities, and they were less advanced than their predecessors in most of the sciences and arts. But they had developed superior metallurgy and weaponry, and they were skilled in riding horses and using war chariots. They grew grains on land near their villages but also kept large herds of grazing animals. The Aryas were divided into five tribes, each led by an independent chieftain who was responsible for defense and internal order. Though they shared a common ethnic identity, the tribes were not united politically. Three social ranks were recognized: priests (brāhmans), the warrior class, and the general population. Membership in these classes was not hereditary.

THE VEDAS

Though the Aryas had no system of writing when they entered India and remained without one for a long time, they brought with them from Iran a tradition of oral poetry and took exceptional delight in their language. By about 1200 B.C.E. certain groups of Aryan priests had begun to memorize with exceptional care the poetry then in liturgical use. By about 800 B.C.E. their religious poetry had been gathered into four collections (saṃhitās) that are known as the four Vedas. Even though preserved in memory only, the texts of these poems were as firmly fixed as if they had been printed. We may thus speak of these recited Vedas as "books."

The Sanskrit of these Vedas belongs to the Indo-European language family. *Veda,* a cognate of the English words *wit* and *wisdom,* means "wisdom"—the sacred wisdom of the Aryas. The Vedic age, when a single cult was dominant in literature, lasted from about 1200 to 600 B.C.E. We shall focus on the religion around 800 B.C.E., when the cult had its greatest following. By this time three collections already had the status of Veda: the Ṛigveda, the Sāmaveda, and the Yajurveda. An independent fourth collection, later called the Atharvaveda, was already in existence but not fully formalized. Each of these Vedas was preserved by a separate guild of priests.

The Ṛigveda

The **Ṛigveda** was the liturgical book of the *hotars,* an ancient order of Aryan priests who originally performed the sacrifices alone. Soon the hotar was given assistants who took over the manual and musical aspects of the ritual, and the hotar became a specialist in hymns of praise. The hotar's lasting role was to recite, at certain key moments in the ritual, one or more hymns in honor of a god or several gods. Each verse of these hymns of the hotars was called a *ṛic,* or praise stanza. This term gave the collection its name, the Ṛigveda, the sacred wisdom consisting of stanzas of praise. The Ṛigveda, most of which is the oldest Veda, is made up of 1,028 hymns organized in ten divisions or books. The preserved names of the poets of these and other hymns indicate that both men and women contributed to them.

The Sāmaveda and the Yajurveda

The **Sāmaveda** is the anthology of the enlarged priestly troupe's specialists—both male and female—in the songs *(sāmans).* The Sāmaveda is a compilation of verses selected almost entirely from the earlier books of the Ṛigveda, arranged in the order in which the singer needed them when performing ceremonial duties.

The **Yajurveda** was compiled for the use of another new participant in the ritual, the **adhvaryu,** whose duty it was to make the physical preparations for the rite and to handle the offerings during the ceremony, at the same time muttering short incantations *(yajuses)* declaring the purpose and meaning of each ritual act. About half of these are fragments extracted from the Ṛigveda; the remainder are new prose compositions.

The weaving together of the individual performances of the specialists became a complicated and worrisome matter. Great powers were believed to be set in play by the priestly utterances, and slips in performance were dreaded, so a fourth priest was added to listen, detect errors, and remedy all mistakes. At first any knowledgeable priest could become such a silent supervisor; soon, however, the position became the monopoly of a group of experts in medicine called **Atharvans.**

The Fourth Veda

The original work of the Atharvans had nothing to do with the great public rituals for which the other three Vedas were composed. The Atharvans had been personal medical practitioners and counselors. In crises they had served both ordinary individuals and kings, warding off battle wounds and threats to the prosperity of their realms. Atharvans often became royal chaplains and as such the supervisors of court rituals. In a natural step they became the silent supervisory priests on the staff of the dignified Vedic sacrifices. Through this elevation of the Atharvans to the status of fourth priests at the great fire altars, the Atharvans' professional lore rose in status also, eventually coming to be regarded as the fourth Veda, the **Atharvaveda.** Incorporating many popular hymns and incantations that had been in use for centuries, the Atharvaveda differs significantly in content and purpose from the other three Vedas. These spells were not suitable for introduction into the Vedic rituals around the sacred fire, but some Atharvans continued to use them therapeutically.

THE VEDIC WORLDVIEW

In the Vedic age people were only beginning to reflect seriously on philosophical problems; the great Hindu systems of thought did not yet exist. Although some metaphysical questions about humanity and the universe were beginning to be asked, the answers were diverse and underdeveloped, as seen in opinions of the time on major topics of concern.

Humanity What is the essence of the human being? The Vedic age was content with commonsense answers. Perceiving that when breath goes, life goes, discussion of the life essence centered on the breath or a similar airy substance believed to permeate the living body. **Prāṇa**, an internal air current of the body, is often spoken of as the basic animating principle. But the favorite term was **ātman**, which is atmospheric in its connotations but less concrete in its reference. Ātman was conceived as a subtle substance existing within the human body yet separable from it.

At death this subtle life-breath leaves the body and rises in the updraft of the funeral pyre to a luminous heaven above the atmosphere. Vedic people expected to reach that lofty place of song and to dwell there with their ancestors indefinitely. All who acted correctly and performed the rituals faithfully could be confident of enjoying in heaven all that was best in earthly life. They did not, however, dislike their earthly bodies or long to leave the earth. On the contrary, worshipers often petitioned the gods for life spans of 100 years. The Vedic religious practices were meant to maximize the earthly life, not to replace it with existence on a different level of being.

The universe The substance, structure, and origin of the universe did not yet receive systematic discussion. Understanding the essence of the universe was not as important to the practical-minded people of this age as being able to control it. But several basic cosmological ideas were well developed and generally accepted. One of the commonest was the understanding of the universe as composed of the **three realms.** These realms were conceived as three horizontal strata, one above the other. The lowest was the earthly realm, the disk on which humanity lived and walked. The second was the realm of the atmosphere, in which birds flew and the chariots of the gods were sometimes seen. Its upper boundary was the vault of the sky, through which birds cannot fly and vision cannot penetrate. Above this vault was the mysterious heavenly realm, the home of the deities and the refuge of the blessed dead. When Yama, the first human, died, he discovered the path to heaven for all who followed him; there he presides over the departed ancestors. It was the god **Vishṇu** who established these great divisions when he marked off the entire universe in three of his giant strides.

Ṛita, the basis of order All natural actions in this three-layered universe are governed by an impersonal principle called **ṛita.** Ṛita enables natural bodies to move rhythmically and in balance, without undergoing the disorganizing effect otherwise implicit in motion. Because of ṛita we have an ordered universe that undergoes change without becoming chaos: the sun follows its daily rhythm of setting and rising; the stars fade at dawn but twinkle again at dusk. Ṛita is a dynamic principle of order, manifesting itself in change, not rigidity.

In human affairs ṛita is the propriety that makes social harmony possible. In speech ṛita is truth, and in interpersonal dealings it is justice. When humans observe ṛita, order prevails and there is peace. In worship ṛita is the pattern of correct ritual performance. Right ritual maintains harmony between humanity and nature, humanity and the gods, and one person and another.

Ṛita is not the command of any deity. The great Vedic god **Varuṇa**, the upholder of order, is the special guardian of ṛita. He punished those who do not speak the truth or who commit improper actions. Not even Varuṇa, however, created ṛita. All the gods are subject to it. Ṛita is a philosophical principle, an ancient Indo-European abstraction that from the beginning was independent of theology. In India the word *ṛita* was eventually replaced by the term *dharma,* "duty," referring to what is right as an unchanging standard. The major Indian orthodoxies still retain the original impersonality of Indian ethical theory. In no other aspect of thought is India more different from the Semitic religions than in this.

The ultimate source of things Vedic composers addressed themselves only casually to the problem of the world's origin and final substance. Their tentative stories about cosmic beginnings varied greatly, though most of their speculations included two original entities: the divine beings and some material with which they worked. As to the nature of the deities' materials, they had no settled answer. Ṛigveda 10.90 traces the main features of the world back to a great primeval sacrifice performed by the gods in which the body of a victim called Purusha ("primal man") was dismembered, his limbs and organs being used to form the parts of the human and natural world. Whence this Purusha may have come and what he was are not explained.

Other speculators considered the possibility of a sexual origin of the world, saying that all things had been generated through intercourse between the Sky Father and the Earth Mother or by a single potent procreator. Such efforts to explain the origin of the world in terms of divine sexuality produced no generally acceptable cosmogony.

They gave rise, rather, to a realization that the **devas** (gods) could provide no answer. Each of the deities was conceived to have a spatial location, and many, even most, were defined by their association with some natural power. Conceptualized as a part of the natural world, a deva could not reasonably be understood to be the creator of that world. This was not monotheism. When at last in the late Vedic passages we find intense consideration of the origin of things, we find seers who perceive, as the primal source, a divine essence rather than a divine person—an impersonal essence from which the divine beings themselves arose. One of the earliest and finest expressions of this dominant view occurs in the last book of the Ṛgveda, in hymn 10.129.

Ṛgveda 10.129: A Hymn of Creation

This hymn reminds us of the first chapter of Genesis. Here, too, there is mention of primeval waters and a sense of the tantalizing mystery of an event so distant in time that it is inaccessible to all the usual means of human knowing. As this daring thought proceeds, however, the thinker's mind reveals its own distinctive tendency as it asks, "What moved on the face of that mysterious deep?" Whereas the Hebrew would reply, "In the beginning God . . . ," the Vedic poet considered the potentialities of all the gods and sought elsewhere for the aboriginal reality:

1. *Nonbeing then was not, nor was there being;*
   there was no realm of air, no sky above it.
   What covered them? And where? In whose protection?
   And was there deep unfathomable water?
2. *Death then existed not, nor the immortal;*
   sheen was there none of night and day.
   Breathless, That One breathed of its own nature;
   aside from that was nothing whatsoever.
3. *There was darkness hid in darkness at the outset;*
   an unillumined flood, indeed, was all this.
   That Creative Force covered by the void,
   That One, was born by the power of brooding.

Contemplating the condition that must have prevailed before the world took form, the seer stresses its otherness from all that is now familiar. Even the three realms (1b)* had not yet been marked out. Neither mortals nor the gods were yet there (2a), nor had day and night made their appearance (2b). Where were these things then hidden, and by what (1c)? That they were sunk away in a formless watery abyss is first suggested tentatively (1d) and then asserted positively (3b). Life and being were represented in that primeval waste by a solitary creative force, vital inasmuch as it breathed and yet breathing as no living thing breathes now (2c). This single source of what has breath was not a personal God but a neuter It (2c). It was not even eternal but arose in the oceanic void through a natural incubating warmth or perhaps through the intense mental activity of unidentified mediators (3d).

4. *Desire came into it at the beginning—*
   desire that was of thought the primal offspring.
   The tie of being in nonbeing found they,
   the wise ones, searching in the heart with wisdom.
5. *Transversely was their severing line extended—*
   what was there down below, and what was over?
   There were begetters—mighty beings!—
   fertile power below, and potency up yonder.

Out of this pool of undeveloped life the actuality of living beings proceeded to appear, through the rise of erotic desire (4a) and then of male and female procreators (5d). The initiating factor again (3d) was power generated by the introspection of meditators whose identity and origin are not explained (4d). In the hearts of these sages, thought gave rise to desire (4b), and this erotic urge became the cord, so to speak (4c), by which creatures were drawn up out of the formless abyss in which they had been hidden. This primal desire was the cord also by which the line of sexual differentiation was drawn across the universe (5a), distinguishing creatures into interacting males and females of great creative power (5c, d).

6. *Who really knows? Who can here proclaim it?*
   Whence is it born? Whence is this creation?

*The number refers to the stanza of the hymn, the letter to the line, in the order *a, b, c, d*. Thus "1b" is the second line of the first stanza.

The gods are later than this world's creation
so who can know from what it came to being?
7. *That from which this creation came to being,*
whether created 'twas, or not created,
He who is its Overseer in highest heaven,
He only knows—or He may know not!

Here the author confesses that his picture of these remote events is not based on the knowledge of witnesses (6a); the gods, the most ancient of all knowing beings, are themselves the products of these processes and cannot testify about the beginning of things (6c). But the author is not sure that even a supreme god, the present ruler of creation, is old enough to be able to bear witness to that time (7d). His only confidence is that all life proceeded from a single divine source, which must have been of a nonphenomenal nature. Though persons were derived from it, it in itself was so different from everything known that it cannot be given a personal name. It can be called only "That One."

The image on this North Indian coin from early in the Common Era represents the Vedic god Indra, a great battle god shaped by the migrating Aryas' military experiences. Note the war god's pike at left, the pommel of his sword at right, and his crested helmet with eagle emblem. (Norvin Hein)

The Devas or Vedic Gods

Each hymn of the Ṛigveda is designated for use in the worship of one or more of the superhuman devas. The word *deva* is derived from the noun *div,* meaning "radiant sky." Thus these beings abide primarily in the heavenly realm. But some dwell in the other two realms as well. The gods of rain and wind, for instance (Parjanya and Vāyu or Vāta, respectively), live in the atmosphere; Soma is a god of the earthly realm; and Agni, divinized fire, has seats in all three spheres—earth, atmosphere, and heaven. All members of the pantheon are formally classified by the realm that is their normal residence. This classification makes it clear that the devas are thought of as existing somewhere in nature as parts of the natural order.

Most of the Vedic deities can be understood as half-personalized conceptions of powers controlling nature. The god Vāyu is the power of the wind. Depicted as a bearded figure in a running pose, Vāyu's loose hair flies backward in wild strands, and his cloak billows. Likewise, the Vedic poet who speaks of Agni, the fire god, has visible fire in mind, whether in the heavenly sun, atmospheric lightning, or the earthly fire ritual. Parjanya is addressed in language applicable to rain and is taken to *be* rain. Sūrya is the sun as seen when the actual solar disk traverses the sky. When the priest in the morning sacrifice faces Ushas, the goddess of the dawn, it is the dawn itself that he faces as he sings:

We see her there, the child of heaven, apparent,
the young maid, flushing in her shining raiment.
Thou mistress of all earthly riches,
flush on us here, auspicious Dawn, this morning.

(Ṛigveda 1.113.7)

Even **Indra**, a great battle god shaped by the migrating Aryas' military experiences, acquired in India a connection with rain. Assuming that all deities operate or can operate in some sphere of nature, India asked this great Aryan warrior god to fight also against the land's most threatening enemy, **Vṛitra**, the evil demon that withholds the waters or the monsoon.

The extent to which the devas are understood to control aspects of nature can be seen in the petitions that we find in the hymns addressed to them. The deities are revered but at the same time are asked to

The Pattern of the Śrauta Sacrifice

Here we shall be content to bring together the most common elements of a śrauta sacrifice in a simple imaginary performance. Let the time be shortly after 800 B.C.E. Already the priestly staff required had reached four. The place is the Panjab. A cattleman has herds numbering in the hundreds, but he is ill at ease. For reasons that are not quite clear, his animals are not increasing and are not in good health. Is it the condition of the pasturelands? His reputation for good husbandry is also at stake. Perhaps, the rancher believes, his fortunes may be suffering by reason of poor relations with the superhuman powers that affect his profession. He has heard of a priest of good reputation who is just now moving from ranch to ranch in the next district. He has invited the brāhman and his staff, and a day has been set.

On the day before the scheduled sacrifice, the adhvaryu of the famous troupe had arrived to prepare a site for the performance, bringing in his cart all the necessary materials and implements: a goat to be sacrificed, a hand drill for kindling a fire, cooking pots, barley meal for making offering cakes, bowls and strainers for preparing **soma,** a sacred inebriating drink, and some sacred grass for seating gods and humans.

In the open air, between the ranch house and the cattle pens, the adhvaryu selected an area for the rite and dug in it three shallow fire pits, one square, one round, one semicircular. With the excavated soil he raised an earthen altar of irregular shape to hold the offerings. Setting slim poles in the ground, he raised a light open shed over the fire pits. On the floor of this booth he strewed the sacred grass. At sundown on this day of preparation, the sponsoring rancher entered the booth to begin a night of purifying seclusion. His hair and nails were trimmed, and after bathing, he put on a new garment. Thereafter he consumed nothing but warm milk, kept his fingers doubled up like those of a baby, and spoke only with a stammer. He conceived himself to be undergoing rebirth into a state of purity fitting him for relations with the gods. (In short, using the model presented in the introductory chapter, he went though the ritual stages of distancing, liminality, and rebirth.)

The next morning, the adhvaryu's first duty was to kindle the sacrificial fires. The house fire could not be used. With much sweat he accomplished this task with a fire drill. As the time of sacrifice approached, a few neighbors assembled to observe the performance. Any Arya might attend such proceedings with merit, but the rite was understood to be the rancher's personal ceremony, and he alone was expected to receive its special benefits.

At the appointed hour the three other priests came: the hotar, the singer, and the supervisor. All took their seats on the grass along with the rancher's wife and the rancher himself, who was now allowed to open his fists and speak clearly. The adhvaryu poured on the fire a libation of melted butter. As the flames shot up, the hotar began the rite by reciting an invocatory hymn:

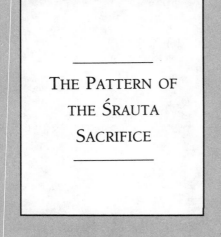

Agni I praise, the household
priest,
the god and priest of sacrifice,
chief priest and bestower of
great gifts.
May Agni, worthy to be praised
by sages ancient and of now,
may he bring hitherward the
gods.
Through Agni may we treasure
gain
and welfare get from day to
day
and honor and most manly
sons.

(Ṛigveda 1.1.1–3)

The fire god, Agni, who can move in all three spheres of the universe, was now presumed to rise from the fire and carry an invitation to the appropriate gods in their heavenly abodes. The divine guests were believed to descend unseen to seats reserved for them on the fragrant grass. There they were entertained with lofty and flattering poetry, such as the following hymn to Indra in honor of his great victory over Vṛitra:

I will proclaim the manly deeds
of Indra,
The first that he performed,
the lightning-wielder.
He slew the serpent, then
discharged the waters
And cleft the caverns of the
lofty mountains.[6]

(Ṛigveda 1.32.1)

(Usually sacrificers praised the god for deeds they wanted the gods to repeat, such as the release of rain by Indra.)

The singing priest then intoned his distinctive and religiously powerful songs, the *sāmans,* while the adhvaryu moved around and offered food and drink as refreshments to the gods. As he did so, he muttered short prose formulas (*yajuses*) that explained his actions. The supervisor did not recite at all but listened carefully, correcting any errors made by the other priests.

To quench the deities' thirst, the adhvaryu periodically poured into the fire libations of milk or the heavenly soma. (The soma plant is said to have been transplanted from heaven to certain high mountains. Its gathered stems were pounded, and the juice was then strained to make a golden inebriating drink.) Cups of soma were given to the priests also, who then sensed a divine presence within themselves:

We have drunk Soma and
become immortal;
We have attained the light the
gods discovered.
What can hostility now do
against us?
And what, immortal god, the
spite of mortals?[7]

(Ṛigveda 8.48.3)

The adhvaryu offered food to the gods by dropping it into the fire. Butter, curds, and cakes were among these offerings. Portions were handed to the patron and the performing priests. At a high moment, the sacrificial goat was untied from its painted post, strangled, and cut up. Portions of its flesh were offered in the fire, but most of it was boiled or roasted and eaten by the participants. Every part had to be consumed, either by the sacrificers or by the fire. As the gods were being praised and entertained in these ways, they were often reminded, pointedly, of the needs and hopes of the rancher.

The ritual completed, the satisfied gods returned to their abodes. The fee for priestly service was now presented. The priests' expected reward was high—the gift of a cow, perhaps. The rancher paid, then bathed and put on his usual clothing. The adhvaryu gathered up the implements of the sacrifice, throwing some into the fire and others into water. He picked up the strewn grass, tossing it into the fire. The sacrifice was over.

apply their powers to the worshipers' needs. In hymns to the dawn goddess Ushas, for example, the composer first observes that as the initiator of each day's work, she controls its success; then the humans pray for material boons:

Mete out to us, O Dawn, largesses: offspring,
Brave men, conspicuous wealth in cows and horses.[2]

(Ṛigveda 1.92.7)

Likewise, a prayer to Pūshan, the sun's light, is well aware of his functions as a guide and a revealer of paths and asks for practical guidance:

Lead us to pastures rich in grass,
Send on the road no early heat.
Thus, Pūshan, show in us thy might.[3]

(Ṛigveda 1.42.8)

To a degree, the worship of these gods and goddesses can be seen as an effort to live successfully amid the awesome forces of the natural world.

This insight does not elucidate the entire Vedic pantheon, however. Particularly, the naturalistic explanations help very little in understanding Indra and Varuṇa, two of the most important deities. These two gods are mentioned mainly in connection with activities that are human and social rather than natural.

Indra is called the chief of the gods. The fact that fully one-fourth of the Ṛigveda's hymns are dedicated to him confirms his preeminence. But Varuṇa is called the foremost of the gods in almost the same terms. Together the two constitute a cooperating pair of rulers whose authority is somehow complementary. They are a committee of two, so to speak, whose authority is the Vedas' nearest approach to that of a monotheistic God.

But neither god's importance rests on control of any vital aspect of the natural world. A seat in nature has been allotted to each of them, it is true. Though Varuṇa's place is the vault of the sky and he is conceived as being present also in bodies of water, he does not *personify* the sky or the ocean. The sky is the vantage point from which Varuṇa surveys human deeds, and he is a water god only to the extent that he inflicts disorders of the bodily fluids on human beings as punishments for violations of ṛita. These marginal connections with nature are not the basis for his vast importance, as will become clear.

Indra has a dramatic connection with the rain clouds, but only in the single myth of his combat with Vṛitra, the demon of drought. But like Varuṇa, Indra in no way personifies rain or clouds, nor is his connection with rain his primary feature. That was visualized 1,000 years later when the emperor Kanishka issued a gold coin bearing Indra's likeness. It shows Indra's fundamental character: the Aryan battle god. In full armor, eagle-crested, armed with both sword and spear, he is a personification of the ideal powers and virtues of the males of the Aryan warrior class.

Unlike Varuṇa, the Indra of the Ṛigveda has nothing to do with morality, either in function or in character. In Vedic mythology he was a ruffian from birth—a lecherous youth and a drunken, boastful adult. After consuming offerings of thousands of buffalo and drinking lakes of intoxicants, Indra lurches off to the wars and there assists his people. He protects them from the power of alien peoples and from terrifying demons. His domain, then, is the hazardous area where his worshipers must cope with hostile outside forces. Immensely strong, Indra promises the warrior class confidence and mastery of battles with foreigners.

Varuṇa is equal to Indra in rank, but there the similarity ends. Whereas Indra protects from dangers lurking at the community's outer boundaries, Varuṇa, his co-ruler, guarantees order by defending the right, guarding the harmony of internal social life. His omnipresent spies examine the truthfulness of what people say and the justice in what they do. Guardian against anarchy, Varuṇa is also the celestial patron of earthly kings, the legitimizer of their authority, and the chief deity addressed in the Aryan coronation ceremony.

Natural danger is not the focal problem in the worship of either Indra or Varuṇa. These two deal, each in his own area, with interpersonal, social dangers—threats to the community from outside or from within. Vedic religion, like other religions, addresses its adherents' most acute insecurities, whatever they be.

In sum, the worship of the Vedic gods is directed toward three types of insecurity. The first is natural: the danger of injury, disease, and want. In this area Vedic worshipers supplemented normal human efforts by invoking the many nature deities and by resorting to the Atharvans' magical rituals. The second insecurity is moral, caused by destructive individualism within the community itself. In the face of such danger, Varuṇa is worshiped as the guardian of ṛita; he punishes antisocial behavior and supports the authority of kings. The third insecurity is military, arising in warfare with alien civilizations. Here Vedic worshipers call to a god of unbounded force, seeking strength and a rallying point in war. In this area they worshiped Indra, just as in economic need they worshiped the nature gods and for social stability they worshiped Varuṇa.

The gods of the Veda have varying moral natures. Varuṇa is a highly moral deity. Nature gods like the solar Savitṛi are amoral, and Indra as a personification of Aryan might is not moral at all. Because Western religions are now highly specialized in dealing with the moral crises of modern societies, many Western students may find it difficult to understand how Vedic worshipers could revere any of these deities save Varuṇa. They should remember that science has only recently become humanity's defense against natural ills. Most religions, past and present, address the whole range of human insecurities. Vedic religion was as broad in its scope as the anxieties of its people.

RITUALS OF THE VEDIC AGE

In rituals we see a religion in action and can often discern a people's deepest concerns and hopes. Life in the Vedic era was rich in rituals of many kinds. About some of them—Aryan ploughing festivals, marriages, funeral rites—we know very little. We know only a little more about the daily fireside rites in each Aryan home, performed for the well-being of the family. In them the husband's role was dominant, but the presence of both the husband and the wife was necessary if the deities were to regard this as a family home and look after it as such. The husband—or presumably the wife in his absence—kept the domestic fire going and offered milk with bits of food in it, accompanied by simple prayers. This tradition of family rituals was to continue, grow in recognition, and at last be described in scripture.

Of another popular ritual we know a good deal because its poetry had the good fortune of being preserved in the Atharvaveda. Most of that Veda consists of incantations that the ancient Atharvan order of priests used at the family hearth when called into the home in a medical or emotional emergency to bring supernatural aid to the suffering family or afflicted family member. Here is an Atharvan's spell for a child with a severe cough:

As the sun's rays fly quickly away,
So also you, O cough, fly forth
In conformity with the ocean's ebb.[4]

(Atharvaveda 6.105.2)

Though gods of the recognized Vedic pantheon are sometimes named in this Veda's verses, they are not approached seriously as personal beings. The divine names are chanted with imperious determination among other awesome words that are thought to empower the ritual. The Atharvan often uses herbs in his treatment also. (The Atharvaveda, also called the Ayurveda, is considered the foundation of the still-used Ayurvedic system of Indian medicine.) In another verse the Atharvan is directing his therapy—herbal as well as verbal—against leprosy:

Born in the night art thou, O herb,
Dark-colored, sable, black of hue:
Rich-tinted, tinge this leprosy,
And stain away its spots of gray.[5]

(Atharvaveda 1.23.1)

The Atharvans had spells also for gaining the affection of a beloved person and for countering a sorcerer's curse. They had charms to control dice in gambling, to cancel the effect of wrongful acts, and to void the disastrous consequences of blunders in performing rituals. This last ability, as we have seen, raised the social status of these magicians immensely.

The Śrauta Rites

Śrauta is the name for the most formal and dignified Aryan sacrifice. The word comes from the noun *śruti,* a synonym for *Veda.* The śrauta rites are those in which the first three collections of Vedic hymns were used. Patronized for many centuries by the Aryas' political and economic elite and served by their most learned priesthood, this type of ritual was handled with such care as no other religious practice of the Vedic age received. Many complicated śrauta ceremonies were developed for use in special situations. There was a royal coronation ritual, a horse sacrifice by which a king could assert and confirm the boundaries of his realm, and an Agnishṭoma rite for times of drought, involving much dripping and splashing and pouring of the ambrosial libation to suggest and induce a downpour of rain. Many śrauta rituals went on for days, and book-length treatment would be required to describe them in full (see "The Pattern of the Śrauta Sacrifice").

LATER LITERATURE OF THE PRIESTLY SCHOOLS

In the early Vedic period, the memorized Ṛigveda was handed down in priestly families. But by 800 B.C.E. a second stage began when professional guilds took over teaching both the literature and the skills of the sacrifice. Recruiting young brāhman boys for the priesthood, the organizations trained their apprentices in their own schools. When the place for education shifted away from the home, brāhman daughters usually remained with the family, and only the boys received the priest's training. In part as a result, a great educational chasm developed between high-caste men and women. This helped to foster a differentiation of **gender roles**: girls were trained in domestic skills in preparation for marriage, and boys were educated in Vedic studies. With different roles came different ideals: women gradually came to value and be valued for characteristics such as fertility and humble devotion to the husband, whereas men were respected for their ritual and literary knowledge.

Preparing for their order's ritual role, the boys memorized the Ṛigveda and learned how to use the text in actual performances. They also heard lectures about the myths and commentaries explaining the Vedic passages, and they were warned about the missteps that are often made by badly trained priests. They heard for the first time that knowledgeable priests were really more important than the gods in producing the boons of the sacrifices. These collateral lectures became traditional in content and form, and the young priests began to memorize them as they memorized the hymns. The lectures too became scriptures, a second stratum of the Vedic religion's holy "books," called **brāhmaṇas.**

The guilds' practical training in ritual performance next underwent a similar codification into a form that could be learned by heart. By about 600 B.C.E. manuals called **śrauta sūtras** were being created that laid down instruction in every act and utterance of the sacrifice. To minimize the effort needed in memorization, these manuals were cast into a very compact new form of literary expression, the **sūtra**, or "thread" of discourse on a particular topic. Composed of a series of succinct and carefully worded prose sentences, a sūtra is easy to memorize. The Śrauta Sūtras of the various guilds became the third stratum of Vedic scripture. Having memorized his Śrauta Sūtra, his guild's brāhmaṇa, and its body of hymns, a young priest was equipped to take his seat at the sacred fire.

THE UNITY OF VEDIC RELIGION

Despite changes in practice and in thinking, the ritualistic religion we have been studying has been held in unity by the unchanging character of its goals. From beginning to end, worshipers at the fire pits strove to maximize the values of this world. They sought to live a healthy, long life amid plenty with a good reputation. When life was done, they both hoped and expected to be accepted into a celestial realm that was not radically different from this world but rather its perfection. Though petitioners at the rites asked generally for personal benefits to themselves, they were not utterly indifferent to the general welfare. The prayer of a king at a royal sacrifice assumes that he and his subjects will benefit together:

> May the cow be rich in milk, strong the draught ox, swift the steed, fruitful the woman, eloquent the youth. May a hero be born to the sacrificer. May Parjanya give rain at all times according to our desire. May the corn ripen.[8]
>
> (White Yajurveda 22.22)

Vedic hearts were not pessimistic about the attainability of such hopes. The gods were thought to be favorably inclined, on the whole, toward dwellers on the earth. Approached through wise priests, they would confer all necessary favor on their worshipers, who even after death would enjoy a blessed life in a place of endless light. Though happy in this assurance, people of the Vedic age were not preoccupied with thoughts of the afterlife, nor did they long either to depart to or to replace this world with a heaven. Rather, Vedic religion showed a firm attachment to earthly values and a persistent confidence in their realizability.

THE RISE OF THE CONCEPT OF BRAHMAN

Over the centuries, as witnessed by the texts, the understandings of how the sacrifice could accomplish its goals changed. As priests reflected on that problem, they arrived at the conception of **Brahman**, the single source of all that is. Brahman was destined to become a key concept in later Hindu thought about final salvation, but when the term first appears, it occurs as a late answer to the question, how do the sacrifices exert their power?

That the sacrifices do produce their promised boons, no Vedic spokesman had any doubt. In early centuries of the Vedic age the explanation was simply that worship is a relationship between persons, human and divine. Just as earthly rulers can be mollified and influenced by praise and presents, gods too can be induced, by ingratiating speech, gifts, and fine entertainment, to exercise their powers for worshipers. But in later literature, beginning with the Yajurveda, authors are found who can no longer conceive of the gods in such personal terms or believe that the fruits of sacrifice are produced by such a personalistic process. It seems likely that the close identification of many gods with natural forces had worked against a deep belief in the gods as persons. Under intense contemplation the gods of wind and rain seemed to some believers to be personal beings by metaphor only or dubious impositions on a broad, ineffable reality. The separateness of their powers, too, was questionable. In thinking of the solar deities—Sūryā as the solar disk, Ushas as the dawn, Pūshan as the illuminator of paths—the separateness of these powers is not self-evident. The deities merge, plausibly becoming a single dynamic force operating in the whole of nature. The gods who exerted their powers for worshipers became mere names to many priests, many of whom now believed that their own insights and powers were more potent than those of the gods in producing the benefits of the rituals. Even the dynamic of the sacrifice came to be viewed impersonally: acts or words of the sacrifice have hidden ties with cosmic realities, and the priest, by manipulating these tokens, can bring about desired effects in the outer world. The symbols in the ritual become handles on the great realities that they symbolize. The masterful priest who knows these secret correspondences can activate the cosmic powers to which the symbols refer and bring about the development for which his client hopes. "This fire is yonder moon," a priest mutters as he casts a libation into the flaming semicircular fire pit. The strained identification seemed nonsense to scholars until they understood that to the priest the fire is a potent moon symbol, by reason of its yellow glow and half-moon shape. The priest's power over the fire gives him mastery over the moon, the cosmic metronome, for instance, that marks off the passage of time. Measuring off the months, the moon consumes the remaining life span of his ailing client. By knowing and using the power hidden in the symbols of his ritual, the priest is undertaking to extend the life of his patron. By such thinking, priests remained assured of the power of their rituals even when they could no longer believe them to be effective through the intervention of personal gods.

In their search for power through the connections to their ritual, the priests became fascinated with what they might be able to do through the outreach of their rituals' words. All people perceive that their words correspond to external realities and sometimes cause things to come into existence or to disappear. Thus it came to be believed that the awesome words of the Vedic hymns could have marvelous effects on aspects of the outer world. An obsession arose in the minds of the ritualists that there might be a word of all-embracing reference that would give access to power over *all* things.

Thus there arose in the late Vedic age a fascination with the term *brahman*. It meant at first a Vedic prayer or a holy spell, but in time it came to mean all liturgical utterances and the Vedas themselves as the collection of sacred sounds. Since *brahman* referred to the entirety of scriptural words, it was believed to have ties with the entire natural world. By the end of the Vedic age, *Brahman* had become a favorite term for the source and moving essence of the whole universe. "That One" of the creation hymn had found a name.

There was as yet no stress on the identity of self with Brahman, no notion of finding eternal peace in Brahman. Success in earthly life remained the end in view. Only the means had changed because there was little faith in the intervention of personal gods. Mastery of the forces that could satisfy one's needs was being sought not by manipulating deities but by manipulating in ritual the microcosmic extension of those forces. Brahman provided a verbal handle on the universe, by which the whole world could be moved and the fundamental needs addressed.

THE VEDAS IN LATER HINDUISM

In the eight and seventh centuries B.C.E. Vedic religion attained its highest development; its acceptance declined after 600 B.C.E as suppressed social classes rose in status and introduced non-Aryan elements into the mainstream. In direct challenge to the brāhman priesthood, Jainism and Buddhism arose as independent religions. The followers of these new religions rejected the materialistic goals and the bloody sacrifices of the Vedic rituals. Even those who remained attached to the Vedas criticized the animal sacrifices. Though few brāhmans questioned the effectiveness of the sacrifices, even among the priests many began to question the value of the boons that were promised. The interest of many members of the priestly guilds turned from the performance of ritual to a fascination with the mystical contemplation of Brahman. A new Hinduism was emerging (discussed in the following chapter).

Nonetheless, some aspects of the Vedic tradition have survived to the present day. The ability to recite the Vedas and to perform the ancient sacrifices has never completely disappeared. Study of the Vedas has remained the most prestigious form of Hindu scholarship. Periodically, Hindu political leaders have revived the rites to legitimize their rule or as a symbol of their loyalty to indigenous custom.

Although today almost all Hindus follow religious practices that originated after the Vedic period, they continue to count on the ancient priesthood. As the old guilds died out, new organizations were formed of brāhmans who were willing to serve as the priests and scribes of new religious movements and who presented themselves as extenders of the Vedic tradition rather than rebels against it. Although the upanishads (later scriptures discussed in Chapters 3 and 4) reflect a new religious faith and a new approach to the problems of life, Hindus understand them to be a continuation and clarification of the Vedic tradition. For this reason the upanishads are referred to as the Vedānta ("end of the Vedas"), extending recognition to the upanishads as the last literary installation of the Vedas.

In time Hinduism produced new religious literature, strikingly different in content from the Vedas, including lawbooks, epics, and Purāṇas (mythological works), with known human authors. The Veda specialists granted such **smṛiti** (human tradition) works great authority nevertheless, considering them necessary and nearly error-free restatements of the meaning of the *śruti* (divine revelation). Indeed, few movements within the broad and diversified river of Hinduism have been openly hostile toward the Vedas. In intention Hinduism is still Vedic, and "the Vedic religion" remains one of the most widely used identifications that modern Hindus apply to their faith.

NOTES

1 All translations in Part One are by Norvin Hein, except where noted.

2 Arthur Anthony Macdonell, trans., *Hymns from the Ṛigveda* (Calcutta: Association Press, n.d.), p. 37.

3 Ibid., p. 32.

4 K. G. Zysk, *Religious Healing in the Veda* (Philadelphia: American Philosophical Society, 1985), p. 45.

5 Arthur Anthony Macdonell, *A History of Sanskrit Literature* (Delhi: Munshi Ram Manoharlal, 1958), p. 197.

6 Macdonell, *Hymns,* p. 47.

7 Ibid., p. 80. With the advantage of modern experience we recognize that soma may have had psychedelic properties. S. Gordon Wasson, in *Soma, Divine Mushroom of Immortality* (New York: Harcourt Brace Jovanovich, 1968), identified the plant with some plausibility as the mushroom *Amanita muscaria* (fly agaric).

8 Arthur Berriedale Keith, *The Religion and Philosophy of the Vedas and Upanishads* (Cambridge, Mass.: Harvard University Press, 1925), vol. 1, p. 290.

Religions of India

CHAPTER 2

Classical Hinduism: The Way of Action

In the sixth century B.C.E., Indian society entered a period of great transformation. The Aryas, who now dominated the entire Ganges valley, had cleared away the thickets and plowed the fertile plains. Tribal chieftains ruling loosely over groups of herders were replaced by kings governing from fortified cities. By the third century B.C.E., these regional kingdoms had given way to vast empires.

In this more settled world the stresses of life also changed. As the people became dependent on tilled fields, rulers could exercise tighter military and social control over them, and economic and political relationships hardened into rigid patterns. India's geographic isolation exacerbated the culture's tendency toward stasis, and its social rigidity generated new stresses and brought alterations in religious life.

The old sacrifices of the Vedic age were all but swept away. Curiously, the brāhmans did not disappear; in fact, they emerged from the centuries of transition more honored and more influential than ever before. Originally the experts only of ritual, the brāhmans came to influence wider and wider aspects of social life, formulating society's ideals and articulating its moral teachings. These ideals and values have provided a pattern for the lives of many Indians even to this day. Indeed, because of their influence, the new religious orthodoxy that emerged by the second century B.C.E., here called "classical Hinduism," has often been called Brahmanism.

SOCIAL CODES OF THE NEW SOCIETY

The brāhmans' abilities to read and memorize gave them a leading role in creating and recording the standards for this new age. Using their compact literary invention, the sūtra, to state these standards, they slowly expanded the range of their authority. In works called **gṛihyasūtras** ("discourses on domestic rites"), which prescribed how householders should perform their home rituals, the priests began to lay down rules for performers other than themselves. In a dramatic new development, between 600 B.C.E. and 200 C.E., works called **dharmasūtras** ("prescriptions on social duty") appeared, in which the brāhmans began to lay down rules for social behavior not related to the rituals. For the next 1,000 years, more expanded verse texts, called **dharmaśāstras**, elaborated on these rules. The most famous, *The Laws of Manu,* attributed to the sage Manu, articulates the etiquette and duties of each class (*varṇa*) and of each age group (*āśrama*) in the new brāhman-dominated society.

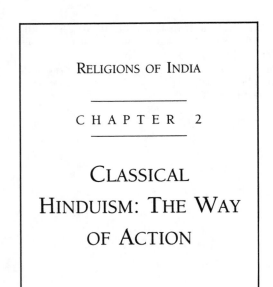

These new texts, which accompanied this era's social revolution, centered on a new term, **dharma**, which inherited much of the meaning of the Vedic conception of ṛita (discussed in Chapter 1). Both words refer to a principle of justice or right that is rooted in the universe, to which humans' actions should conform. But there the similarities between the two terms end, for their respective conceptions of the universe and the patterns of life they envision are profoundly different. *Ṛita* comes from a verbal root that means "to run, go rightly, fit in." To follow ṛita is to run with the harmonious flow of things in a world that forever changes. *Dharma* is formed from a verb meaning "to hold steady, make firm, restrain, preserve." The duties to which it refers are components of a sacred world that is imagined to be firm, stable, steady, and unwavering. Like all else that is good in such a world, the path of dharma does not change over time. Indeed, one's sacred duty (dharma) is an eternal duty (*sanātanadharma*), and sanātanadharma has become a favorite name for this orthodox religion itself. Adherents believe that the world and their lives are based on a blessed pattern that is eternal. The virtuous person is restrained and never allows passion to sway him or her from that path. By remaining in traditional duties one supports the firmness of the universe. This notion that social duties are unchanging reinforced the fixity of the new social patterns. Henceforth, classical Hinduism would view change as destructive and would resist open innovation.

This cobbler follows one of the most visible of the outcaste occupations. His usefulness is great, but his social standing is low for he handles leather. Because of this sanitary scruple, high-caste Hindus avoid touching shoes with their hands. (Allan L. Price/Photo Researchers)

THE CASTE SYSTEM

For over 2,000 years the caste system has provided the pattern for Hindu society. Castes (in Sanskrit, **jātis**, or "births") are hereditary occupational groups hierarchically ranked by popular estimation of the purity and dignity of each group's traditional work.

Firm hereditary occupational distinctions did not exist among the Aryas. During most of the Vedic age, class distinctions were few and flexible. The Vedic poems, however, did mention three social classes: the brāhmans, or priests; the **rājanyas** or **kshatriyas**, rulers and warriors; and the **vaiśyas**, or common people. Although the sons of warriors and priests generally adopted their fathers' occupations, they were not forced to do so. For example, sons of commoners could become priests, and a priest's child could become a potter.

Origin of the Social Classes

The earliest indication of a turn toward caste occurs in a late hymn of the Ṛigveda. Ṛigveda 10.90 tells of a sacrifice in which the giant Purusha, a cosmic man, was the victim. From Purusha's limbs and organs all the prominent features of the world were formed, including the social classes:

The brāhman was his mouth;
His two arms became the rājanya;
His thighs are what the vaiśya is;
From his feet the śūdra [menial class] was produced.

We should note in this verse the appearance of a new, distinctly Indian order of class precedence. In Aryan societies of the Middle East and Europe, the warrior class always occupied the highest level of leadership, but in India the priesthood has from this time onward been supreme and has served as the model for much that is distinctive in Hindu civilization.

In this verse, a new depth of class consciousness is shown: the moderate social differences of earlier Vedic times have been sharpened. In addition to the original three classes, we now see a class of menials, the **śūdras**, who ranked lower than ordinary citizens and were to perform the humblest tasks. There are now four social divisions or **varṇas** (literally, "colors"), each with a characteristic occupation.

Scholars have still not determined the reason for this development. It may have been a way to justify the Aryas' control of an indigenous serf population, or the four-class theory of Ṛigveda 10.90 may be a hint of the rising influence of discriminations that survived from a pre-Aryan culture.

Duties of the Social Classes

The author of *The Laws of Manu* cited Ṛigveda 10.90, making its scheme of the four varṇas the theoretical framework for the new Hindu society. The classical social order that Manu describes goes far beyond the Vedic idea, however. The varṇas are now hereditary, and their inequality in dignity is proclaimed with a new emphasis. There is special stress on the exceptional rights of the brāhmans, whose duty is to perform sacrifices, to study and teach the Vedas, and to guard the rules of dharma (*Manu* 1.88–101). Because their work is sacred, the brāhmans are supreme in purity and rank, and injuries committed against them are punished more severely than offenses against members of other castes. Personal service by śūdras is their right at any time. If brāhmans are in economic difficulty, they are permitted to take up livelihoods proper to the kshatriya and vaiśya classes (*Manu* 10.81 ff.).

The kshatriyas are warriors, the protectors of society—kings were typically of this varṇa. They were to rule according to the dharma codes, heeding the counsel of brāhmans. Warriors must never do the work of brāhmans, but in times of misfortune they may enter the occupations of vaiśyas and śūdras.

Members of the vaiśya caste, according to Manu, were to be traders, herders, and farmers. In later times they turned over their farming and herding roles to the lower groups; trading became their distinctive occupation. In distress, they may resort to the work of śūdras. Vaiśyas are considered to be full citizens of Hindu society and are allowed to study the Vedas.

In the Vedas the śūdras were a beggarly group, the lowest of the varṇas; Manu's description accords in part with that picture. In dignity there is a great gulf between them and the elite classes above them, whom they were to serve meekly. Śūdras were not to study the Vedas or attend any Vedic ceremony. It was not proper for them to be wealthy, though they were to be protected from outright starvation. Over time they have traditionally been herders and farmers as well as artisans and manual workers. Manu described their many groups of artisans as jātis, or hereditary occupational groups, and suggested that they arose from ill-behaved members of the higher varṇas who were punished by demotion to the śūdra rank. But to suppose that a major portion of the population of a vast country was created by such a process is very hard to believe.

Manu completes his social picture by sketching the life of a group even lower than the śūdras. These are the corpse handlers, executioners, hunters, leather workers, and fishermen. Because their occupations are associated with dead bodies and filth, which are considered contaminating, they cannot be dignified with the name of any Aryan class. Their houses must be built outside the village limits. They may not enter the village at night. No one may teach them the sacred texts. Their personal morality is of little concern. Manu calls them "no-class people"; they are today called **outcastes**. Again unconvincingly, Manu traces these groups—essential to the economy and significant in number—to forebears of the Vedic varṇas who were punished for offenses by being stripped of all Vedic rank.

Clearly, the Aryas had incorporated into their social system a subjected people who had a ranking system of their own based on hereditary occupations. Out of the two stratifications, a single social hierarchy developed, the three original classes of the Aryas becoming the aristocracy. But probably as a remnant of the indigenous system, all the varṇas in time became subdivided into specific hereditary occupational groups.

Manu on the Stages of Life

The tendency of classical Hinduism to identify people in terms of social rank expresses itself further in a conception that each individual's personal career is divided into four stages of increasing dignity. These are the **āśramas**, or stages of spiritual effort. One must honor as superior, the law books say, those who have attained a higher āśrama than one's own. Even within the familiar circle of one's own caste or family, age, gender, and effort bring elevation and differences in status. Thus the law codes strive, using many devices, to remove all ambiguities about the social position of any person and to eliminate controversies about rank. Thus when two orthodox Hindus meet, one almost certainly owes deference to the other—if not by reason of caste, then by reason of seniority. The person in the inferior position will greet the other using an appropriately respectful salutation. The languages of India are rich in words by which one can honor those to whom respect is due.

The Student Stage Between the ages of 8 and 12 a boy of any of the three upper varṇas is expected to apply to a teacher and begin formal study of the Vedas. The teacher is to instruct the boy in the recitation of the sacred texts. In return, the pupil must obey, serve, and show respect for his teacher.

The Householder Stage When the young man concludes his studies, he should marry. In doing so, he enters the second āśrama, that of the householder. He must beget sons and earn a living for his family through work appropriate to members of his caste. In addition, he must give alms to those who have passed into the higher āśramas.

Since the Hindu woman was not taught the Vedas and hence could not enter the student stage, the householder stage was the only one in which men and women, as husband and wife, shared a common purpose of life. Even so, the respective roles of the husband and wife were different and socially unequal. Manu stipulates that the husband must protect the wife, as did her father and as would her sons later in life. Her husband is to provide her with adornments and to "approach her" in due season. The woman is described by Manu as a subject: "In childhood a female must be subject to her father, in youth, to her husband, and when [he] is dead, to her sons; a woman must never be independent" (*Manu* 5.148).[1] Even if he was an unscrupulous libertine, "a husband must be constantly worshipped as a god by a faithful wife" (*Manu* 5.154).

The Stages of the Forest Dweller and the Sannyāsī When a man is a grandfather and his hair is white, ideally he should leave his home and thereafter devote his life to spiritual practices in the forest (*Manu* 6.2). In actuality, many people deferred this departure from society until a future life, but it remained a cherished ideal. We describe these two āśramas together because in both the literature and modern practice, the former runs into the latter.

The stage of the forest dweller designates an early phase of the full-time monkish life. Here one may still perform one's old habitual rituals and live in forest settlements but must attempt to quell passions and to generate spiritual power. A man's wife may accompany him at this stage, though he is to begin to detach from her even as she serves him.

When the forest dweller has overcome all spiritual impediments, he may cease all ritual and ascetic practices, sever all remaining social ties, and enter the final stage of life. This is the stage of the **sannyāsī**, the total renouncer of the world, when final liberation itself is his goal. Homeless and not careful about bodily comforts, he is to devote himself to study of the upanishads and to meditation on the soul within himself and all beings. His goal is a serene liberation that will continue eternally, even beyond death.

Men who live in either of these stages have left caste, social status, and family behind. It is nonetheless a highly revered life style. For women, the stage that follows the householder stage is more ambiguous. Since her reason for living was to keep her husband alive and well, if he dies or leaves her for the spiritual path, she is seen by the tradition as living without a purpose. In widowhood, a position held in low esteem, a woman was to shave her head, dress plainly, and serve her sons.

KṚISHṆAPUR: A TWENTIETH-CENTURY CASTE COMMUNITY

Hindu communities of the age of the dharmaśāstras were characterized, as we have seen, by a systematic stratification of society, firm assignment of hereditary social roles, and conceptions of justice that included unequal privileges. Society restricted one's choice of occupation and of marital partner, and it extended freedoms unequally according to social rank. The dignity and wealth of any person depended heavily on his or her caste; the unequal service that was required of the various classes was rationalized as a requirement of the divine law.

Evidence shows that the picture we have just seen accurately portrays Hindu social life even into the present century. The ranked caste system and the āśramas have remained the persistent background of Hinduism's beliefs and practices and indeed have been the framework in terms of which those beliefs and practices often get their meaning. Modern sociologists' fieldwork in village India has shown the continuing reality and importance of the social ideals proclaimed by Manu.

Based on those sociologists' reports, let us construct a picture of an imaginary village that typifies traditional caste life, both to show its continuities with the ancient ideals and to show realities of its life not recorded in the ancient texts. We will call our village Kṛishṇapur.

Located in the plains of northern India, Kṛishṇapur has about 1,500 inhabitants belonging to some 30 castes. Varṇas exist in Kṛishṇapur not as organized social groups but as collections of jātis (castes). Public opinion assigns each caste to one of the four varṇas or to none. The members of some castes believe that their caste deserves a higher varṇa classification by reason of its unappreciated virtues and secret noble origins, but the general opinion of their neighbors compels them to be silent. At certain public events in the village, caste representatives participate in the order of their precedence, thus publicly acknowledging their rank.

Most of the inhabitants have heard of the dharmaśāstras, but almost none have read (or could read) those ancient books. They do not turn constantly to the texts for guidance; rather they assume that the requirements of those respected texts were long ago incorporated into the local rules governing village behavior. The ancient pattern of the four varṇas provides the community's broad theoretical framework, but the active organizations of the village are the jātis, whose members earn their livelihood by one or another of the village's several dozen occupations. When the dharmaśāstras were written, only the lowest varṇas were thus subdivided, but the model was infectious, and now even the high varṇas are subdivided into occupational castes.

Among the brāhmans we find different castes of priests who perform the rituals of childhood, adulthood, and death, respectively. In addition, a village may have among its brāhmans an astrologer and a physician practicing traditional Indian medicine. Most of the kshatriyas are landowners engaged in farming; a few brāhmans, exercising their special privilege, also own land. The third varṇa, the vaiśyas, includes the local groups who keep official records, as well as moneylenders, goldsmiths, and dealers in grain. The śūdra castes contain the groups that perform manual tasks not regarded as impure or morally tainted, such as florist, truck gardener, carpenter, herder, barber, and tailor. Finally, there are the outcastes, those who have no varṇa, whose jobs are deemed grossly unclean. They include washermen, sellers of liquor, fishermen, tanners, toilet cleaners, and handlers of dead bodies.

Each caste is represented by a small group of families, and each governs its internal life by its own traditional caste law. This is an unwritten code that lays down rules for personal habits and for relationships within and between families. Intimate matters that in many societies are left to personal taste, custom, or etiquette are firmly regulated in Kṛishṇapur. Each caste has its own rules regarding foods that may not be eaten and persons who may not join caste members at dinner. Restrictions on the company in which orthodox Hindus may dine are so severe that few ever eat with any but members of their own caste. Bodily contact with persons of a lower caste communicates contamination to any individual of higher rank, and from such a tainted person some degree of impurity could be spread to other members of the caste.

A member who has undergone serious contamination must promptly remove the taint by bathing or undergoing more drastic rites. Members must select mates for their sons and daughters from certain families of the same caste. Caste rules are enforced by a council of caste elders, who punish offenders with fines and social boycotts.

Another important unwritten code is the traditional village law. It prescribes all villager's duties to castes other than their own. It covers economic relations, professional services that each caste is expected to render, and the services or goods that are to be provided in return.

Economically, the castes fall into two broad groups: food producers and providers of services. The former group consists primarily of farmers. The latter contains the many artisans and laborers who offer the goods and services needed to maintain farms and to equip homes. An ingenious exchange of food, goods, and services is the basis of economic life, rather than money payments. The village code outlines the duties of each worker and his share in the farmer's harvests.

Representatives of the town's most prominent castes make up the village council. Workers who fail to make the traditional contributions of food or services are brought before the council. After hearing the complaint, the council can bring a rule breaker into line by ordering all castes to shun the offender, cutting off all services.

Kṛishṇapur is a restrictive society that limits personal freedom—for example, in the choice of mates and occupations—even more severely than the ancient dharmaśāstras did. The caste and village codes establish an order of precedence so precise that no one in the community has an exact equal. Another person is always either superior or inferior. Talent, wealth, and seniority ordinarily bring leadership in one's own caste, but they do not necessarily give eminence in the village as a whole. Formal precedence belongs to those who are born to it, and economic advantages are distributed unequally. The freedom to enter alternative occupations, just as in the teaching of Manu, belongs to the castes of the upper varṇas alone. The brāhmans and kshatriyas of Kṛishṇapur have used this freedom to acquire and farm the land, a freedom that has helped them in the struggle to survive.

In the present century industrialization has introduced a money economy into rural India and affected the livelihoods of many of the castes. For at least 2,000 years, however, Hindus have accepted the life of communities structured in the traditional pattern, which has been the persistent social background of Indian religious thought. This distinctive society has greatly influenced the content of Hindu religion. Sometimes its presence is reflected in the categories in which Hindus think. Sometimes its influence is seen in the provision of religious remedies for the special tensions of this society or rational justifications for its social lots. The explanations of Hindu religious doctrine have allowed this unusual social order to survive and have enabled Hindus to live happily, generation after generation, in one of the most unequal and yet enduring societies the world has ever known.

Karma and Rebirth

The intimate connection between Hindu doctrine and Hindu society is illustrated dramatically in the belief that human beings are born again and again to lives of varied fortune in a course controlled by the moral quality of their accumulated deeds. It is an idea central to Hinduism. With slight variations, it is accepted by Buddhists and Jains. The belief in reward and punishment through rebirth appeared in the very age in which the classical Hindu caste system was being organized. Several upanishads that describe the concept as a new teaching belong to the period when the dharmasūtras were outlining the new social system.[2] From that time onward, **karma**, rebirth, and the caste system developed in a combination that became the central pillar of classical Indian culture. To understand the doctrine of karma and rebirth solely as a philosophical concept would be to understand only a fraction of its function and power.

In its most rudimentary sense, *karma* means "an action." In ethical discussions it means an action that is morally important because it is required or prohibited by the codes of dharma. Karma means, next, an unseen energy believed to be generated by the performance of such a dutiful or undutiful act. Long after the act has been completed, its energy continues to exist. At an appropriate time, it discharges itself on the doer, causing the person to receive the consequences of the original act. Accumulated karma gives to some meritorious persons sharp minds, good looks, and long and healthy lives. It brings the opposite to others, for equally valid reasons.

Karma is believed to exert itself with particular force at the times in our individual careers when we are about to be reborn. At the moment of our conception in the womb, the accumulated moral force of our past deeds is believed to move us into a family of an appropriate caste. All persons born into one of the castes of Kṛishṇapur are believed to have been brought to that special lot by karma, of their own making, and that alone justifies their social rank.

Some Hindu writers conceive of karma as an energy that emerges from the doer of an act; it hangs overhead like a thundercloud. Without warning, like a thunderbolt out of the blue, that karma descends on the doer at the proper time to effect its perfect retribution. Other Hindu thinkers describe karma as a force within the doer that operates by conditioning personal disposition and drives that then cause those who are on wrong paths to persist on them until they are ruined by natural processes. Monotheistic Hindus hold that God oversees the retributions of karma. The only inevitability is that we shall bear the consequences of our good and evil deeds.

Whatever their understanding of how karma operates, Hindus believe that human beings are not totally helpless before it. To continue in wrongdoing is easy but not inevitable. By persistence—over many lives, if necessary—we can master our evil tendencies.

The Hindu belief in rebirth according to karma has convinced the people of Kṛishṇapur that their places in society are appropriate and advantageous. Each villager is understood to have a long personal history of good and evil deeds done in former lives, and each one's present situation is seen not only as just but also as that person's best opportunity for betterment. Because they are limited in their capacity by their past karma, people are fit only for the particular opportunities offered by their present caste and sex. To attempt to take on the duties of another social station would be not only unjust but also dangerous, since it would lead to poor performance and then to even more restricted future rebirths.

About the afterlife the inhabitants of Kṛishṇapur accept for the most part the beliefs set forth by Manu: offenders against the dharma rules will, when reborn, be punished. Some may be reborn as lesser animals—tortoises, fishes, snakes, lizards, spiders. Some may come back as grasses or shrubs. Very great offenders will be condemned by Yama, the judge of the dead, to dreadful hells where they will be scorched in hot sand, boiled in jars, or devoured by ravens. A person who has performed his or her dharma well may be reborn as a noble animal or into another human life. The very virtuous may be born into pleasant celestial realms. Manu describes several, the highest of which is the marvelous heaven of Brahmā the creator. Though ideas about the afterworlds vary greatly, most Hindus believe that the processes of retribution are highly developed and extremely thorough.

The idea of karmic retribution, the promises and dangers of a life lived virtuously or otherwise, and the justification of one's present status based on past deeds have undergirded the caste system's structures and controls and have helped to make Hinduism's culture a lasting one.

THE RITUALS OF CLASSICAL HINDUISM

A natural sequel to our study of the social institutions of the post-Vedic culture would be a survey of the religious ceremonies that are common in communities like our hypothetical Kṛishṇapur.

The social transformation that occurred at the end of the Vedic age was accompanied by equally radical changes in worship practices. The Vedic sacrifices fell from vogue and became rarities. Dozens of the Vedic gods were quietly retired from active worship. Rituals of unprecedented types emerged into literary notice—rituals that have endured even to the present. Some words and phrases of the Vedic hymns persisted in these new rites as linguistic ornaments, but the warp and woof of post-Vedic liturgies seem to have come from other sources, perhaps from the subjected non-Aryan classes. Whatever their source, they have been handed down for centuries by the brāhman caste, who either teach the rituals to the householders or perform them on the householders' behalf. We shall learn what we can about rituals that are prevalent in traditional Hindu homes and go on to speak of activities in special houses of worship.

The Sandhyās ("Meditations of the Twilight") The **sandhyās** are personal meditations to be performed at the important transitional hours in the sun's daily passage—dawn, noon, and evening. The dawn meditation still survives among devout high-caste Hindus, who rise very early for this purpose. First they spend a few moments in formal breathing exercises (*prāṇayāma*). Just as the rim of the sun appears on the horizon, the worshiper stands and recites the lines of Ṛigveda 3.62.10, called the Gāyatrī mantra:

Let us meditate on that excellent glory
Of the divine vivifying sun;
May he enlighten
Our understanding.

In the final moment of the rite the worshiper pours out from joined palms an offering of water to the sun.

The Sandhyās are personal meditations to be performed at dawn, noon, and evening. The dawn meditation survives as seen here as the worshiper pours out an offering of water to the sun. (Kit Kittle)

The Saṃskāras ("Rites of the Rounds of Life") The **saṃskāras** mark the important transitions in the lives of Hindus of the three highest castes, from the moment of conception to death. They enable families to surround their members with affection and to try to protect them from harm at times of change. These rituals are performed in the home, usually near the family hearth. Even funeral observances, which culminate at a cremation ground, begin and end at the home. The father and the mother are the primary actors in many of these performances, and the father himself may officiate at them if he knows how. Apart from funerals, almost all such observances are happy occasions involving a joyous gathering of relatives.

Today many of the ancient rites have dropped out of use. But the traditional marriage and funeral ceremonies are part of every Hindu's career, and other saṃskāras are still practiced by a minority of high-caste families. (The initiation, wedding, and funeral ceremonies are described in the accompanying box, "Rites of the Rounds of Life.")

Pūjā, the Ritual of Image Worship The most frequently performed of all Hindu ceremonies is a form of worship called **pūjā**, which is addressed to an image of a deity. The use of idols—pūjā's main innovation—is of uncertain origin. It arose in connection with a belief that the celestial deities, if properly approached, could be induced to adopt earthly residences and thus become more permanently available to their worshipers.

To enable a particular celestial being to descend and remain on earth, first a sculptor has to create a form displaying the known features of the deity. Next, a rite of installation induces the divinity to descend into the image and become available to worshipers, to remain as long as the god is cared for and honored. It cannot be neglected: it must be given personal attention and offerings of food and drink. The provision of these necessities through a daily routine of rituals is the basic activity in pūjā. If requisite ritual care is not given, the deity will abandon the image.

In pūjā, as in the Vedic sacrifice, the object of worship is a single deity or at most a pair, and the worship is not done as a congregation but as an individual worshiping for personal reasons or for the benefit of a household. The types of gain sought in the earliest pūjā that we know about were the same as those pursued in the older sacrifices: health, wealth, safety, and blessed afterlives in heavenly places. But in accordance with the new cosmology, the desire to accumulate good karma was soon added.

One of the most common sites of pūjā is a home shrine where at least once a day the image, kept in a niche or a cabinet, must be accorded the proper rites, usually by a family member. Near the deity certain utensils are stored: a vessel for water with a ladle for purifying the area with sprinklings, a bell, an oil lamp to be circulated before the image, and trays on which flowers, fruit, or cooked meals may be offered. The deity's image is cared for throughout the day. It may be roused from sleep, bathed, fed at mealtimes, wreathed with flowers. Often an evening song is sung while the god enjoys the spiritual essence of the food it is served; then a courteous goodnight wish is expressed, and the ceremony ends with a circulation of lamps.

Rites of the Rounds of Life

From birth to death, the primary transitions in the Hindu's life are signified by the saṃskāras, the rites of the rounds of life. Here are three common ones.

THE INITIATION CEREMONY

The initiation ceremony, or *upanāyana,* is one of the great events of upper-caste Hindu boyhood. Performed between the ages of 8 and 12, it is the ritual occasion at which the boy is presented to his religious teacher to begin instruction in the Vedas. The ritual begins when the boy spends the night before the ceremony in complete silence (symbolic distancing). At breakfast he eats with his mother for the last time; henceforth he will eat with the men. He then bathes and is led to a canopy under which he formally accepts his **guru**, or teacher (thus entering the liminal phase). The guru drapes over the boy's shoulder and chest a sacred thread to be worn thereafter as a mark of a twice-born Hindu man. After this ceremony, the boy may begin to study the Vedas, through which he will be spiritually born again into the heritage of Vedic learning. After his period of studentship, he is no longer considered a boy but rather an adult.

THE HINDU WEDDING

The Hindu wedding is a group of social customs focusing on a central uniting sacrament. The first action is the parent's settling on a suitable match for the child. Because chastity is so highly valued in wives, this is often done when the girl is just reaching puberty or even earlier. The groom may be of any age. A sizable dowry must be negotiated, to accompany the bride from her father's family to her husband's.

On the wedding day the groom travels in procession with friends and relatives to the bride's house, where he is received with formal honors. In the rites that follow, conducted by a brāhman, the prominent elements are intended to unite

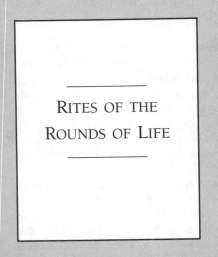

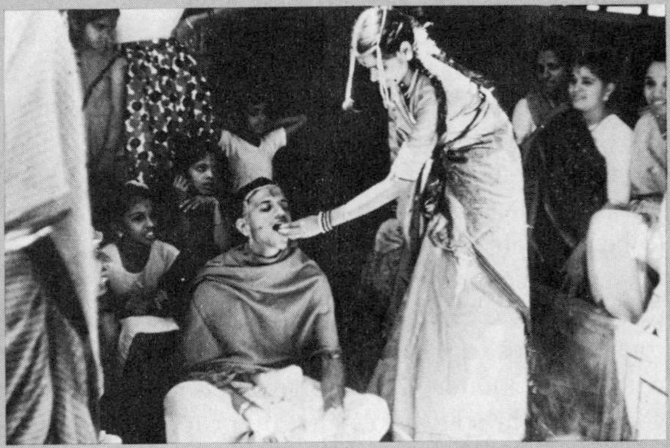

The Hindu wedding ceremony involves many symbols of undertaking new obligations. One of the wife's duties is to feed her husband and family; this is represented in the episode shown here. (James Martin)

In the Hindu "rite of the translated body," the body is placed on the carefully constructed funeral pyre and the eldest son sets the pyre aflame while reciting the traditional prayer. (Reuters/Bettmann)

the new couple visibly, to sanctify their union with a commingling of divine energies, and to ensure that their life together will be long, fertile, prosperous, and undisturbed by harmful superhuman forces.

Standing before the fire that is the visual focus of the ceremony, the groom clasps the bride's hand and says, "I seize thy hand . . . that thou mayest live to old age with me, thy husband." The bride places her foot on a stone to symbolize the firmness of her resolve. The ends of their flowing garments are knotted together, and they then enter into the ceremony's climactic and binding act: walking arm in arm three times around the sacred fire, each time in seven steps. The groom then touches the bride over the heart, saying, "Into my heart will I take thy heart; thy mind shall dwell in my mind." He paints on her forehead the vermilion cosmetic mark of a married Hindu woman. To symbolize their union, they eat a common meal while sitting together, though such commensal eating will not be their general practice as husband and wife. On the evening of their wedding day the two go out under the sky and look up together at the unchanging Pole Star, their model in a marriage that is indissoluble.

FUNERAL RITES

In any home, when a mature person has died, an observance follows that is called *aurdhvadaihika*, the "rite of the translated body." Within a few hours a procession of hurriedly summoned relatives and friends starts to move toward the local cremation site, led by the eldest son of the deceased as the chief mourner. The body is carried on a litter. The grieving marchers cry out the name of the god Rāma or sometimes the name Hari (Vishṇu). At the cremation ground the body is laid on a pyre of wood constructed according to strict rules. The son then performs the difficult duty of setting the pyre aflame with a firebrand that has usually been carried from home. He prays, "O Fire, when the body has been burnt, convey the spirit to its ancestors." The mourners return in a group toward their homes, without looking back, and they bathe in their clothing before entering any dwelling. Following this rite, ritual offerings are made every month for a year and once yearly thereafter.

THE HINDU TEMPLE AND ITS RITUALS

Another common site of pūjā, and a much more exalted one, is the Hindu temple. For 2,000 years the creation of temples and their images has been Hindu artists' principal outlet. In the outer walls of a temple, dozens or even hundreds of images may be set. But temple worship focuses on its main image, which is housed in a windowless cubic sanctuary at the temple's center. This cell is almost always topped by a spire, sometimes of soaring dignity.

In the tiny sanctuary there is neither room nor provision for assemblies of communal worshipers, as is found in churches, mosques, and synagogues. Hindus come as individuals, bringing personal salutations, petitions, and gifts and hoping to enjoy the benefits of viewing a deity. A priest enters the sanctuary and presents the offerings on the worshiper's behalf.

Temples are public institutions in the sense that Hindus of any varṇa may enter and worship. (Temple ceremonies, unlike the Vedic sacrifices, have always been open to the participation of śūdras, though only since India's independence have outcastes been welcome inside.) But in other respects the temples do not express the collective Hindu life. As a rule they are built by individuals, and worship there is the worship of individuals.

Pūjā is understood in many ways, and it is performed for many purposes, both self-interested and self-sacrificing. Some worshipers seek earthly favors through the deities' goodwill, to be won through human gifts. Others seek, by the merit of their worship, to attain after death a more fortunate rebirth on earth or in blessed realms above. Pūjā also serves as a form of expression for salvation seekers who dare to hope for liberation through the power of a personal God. Even Hindu monists (see Chapter 3) often participate in temple worship as a useful discipline.

All Hindu temples, both old (top) and new (right), possess the porch for shelter of worshipers and the spire rising above the cell where the icon of the deity is kept. (James McKinsey; Religious News Service)

RITES OF THE VILLAGE GODLINGS

In rural India another type of pūjā survives. The deities involved are minor beings unknown to Sanskrit literature. Our information about them comes from observations of Hindu life. Travelers approaching a typical Hindu village may see beside a well a pile of stones daubed with red paint or a conical mound of earth into which a red pennant has been thrust. Some such structures are earthen cells containing mud figurines. All are shrines of local godlings who must be worshiped in their own humble abodes.

These godlings are thought of by many people as destructive forces that from time to time disrupt the security of their villages. Human afflictions of unknown cause are believed to be the work of such local spirits who have been offended. When a calamity occurs—an epidemic, a drought—someone with shamanistic gifts must be found who can learn the identity of the irritated spirit and the cause of its anger and then prescribe the rites and offerings that will appease the vengeful deity.

Many of these spirits are believed to be female. The most powerful fall into two major classes: goddesses who protect particular villages and those who inflict particular diseases and other kinds of harm. The rites addressed to the village godlings are pūjās in general outline, but they differ from the pūjā rituals described so far. The officiating priest is not a brāhman but a person of low caste. The liturgical language is not Sanskrit but the local dialect. Animals are often sacrificed, and deliberate cruelties are sometimes inflicted on them in an apparent effort to satisfy the fury of the godlings through sufferings less grave than the loss of human life. The sole aim of such rites is to avert dangers; no notion of salvation or even of generating merit is involved.

It may be tempting to identify these rituals with magic rather than with religion, but the rites are religious in that superhuman beings are addressed by ritual. Another factor that is often considered characteristic of religion is social concern. In the worship of these deities, the usual individualism of Hindu religious activity is set aside for collective action to meet a common crisis, and local populations are drawn together in rare unity. During the short span of these gory performances, the fragmented Hindu village becomes a community in the fullest sense of the term. Thus, although these cults are often called forms of "lower Hinduism," in this one respect their achievement is high. Today, however, such practices are on the wane, giving way to the more effective remedies of modern science.

THE PLACE OF RELIGIOUS PRACTICE IN HINDUISM

In the eyes of outsiders, Hindu religious duties fall into two classes: ritual obligations and social obligations. Hindus do not regard this distinction as important; their aim is simply to fulfill the requirements of dharma, which applies to all the acts required by tradition. All the duties described in this chapter, whether ritual or social, are alike in that they are viewed as the requirements of dharma. The householder's offerings of water at the domestic shrine, a king's defense of his realm, and the work of a potter are all sacred duties; all produce merit or demerit, and all determine the future of the doer, for good or ill.

In Vedic times Hindus believed that through the pleasure of the gods, the observance of the traditional duties would surely lead to immortal life in heaven. But later Hindus conceived of the process of reward more mechanically, in terms of the accumulation of karma, and concluded that everlasting blessedness could not be earned by good deeds, whatever their number. The good karma produced by one's deeds will remain finite in quantity, no matter how long the life of virtue continues. Final liberation is infinite in length and in worth, and in a just universe one's merit, which is always finite, cannot deserve or attain this infinite reward. Good actions alone cannot bring final salvation from the round of births and deaths. At most, good actions can lead to blessings in this life and in future lives. Thus Hindus joined thinkers of other religions who have held that salvation cannot be obtained by good works alone.

Desolated by this loss of hope, Hindus groped for new paths to a life beyond all deaths. In time they established their classic plans of salvation: the Way of Knowledge (*jñānamārga*) and the Way of Devotion (*bhaktimārga*). Those seeking eternal beatitude shifted their hope from the life of religious duty to one of these new paths. After the Way of Knowledge and the Way of Devotion were recognized as divisions of Hindu life, the older discipline of the customary duties came also to be thought of as a way— the *karmamārga,* or Way of Action. It is the Hinduism of the Way of Action that we have been examining until now.

The conception of the three mārgas is one of the favorite Hindu formulas for identifying the distinctive forms of Hindu religious life. We shall use its categories to outline the subject matter of the next two chapters. In using the idea of the three mārgas we should not suppose, however, that all three ways begin at the same point or lead to the same destination. All Hindus are born into the pattern of customary living that makes up the karmamārga, and all travel on this way in their early years. Ideally, they become aware in time that the Way of Action does not end in salvation but in rebirth, and they consider taking up one of the two paths that do promise salvation.

It is not possible to divide all Hindus clearly into three definite groups according to mārga. Most Hindus, moreover, participate in two of them: millions continue to perform faithfully all the duties of the Way of Action, yet they have made a strong commitment also to one of the two ways of salvation. And in the understanding of the Way of Devotion, the requirements for liberation can be met while remaining completely faithful to all the duties of the Way of Action. The concept of the three mārgas is more useful in distinguishing types of Hinduism than in separating individual Hindus into types.

NOTES

1 All translations of *The Laws of Manu* in Part Two are from G. Bühler, trans., *Sacred Books of the East, Vol. 25: The Laws of Manu* (Oxford: Oxford University Press, 1886).

2 Chāndogya Upanishad 5.10.7 and Bṛihadāraṇyaka Upanishad 3.2.13, 4.4.5, 6.2.1–16. Unless specified otherwise, extracts from the upanishads have been translated by Norvin Hein from the Sanskrit texts published in S. Radhakrishnan, *The Principal Upanishads* (New York: Harper, 1953).

Religions of India

CHAPTER 3

Classical Hinduism: The Way of Knowledge

The distinctive form of Hinduism known as *jñāna-mārga,* the Way of Knowledge, first appears in the **upanishads**, a series of texts that began about 600 B.C.E. They arose after the Vedic period (Chapter 1) and were roughly contemporaneous with the development of the caste system (Chapter 2). The doctrines of this discipline have been respected in all segments of India's highly structured society ever since. The followers of the Way of Knowledge have typically been persons, like those born in Kṛishṇapur, who grew up in the Way of Action. In studying the religion of the upanishads, we are thus not looking at a different religion but are rather exploring another aspect of the religious life of the same society. The religious life of Kṛishṇapur and the mystical practices we shall now observe are complementary, two parts of the religious whole of classical India.

In contrast to the Way of Action, the Way of Knowledge implies a new kind of religious life that does not center on ritual and social duties but rather on mental disciplines involving *jñāna,* knowledge. This does not imply a stress on training in doctrines or putting one's trust in philosophical methods. The word *jñāna* is rendered most accurately by the Greek word *gnōsis,* as conceived of by the ancient Gnostics; both terms imply a religion based on secret wisdom, taught by sages and drawn from mystical experiences and esoteric sources not available to ordinary people.

The spirit of this path has been described well by the author of the Mārkaṇḍeya Purāṇa:

> He who thirsts after knowledge thinking "This should be known!" "This should be known!" does not attain to knowledge within a thousand *kalpas* [cosmic ages]. . . . He should seek to acquire that knowledge which is the essence of all, and the instrument for the accomplishment of all objects.[1]

THE UPANISHADS

The word *upanishad* means "a secret teaching" and has come to apply to scripture that contains such confidential teaching. The upanishads offer secrets in the sense that they tell of realities that are not perceived by ordinary persons, and their teaching can be understood only by persons who have entered into the life of meditation. They are the particular scriptures of the followers of the Way of Knowledge. More than 100 mystical writings of many ages are called upanishads, but the status of revealed scripture *(śruti)* has been given only to a canon of 13 of the earliest of these, composed in the four centuries ending about 200 B.C.E. These principal upanishads are believed to have been revealed in the same superhuman manner as all the Vedas and thus to be part of the Vedic corpus.

In part because their Sanskrit is now standard, the upanishads are the oldest literature that today's educated Hindus can comprehend readily. Hindus therefore tend to derive their impression of the substance of Vedic teaching from the upanishads. Deemed to contain the culmination of Vedic teaching, these works are called the **Vedānta** ("Vedas' End").

The 13 original upanishads have been used as authoritative sources to justify the doctrines of many later forms of Hindu metaphysical thought. We do not have space to give attention to one of them, the fascinating Sāṃkhya system, which now has little direct following and had only slight support in the upanishads. As our example of a system of the Way of Knowledge, we will focus instead on the Vedānta system, which evolved from the upanishads, and has long been the predominant form of this path.

The upanishads came into being in a post-Vedic social world and deal with problems that arose during that period. This is the era during which the dharma-sūtras were composed; the stratified caste system had taken form as well, supported by belief in rebirth governed by karma. The sacrifices, though still well remembered, attracted very few people, in part because they did not address the anxieties that then prevailed. To meet these new concerns, daring new lines of thought were being proposed in upper-class Aryan circles. Priestly lessons were being interrupted by persons who insisted on asking new questions. Fathers and sons were exploring new issues. Kings were sponsoring metaphysical debates at their courts. The most noted spokespersons of the new thinking, however, were not courtiers but forest wanderers, who made only brief and rare appearances in the assembly halls. People who were inspired by their message also left their homes, dwelling henceforth in secluded places, living on alms, and spending their hours in meditation. Unlike their Vedic predecessors, their strivings were internal. They sought control of their destiny by the power of *jñāna,* knowledge.

Scholars for a century have tried to discern the nature of this storm against tradition. Some saw in it a parallel to the Christian Reformation—a drive to compel the leaders of an old religion to give up their monopoly on religious leadership. Religious leaders of the kshatriya caste, according to this theory, were the prime instigators of this revolt. The rituals of the brāhmans were being swept away to make room for new, more vital religious movements. These scholars who saw a class struggle in the upanishads pointed to some kshatriya names among the leaders of the new movement and to some bitter words against arrogant brāhmans.

But this theory has not earned general acceptance. Recent studies show that most of the leaders of the new faith were in fact brāhmans and that the texts of the upanishads were preserved in the brāhmans' priestly schools. Criticism of the priests of Vedic sacrifice is seldom vehemently hostile. Nor are brāhmans accused of fraud: sacrificers do obtain the promised benefits. The upanishadic charge is rather that the fruits of sacrifice are of no lasting worth. They do bear sacrificers to heaven, as the priests promise, but the rituals' merit will eventually waste away. Heaven will end, and we will return to earth to have to endure again the wretched process of aging and dying (Muṇḍaka Upanishad 1.2.7–10).

The explosive factor in the upanishads is not the rise of a new class of leaders but the rise of a new class of problems. The old way of dealing with death has broken down. The new doctrine of karma, so useful for its justification of the discriminations of the new stratified society, has had the unintended effect of destroying the Vedic faith in a permanent refuge from death. For the person of the Vedic tradition, all that is visible on the horizon now is an eternal return to deaths (*punarmṛitu,* literally "again-death") and, as bad, to circumscribed lives of little freedom and minimal satisfaction.

Death is of course considered unpleasant in most cultures. But in India the doctrine of rebirth gave the problem special distressing dimensions. Vedic salvation came to be seen as transient, and old age, suffering, and death came to seem unpleasantness without end. The assurance that one will return from death to new lives brought no consolation to people of this new age. They knew life's weariness too well. No compensation lay ahead—in this life or the next ones—for the misery of multiple deaths. When one asks, "What is these people's greatest distress?" the upanishads' answer is clear: "May the evil of death not get me!" (Bṛihadāraṇyaka Upanishad 1.5.23); "To hoary and toothless and drooling old age may I not go" (Chāndogya Upanishad 8.14). These people longed for freedom in a stable, unchanging existence of another nature. The upanishads offered a solution for that problem, a gospel of liberation **(moksha)** from the endless round of worldly life. We must see what that salvation was and how it was attained.

Discussions of Brahman

The hope for eternal life rested on the discovery of a secret bridge between the human soul and an immortal spirit in the outer universe. On the one hand, the seers searched the outer universe for the fundamental principle of the cosmos; on the other, they conducted internal probes for the essential self. They thus employed an already ancient Indian method of searching for hidden correspondences between the worshiper and the cosmos.

The search for the fundamental outer principle centered on the term *Brahman*. Already much discussed in the Vedic era, the term was first used to refer to a mysterious power that was felt when one heard the sonorous sounds of the recited Vedic hymns. These awesome words were thought, like all words, to have ties with realities in the outer universe and to have power over them. As time went on, Vedic thinkers conceived of the totality of the sacred words of the Veda as a single power suffusing the outer universe. They called this all-pervasive unseen power *Brahman*. Imagined at first by priests interested in giving unlimited power to the sacrifice, Brahman came to be seen also as an energy that was the essence of the entire world and, as such, a powerful resource for the solution of the age's new anxieties.

Famous passages of the upanishads elaborate further on the concept of Brahman. It becomes the usual name for the mysterious "That One" who in Ṛigveda 10.129 lay originally on the waters of nonbeing and became the single source of all that breathes. One upanishad makes the point that Brahman is the whole of the power that resides in gods. Even the greatest of the Vedic deities appear and confess that they have no power aside from their share in the power of the mysterious Brahman dwelling in them (Kena 3). Asked how many gods there are, the sage Yājñavalkya reduces the traditional high number first to 33, then to three, and finally simply to one: Brahman (Bṛihadāraṇyaka Upanishad 3.9.1–9). The Brahman of the upanishads is the successor to the Vedic gods as the object of religious aspirations. It is more than a sacred power, however. It is the universal essence, the ultimate source of souls, the being from which all things spring, yet it remains one and makes the universe one. Chāndogya Upanishad 6.2.1 calls it "One only without a second."

The upanishads go on to stress that Brahman is not a material thing. We might say that Brahman is pure spirit. As the unifier of material things, Brahman cannot itself be material but must be a reality of a different, invisible, superior order. In one passage the boy Śvetaketu, who has never before heard of a "world soul," doubts his father Uddālaka's constant talk about a universal presence that cannot be seen. The father then demonstrates by example that realities that elude the senses do exist. He gives his son a lump of salt, asking him to drop it into a cup of water. After some time, Uddālaka asks Śvetaketu to return the salt to him. The boy gropes in the cup but cannot find the salt; he declares it gone. The father then asks Śvetaketu to sip from one side of the cup and then the other, and he complies. Then the boy admits that the salt is indeed there, in every part of the water, though nonexistent to touch or sight. Like that, says the father, Brahman can be present throughout the universe, though nowhere seen. Through the vision of the mystic only can its presence be directly known.

A second great affirmation is that Brahman is generative: itself a seeming nothing, it gives being to everything. It is the source of the whole phenomenal world. Uddālaka again offers his son a demonstration. Standing under a huge spreading banyan tree, Uddālaka asks his son to pluck one of its seed pods from a branch, then to crush the pod and extract a seed, then to split the seed open. "What do you see there?" the father asks. Seeing no seed kernel inside, Śvetaketu says, "Nothing at all, sir!" Just as from this "hollow" shell sprouts this mighty banyan tree, says the father, such is the case with great "world tree." It arose from an empirical nothing that no one can see and that some deny. The invisible Brahman has brought forth endless worldly forms—yourself included—and now sustains them (Chāndogya Upanishad 6.12).

Many passages in the upanishads dwell on the failure of all human language to describe Brahman. Those who search through the material world can report their discoveries in familiar terms, but spiritual realities are a different matter, for they lie beyond the competence of our descriptive words. Adjectives that speak of form, color, sound, smell, and so on can only misrepresent Brahman, for it cannot be described in sensory language. The truest words about Brahman are that it is indescribable. One can know the bliss of Brahman, but from Brahman itself both words and the mind fall back in defeat (Tattirīya Upanishad 2.4.1). Even those happy persons who have actually known Brahman can only point and say in ecstasy, "This is it!" (Kaṭha Upanishad 5.14).

Thus the searchers who sought the final cosmic principle reported that all being rests in Brahman, a spirit that is one throughout the universe, the life-giving principle, the source of all, a reality that can be experienced but not described in the words of any lexicon.

The Search for an Undying Soul

The spiritual seekers on the Way of Knowledge probed the inner world as ardently as the outer in hope of discovering a basis for immortality. After asking, "What is the universe?" they asked, "What, ultimately, is my very *self?*" The word is *ātman,* the reality that is the lasting and indispensable basis of one's being. *Self* is a possible translation of the word, but *self* does not suggest the religious nature of the quest for ātman. Let us speak of the drive to know the *soul,* though *soul,* too, is not a perfect rendering, for it misses psychological dimensions of the Sanskrit word. In using *soul* we should stand ready to attach new meanings to it.

The upanishads searched within for the basis for permanence in the individual. Asking, "What is the real person?" the authors first scrutinized the processes of birth, growth, decline, and death, seeking some enduring physical factor. Some said that there is a tiny inner person, the size of a thumb, that is the soul from which we are reconstituted again and again after death. Others found the essence in the old Vedic thinking about *prāṇa,* life-breath. Of course, in such physical constituents, real or imaginary, no basis for immortality was ever shown to exist. Hence the search for something deathless turned inward, to realities reported by persons given to introspective meditation. Indian thought has always accepted observations made in introspection as just as valid as observations of the outer world.

For lack of experience in meditation, outsiders often find the upanishads' descriptions of subjective explorations difficult to understand. Yet even outsiders can see a certain conceptual pattern occurring again and again: the soul is a core reality concealed from ordinary observation by multiple obscuring sheaths. These sheaths are impediments that must be overcome in order to apprehend the existence of the soul. Something akin to concentric rings are involved, in the midst of which the soul stands like the bull's-eye of a target. Three very different but complementary traditional sketches of the soul behind triple barriers have their beginnings in the upanishads.

The soul veiled by material stuff Three concentric shells of progressively coarser material are understood to be gathered around the soul. First and finest is the *causal body,* consisting of one's accumulated karma, in the form of deposits of very fine matter. This karma stuff clings to the soul throughout rebirths and even through dissolutions of the cosmos, causing one to be born again and again according to one's just desserts. Only when one enters final liberation will that innermost sheath be dissolved so that only one's soul, one's true self, will continue.

Just outside the causal body lies the sheath called the *subtle body,* made up of irreducible atoms, so to speak, of five kinds. Each kind of atom, when present in a compound thing, is detectable to a specific sense—sight, taste, touch, and so on. When not combined—as when making up the subtle body—these atoms elude all senses. So subtle bodies are not seen by the eye. They are the ghostly bodies of deceased persons. After death, in one's conjoined causal and subtle body, one goes to retribution in heavens or hells.

When reborn into the world according to one's remaining karma, one takes on again the third kind of body, the *gross body,* the outermost of the rings. That course sheath is the only self that ordinary persons see. The gross body is made up of five kinds of molecules, so to speak, each compounded from the atoms of which the subtle body is made.

This picture of three concentric bodies has influenced Hindu mysticism and shows how different the soul is conceived to be from any material substance. It also suggests how inaccessible the soul is to all of our ordinary means of knowing.

The soul as pure consciousness Chāndogya Upanishad 8.7–12 describes four levels of consciousness. In the *waking consciousness* we experience everyday life. The material world dominates, and the soul is utterly unknown. At night we sometimes dream, thus entering the *dreaming state,* in which we continue to perceive subtle material forms. Even in the dreaming state, however, material entities may still give us nightmares and thus distress us. Third is the *dreamless sleep* state of consciousness. In it the whole panorama of worldly things, both subtle and gross, vanishes. A blissful state, it is a premonition of the blessedness that will be known in the ultimate unity. Yet we remain residually aware that it is we who are in this blissful condition; we retain a remnant of self-consciousness.

Something lies beyond this state of deep, dreamless sleep—an ultimate state of consciousness. That highest state of awareness has no descriptive name. The upanishads simply call it *turīya,* "the fourth." In this state, blissful consciousness exists alone, without awareness of any object or concept. There is no awareness of material objects, gross or subtle, or of the individual who is conscious. There is neither longing for nor loathing of material objects. Only consciousness itself exists, the consciousness that is the very nature of the soul. Omnipresent, a reality without a second, its unity is like that ascribed to the cosmic Brahman.

The soul seated in a web of psychic organs Individuals make their appearance in the world by an evolutionary extension of consciousness from the soul into psychic faculties. They remain imbued with consciousness by reason of continuing contact with the soul from which they have emerged. The course of the evolution of the individual brought into existence first the conscious intellect called the **buddhi**, by which a person ponders information, decides, and initiates action. Then, by extension from the buddhi emerged the **manas**, or lower mind, which receives stimuli from the senses and identifies sense objects. Finally, the senses themselves—the faculties that have eye, ear, nose, tongue, and skin as their physical organs—emerged and began their work of apprehending the realities of the physical world.

But none of these faculties have any power to give one reflexive knowledge of the soul itself. They were so formed and so directed that they point outward only, making contact solely with the phenomenal world. The soul lies at the inward, not the outward, end of the line that is the sense process. To seek the soul through the operation of the senses is as foolish, to use modern terms, as to try to catch the operator of a powerful searchlight in the beam of the searchlight itself.

A searcher for the soul who looks outward to the phenomenal world only misdirects the power of knowing by which the soul itself could be revealed. How then *could* the soul be revealed? The pattern just outlined suggests that only introspection could be of any use—the tactic of retroversion to which the mystic must and does resort in the discipline called yoga. If consciousness can be withdrawn from things and turned back toward the center of our being, our power of knowing might be intensified and focused intensely on the soul. By such introspection we might merge our consciousness in that central pool of radiant consciousness from which the consciousness animating all of our psychic organs once emerged. As the Kaṭha Upanishad suggests:

The Creator pierced the sense-holes outward,
So one looks out, not toward the soul within.
Some wise man seeking deathlessness
With eyes inverted saw the soul direct.

No verse of the upanishads reveals the self-understanding of its mystics more effectively. Not the casual report of an explorer, it is the proclamation of a discoverer, testifying to a culminating inner experience. In the upanishads there are many such attestations to the experience of the oceanic trance. To post-Vedic India this experience brought relief from great distresses—particularly to a burning question about the afterlife. The obscuring sheaths have been penetrated and the true self has been found in an interior ocean of light that has no islands and no shores; immune to the changes wrought by time, that universal consciousness is all that one has ever been or ever will be. Hope for a stable afterlife, lost at the end of the Vedic age, is regained on a different basis, and the world's sufferings and oppressions can now be seen as fantasies of no importance. Peace is suggested in Chāndogya Upanishad 7.35.2:

Not death does the seer see
Nor illness nor any sorrow.
The seer sees just the All,
Attains the All entirely.

The reference to the All indicates that searches for the final reality within and the final reality without had led to a single conclusion: a reality that is immaterial, indescribable, generative, and yet eternally one. "Thou art That" was Uddālaka's final word to his son. Your soul is the world soul, Brahman, and shares its eternity and bliss. The discovery opened the way for a new kind of religious effort that became a way of salvation, the Way of Knowledge. (See the accompanying box, "The Way of Knowledge in a Upanishad Text.")

Of course, the trance that dissolves the mystic's fears appears to dissolve the mystic himself. The sage replies that nothing that ever truly was will vanish through this discovery. All that disappears—and rightly—is the ignorant supposition of individuality

The Way of Knowledge in a Upanishad Text

If you have become interested in this mystical religion, you should undertake, early, some direct reading in the upanishads. If you have little background in the meditative life, the ideas and references in these texts may be puzzling, but the struggle to understand may be fascinating. The following passages are from the sixth chapter of the Maitrī Upanishad, a scripture that expresses some of the teaching we have presented in this textbook—on Brahman, on the practices and processes of yogic meditation, on the final vision, and on the benefits that spring from the attainment of long-hidden knowledge of Brahman (here spelled, in stem form, *Brahma*).

3. There are, assuredly, two forms of Brahma [Brahman]: the formed and the formless. Now, that which is the formed is unreal; that which is the formless is real, is Brahma, is light.

17. Verily, in the beginning this world was Brahma, the limitless One—limitless to the east, limitless to the south, limitless to the west, limitless to the north, and above and below, limitless in every direction. Truly, for him east and the other directions exist not, nor across, nor below, nor above.

Incomprehensible is that supreme Soul (Ātman), unlimited, unborn, not to be reasoned about, unthinkable—He whose soul is space! In the dissolution of the world He alone remains awake. From that space He, assuredly, awakes this world, which is a mass of thought. It is thought by Him, and in Him it disappears. . . .

To the unity of the One goes he who knows this.

18. The precept for effecting this [unity] is this: restraint of the breath (prāṇāyāma), *withdrawal of the senses* (pratyāhāra), *meditation* (dhyāna), *concentration* (dhāraṇā), *contemplation* (tarka), *absorption* (samādhi). *Such is said to be the sixfold Yoga. By this means*

When a seer sees the brilliant
Maker, Lord, Person, the
Brahma-source,
Then, being a knower, shaking
off good and evil,
He reduces everything to unity
in the supreme
Imperishable.

19. Now, it has elsewhere been said: "Verily, when a knower has restrained his mind from the external, and the breathing spirit (prāṇa) *has put to rest objects of sense, thereupon let him continue void of conceptions. Since the living individual who is named "breathing spirit" has arisen here from what is not breathing spirit, therefore, verily, let the breathing spirit restrain his breathing spirit in what is called the fourth condition* (turīya)." *For thus it has been said:*

That which is non-thought, [yet]
which stands in the midst of
thought,
The unthinkable, supreme
mystery!
Thereon let one concentrate his
thought
And the subtle body, too,
without support.

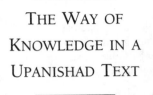

20. Now, it has elsewhere been said: "One may have a higher concentration than this. By pressing the tip of his tongue against the palate, by restraining voice, mind, and breath, one sees Brahma through contemplation." When through self, by the suppressing of the mind, one sees the brilliant Self which is more subtle than the subtle, then having seen the Self through one's self, one becomes self-less. Because of being self-less, he is to be regarded as incalculable, without origin—the mark of liberation (moksha). *This is the supreme secret doctrine. For thus has it been said:*

For by tranquillity of thought
Deeds (karma), *good and evil,*
one destroys!
With soul (ātman) *serene,*
stayed on the Soul (Ātman),
Delight eternal one enjoys!

24. Now, it has elsewhere been said: "The body is a bow. The arrow is [the sacred sound] Om. *The mind is its point. Darkness is the mark. Having pierced through the darkness, one goes to what is not enveloped in darkness. Then, having pierced through what is thus enveloped, one sees Him who sparkles like a wheel of fire, of the color of the sun, mightful, the Brahma that is beyond darkness, that shines in yonder sun, also in the moon, in fire, in lightning. Now, assuredly, when one has seen Him, one goes to immortality." . . .*

28. Now, it has elsewhere been said: "Having passed beyond the elements, the senses, and objects of sense; thereupon having seized the bow whose string is the life of a religious mendicant and whose stick is steadfastness; and with the arrow which consists of freedom from self-conceit having struck down the first warder of the door to Brahma [egoism]—he who has confusion as his crown, covetousness and envy as his ear-rings, lassitude, drunkenness, and impurity as his staff, lord of self-conceit, who seizes the bow whose string is anger and whose stick is lust, and who slays beings here with the arrow of desire—having slain him, having crossed over with the raft of the syllable Om *to the other side of the space in the heart, in the inner space which gradually becomes manifest one should enter the hall of Brahma, as the miner seeking minerals enters into the mine. Then let him disperse the fourfold sheath of Brahma by the instruction of a spiritual teacher* (guru).

"Henceforth being pure, clean, void, tranquil, breathless, selfless, endless, undecaying, steadfast, eternal, unborn, independent, he abides in his own greatness.

"Henceforth, having seen [the soul] which abides in his own greatness, he looks down upon the wheel of transmigrating existence (saṃsāra) *as upon a rolling chariot-wheel."*

For thus has it been said:

If a man practices Yoga for six
months,
And is constantly freed [from
the senses],
The infinite, supreme,
mysterious
Yoga is perfectly produced.

But if a man is afflicted with
Passion and Darkness,
Enlightened as he may be—
If to son and wife and family
He is attached—for such a one,
no, never at all!

Source: Robert Ernest Hume, *The Thirteen Principal Upanishads* (New York: Oxford University Press, 1931), pp. 424–443.

and personhood. Over millennia that experience and that reasoning about the true self have been accepted gladly by millions of persons who found little satisfaction in the careers available to them in their place and age.

Millions of other Hindus, it will be noted, hesitated to make that drastic sacrifice. Lovers of the world or lovers of persons human or divine, they turned away from such disappearance of persons and raised up other understandings of salvation.

THE VEDĀNTA TRADITION

When the canon of the great upanishads was completed, the new and powerful religion called the Vedānta began its long history. The Vedānta is based on a distinctive kind of mystical experience and on belief in the underlying unity of all reality. This belief in an all-inclusive oneness left thinkers with a paradox. The upanishads often speak, on the one hand, of the complex world as an actuality. On the other hand, the undivided and all-inclusive Brahman they declare to exist alone. But how can the universe be divided and not divided at the same time? If Brahman, the sole reality, is one, must not the multiform world of experience be ruled out as nonexistent? And if the many things of the world are real, then must not the universal Brahman be a fiction?

The Vedānta tradition quietly grew for 1,000 years, recording its thinking on these disturbing questions in aphoristic texts on Brahman known as the **brahmasūtras**, the earliest of which is the Brahmasūtra of Bādarāyana (c. 200 C.E.). The first full presentation of the Vedānta system is a commentary on this work by the founder of the important Advaita (nondualistic) Vedānta School, Śaṅkara, writing around the year 800. Śaṅkara mediated between the two sides of the paradox, on the one hand the claim that plurality is real and Brahman is unreal versus the claim made by some Mahāyāna Buddhists (see Chapter 8) that the world is an unreal phantasm. He taught a *monistic* system: all things *do* have a substantive ground (Brahman), and that substance is one.

"What am I?" That is a basic question in any Indian outlook. Śaṅkara saw that we take ourselves to be separate individuals, each with a separate body that is a real and lasting part of ourselves. Therefore, we associate ourselves with the history of our changing bodies, thinking that our real selves undergo disease or death. Because our bodies are separate, we see ourselves as separate from others, and we are filled with thoughts of "I" and "mine." We think we can make ourselves happy with physical comforts, pleasure, or wealth. If we fail to attain these goals, we become dejected; if we succeed, we are elated, though only for a moment. We are, in short, never satisfied. We are constantly miserable but unaware of the reasons for our misery. We want liberation from rebirth but do not know how to attain it.

What the revealed upanishads assure us, says Śaṅkara, is that we are not separate individuals, winning or losing life's competitive struggles. In fact we are eternally one with the universal and immortal Brahman, the only reality. That perfect being is always characterized by consciousness, existence, and bliss. Since Brahman is the self in all of us, its blessed characteristics are ours also. In our daily life, however, we do not perceive the blessed unitary Brahman, and we do not know its bliss. How, then, can we believe the upanishads' statements about Brahman to be true?

Levels of Knowledge

In reply, Śaṅkara pointed out that even in everyday experience our senses can deceive us. There are several levels of what we call knowledge, and they are of unequal value in revealing truth. Even as unenlightened persons we are aware of one grade of experience that yields only *deluded knowledge.* For example, when we look out over a hot shimmering plain and see in the distance a lake that is only a mirage, our knowledge of the lake is deluded knowledge. Or we may mistake a shell on a beach for a shiny coin. Such perceptions are based on apprehension, but the object of experience is misperceived. Perceptual mistakes like these are corrected by comparison with later experiences and with the experiences of others. Śaṅkara's point is that experience can be deceptive and that seeing is not necessarily believing.

Empirical knowledge is the kind of knowledge that we get when we see real lakes or real coins. Their reality stands the test of repeated observations or other people's descriptions. It is this empirical knowledge that convinces us that we are all separate persons. It convinces us, too, that in our real selves, we are bodies—bodies that suffer injuries, grow old, and die. Therefore, Śaṅkara asserted, empirical knowledge is open to correction. Fortunately, empirical knowledge too can be superseded when we rise to the insight of a still higher grade.

Supreme (pāramārthika) knowledge is the final and highest form of experience open to us. It yields knowledge that is absolute truth. Unlike empirical knowledge, pāramārthika knowledge is not obtained through the senses, the mind, or the intellect but directly through consciousness, ātman. This supreme experience comes when our fallible senses are made to cease their operation and the conceptualizing activities of the intellect are stopped. When our psychic organs are put to rest and all our power of consciousness is concentrated in our innermost self, a unique state of consciousness called **samādhi** is reached. In this introverted state, a distorting film is removed from consciousness, and we can apprehend reality as it actually is. The understanding of what is real and what is unreal undergoes a remarkable reversal:

In what all beings call night
the disciplined sage awakes;
That wherein beings awaken
that the silent one sees as night.

(Bhagavadgītā 2.69)

Direct perception, then, convinces the mystic that the separateness of persons is false and that the oneness of all is the truth. Just as the upanishads teach, reality is a single ocean of consciousness without any real division. Utterly homogeneous, it is beyond any effect of time and change. This one immortal being is not only pure consciousness but also pure bliss. In it one is immune to all ills. The defects of our bodies and our bodies themselves are delusions comparable to a mirage. There is liberation from all distress for those who have attained this knowledge, for once gained, it is never lost. Those mystics are at peace now and forever who realize their oneness with the blissful Brahman.

Śaṅkara's Doctrine of Māyā

If universal oneness is the reality, why do we so persistently misconceive of ourselves as separate individuals? Because the effect exists (because there *is* delusion), it must be inferred that a cause exists, a factor that makes us project onto the unitive Brahman the many figments that make up our everyday world. Analogous to the factor that makes us see lakes and coins when the reality is something else, a cosmic factor causes our social delusions of plurality. Śaṅkara calls it **māyā**, "illusion," which he uses in several different senses. First, māyā is the factor creating cosmic delusion. It is māyā that is operative when our consciousness misinforms us that the universe is composed of many things. It is māyā also that causes us to apprehend ourselves wrongly as separate individuals, each composed of a separate body and soul. To māyā as a factor distorting our subjective understanding Śaṅkara also applies the term *avidyā,* or ignorance.

Even though its metaphysical status is a mystery, this factor cannot be conceived of as real (that is, included within Brahman) because Brahman includes no second thing. Nor is it unreal (apart from Brahman), for no thing—except nothing—is apart from Brahman. Clearly, māyā is not nothing: it acts, with catastrophic consequences. Neither real nor unreal, māyā is a unique entity that is the cause of all human sin and misery; it is the supreme impediment to our salvation. It causes individuals to appear separate, to believe in their separateness, and to act selfishly. It causes a material world to distract souls into love and hate for its figments. It binds illusionary individuals to illusionary bodies and illusionary worlds and to illusionary responsibility for their illusionary acts. Our one noble desire is the desire to end the ignorance that makes us desire individual material gain. We can hope to attain liberation only if we are willing to renounce the world and adopt the arduous life of seekers of salvation through the Way of Knowledge.

The Sannyāsī, Renouncer of the World

It was recognized from the start that seekers of the extraordinary knowledge of the hidden oneness of things must use extraordinary means. Old values were to be purged; new sensitivities were to be developed; the mind was to be retrained with full-time dedication. In the upanishads the original proponents of the new mystical religion are presented as men who abandoned house and property and wandered off into the forest. Residence in secluded places is described as advantageous to the practice of meditation, and as time went on the mystical literature became more and more insistent on a clean break with the workaday world. At first the leaders of the mystical movement are spoken of in general terms as wanderers or ascetics, but the later dharmaśāstras give them the specific and standard name *sannyāsī,* "renouncer." The caste society since its first creation has generated, through its heavy restrictions and its imposed tasks, a massive secession from strictly ordered life. The renunciation **(sannyāsa)** that sannyāsīs have undergone is understood to have been a severe and permanent renunciation—not merely of desires or of one's profession but of the world. The term *sannyāsī* to this day, when applied to a religious mendicant, credits that person with serious study of Vedānta teaching and a sincere desire for final liberation. That is the kind of monk we shall be discussing. (Female renunciants have always been rare.)

For 2,000 years most Hindus have believed that some day, in some rebirth or other, they should abandon the life of the householder for the life of the wandering monk. And throughout those millennia, mendicants in saffron robes, carrying a staff and a begging bowl, have been conspicuous on the Indian scene and have had the respect and support of Hindus.

Becoming a sannyāsī is therefore a much-honored act, but it is an act of free personal choice. At what age, or even in what life, the move must be made, the scriptures do not say. As the upanishads grew more influential, a massive number of young persons on the very verge of adulthood began to adopt the forest life. By the second century C.E., as expressed in the Bhagavadgītā, many in Hindu society were dismayed at the loss of the services of the young renunciants. The dharmaśāstras drew up a defensive rule that world renunciation should be delayed until the declining years of life, when one's skin is wrinkled and one's hair is white *(Manu* 6.2). This delaying of the turn to the monastic life has remained the ideal, but in practice insistent young persons have always been allowed to make the move. The one essential qualification is an inner one: disillusion with worldly pleasures and a deep longing for liberation from further births.

Even while still living the life of a householder, Hindus committed to the Way of Knowledge are able to make preparations that should hasten the time of their salvation. They should curb the ego, calm their minds by selfless performance of their duties, and avoid bad conduct, which destroys serenity (Kaṭha Upanishad 2.24). The same need of mental calm before even attempting advanced meditation underlies a requirement that one must perfect in oneself five moral virtues: nonviolence, truthfulness, honesty, chastity, and freedom from greed. These five virtues, together, are always identified as the first of the traditional eight-limbed yoga. They may be perfected while one is still living in the world. The same is true of five further essential virtues, of mental nature, that comprise the second step: cleanliness in body and in diet, the practice of being contented, austerity (developing powers of self-denial and endurance), study of religious texts and doctrines, and meditation on the Lord. This last, meditation on a personal deity, is thought to be useful for beginners on the Way of Knowledge, even though they will eventually surrender the personal concept for an impersonal conception of the divine.

Instructions for the life of laypersons are often given in terms that are less formal than these lists. Śaṅkara simply says that spiritual seekers should meditate on Vedānta truths constantly, study the upanishads, and ponder such scriptural statements as "I am Brahman."

After years or lifetimes of such preparation, it is believed, a householder will suddenly perceive that it is time to renounce the world. The precipitating factor is often some dramatic manifestation of the transience of life—there is a death in the family, or a king looks in the mirror and finds the first gray in his beard. At root there may be some catastrophic reversal of fortune—great financial loss or the collapse of a reputation. The event may be a domestic quarrel or even a single chiding word. The routine duties of a person's life suddenly become suffocating and meaningless, and the tools of his trade are dropped, never to be picked up again. Or a drive for great wealth succeeds, and success brings a realization of the vanity of possessions and the need for something eternal. The lives of famous saints often tell the story of these spectacular turning points in spiritual careers.

The actual departure of the would-be sannyāsī from his family and village is a solemn ritual. In a round of farewell calls, the departing one gives away his prized possessions. He performs his last ritual as a householder. In a formal separation, he leaves his village on foot, and his son escorts him for a stated distance on his way. Finally, at a certain spot father and son take a back-to-back position, the son facing toward the village, the father toward the unknown. Both stride off resolutely in their respective directions without looking back. The father must walk straight ahead until the end of the day without stopping. Theoretically, he should never again mention the name of his village or even think of it.

For him a completely new life begins. He becomes a wandering beggar, building no fire and cooking no food. Appearing at a house door just after the time of dinner, he eats whatever scraps he may be given. He sleeps wherever night overtakes him—ideally under a tree, but perhaps at a temple or a charitable shelter for monks. Rarely, such seekers reside for extended periods in a monastic establishment, but in contrast to Buddhist and Christian monasticism, no special value is attached to cloistered living. Mendicants rove at will, visiting temples, attending religious fairs, or lingering on mountains noted as places of meditation. The monk has no family obligations, no ritual duties, and no work to do. He has faith that he will attain in his own time, alone, the liberation he is seeking.

In this spontaneous new life, the irritations of a restrictive society are eased. The former caste of the holy man is forgotten, and its restrictions no longer oppress him. If gifted, the holy man may become an eminent teacher or spiritual guide. He is now his own master, free to roam and to live on alms, on the sole condition that he forever separate himself from society's concerns. Sannyāsa has been the outlet for millions of sensitive Hindu men who could not endure the confinements of caste life. It has also been the safety valve of the caste community, siphoning off the discontent of people who might otherwise have destroyed it. Sannyāsa, like the doctrine of karma, has been a strong supporting pillar of the classical Hindu culture.

Since the skills developed in the worldly life do not help in the inner explorations now to be carried out, the renouncer quickly seeks out the expertise of a teacher who has made the mystical journey and reached the other shore. It is believed that destiny provides each seeker with his own true teacher and that this guru and his disciple will recognize each other when they ultimately meet face-to-face.

The guru now administers the rite of initiation into the final stage of life. It is irreversible, a ritual death to the world and a rebirth into the realm of transcendence. The teacher rips off the disciple's sacred thread and cuts off his queue, the signs of honorable status as

This Hindu ascetic sits in the characteristic meditation position. He remains motionless and seemingly oblivious to the world. (Religious News Service)

a conforming Hindu. Henceforth the disciple will no longer belong to any caste. The names by which he has been known are uttered for the last time, and the teacher confers on him a new name devoid of caste significance but evocative of some religious truth. The guru should instruct his disciple in doctrine and in proper monkish living. When the disciple is deemed ready, he is guided in the advanced meditational discipline that is called yoga.

Yoga

The term *yoga,* like its English cognate *yoke,* means "to join, unite" and also "to harness up, set seriously to work." Followers of the monistic Vedānta tradition understand yoga as training that can bring about conscious union of one's own soul with the universal soul. There are several systems of yoga.

Haṭhayoga is a physical discipline used to tone the body; it may or may not be followed by deeper meditations. The Tāntric schools, whose position is marginal in Hinduism, practice a *kundalinī* yoga that has its own unusual imagery. Some modern mystical movements have developed their own unusual yogic practices. But for most Hindus yoga refers to a version of the eight-stage meditational discipline attributed to the ancient sage Patañjali. An early variation on the formula was seen in the box "The Way of Knowledge in a Upanishad Text," in Maitrī Upanishad 6.18. Patañjali's *Yoga Sūtra* outlines the "limbs" or stages of the yogic path more fully: moral restraint, mental discipline, posture *(āsana),* breath control *(prāṇāyama),* withdrawal from sense objects *(pratyāhāra),* steadying of attention *(dhāraṇā),* meditation on religious insights *(dhyāna),* and concentration on or mystical merging with the ultimate *(samādhi).*

The first two, discussed earlier, are preliminary stages, consisting of moral and meditational preparation. The third stage prescribes physical postures that are thought to be conducive to serenity. The meditator is to take a bodily posture such as the lotus position (legs crossed, hands cupped with palms upward in the lap), which is designed not to strain the body but to make it possible to forget the body so that a higher identity may be known. Next comes the control of breath, which is related to a common belief that breath is at the root of life and that breath control can therefore bring one nearer to the basis of one's being. More obviously, breath regulation brings one's attention into sharp focus and creates calmness.

Mental calmness is also the goal of the fifth step, the withdrawal of the senses from attention to all objects of sense. The process is compared to a turtle's retraction of its limbs into its shell. Immunity from the upsetting effect of outside circumstances is the end in view, and freedom to concentrate one's attention on inward matters. The sixth step, the steadying of attention, assumes that freedom from distractions has been achieved and involves development of the ability to hold one's attention firmly on one focal point as long as desired. The seventh stage provides for positive meditation on chosen religious themes such as the thought "Thou art That" or "I am Brahman"—great words of the upanishads—or the sacred syllable *Om,* the sound symbol of Brahman. Such meditations, long continued, are designed to bring the nation of individual selfhood near to extinction. If the meditator is bold enough to accept that extinction and press on, he is said to enter into the culminating experience of monistic meditation that is called samādhi. This last stage of yoga begins when the yogi's awareness, long focused on a single point, swells explosively to encompass a limitless reality. A sense of all-reaching participation in a living cosmos sweeps over him, and his individuality appears

Two modern advocates of the doctrine of monism: left, the Shankaracharya of Dwarka Peeth, the abbot of one of the monasteries founded by Śánkara; right, Sarvepalli Rādhākrishnan, creative modern philosopher. The abbot's accoutrements indicate that, despite his commitment to the impersonal Brahman, he allows or practices the worship of the personal god Śiva. Note the forehead lines, the large beads, and the trident held by his attendant. (Religious News Service)

to be dissolved in the light of a luminous ocean. The sense of infinite oneness is understood by the mystic to be a revelation taking precedence over all earlier insights: it is the final truth about the nature of things. Plural things and plural souls are no longer seen as real. But the disappearance of individuality does not bring nothingness. The real person is found in a universal consciousness in which there are no distinctions, no possibility of change, and no sense of time. Births become phantasmal events that do not really occur, and deaths become appearances without reality. Meditators who know this experience understand themselves to be forever free. Life beyond death will be a continuation of this experience, which is a revelation to the living of the nature of moksha, final salvation.

In the assurance of immortality implicit in the unitive mystical experience, seekers of the age of the upanishads recovered, substantially, the paradise that had been lost at the end of the Vedic age. Attained by different means, it was a different paradise that could be enjoyed only by renouncing all earthly values and even personal existence itself.

People who undergo this experience are called *jīvanmuktas* (the liberated while still living) or simply "enlightened." Irreversibly stripped of all sense of self and incapable of any self-serving act, they will acquire no new karma. When their old karma is expended, their bodies will die for the last time. They will then enter into final liberation in Brahman, never to be born again.

Some of the most famous Hindu saints have been natural mystics who had no need to practice yoga but achieved the unitive experience spontaneously and without conscious effort. There are some teachers today who deny the necessity of yoga and urge their disciples to await such a natural revelation.

Will all who take up the search for mystical enlightenment achieve it? Hindus have usually held that the chance of success is small for those who remain in society as householders (Maitrī Upanishad 6.28). It is admitted that even renunciation of the world and a lifetime of meditational effort are often insufficient. Although meditation practices may help, the outcome of yoga ultimately lies beyond human control. If realization is not achieved in the present life, however, all agree that the efforts of strivers are not lost. Reborn to more favorable situations, these people will eventually attain illumination and the liberation that is their goal.

NOTE

1 Manmatha Nath Dutt, *A Prose English Translation of Mārkaṇḍeya Purāṇam* (Calcutta, 1896), p. 181.

Religions of India

CHAPTER 4

Classical Hinduism: The Way of Devotion

The third of the Hindu mārgas, the Way of Devotion or *bhaktimārga,* places its hope for liberation in the power of a personal God of the universe. Two great theistic movements in Hinduism—one centered on Śiva, the other centered on Vishṇu—have been exceedingly popular for 2,000 years. Together they probably hold the allegiance of a majority of Hindus today. These two forms of Indian religion are the most similar to the faiths of the West.

Like the Way of Knowledge, the Way of Devotion was a product of the stressful period when followers of the Vedic religion for the first time experienced a regimented social order and when even the heavens no longer offered hope of lasting freedom. The Way of Knowledge and Buddhism offered release from karma and the unwanted round of lives, but at the cost of continuing existence as a person. Many Hindus cherished their own individuality too highly to find satisfaction in such liberations. In intellectual struggles they gradually worked out a different plan of salvation through a personal God of new stature. This development was difficult for people reared in the Vedic tradition because the comprehensive forces that control human life—ṛita, or dharma, and karma—were conceived of as impersonal principles. The personal gods of the Veda, by contrast, were thought to reside in some specific region of the natural world, exercising only limited powers and functions. Even the greatest gods were believed to control only a portion of the universe.

Speculation about a cosmic god with universal jurisdiction is evident in the late Vedic hymns, but the notion of such a deity developed into monotheism only slowly. The rise of the concept of a universal "world essence" helped greatly in the emergence of monotheism when, in the Śvetāśvatara Upanishad (around the fifth century B.C.E.), the Vedic god Rudra (now known as Śiva) is described as Brahman, the totality of all being and all power. As such, the Lord Śiva rules over all. He pervades persons, is present in their hearts, and thus may be perceived by meditators who practice yoga. When we see him in ourselves as Śiva the Kindly, we respond with devotion (**bhakti**); God in turn responds with gracious help. It was he who created karma, and what he created he can break. When the fetters of karma are broken, there begins a life of freedom, including freedom from death. A century or two later, the writings known as the Bhagavadgītā expanded this idea about Brahman into a monotheistic theology: Brahman became the universal power of God. This doctrine soon entered all branches of the bhaktimārga.

The term *bhakti* derives from a verb meaning "to divide and share," as when food is divided and shared at family and caste gatherings. The noun *bhakti* recalls the loyalty and trust that prevail at such meetings—the generous portions of food, the junior members' willingness to serve, and the protectiveness of the elders. *Bhaktas,* devotees who follow the Way of Devotion, have discovered such affection at the center of the universe in "the great Lord of all the worlds, a friend of all creatures" (Bhagavadgītā 5.29). While sharing this common attitude toward God, the Way of Devotion has from the beginning consisted of two separate streams: the worshipers of Śiva, known as **Śaivas**, and the worshipers of Vishṇu, called **Vaishṇavas.** Let us begin with the Śaivite tradition.

THE WORSHIP OF ŚIVA

Śiva is known in the Vedas as Rudra, the Howler, a power operating in destructive rainstorms. His face is red, and his neck is blue. He dwells isolated in the mountains, and his retainers include robbers and ghosts. His weapons include sharp arrows and the dreaded thunderbolt, and in the Vedic hymns none who worship him assume that they are safe from him. He attacks with fever, coughs, and poisons, yet he is also a physician who possesses 1,000 remedies.

Persons impressed by life's harshness and brevity have been drawn to the worship of Śiva. For his worshipers, safety can be found—if at all—only by dealing with the one who presides over such dangers. They see Śiva as the special divine force behind all natural processes of destruction; consequently, Śaivism attracted small groups of Hindu society's alienated, morbid, and misanthropic members, drawn by the religion's stark realism. Yet there are many more optimistic souls who are also part of the Śaivite circle who worship him as the supreme monotheistic deity.

The Liṅgam and Yoni Emblem

Shrines dedicated to Śiva began to appear in the first century B.C.E. In some shrines the object of worship was a stone pillar resembling the male generative organ: Śiva had come to be regarded as a source of procreation as well as destruction! Images of Śiva in human form were also common. Worship of the phallic emblem did not become dominant until it had evolved into an only vaguely phallic upright cylinder rounded at the top, called a **liṅgam**, which is clearly a symbol rather than a representation of the sex organ. Four faces often look out from the sides of the shaft. These indicate the omniscience of the god, who faces in all directions.

Within a few centuries it became customary to seat the cylinder in a shallow, spouted dish that was at once a basin for catching liquid oblations poured over the liṅgam and a symbolic **yoni**, or female organ, representing Śiva's **śākti**, or female reproductive power. A combined liṅgam and yoni icon usually stands at the center of shrines to Śiva. Modern Hindu scholars insist that this emblem refers to metaphysical truths only, even though it uses symbols of the human genitals. Indeed, the rites of liṅgam worship have never been orgiastic or erotic. The icon makes a statement about the cosmos: Śiva's potent generative power is eternally at work, and it is feminine as well as masculine, a force for life as well as for destruction.

Because the people of the Indus valley civilization used similar phalluses in their cult, many scholars speculate that the liṅgam and perhaps other aspects of Śiva worship entered Hinduism from this old source.

A more dramatic but less common recognition of femininity in Śiva's nature is the icon of the half-woman Lord (Ardhānārīśvara) in which the image's left half is full-breasted and wears the ornaments and clothing of a woman while the right half is presented as male. The same tendency manifests itself in the development of many new myths about Śiva's powerful wife, called, Umā, Pārvatī, or Durgā.

Śiva's feminine side was conveyed also in the growing body of Śiva mythology produced between the first and fifth centuries C.E. In the epics and Purāṇas, Śiva develops a dual nature, showing a kindlier side while maintaining his destructiveness. He haunts the cremation grounds and smears his body with the ashes of the dead. (One still prepares for the worship of Śiva by rubbing ashes over one's body and marking one's forehead with three horizontal stripes of white ash.) Śiva wears a necklace made of the skulls of past deities, whom he has outlived and whose creations he has brought to an end. Stories of his wildly destructive acts continue to be told, and he is given new names that stress his ferocious and unpredictable nature. Some orders of ancient Śiva devotees shocked their contemporaries by dwelling in creation grounds, practicing bloody sacrifices, or using skulls as alms bowls.

As Śiva became a universal God, however, new myths showed him using his dreadful powers in

Though Śaiva artists sometimes give Śiva a human form, this simpler representation appears in the usual shrine. Śiva is seen here as the universal male power in everlasting union with his female energy. By their combined force, the world comes into being and evolves. (The Metropolitan Museum of Art, gift of Samuel Eilenberg, 1987)

constructive ways. One favorite myth tells how Śiva saved the world from danger: when the sacred River Ganges fell in a destructive torrent, Śiva caught it in his heavy hair. Thus Śiva's role as the protector is often symbolized by a gentle river spouting from his matted locks.

Śiva as the One God

After 400 C.E. several new groups arose that worshiped Śiva as the supreme God. Some sects composed Sanskrit manuals called *āgamas* that articulated their beliefs and guided their members in rituals, image making, and temple building. Another sect, the South Indian Śaivasiddhānta theological tradition, developed in the seventh century; it still thrives. But the most significant development in Śaivite religion was the appearance of a series of remarkable religious poets who wrote in the South Indian Tamil tongue. Beginning in the seventh century with Appar and Sambandar, their beautiful hymns are still sung. As recently as the seventeenth century, there were new surges of devotion in Tamil literature, and a poet named Śivavākkiyar praised the uniqueness of Śiva in these lines:

Not Vishnu, Brahmā, Śiva,
In the Beyond is He,
Not black, nor white, nor ruddy,
This Source of things that be;
Not great is he, not little,
Not female and not male—
But stands far, far, and far beyond
All being's utmost pale![1]

The early Tamil poets' belief in a personal God was challenged, however, by the philosopher Śaṅkara's arguments for an impersonal Brahman (see Chapter 3). Śaivite theologians like the South Indian Meykandār and his disciple Aruḷnandi in the thirteenth century defended Śaivite beliefs: by calling Śiva *Paśupati,* the Lord of Cattle, the Śaivasiddhānta theologians wished to emphasize the protective aspect of Śiva's nature. Like Western religions' notion of a "good shepherd," it stresses Śiva's concern for human souls; like a shepherd, Śiva seeks to free them from the tethers that prevent them from attaining liberation.

Souls, according to the Śaiva theologians, are deluded about their nature, imagining themselves to be physical beings only and thus separated from others. They are not aware that God dwells in and guides them all. Ignorant of Śiva's helping powers, they are bound by the three tethers of ignorance (believing they are isolated beings), the karma of past actions, and māyā (the physical world and its pleasures, which dominate human attention).

Śiva, as *pati,* or Lord, offers many kinds of spiritual assistance to help humans liberate themselves from these bonds. In many shrines in southern India, the principal Śaiva beliefs are expressed in images of Śiva as the supreme dancer. Śiva is worshiped there as the creator, preserver, and destroyer of life and as a gracious guide. As he dances, Śiva continually creates, preserves, and destroys all things physical so that souls may live and learn.

The union with God of which these Śaivas speak is not like the mystical union with Brahman of the Advaita (Chapter 5) because it entails neither a loss of individuality nor any sense that the worshiper has become divine. Śaiva teachers agree with Muslims and Christians in saying that it would be blasphemous for human beings to identify themselves with God.

THE ŚĀKTAS

We take up Śāktism at this point because much of its thought was contributed by the Śaivas, with whom the Śāktas have interacted for 2,000 years. The **Śāktas** accept and use Śaivite myths and symbols and share their apprehension of the world as filled with both natural and supernatural menace. The Śāktas also acknowledge Śiva as the supreme deity; yet they worship not his masculine aspect, which they understand to be passive, but rather Śiva's active feminine reproductive power, śākti. That śākti is often identified with the great goddess **Durgā**, the active power that actually determines the course of the natural universe.

Our earliest evidence of the Śākta movement is from Sanskrit literature of the early first century C.E., which mentions that fearsome goddesses were being worshiped in rural villages. The **Mahābhārata** epic (c. third century epic narrative that became a compendium of legends and literature) takes more serious note of them, even naming some of these non-Vedic deities, including the wild-haired **Kālī**, who roams battlefields devouring human flesh and drinking the blood of the fallen; the gaunt Cāmuṇḍā, enemy of all life, who kills especially by famine; and Durgā, whom wild tribes worship with offerings of meat and liquor. Though sometimes the goddesses look down on people with motherly tenderness, they are ordinarily depicted as full-breasted, fanged, and dangerous. Fundamental to Śāktism is a starkly realistic approach to the grimmer aspects of the world.

Early Śāktism conceived of many śāktis and consorts of Śiva, but Śaivism's quite early effort to unify the universe as the realm of a single deity influenced Śāktism also, in time. The appearance, in about the sixth century, of the *Devī Māhātmya,* a Sanskrit poetical work on the heroic deeds of Durgā, marked the emergence of Śāktism into Brahmanic culture and the appearance of a monotheism focused on the goddess Durgā. Durgā thenceforth became the one cosmic Śākti, and other goddesses, though still named and worshiped, were regarded as various forms that Durgā assumed from time to time to cope with various demonic forces. Kālī in particular continues to be worshiped very widely as one of Durgā's most dreadful and powerful manifestations.

In late September and October, the entire Hindu population of Bengal celebrates the annual Durgā Pūjā, a festival in which Durgā's deliverance of the world from the attack of the buffalo demon Mahisha is celebrated. Local enthusiasts in each neighborhood erect clay images of Durgā brandishing many weapons in her many hands and retell night after night the story of her combats. On the last night of the recitations, the festival is concluded by sacrificing a goat or a buffalo as an offering to Durgā. In this rite survives the sole remnant of animal sacrifice in modern Brahmanic Hinduism.

Here Śiva emerges from the world pillar as the world's central power. Infinite in outreach, he is beyond the comprehension of the greatest of the gods. Brahmā is represented in the upper left as a swan and Visṇu is represented by a boar at the bottom. (Reunion des Musees Nationaux, Paris)

Śiva as the Dancer who activates the rhythms of the universe. His sending forth of the cosmos is suggested by the drum in his right hand. In his left, a flame indicates his power of destruction. At center, one hand makes the sign of reassurance, while the other points to his feet, at which worshipers may fall and receive his help. (Cleveland Art Museum)

In Śākta worship two quite different moods are found. Sometimes the furious goddess is seen as taking the field as the champion of life. At other times Śākta believers perceive her rage as directed against themselves, and they pray that her wrathful visitations may be averted.

The assurance given by Śākta teaching enables believers to accept harsh experiences with equanimity. Such calm acceptance of the tragedies of life is found in the Bengali poetry of Rāmaprasād Sen (1718–1775), the greatest modern poet of Kālī devotion, who expressed his view of his own sufferings in these words:

Though the mother beat him,
the child cries, "Mother, O Mother!"
and clings still tighter to her garment.
True, I cannot see thee,
yet I am not a lost child.
I still cry, "Mother, Mother." . . .
All the miseries that I have suffered
and am suffering, I know, O Mother,
to be your mercy alone.[2]

Although the Hindu conceptions of Durgā and Kālī are shocking, reflection will show us that the needs at the center of Śākta worship have been deep concerns in other religious traditions as well.

Śāktism is of particular interest as the modern world's most highly developed worship of a supreme female deity. The worship of Durgā has most of the characteristics of monotheism. Her power alone is understood to create, control, and destroy all phenomenal things, and thus no Śākta worship is directed to any being who is not one of her forms or appearances. But Durgā is not understood to be the whole of the divine nature; the realm of the transcendent and changeless is Śiva's, and those who seek liberation from the world (moksha) must seek it by meditation on Śiva in yoga. Śāktas, however, express little desire for moksha. As people concerned about the world, they seek from the goddess health, wealth, and general well-being.

Tāntrism

A closely related form of religion called **Tāntrism** arose in ancient times out of the same popular goddess worship from which Śāktism was born. Tāntrists often follow Śākta patterns in their public life. They are equally feminist in their theology. But Tāntrism has moksha, or liberation, as its goal, and it is set off from Śāktism by erotic ritual practices and by an elaborate yoga that is sexual in its concepts. Although it had an important parallel in Vajrayāna Buddhism (see Chapter 8), Tāntrism was disdained by most Hindus and was never more than a marginal development with a small following.

THE WORSHIP OF VISHṆU

Vishṇu in the Vedic Age

The second of the two great bhakti traditions has long honored the name of the Vedic Vishṇu and has absorbed much of the lore of that kindly deity. The Vishṇu of the Vedas is associated with the sun and is seen as promoting growth. He is present in plants and trees, provides food, and protects unborn babies in the womb. Although he rides a sun-eagle and is armed with a discus that represents the orb of the sun, he is not the sun itself. His jurisdiction is not limited to a single part of the natural world.

Although not a great god in the Vedic pantheon, Vishṇu appealed to many in post-Vedic times because of the stories of his deeds on behalf of humanity. For example, Vishṇu assumed the form of a dwarf and went as a beggar before Bali, the king of the demons, and asked as alms the gift of as much space as he could mark out in three steps. The demon granted him this seemingly small favor. Vishṇu then resumed his cosmic stature and paced off in the first giant step the whole earth, as an abode for living persons. Then he marked off the atmosphere, and in the third step he established the high heavenly world as a pleasant refuge for the deceased. Vishṇu was the one god of the Vedic pantheon who was known to care about the happiness of the dead.

The cult of Vishṇu attracted persons concerned about the problem of immortality and also those who had at heart the welfare of society. Vishṇu worship appealed to those who saw the universe as friendly and good. Salvation seekers of the post-Vedic age who could not conceive of the violent Śiva as their savior found an alternative in one or another of Vishṇu's forms. Vaishṇava religion attracted the more settled citizens and civic leaders of the Hindu world.

Origins of the Vaishṇava Tradition

The Vaishṇava religion did not arise directly out of Vedic circles that worshiped Vishṇu, however. Its institutional history began with the Sātvatas, a tribal people who from the fifth century B.C.E. worshiped the non-Vedic deity **Kṛishṇa Vāsudeva**. In its early phases, this religion was often called the Sātvata faith or sometimes the Bhāgavata faith because its great god was given the title *Bhagavat,* "Bounteous One."

Due to its military prowess, this non-Aryan Sātvata tribe eventually attained kshatriya (warrior) status, and with that came participation in life around the courts and contact with brāhmans. Some brāhmans became active adherents and even teachers of the Sātvata faith, assisting the sect in establishing its simple monotheism on the basis of the upanishads' doctrine of the oneness of the world in Brahman. The **Bhagavadgītā**, a work of the second or first century B.C.E., was the literary legacy of this creative encounter between the monotheistic and monistic religious traditions. It was received with such favor that it was incorporated immediately into the great epic, the Mahābhārata, that brāhman editors were beginning to enlarge at that time.

THE BHAGAVADGĪTĀ

The Bhagavadgītā consists of 18 short chapters of Sanskrit verse. Often printed separately from the Mahābhārata, it has become the most widely used of all Hindu scriptures. One reason is its anonymous author's ability to find positive value in the teachings of other Hindu forms of religion; this text's pluralistic spirit has allowed it to be appreciated and used by millions of Hindus who are not devotees of Kṛishṇa at all. But the main reason for the wide acclaim that the work received at the time of its writing was the solution that it offered to a critical social problem: many young men and women, inspired by the message of the late upanishads and other religions, had renounced their social station and had become forest hermits in order to seek liberation. The Bhagavadgītā discusses this practice in detail.

The author knew the major upanishads well and believed that Kṛishṇa himself had revealed them (15.15). He was inspired by their message that the universe had a metaphysical unity in Brahman, but he did not regard all teachings as equally true and effective. Politely but firmly, he subordinated the impersonal Brahman of the upanishads to the control of a personal Lord (14.27; 13.12). With great emphasis he corrected the view that seekers of liberation must abandon the world and cease performing their duties. His method is an ingenious analysis of how doing our duty can damage us and how we can perform our duty without harm.

The Bhagavadgītā opens with a scene that exemplifies this great problem. Arjuna, a sensitive warrior, is contemplating the grim duty that Hindu society requires of his military caste, and he recoils at the thought of the injuries and guilt that will follow his fighting. Arjuna is the hope of the army of the Pāṇḍavas and is bound by duty to fight the forces of the Kaurava prince, Duryodhana, who has committed great wrongs. But as Arjuna looks down the ranks of opponents he is expected to slay, he is paralyzed by the thought of the dreadful harm that he is likely to inflict on the relatives and respected teachers that he sees among them. Dropping his weapons, Arjuna throws himself down, saying it would be better to live by begging as monks do than to commit such deeds (2.5). Confused about what is right, he asks for the advice of Kṛishṇa, who is serving as his chariot driver.

Though it is the duty of a warrior that is discussed in this story, the case of Arjuna epitomizes the moral problem of the members of every occupation. Must we, as the upanishads taught, abandon our worldly work with its imperfections and endless retribution if we aspire to liberation?

Cāmuṇḍā, one of the Seven Mothers, with her weapons (note the sword above her head) and the bowl from which she drinks blood. Śāktas understand her to be a manifestation of Durgā, the universal mother, and try to accept natural destruction at her hands with trustful worship, like the figure at the bottom. (Trustees of the British Museum)

Kṛishṇa responds first with conventional arguments: disgrace descends on all who flee their duties; in using arms no real harm is done, since the soul cannot be slain. Kṛishṇa then begins to reveal the real reason why the duties of life need not be abandoned: because they can be performed in a new spirit that prevents the acquisition of karma and makes them a means of liberation rather than of bondage. It is the selfish desire with which we act, not the action itself, that binds acts to us and makes their impurity our own. If we can perform our duties simply because the scriptures require us to perform them or simply as a service to God, with no desire to make any personal gains, then those acts will have no real connection with us in the operation of the processes of retribution. No karma will be created by those acts, no ties with the world will be deepened by them, and no future births will ensue. After a life lived in the selfless performance of one's social role, the dispassionate soul, unfettered still despite a fully active life, is forever freed.

Kṛishṇa explains that he himself as the Lord of the Universe creates and maintains the world in that desireless spirit: it is only to secure the welfare of the world that he carries on his eternal cosmic activity (3.20–25), and it is only to save the world from evil that he descends to mundane births in age after age (4.5–15), and thus his work entails no bondage.

Human workers in the world can emulate that selflessness and share in that freedom. The author explains how meditation can be used to achieve mastery of desires. The necessary discipline involves turning one's attention away from sense objects and redirecting it toward the soul, Brahman, or, best of all, the personal Lord. Even simple devotees can make a beginning in such refocusing by contemplating Kṛishṇa's deeds and singing his praises and then moving on to deeper exercises. The author knows and teaches progressive introspections much like the eight-stage yoga of the Way of Knowledge. He insists on modifications. He omits the tactics that lead to preternatural luminous visions and seeks rather an experience of utter tranquillity into which one enters through complete elimination of desire. That supreme serenity is the experience of Brahman, the very state of consciousness that *is* Brahman. Created by desirelessness, it is a moral state and a basis for desireless action in a continuing life of devotion to duty.

Brahman entered by the serene meditator is not

merely a psychological state, however; it is also a metaphysical one. It is the stuff of the universe, divine in nature, and one's state in final liberation. But it is not autonomous, nor is it the highest reality; it is God's stuff contained in him, the stuff with which God creates the world. The divine stands above it and uses it, and even the human being does not vanish as an individual upon attaining it (6.30). All who consciously participate in this universal Brahman discover also their tie with all other living beings and feel empathy with them:

O Arjuna, he who sees in all
Sameness with himself
Whether in happiness or sorrow,
His is the highest yogī.

(Bhagavadgītā 6.32)

We compare with this the understanding of the Brahman seeker of the upanishads, who found in Brahman only assurance of his own immortality.

In realizing Brahman, the successful meditator also discovers a tie with God, for Brahman is God's "world essence." A passage at the end of the text (18.54) shares the general Vedānta view that the experience of Brahman is the state of eternal liberation but at the same time teaches a special understanding of how that liberation comes about. When the mystic discovers the reality of his relationship with God, devotion to God arises, and one enters final liberation, which is life in and with the Lord.

Arjuna does not respond very quickly to his charioteer's arguments, but when he is granted a vision of Kṛishṇa not in his worldly form but in all his cosmic greatness as the be-all and end-all of existence even greater than Brahman (11.37), he is awed. Arjuna at last understands Kṛishṇa to be the very source of the duty (14.27) that he is resisting. Arjuna is moved, and in verse 18.37 he vows to Kṛishṇa, "I shall do your word."

Like Arjuna, many generations of Hindus have been moved by the charm and reasoning of the Bhagavadgītā to remain faithful to their duty. With great creativity the unknown author of this small scripture adapted the metaphysics and the mysticism of the upanishads to the religious needs of a civil society. In doing so he transformed his small sect into a major support of the Brahmanic order.

THE LATER VAISHṆAVA TRADITION

The subsequent history of the Vaishṇava religion centered on two kinds of developments: (1) a gathering of congenial groups around the original users of the Bhagavadgītā and (2) special responses to pressures and needs that arose later. During a history of 2,000 years, the Vaishṇava tradition grew into a great family of religions bound together by common acceptance of the Bhagavadgītā and several other scriptures and by allegiance to Vishṇu.

The Identification of Kṛishṇa with Vishṇu

The author of the Bhagavadgītā, in a few subtle statements, indicated that to him Kṛishṇa in his heavenly form was the Vedic deity Vishṇu (11.24, 11.30, 11.46). At stake in this and other efforts to establish a tie between Kṛishṇa and the Vedic god was the orthodoxy of Kṛishṇa's sect in the eyes of other Hindus. The deciders of such claims were neither the Sāṭvatas nor the general population but learned brāhmans, for the brāhmans, by arriving at a consensus, could authenticate a religion. If Kṛishṇa (even under another name) or some other deity was understood to have been mentioned in the Vedas, then worship of that deity could be deemed a form of Vedic religion and hence orthodox. Brāhmans could then serve the sect as priests, and the religion and its texts could be considered part of the revealed Vedas.

After five centuries of negotiation with brāhmans, the worshipers of Kṛishṇa won full recognition of their tie with Vishṇu and thus won the right to be called Vaishṇavas ("Vishṇuites"). In that final settlement, not only the brāhmans made concessions. The Vaishṇavas stopped exalting kshatriyas as religious leaders, and they restrained their earlier tendency to minimize the importance of caste rank. Through such compromises brāhmans and Vaishṇavas together became the mainstays of the caste civilization.

The Avatars

One of the most distinctive and most important of the Vaishṇava ideas is that the deity descends to earth and is born there in many different forms or incarnations (**avatars**). This belief first appears in the

Bhagavadgītā, where Kṛishṇa speaks of his alternation between two realms:

Though I am an eternal unborn Soul,
the Lord of Beings,
relying on my own materiality
I enter into phenomenal being
by my own mysterious power [māyā].
Whenever righteousness declines
and wickedness erupts
I send myself forth, O Bharata [Arjuna].
To protect the good and destroy evildoers
and establish the right, I come into being
age after age.

(Bhagavadgītā 4.6–8)

In the Bhagavadgītā, Kṛishṇa is addressed as an avatar ("descent") of Vishṇu (11.24, 11.30). Most Hindus believe that Vishṇu is the heavenly source of all avatars.

This idea of an avatar is clearly post-Vedic. Even the ideas that were necessary for its creation are post-Vedic—the conception of a supreme deity, of repeated births, and of a metaphysical link between the divine and human states.

The number of the avatars has never been settled. Most Hindus today recognize ten, named in this order: Matsya, the fish; Kurma, the tortoise; Varāha, the boar; Narasiṃha, the man-lion; Vāmana, the dwarf; Paraśurāma, an ax-wielding man; Kṛishṇa, whom we have already met; Rāma, a folk hero; Gautama Buddha, the founder of Buddhism (a desire to include Buddhists in the Vaishṇava faith is apparent here); and Kalki, the avatar yet to come. The myth of Kalki is particularly interesting. Pictured as a swordsman on a white horse (or a horse-headed figure), Kalki is to appear at the end of the present evil age to unseat from their thrones the wicked barbarian rulers of the earth and to restore the righteous Brahmanic order. This hope in Kalki expresses Hindu India's revulsion in the first three centuries C.E. to the long and often hostile rule of foreign dynasties and faith in a deity concerned with the world.

Although the ten figures are recognized as divine by all traditional Hindus, only the Vaishṇavas feel obliged to worship any of them, and among Vaishṇavas it is customary to select one favorite avatar for personal or family worship. Currently, the worship of only Rāma and Kṛishṇa is widespread; they are the most popular of the Hindu divinities. The Bengal Vaishṇavas and some others deny that Kṛishṇa is an avatar of Vishṇu but, pointing to the Bhagavadgītā, believe that Kṛishṇa Vāsudeva himself is the supreme deity and the source of all avatars.

Defenders of Vaishṇava Belief

The sect that produced the Bhagavadgītā continued to grow for 1,000 years. Its identification of Kṛishṇa with the Vedic deity Vishṇu—rapidly ac-

Kalki, the tenth avatar, is envisioned as a swordsman on a white horse. Kalki is to appear at the end of the present evil age to unseat the wicked barbarian rulers.

cepted—placed Vaishṇava religion within the pale of Vedic faith in the eyes of most Indians. The incorporation of the upanishadic notion of Brahman into the Bhagavadgītā created another tie with Vedic literature.

Yet even though the Bhagavadgītā made Brahman out to be a secondary aspect of a supreme being who is personal, the great monistic teacher Śaṅkara, writing around 800, thought otherwise. He maintained that the ultimate was the impersonal Brahman and that plural things and persons—even the divine person—are miragelike appearances imposed falsely on Brahman. To Śaṅkara, worship of a personal God was useful only to persons of weak intelligence and should not be persisted in, for it focused on an illusion. The respectability of the Vaishṇava worship of a personal God was again in danger.

Stung by this belittling of their faith in a personal God, leaders of Vaishṇava movements for centuries wrote responses in the form of new commentaries on the Vedāntasūtra. These became fundamental documents in the theologies of great sects. We shall explore the first and most famous of these commentaries, written about 1100 by Rāmānuja for the use of his Śrīvaishṇava community of South India.

Rāmānuja's examination of Śaṅkara's monist argument might run as follows: Where does this māyā you speak of—this creator of all plurality and persons—exist? Does it exist in Brahman? That is impossible: Brahman is homogeneous and can have within it no separate thing. Brahman is perfection and can have within it no evil thing. Brahman is knowledge and could accommodate ignorance within itself only by destroying itself. Brahman is the real and contains nothing that is not real; if māyā exists in Brahman, it is real, and its alleged products—personal beings, the personal God, and the plural world—are also real, as we Vaishṇavas hold. Is māyā then located outside Brahman? Outside of Brahman, the sole reality, there is only nothing. If māyā is nothing, it has produced nothing—not even the illusion that you hold our world to be.

By these and many other arguments, Rāmānuja exposed weaknesses in the logic of Śaṅkara's teaching and defended the Vaishṇava belief in the reality of persons, both human and divine. Rāmānuja declared the divine, all-inclusive reality that the upanishads call Brahman to be no neuter reality but rather the personal Lord. Brahman was simply one of the many names of Kṛishṇa Vāsudeva, the basis of all being.

Rāmānuja's understanding of the nature of mystical experience and its place in the religious life is a representative Vaishṇava view. Vaishṇavas aspire to *darśana,* a physical or spiritual "seeing" of the beautiful form of the Lord. In its lower grades, darśana can be merely a reverential viewing of an image in a shrine. At a higher stage of contemplation, darśana can become a powerful inner meditative vision of a deity. Rāmānuja's comment on this higher darśana is that it is not a direct perception of the deity but a subjective vision shaped out of recollections of one's previous experiences. It is not a direct means to liberation; rather, its importance is that it is a powerful generator of devotion (bhakti), which is the last human step toward liberation. Not all Vaishṇavas state as clearly as Rāmānuja did that such visions of deity are subjective, but all followers of the Way of Devotion agree that final liberation does not arise from the power of such visions but from the power of God, who responds to the devotion that such visions can generate.

The Cult of Gopāla

Our account of Vaishṇava history has so far followed a tradition that flowed for centuries from the Bhagavadgītā and promoted its values. We confront the real complexity of the Vaishṇava movement, however, when we encounter a powerful new development in Kṛishṇaism: the worship of Kṛishṇa as **Gopāla**, the cowherd boy.

The *Harivaṃśa Purāṇa,* written around 300 C.E. began the new tradition. The author says in his introduction that he is filling in the omissions of the Mahābhārata, which had failed to tell the whole story of Kṛishṇa. The author then proceeds to relate dozens of new stories about the early exploits and antics of Kṛishṇa, from his birth to his unseating of his wicked uncle Kaṃsa from the throne of Mathurā. All are retold more fully in the *Vishṇu Purāṇa* and again in the *Bhāgavata Purāṇa* (eighth or ninth century). Distinctively lighthearted, these tales recount the child Kṛishṇa's impudence in stealing butter from his mother's pantry and evading punishment through alibis and of his wheedling tasty curds from the cowherd women. In the accounts of Kṛishṇa's adolescence, his naughtiness takes a flirtatious turn. He teases the *gopīs* (cowherd girls) shamelessly and does audacious things to excite their romantic feelings (see the accompanying box, "Krishna and the Gopīs").

COMPARISON

Kṛishṇa and the Gopīs

The story of Kṛishṇa's dance with the gopīs (girls of the cowherd caste) is the most sacred of the Gopāla cult's myths and the source of much of its symbolic language. The favorite version, found in *Bhāgavata Purāṇa* 10.29–33, is retold in popular poetic recitations, songs, and operatic performances.

On a certain full-moon night in autumn, Kṛishṇa stood at the edge of a forest near the settlements of the cowherds. With a mischievous smile he put his flute to his lips. The flute's enchanting notes carried afar until they reached the houses of the cowherds, where the dutiful wives of the herdsmen were preparing food and faithfully attending to the needs of their families. But when they heard the bewitching notes, they were helpless. They dropped their wifely tasks and hurried into the dusk. At the forest's edge they came upon Kṛishṇa. He feigned astonishment and addressed the gopīs thus:

KṚISHṆA: O ladies, you surprise me. What service can I do you?
GOPĪS: You have called us, and we have come.
KṚISHṆA: I was playing the flute merely for my own pleasure. Why have you come here?
GOPĪS: Why do you ask why we have come? You have called us. It is to see *you* that we have come!
KṚISHṆA: Now you have seen me. It is a dark night, this is a dangerous forest, and it is not a time for ladies to be roaming. Go home now to your husbands.

The gopīs protest that Kṛishṇa is a rogue for enticing them and then rebuffing them. They hang their heads, falter in their speech, and finally are able to stammer out the real justification for their presence in the forest: "You are our real husband, our only husband, the only husband of the whole human race, and it is only you that we wish to serve!"

Kṛishṇa is pleased by this declaration and agrees to sport with the gopīs. Rādhā, their leader, joins him in organizing them for dancing. They form a revolving circle. Pleasure and excitement grow as the dance whirls on. The gopīs begin to be proud that they are in the company of the Lord of the Universe. Not content to think of themselves as the luckiest women in the world, they begin to think of themselves as the best and most beautiful women in the world. They demand services of Kṛishṇa, saying, "Fasten my earring!," "Comb my hair!," "Carry me!" Suddenly leaving their midst, Kṛishṇa disappears into the forest. Forlorn and humbled, the

For many centuries after this first blossoming, it was this child Kṛishṇa and not the Kṛishṇa of the Bhagavadgītā who captured the attention and creative talents of the Vaishṇavas. No Vaishṇava flatly rejected the Bhagavadgītā, of course, but it was now the naughty little prankster, not the lecturer about duty, whom Vaishṇavas worshiped with delight. Scholars have been puzzled by this radical change in the moral content of Kṛishṇa worship. Why did the civic-minded Vaishṇava community turn from the morally inspiring divine teacher of the Bhagavadgītā toward worship of an uninhibited young prankster Kṛishṇa?

We must consider how, in 400 years, the distresses of the average Hindu of Vaishṇava faith had changed. The second century B.C.E., which gave rise to the Bhagavadgītā, was a time when many Hindu youths

gopīs search for him in the gloom, calling out his name as they wander through the dark glades and asking the trees and vines for hints of where he may have gone. Unable to find him, they gather in a clearing in the forest and begin to console themselves by telling each other about Kṛishṇa's deeds. Peering through the trees, Kṛishṇa observes the gopīs' new humility and devotion; he relents and returns to their circle. Then he begins the magnificent Mahārāsa, the rāsā dance in its most splendid form. Moving into the circle of the dance, Kṛishṇa multiplies his own form until there is a Kṛishṇa at every gopī's side. As the partners whirl on, romantic feeling rises to a crescendo with the music. Every gopī's longing for Kṛishṇa is satisfied by his special presence beside her.

This tale of Kṛishṇa's meeting with the cowherd women uses the language of romantic love, but it refers to nonsexual aspects of the religious life.

(Photo: Cleveland Museum of Art, Mr. and Mrs. William H. Marlatt Fund, 60.45.)

were alienated from their world and fleeing their caste duties. Politically, Greek and Buddhist rulers of India were indifferent to brāhman social ideas and were threats to brāhman social leadership. Responding to this situation, the Bhagavadgītā had rallied Hindus behind the brāhmans' leadership and called for acceptance of the caste patterns. The Vaishṇavas helped reverse the retreat from the Brahmanic social order.

The whole situation changed following the second century C.E.: the last foreign dynasty crumbled, and the Gupta emperors—who were Hindus—came to power. Henceforth caste rules regarding occupations were enforced by the state, and brāhmans became the judges of law and social mores. At this point the Bhagavadgītā's social hopes had become the rule of the land. Its moral ideals, far from repudiated, were in fact realized.

India now enjoyed the rule of religion in both professional and family life, as well as in relations between the sexes.

But what Hindus now lacked was personal freedom. Caught in the grip of Brahmanic rectitude, Vaisṇavas did not respond with the old enthusiasm for the Bhagavadgītā's divine moralist. Their hearts were uplifted, rather, by the new lore of a roguish young god who used his divine prerogative to live in unbounded freedom. In new myths about this libertine god, they created a refreshing and wishful picture of their own ultimate liberation, and in the meantime they could enjoy a certain freedom of mental fantasies. The transformation of Kṛishṇa reminds us of the transformation of the battle god of the Aryas of ancient Iran, who in India became Indra, the god of rain. Gods often change as the needs of a people change: they change, or they cease to be worshiped.

Especially during the Muslim domination in India (c. 1200–1700), large sects of worshipers of the child Kṛishṇa were founded. They continue to have a great following today. The adherents of one sect are well known in the West for chanting the name of Kṛishṇa in public places and are therefore often called the Hare Kṛishṇa people.

The religious practices of the Gopāla faith center on contemplation of Kṛishṇa's *līlās,* or frolics. Sometimes in Sanskrit but more often in vernacular versions, the narratives of the tenth book of the *Bhāgavata Purāṇa* are read, sung, or performed in operetta style with dance preludes in an unusual kind of miracle play called the *Rāslīlā.* To rehearse Kṛishṇa's līlās mentally and to envision them before the inner eye are the Gopāla cult's equivalent of yoga. Kṛishṇa devotees seek to obtain visions of their God in the course of private meditations or at climactic moments of these emotional religious assemblies. Sometimes religious ecstasies overwhelm some spectators; these are cherished as tokens of divine favor. Mathurā and Vrindāban, cities sacred to Kṛishṇa, have become great centers of pilgrimage and retirement for those who wish to pursue the spiritual life in these ways.

THE WORSHIP OF RĀMA

The story of Rāma occurs for the first time in a Sanskrit epic poem called the *Rāmāyaṇa,* written by Vālmiki around the fourth century B.C.E. It may be based on memories of an actual prince Rāma of the North Indian

During the Muslim domination of India, large sects were founded that worship the child Kṛishṇa. Hare Kṛishṇa people are well known in the West for chanting the name of Kṛishṇa in public places. (UPI/Bettmann)

kingdom of Ayodhyā. In the spirit of heroic legend rather than myth, Vālmiki tells of Rāma's great southern expedition to defeat a demon, Rāvaṇa, who had abducted his wife, Sītā. After many heroic trials, Rāma returns to his kingdom of Ayodhyā in the north and rules with model righteousness in a golden age of prosperity and justice.

The characters in the epic include numerous members of an illustrious royal family who almost without exception exemplify the Hindu ideals of good behavior. This is especially true of Rāma's wife, Sītā, whose virtue and unhesitating willingness to serve her husband have served as a model for millions of Hindu women. Functionally, the *Rāmāyaṇa* serves as a supplement to *The Laws of Manu,* reinforcing the codal prescriptions with word pictures of ideal lives.

The first and last books of the epic, added about the time of Christ, show the beginnings of a worship of Rāma as a god, deemed the eighth avatar of Vishṇu. In North India in particular, Rāma worship has become a major form of religion through the impact of an extremely popular version of the *Rāmāyaṇa* called the *Rāmcaritmānas* by Tulsī Das (c. 1575). It is the most widely read of all Hindi books. Yet even the illiterate learn Rāma's story at a great autumn festival called the Rāmlīlā, in which the entire *Rāmcaritmānas* is recited and enacted annually. The great popularity of this *Rāmāyaṇa* has broken the hold of Śāktism in North India and made this heartland of India predominantly Vaishṇava.

The relation between the cults of Rāma and Kṛishṇa is one of mutual support. In heavily Vaishṇava communities today, the people participate in the festivals of both deities, and the worship of Rāma and Kṛishṇa has become loosely joined in a composite religion. With theological consistency, Vaishṇavas can include both Kṛishṇa and Rāma in their devotions, explaining that as different avatars of one and the same deity, they are identifiable with each other and are not different objects of worship. It is the difference between these two deities, however, that makes it easy to combine their worship. As moral beings seeking self-control and social order, Hindus worship Rāma. As intellectual beings seeking reasoned understanding, they turn to the thoughtful Bhagavadgītā and to the systematic theologies of the Kṛishṇa cult. As emotional beings oppressed by the heavy restraints of Hindu social life, they worship Gopāla Kṛishṇa, the carefree divine prankster.

ACTION, DEVOTION, KNOWLEDGE: A RETROSPECT ON THE THREE WAYS

In Chapters 2 through 4 we have seen among followers of Hinduism's three ways some dramatic similarities and differences. Longing for liberation from the world has remained an acute distress among followers of the Way of Knowledge and a persistent concern of followers of the Way of Devotion as well. Only those who live their lives in the routines of the Way of Action say little or nothing about liberation. Even so, one cannot say that pangs of such longing are entirely absent in them. It is a matter of degree, and it is not wrong to say that transcendence of the world is the goal of traditional Hinduism.

Those who do strive for liberation differ on the means that will bring about that happy event. The knowledge seekers rely on the power of rare insights generated in the course of difficult introspective meditations. Devotees, by contrast, seek, through worship, to establish intimacy with a God of cosmic power who can release them from the bondage of retribution for past acts.

Whether one elects to seek liberation through knowledge or through devotion entails differences in the form and content of one's practical religious life. The Way of Knowledge requires deep and long-continued meditations, usually in seclusion. Knowledge seekers have thus characteristically been sannyāsīs, renouncers of the world. Devotees also sometimes renounce the world if their feeling of alienation is intense, but isolation in the forest is not really helpful to the development of emotion in worship. Devotees more typically seek out what they call *satsang,* the company of the good; they are most often found not in forest solitude but in these emotional gatherings for worship in story and song.

Also in their conceptions of the ultimate life of the liberated there is a difference between devotees and followers of the Way of Knowledge. For the latter, final beatitude is a merging in Brahman, where no second being is known. Devotees also seek transmutation to a transcendent realm and status, but for them the ultimate blessedness is a life of fellowship in which the love between the deity and the worshipers can be sustained. Some speak only generally of attaining God's realm or presence. Others elaborate on that simple faith, often describing in vivid details the eternal life of the liberated in the special heaven of their deity, be it Śiva, Śākti, or Kṛishṇa Gopāla.

However traditional Hindus conceived of their goal—as a personal or an impersonal state—none imagined that this workaday world itself could ever be the site of life's final blessedness. Even for the world-concerned author of the Bhagavadgītā, the hope of humanity lay elsewhere, in the transcendent:

> *Transient and troubled is this world;*
> *On reaching it, venerate Me.*
>
> (Bhagavadgītā 9.33)

NOTES

1 Robert Charles Caldwell, trans., "Tamil Popular Poetry," *Indian Antiquary*, April 5, 1872, p. 100.

2 Quoted in Dinesh Chandra Sen, *History of Bengali Language and Literature* (Calcutta: University of Calcutta, 1911), pp. 714 ff.

Religions of India

CHAPTER 5

Modern Hinduism

We have completed a study of a remarkable cultural tradition that shaped the lives of millions of human beings for several thousand years. Hinduism's cosmologies are among humanity's most sophisticated intellectual constructions; ingeniously integrated with a highly organized society, they laid the basis for a tranquil civilization of long endurance. If our only aim were to become acquainted with the world's great alternatives to Western religion and culture, our purpose would be accomplished at this point.

But we hope also that our study will prepare us to meet Hindus as they are today; for that we need to supplement our study. India during the past 800 years has undergone an almost unprecedented breaching of its natural defenses and has suffered powerful incursions of foreign peoples. These events have brought it new problems and great changes.

The first of these great invasions was that of the Muslims, who conquered most of India from the northwest and ruled for five centuries. They zealously promoted their faith, and by 1700 several parts of India had become predominantly Muslim. Yet the subcontinent as a whole remained loyal to Hinduism.

After the death in 1707 of Aurangzeb, the last great Mughul emperor, the Mughul Empire declined rapidly. For the next 50 years, India lay in a state of anarchy. European merchants, protected by a few soldiers, had long operated trading posts along the Indian coastline. Now, raising mercenary armies, the Europeans began to move into the political vacuum left by the Mughul Empire's disintegration. By 1757 the British East India Company had gained control of India's most prosperous provinces, and by 1818 the British had eliminated all serious rivals for the control of the entire land.

THE BRITISH PRESENCE

Two centuries of British rule (1757–1947) were much more disturbing to the old Hindu civilization than the previous 500 years of aggressive Muslim control. There were two reasons for this. First, the British, unlike the Muslims, brought to India powerful new economic institutions. Their ships and trains drew India into a worldwide commercial network, and soon Calcutta, Bombay, Madras, and inland cities as well became huge trading centers.

This development brought with it a great increase in the proportion of the population engaged in trade and making a living outside the tightly knit economy of the villages. Large numbers of people in the new cities became immune to the traditional penalty for nonconformity, termination of livelihood. Family and caste assemblies could still bring heavy pressure on their individual members, but once the industrial revolution reached India and factories became a major employer in the towns, millions of Hindus became freer to exercise personal choice in employment—and in religious matters as well.

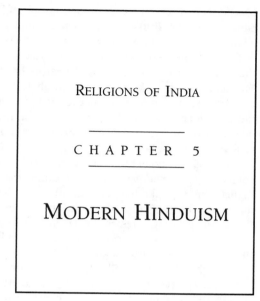

The second reason for the strong impact of British culture was the British government's promotion of education. Although by today's standards the schools of British India were not extensive, they far exceeded the public education available under earlier Hindu and Muslim rulers. As early as 1817, the Hindu College was established in Calcutta to instruct young Indian men in the English language and literature. The local response was positive, and Christian missionaries soon opened similar schools and colleges.

In 1835 a momentous decision was made to conduct government-supported education mainly in English and to make the Western arts and sciences a main part of the curriculum. In the same period European printing presses made the literature of Europe easily available to the increasing numbers of Indians who could read English.

To appreciate the collision of ideas that then occurred, we need to examine the Hinduism prevailing around 1800 and note the shocking contrasts it had to confront. Many of the popular Hindu practices sought protection against the dangers of the natural world. The central Hindu ideas had the function of supporting the caste system. Belief in karma and rebirth rationalized the assignment of hereditary work and unequal distribution of opportunities and honors and justified the subjection of women and the harsh treatment of widows. The deprivations that old Hinduism imposed on many were made tolerable by reflections on the evil of material desires, by thought about loftier satisfactions in transcendent realms, and by denying the significance—or even the reality—of the whole physical world. Hinduism provided no rational justification for attempting to change the world. The way to happiness did not lie in transforming the world but in liberating oneself from it. It was the soul, not the world, that was capable of salvation.

The idea of one's *nation* traditionally had little importance—in fact, the major Indian languages had no precise word for that idea. In the traditional Hindu conception of identity, the notion of one's nation scarcely figured. One understood oneself to be submerged in the collectivity of family, clan, and caste; nationality was not a central aspect. With the coming of the British there arrived in India a conception of one's nation as a prime aspect of personal identity, as an entity to which one owed heavy moral responsibility, and as an essential unit to be involved in struggles for a better life.

The British brought with them also an optimism, unusual even in the West, about the possibility of social improvement—of freedom from disease through medical science, of freedom from poverty through industrialization, and of freedom from injustice through reform.

The Europeans of that time not only proclaimed faith in the world's regeneration but also took actions toward that end, with impressive results. The power of Western learning was as obvious to Hindu observers as the power of the new steamboats that could transport huge cargoes upstream on Indian rivers. Vaccination was clearly more effective than offerings to the smallpox goddess. Young Hindus did not take long to decide that they wanted to absorb Western knowledge and to participate in its power.

This clear decision among the early generations of Western-educated Indians soon began to give rise to new movements within Hinduism. Between 1800 and 1947 there were few Hindu champions of innovation who were not also reformers of religion. The first Hindu movement that reflected the Western impact was the **Brāhmo Samāj** (Society of Believers in Brahman), founded in 1828 by a Bengali brāhman named Rām Mohan Roy (1772–1833).

THE BRĀHMO SAMĀJ

Rām Mohan Roy's family had for generations served Muslim rulers, so they of course sent their son to Muslim schools, where he learned Persian and Arabic and absorbed Muslim attitudes, including hostility toward the British. In 1803, however, their son took employment with the British East India Company, and under the guidance of a friendly British official, he studied English and Western literature and thought. Reversing his prior opinion of Western culture, Roy became an advocate of Western education and eventually founded many schools that taught the Western arts and sciences.

In 1814 he retired from his post to focus more intensively on religion and morality. He studied the Bible and, though he did not accept Christian theology, developed an admiration for the example and teachings of Jesus. The Brāhmo Samāj, which he founded in 1828, used in its worship the upanishads—which he regarded as Vedic scriptures, of course—and he and

Rām Mohan Roy founded the Brāhmo Samāj (Society of Believers in Brahman) in 1928. This was the first Hindu movement to reflect the impact of Western influence on India. This detail is from a painting by Rolinda Sharples (City Art Gallery, Bristol, England)

his circle of educated people were convinced that the Vedas were not polytheistic but, like the Bible, monotheistic. Their new religious association, like a church, met weekly for congregational worship—a novel pattern in Hindu religious life. The new association denounced idols and idolatry, gave up all claims to privilege on the basis of high caste rank, and undertook to provide education for men and also for women.

After the death of Rām Mohan Roy, the members of the society undertook a more thorough study of the entire Veda and concluded that its outlook was in fact polytheistic after all. They thereupon relinquished their use of Vedic scripture—and their claim to be orthodox Hindus—and resorted to reason and conscience as their final authorities in religion. Their social teachings became more radical: they asked their members to drop their caste identities completely, they developed new nonpolytheistic family rituals, they pressed for laws forbidding the marriage of children, and they supported a British edict forbidding **satī**, the burning of widows. Through the nineteenth century the Brāhmo Samāj kept the Hindu upper classes in an uproar of argument for and against their daring demands. The views of the Brāhmo Samāj on the gods and the scriptures were in the end seldom adopted, but the association won its battle for social reform.

THE ĀRYA SAMĀJ

While the reformist commotion of the Brāhmo Samāj was at its height in Bengal, Svāmī Dayānanda (1824–1883) launched a very different kind of reform movement in northwestern India. (*Svāmī* is a respectful title for a religious teacher.) Even as a child in Gujarat, Dayānanda spurned the devout Śiva worship of his family. Soon he became an ascetic and wandered about in search of a teacher. He found his guru finally in a fiery eccentric teacher named Virajānanda who allowed his disciples to study only the oldest Vedic scriptures and taught them to loathe the Purāṇas and dharmaśāstras and all the gods of popular Hinduism. In 1863 Dayānanda began his own reformist campaigns, lecturing in Sanskrit against idolatry, polytheism, *pūjā,* and pilgrimages and denying the divinity of Rāma and Kṛishṇa. In 1874 Dayānanda wrote *The Light of Truth* in Hindi, and in 1875 he founded the **Ārya Samāj** (Aryan Society), a religious society that spread rapidly throughout northern India proclaiming the doctrines of his book. Let us summarize the main teachings of the society:

The Vedas alone are the Word of God and the only basis of Hinduism. By Vedas Dayānanda meant only the saṃhitās, the four early books of hymns. Only when they are in complete agreement with the four Vedas do the brāhmaṇas and the upanishads have any force. Later scriptures—even the Bhagavadgītā—have no place at all in Hinduism. The Vedas teach the worship of one personal God only. They do not mention or justify the *jātis* or professional castes, and even brāhmans have no right to any inherited privilege. The varṇas are mentioned in the Vedas as social classes, but admission to them is by merit, not heredity.

The Vedas are the source of all truth, scientific as well as religious. Employing unusual translation methods, Dayānanda maintained that the sages who wrote the Vedas already knew the steam engine, telegraph, and other inventions. The Vedic sciences were later forgotten, but Indians who study them now are not taking up Western ideas but merely recovering lost Vedic knowledge.

The ancient Vedas record the undefiled original religion of humanity. This religion, diffused throughout the world, was distorted as it spread. But the Vedas remain the ultimate source of all the fragmentary and corrupted truths that non-Hindu faiths teach. Adherents of those faiths should return now to the uncontaminated source of all truth, the Vedic religion of the Ārya Samāj.

Dayānanda vilified Kṛishṇaism, Islam, and Christianity. He was particularly incensed at efforts to spread these two latter faiths and indeed at all foreign influences in India. The society has persistently opposed child marriage, polygamy, and the suppression of women and has justified widow remarriage and intercaste eating and marrying.

The Brāhmo Samāj and the Ārya Samāj are small organizations now—the former with a few thousand members, the latter with half a million. But they are small because they were so successful. Their social demands were so widely accepted that liberal Hindus are no longer driven from their families and castes and compelled to seek refuge in radical brotherhoods like these. Thanks to a century of reformist agitation (and industrialization), the old rules regarding occupation and social mingling are relatively ineffective in the cities and resistible in the countryside. Caste continues to be important in marriage matches, however, and often provides the competing units in political struggles.

The Ārya Samāj is now a nonpolitical religious association, but it has revived in Hinduism a long-lost understanding that political concerns are religious concerns, and it has produced important political leaders. It also began an important modern Hindu tendency to glorify the Hindu past and to seek ancient models for political action. As India faced the prospect and then the actuality of self-government, reformed Hinduism led in the effort to bring the resources of religion to bear on the truly critical problem of organizing a harmonious Indian nation and led in the tendency to abandon to science Hindu religion's former obsession with matters of health and economic well-being.

HINDU RELIGIOUS NATIONALISM

Dayānanda's resentment of Western influence was a light squall preceding a hurricane. In the late nineteenth century the sons of upper-class Indian families began to graduate from Indian universities with a new ambivalence toward Western culture. Western studies, like flowers transplanted from another climate, did not root easily in Indian soil. Even students who acquired a deep knowledge of the West were often offended by the aloofness of Europeans, who did not grant them the dignity of full social acceptance.

About this time, Western orientalists' search for India's forgotten past was uncovering records of a happier and greater India of pre-Islamic times, when enlightened Hindu rulers had patronized brilliant systems of thought and great works of literature and art. Hindu religious leaders now called on the young men of India to identify themselves with that brighter ancient heritage. Beginning about 1890, a passionate nationalism with religious overtones began to grow in the minds of many literate young Hindus. They viewed the West as a crass and worldly civilization, advanced only in the natural sciences, and saw the East as a spiritual culture destined to teach the world the art of lofty living. All the emotional devices of the Way of Devotion were brought into the service of a new object of devotion, the Indian nation. Seeing foreign rule as a moral outrage, the liberation of India became the goal of this semireligious nationalism.

India was sometimes conceived of as a divine mother in the form of the goddess Kālī. Beginning in 1905, secret societies dedicated to violent revolutionary action were organized. At altars of Kālī bearing heaps of revolvers, recruits vowed to bring bloody offerings to the Mother. A training manual titled *Bhavānī Mandir* (The Temple of Kālī) assured future assassins that their acts would attract the world to the light of Hinduism. Those less accustomed to making blood offerings cultivated a reverence for a milder figure called Bharat Mātā (Mother India).

The first great leader of Hindu ultranationalism was a brāhman of western India named Bāl Gangādhar Tilak (1856–1920). It was he who first made Hindu festivals occasions for political agitation, and he revived understanding of the Bhagavadgītā as an inspiration to military action (as in "Fight, O son of Bharata!" 2.18). Tilak's militant Hindu spirit all but dominated the Indian independence movement between 1908 and 1917. During those years, more than 100 officials of the British government were killed or wounded by assassins of this outlook. The resort to bloodshed was put down, but the spirit lived on through the next decade in political movements that were more circumspect, notably the ardently Hindu society for the promotion of nationalism called the Hindu Mahāsabhā—formed in the 1920s but still a powerful nationalist organization—and its paramilitary auxiliary, the Rāshṭriya Svayamsevak Saṅgha. These twin organizations have been a hotbed of revisionist thinking about the re-creation of India as an exclusively Hindu nation. They insist that India must be one undivided nation geographically and racially, with one language, one culture, and one religion—Hinduism. Religious minorities are to be treated as foreigners, without civil status or automatic rights. Since the advent of self-government in India in 1947, Hindus of this chauvinistic outlook have formed political parties with similar agendas. Opposing the more religiously neutral parties founded by Mahātma Gāndhi and Jawaharlal Nehru, some of these Hindu nationalism parties have become powerful.

MAHĀTMA GĀNDHI

Fortunately for the outside world, India's independence was not won by such ultranationalists but by forces led by Mohandās Gāndhi (1869–1948), a religious leader of a radically new type. Born in Gujarat into a family of the vaiśya (merchant) class, Gāndhi was first a lawyer and later a social reformer and political leader. Neither a brāhman nor a scholar in Hindu literature nor even a systematic religious thinker, Gāndhi's religious leadership has nevertheless touched to some degree all present-day Hindus, who everywhere speak of him reverentially as Mahātma (the "Great-souled One"). After studying law in England, Gāndhi moved his practice to South Africa, where for many years he led a nonviolent movement to protect the rights of Indians there. Returning to India, he became in 1920 a leader of the Indian National Congress. Thanks to his skillful direction, India at last became a free republic in 1947. The following year, while conducting a prayer meeting in New Delhi, he was assassinated by a fanatical Hindu nationalist of the outlook just described, who resented Gāndhi's kindness toward Muslims.

The scriptures that Gāndhi loved most were the *Rāmcaritmānas* of Tulsī Das, the Sermon on the Mount in the New Testament, and, especially, the Bhagavadgītā. His choice of scriptures reflects the centrality of moral and social concerns in his religious life. Yet Gāndhi was not bound by the authority of any of these scriptures but held rather that one should check their teachings against the inner voice of conscience, for it could reveal the way of right action. Though Gāndhi's assumptions about the nature of God and the universe were generally those of the Vaishṇava monotheists, he was not interested in theoretical discussions and preferred the simple statement "God is truth." By this he meant that God is the basis for order and law and the force that supports moral righteousness in the world. Yet God for him was not an abstract principle but a spirit filled with purpose who hears prayers and supports and guides people who struggle in the cause of right in all areas of life, including politics.

To Gāndhi, all religions originate in the inner voice, which is universal. They differ only externally, in their linguistic and cultural expressions. Yet those different expressions make each religion uniquely effective for its followers: the religion of one's own culture cannot effectively replace the religion of some other culture.

Gāndhi's courageous tactic for social reform was called **satyāgraha** ("holding on to truth"). It was based on his confidence that God, in the form of truth *(satya)* and the inner voice that utters it, is present also in the hearts of wrongdoers. Gāndhi taught that believers in satyāgraha must seek to awaken the inner voice in the oppressors so that they will themselves perceive their wrongdoing and voluntarily stop it. One should not seek personal victories over opponents but the victory of truth, which belongs as much to one's opponent as to oneself. Such victories cannot be attained by violent means. Gāndhi's great campaigns for national independence were often launched under the guidance of his own inner voice; in essence, they were demands that the British rulers consult the voice within themselves with regard to what was right. Gāndhi's faith so impressed the world that in the 1960s, Martin Luther King, Jr., made effective use of satyāgraha techniques to advance the goals of the American civil rights movement.

RECENT RELIGIOUS LEADERS

In the modern period, the religious life of most Hindus has followed traditional patterns under the guidance of old-style leaders. Let us look at several key leaders.

Rāmakṛishṇa Paramahaṃsa

This many-faceted holy man has had great impact on modern Indian cultural history. Little concerned with Western ideas, Rāmakṛishṇa Paramahaṃsa (1836–1886) was a man of visions who experienced many kinds of trances and apparitions. He was born of poor brāhman parents in rural Bengal and lived for most of his adult life in a temple of the goddess Kālī near Calcutta. As a young man, he fell into a despair approaching madness following the death of his father. He appealed to Kālī to give him some token of her regard, and on one dark day he snatched a sword from the temple wall, intending to commit suicide by offering the goddess his life's blood. At that moment, Rāmakṛishṇa reported, the goddess emerged from her image in an ocean of light and enveloped him in wave after wave of her love. This experience ended his fears; he became a composed and effective teacher.[1]

Although Rāmakṛishṇa was a devotee of Kālī, he had visions of many other deities and types. He experienced, for example, mystical trances of the Advaita type, in which personal deities played no role. He also had visions of Christ and of Muḥammad, which led him to believe that he fully understood Christianity and Islam. Thinking them to be mystical religions of Hindu type, he concluded that they were valid faiths; he therefore taught the unconditional equality of all religions, a position from which his followers later withdrew. Rāmakṛishṇa's vivid testimony to direct religious experiences drew back into traditional Hinduism many of his contemporaries who had been drawn to the Westernized cults.

Svāmī Vivekānanda

Foremost among Rāmakṛishṇa's disciples was Vivekānanda (1863–1902), who organized an order of monks, the Rāmakṛishṇa Order, to carry on the master's teaching. Vivekānanda had a university education and shared the patriotic feeling and social concern of India's English-educated elite.

In dedicating itself in India to works of social service, the Rāmakṛishṇa Order has proposed by its example a new activist ideal for the life of the sannyāsī. The monks carry out relief work at times of famine and flood and operate excellent hospitals and clinics. Rather than focusing on Rāmakṛishṇa's worship of the personalistic Kālī, they emphasize his Advaita form of mystical experiences of absolute oneness and teach a modified Advaita Vedānta doctrine: unlike Śaṅkara's, their account of māyā permits an acceptance of the world as real.

For many educated Hindus, their neo-Vedāntic outlook has served as a new rallying point. In this view, other religions may be valid as far as they go, but they are incomplete; in the end they must be completed in the Advaita experience of absolute oneness. This perception that monism is the ultimate religion that completes other faiths has become the basis for a Hindu mission to the world. In 1893 Vivekānanda represented Hinduism at the World Parliament of Religions in Chicago and remained to become the first great Hindu missionary to the West. In the United States at present there are 11 centers of the Rāmakṛishṇa a Mission, where meditation and Advaita Vedānta philosophy are taught.

Maharishi Mahesh Yogi

A recent and very aggressive promoter of the Advaita outlook is Maharishi Mahesh Yogi, who at the time of this writing is still alive. His organization, the Transcendental Meditation Program, has trained thousands of westerners in a simple form of Hindu meditation. Maharishi has removed the aura of exoticism that formerly surrounded yoga. His extraordinary impact on Europe and America is based on the simplicity and effectiveness of his meditation techniques, his organizing ability in establishing meditation centers, and his willingness to allow yoga to be used not only for spiritual rewards but also for the attainment of emotional equilibrium and physical health.

Rabindranāth Tagore

A very different kind of influential Hindu has been Rabindranāth Tagore (1861–1961), who received the Nobel Prize in literature for his *Gitāñjali* ("A Handful of Song-Offerings"), a booklet of devotional poetry in English. A prolific poet in Bengali and in English, Tagore poured forth his personal faith, using many of the images of the Gopāla cult but using language with universal intelligibility and appeal. He was born into a leading family of the Brāhmo Samāj and remained true to the family's belief in a personal

Rabindranāth Tagore, a noted Hindu poet, wrote in both Bengali and English. The poetry makes use of the images of the Gopāla cult but has worldwide appeal. Rejecting the notion of the world as illusion, Tagore celebrated a unifying divine presence in nature and in humanity. (Wide World)

God. In time he moved quietly away from the rationalism of the Brāhmo Samāj, however, toward a mystical substantiation of his faith. Yet his mysticism was not that of yogic introspection. Awareness of the divine presence came to him in open-eyed moments of loving contemplation of the beauty of nature and of living beings:

> *When I go from hence, let this be my parting word, that what I have seen is unsurpassable.*
> *I have tasted of the hidden honey of this lotus that expands on the ocean of light, and thus I am blessed—let this be my parting word.*
>
> *In this playhouse of infinite forms I have had my play, and here have I caught sight of him that is formless.*[2]

A person of cosmopolitan spirit, Tagore had a distaste for religious and cultural jealousies and stood aside from nationalistic forms of Hinduism.

THE MORALE OF CONTEMPORARY HINDUISM

There was a time, a century ago, when the population that was nominally Hindu was filled with restlessness and resentment. It was by no means clear that the coming generations would continue to call themselves Hindu or that Hinduism would be an important shaping factor in their lives. It is clear now that Hinduism has passed through a century of severe testing and survived. The once-restrictive social orthodoxies that generated disaffection have been broken by reformers, and idealists have found ways whereby the force of religion can be directed to problems that have disturbed modern people. No Hindu is now compelled to subscribe to medieval cosmologies, prescientific approaches to nature, or the privileges of an ancient aristocracy.

Hindu despisers of their tradition are now rare. It is true that a vehement hostility toward brāhmans is sweeping the Tamil area in the south, but brāhmanism is not the whole of Hinduism, and the hatred has not spread beyond the Tamil area. Significant numbers of people of low social rank continue to become Muslims or Buddhists—but these are groups who had never, in fact, had membership in the Hindu community. It could also be said, of Hinduism as of other religions, that a great central mass of its people knows little and cares little about the religious tradition, but the rank and file that formerly ran from the indifferent to the disaffected now runs from the indifferent to the ardent. Young persons are willing to identify themselves as Hindu without hesitation.[3] With their participation, the ritual life of families and villages goes on, with some simplification. Attendance at temples is high, and new temples and monasteries are being built at an unprecedented rate. Hordes of astounding size throng the pilgrimage trails and attend religious fairs. With a new freedom, charismatic religious leaders rise up and become gurus, instructing thousands not merely in meditation but also in the moral life, thus helping to fill the vacuum left by the decreasing relevance of the dharmaśāstras. The India of the foreseeable future will be predominantly a Hindu India.

Just what the word *Hindu* will come to mean, however, is not clear. It is idle to suppose that Hinduism will not be a national, and even a nationalistic, religion because the problem of uniting and preserving the nation is an acute one, and religions deal with acute problems. But it is also hard to believe that India, which in religion has entered into dialogue with the world, will spurn the world concern of such great figures as Rāmakṛishṇa, Maharishi, Tagore, and Mahātma Gāndhī. The moderation of these leaders of international mind will surely moderate the spirit of a national Hinduism. All depends on choices yet to be made by millions of people, who will make Hinduism what they wish it to be.

NOTES

1 *Life of Śrī Rāmakṛishṇa* (Calcutta: Advaita Ashram, 1964), pp. 69–72.

2 Rabindranāth Tagore, *Gitāñjali* (New York: Macmillan Publishing, 1971), pp. 108–109, verse 96.

3 Philip H. Ashby, *Modern Trends in Hinduism* (New York: Columbia University Press, 1974), ch. 3.

Religions of India

CHAPTER 6

Jainism and Sikhism

Jainism

THE FOLLOWERS OF THE VICTOR

Jainism is a religion of asceticism par excellence. It exemplifies, in the extreme, what in India is called *karmamārga,* the Way of Works. In this religion of approximately 2 million principally Indian adherents, a model of liberation through rigorous personal discipline and denial of the body is taken to the extreme and made a key part of the faith. Jain asceticism is closely linked to a second principle, the doctrine of **ahimsā**: noninjury of any living being.

Scholars believe that the religion appeared more or less in its present form in northeastern India about 2,500 years ago in reaction to changing conditions of Indian life and religious systems. It was a time of ferment, the era of the Buddha, the upanishads, and new religions emerging to satisfy new religious needs. In the panorama of Hindu thought, Jainism was constituted from non-Brahmanic, lay, and unorthodox themes. The hereditary priesthood, along with its sacrifices and other rituals, was rejected. Moreover, it included very early religious traditions, probably dating back to pre-Aryan, Dravidian times.

As compared with the vast diversity of Hindu mythology and reflection, Jainism has been more carefully disciplined and systematic. An ethical religion, it has been properly described as a philosophy but not a theology—there is no God. Instead experience is controlled by an all-inclusive and morally determined chain of cause and effect.

The Jains unify what we in the West usually split into two: matter and emotion. For them, the physical world is a nonliving realm consisting of matter, space, time, and the agents of motion and rest. The key, though subtlest, form of this is **karmic matter**, which is a side effect of each person's desires, passions, and attachments. Greed, for example, is considered the result of binding attachment. Thus if one is moved by a greedy desire, one takes on the subtle material form of such negativity and carries it like baggage. This shapes one's future in this life and succeeding lives, for, like Hindus and Buddhists, Jains believe in transmigration of the soul (rebirth after this life into another earthly life). The goal of the religion is to be liberated from all passions and desires and hence to be freed from the subtle bonds of matter. When truly freed, one gains a permanent state of moksha ("release" or "enlightenment").

According to Jains, the transformative path of self-mortification was originally laid out by the "ford finders," **Tīrthaṃkaras**, who crossed over—transcended—the river of life and found release from matter's clutches. According to Jain theory, there were 24 Tīrthaṃkaras in all, beginning with Ṛisabha, who lived for 8.4 million years. The nineteenth

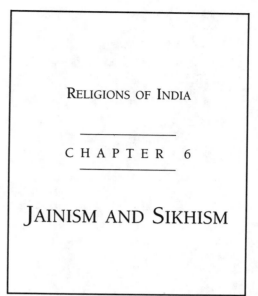

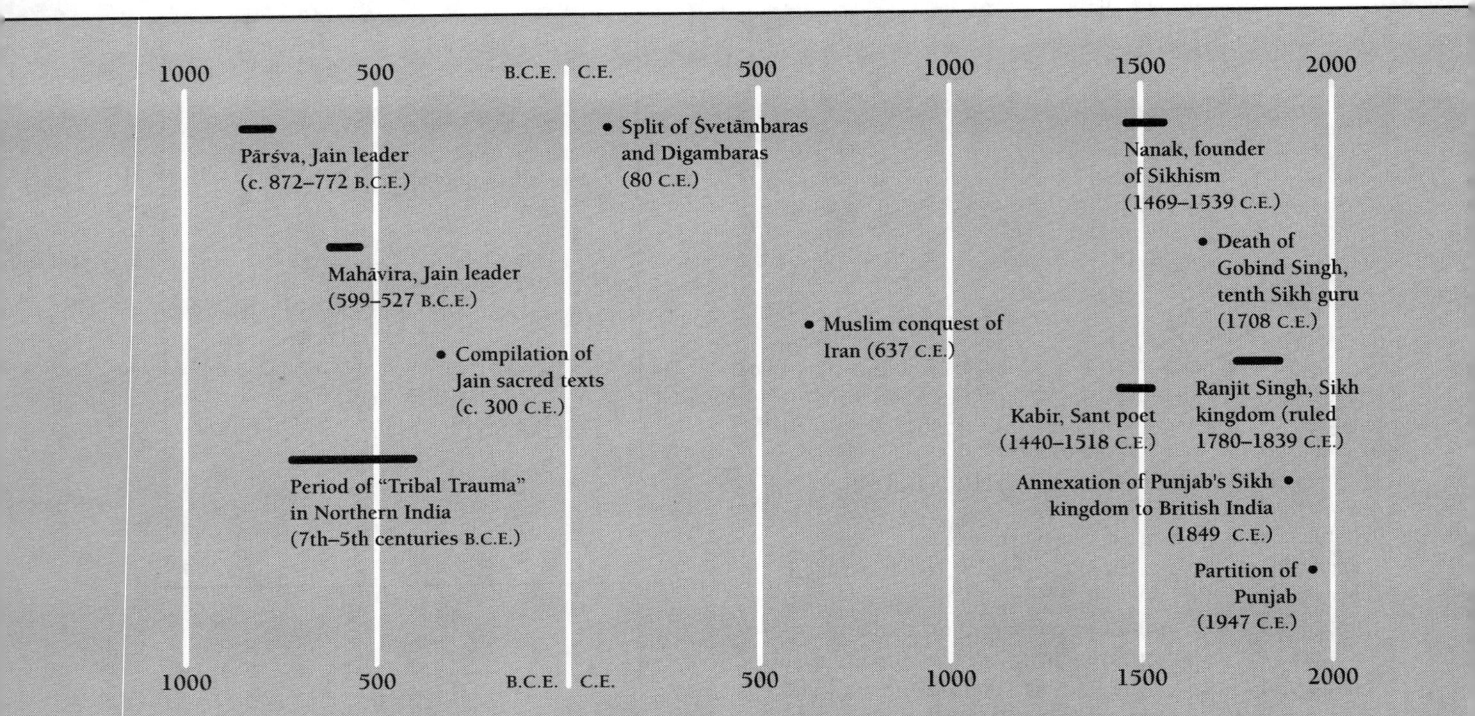

JAINISM AND SIKHISM TIME LINE

Tīrthaṃkara, Mallinātha, is said to have been a woman. Modern scholars believe that the first 22 Tīrthaṃkaras are mythic figures, but they do accept Pārśva (born about 872 B.C.E.) and Mahāvira as historical.

But neither evoking the ancestral ford finders nor following their path can rid a person of passions. Since the gods are themselves regarded as finite beings subject to rebirth, they cannot help others on the solitary crossing toward freedom. One must do it oneself: "Man, thou art thine own friend. Why wishest thou for a friend beyond thyself?"

Rather than relying on anyone else, the Jains practice austerity: meditation, long periods of fasting, control of the emotions, and other ascetic techniques. Such efforts help to purify the self, thereby aiding release from one's passions, matter, and one's karmic accumulations.

Like Buddhism, Jainism first grew up as a monastic and an ascetic religion and only later developed a lay following. Connected to their desire to accumulate no bad karma is the Jains' emphasis on ahimsā, "non-injury." Jains are famous for their attempts to avoid injuring any living creature, since they believe that every living thing has a soul. A Jain monk covers his face with a gauze mask or handkerchief to guard against breathing in (and thus killing) insects. He carries a broom to sweep the path ahead of him to avoid stepping on any living beings. At night Jains refrain from drinking water for fear of unintentionally swallowing a gnat. Jains are strict vegetarians; they refuse not only to eat meat but also to use leather. They were also the first advocates of "animal rights," so popular in the West in recent years.

MAKERS OF THE RIVER CROSSING

Scholars believe that Jainism was given its present form by Nataputta Vardhamana, known as **Mahāvira** ("Great Hero") and as **Jina** ("Victor"). Tradition establishes his life from 599 to 527 B.C.E., although some modern historians place him about 60 years later. Either way, he was roughly a contemporary of the Buddha. The era in which these great religious leaders lived was characterized by rapidly changing conditions of Indian and religious systems, the growth of cities and their merchant class, and a decline in Vedic ritualism.

Mahāvira was preceded as a ford finder by **Pārśva**, often referred to as Pārśvanātha (the Lord Pārśva), who was born in about 872 B.C.E. in what is now the city of Banāras. Tradition has it that Pārśva was married to the daughter of a king but was not interested in the luxuries of the court. At the age of 30 he renounced worldly pleasures and began a life of austerity. Pārśva wandered throughout India, gathering disciples and teaching them to observe the four vows: not to take life, not to lie, not to steal, and not to own property. At last he finally purified himself of his karma and achieved liberation (moksha) on Mount Sammeda in Bengal, which is revered by Jains today as the Hill of Pārśvanātha.

It was some three centuries after Pārśva that Mahāvira gave Jainism its present shape. As noted, he was born in the sixth century B.C.E. near Vaisali (in present-day Bihar), in northeastern India, into a Jain family of the warrior caste. After tearing out his hair by the roots, Mahāvira donned a monk's robe. Stripping off his robe 13 months later, he began to go about naked. Such nudity, long regarded as an ideal, was interpreted as a sign of renunciation of all worldly possessions. (Such public nudity is no longer practiced.)

For the next 12 years Mahāvira led an austere and disciplined life of meditation and asceticism. His reward was moksha, when he finally became a victor over his body and his passions (the name *Jain* means "follower of the victor"). After this enlightenment, Mahāvira began to preach and teach, converting many to the Jain way of life.

After Mahāvira's death, the sacred texts of Jainism, said to have been composed by him, were at first preserved in oral form and written down only two centuries later. At about that time, around 300 B.C.E., the Jain monks began to quarrel, ultimately splitting into the **Śvetāmbaras** ("white-clothed") and the **Digambaras** ("sky-clothed"), who took the vow of nudity. About 80 C.E. the split between the two became irreversible; indeed, it persists today. The Digambaras' center is in Mysore in the Deccan region of southern India. Śvetāmbaras are found mainly in India's western cities. Both sects have their own sacred books and commentaries.

Nataputta Vardhamana, known as Mahāvīra ("Great Hero") and as Jina ("Victor"), is credited with giving Jainism its present form. Here he is represented surrounded by the other Tīrthaṅkaras. (Seattle Art Museum. Eugene Fuller Memorial Collection)

Each Jain monastic community is governed by an *acarya,* or superior, who decides disciplinary and doctrinal matters. The details of the Jain monastic life pattern are carefully defined with rules for truthfulness, study, wandering, and begging as well as confession and penance. The monks do not travel around the countryside during the season of the monsoon rains. At that time, because the wet soil is swarming with small creatures, monks take refuge in a fixed place and, along with members of the laity, receive religious instruction. Their days and nights are divided into periods of requesting alms, eating, studying, meditating, teaching, mortifying the body, and confessing faults. Monastics are easily identified by their shaved heads. Many Jain sects have communities of nuns who follow many of the same practices, despite the Jains' typically ascetic condemnation of women as the greatest temptation and the cause of most sinful acts.

JAIN PHILOSOPHY AND COSMOLOGY

Jain monks in their reflection developed a wide variety of philosophical subtleties. The Hindu idea of māyā, the world as illusion, was rejected. Instead, in their realism, Jains affirm that mind and matter are and will remain eternally separate. The visible universe—made up of souls, matter, space, and the principles of motion and rest, as well as time, which is eternal and formless—is continually in the process of change but indestructible. It operates on its own internal principles. Beyond it, unperceived by the senses, is the indestructible and eternal realm of limitless knowledge and infinite power, the pure state of endless release.

Jain philosophy is described by westerners as a pluralistic substantialism that emphasizes particularity and refuses to give up the continuing reality of change. It is especially interesting because of its both/and rather than either/or orientation. The key principle, *syādvāda,* indicates that all judgments are made from a certain angle and hence are relative. Reflection is led to a yes-and-no position that allows no absolute judgments. Everything has an infinite number of qualities, it is premised. Hence reality must be viewed from many different perspectives. Any attempted definitive statement will inevitably be one-sided, excluding important aspects. At the same time, the Jain emphasis on intuitive religious knowledge has led to definite conviction.

For example, Jains view the universe as eternal and uncreated, rejecting the concept of a supreme being or a creative spirit. Temporal spans are vast. Jains understand the present era as a degenerating and descending one, but they believe that it will be followed by a more ascending, expansive period. They use the figure of a wheel with 12 spokes to symbolize different world ages. The growth of happiness and knowledge during the positive part of the cycle is represented by the first six spokes; as the wheel turns, however, it is followed by retrogression until the cycle begins again. Jains even speculate that 24 new Tīrthaṃkaras will live on earth in the new augmenting period.

The cosmos, immense and enduring through eons, is envisaged as a colossal standing human figure. At the base are the hells, populated by overwhelmingly wicked beings. The middle world in which humans live is represented by a thin disk. It is only at this level that the conquest of karma can be accomplished. Deities (no one absolute) come and go as they visit it. Where perfected souls dwell, the top of the world, is represented by the figure of a crescent moon or an inverted umbrella.

As noted, all actions in people's present and previous existences produce particles of karma that weigh them down and bind their jīvas to an endless cycle of existence. When at last freed from karma, the person's soul rises up to the zenith of the universe, where it remains forever, motionless and free of suffering. Actually, Jains believe that many souls will never achieve final release; instead they will migrate and wander forever.

JAIN ETHICS

In principle, Jains are forbidden to have any occupation that involves the destruction of living beings. They may not eat meat or eggs. Even farming is taboo, since operations like tilling the soil and weeding the crops may harm living creatures.

Whereas monastics take only five vows, laymen affirm a longer list of 12 oaths, expanding those of the monastics: (1) never intentionally take a life or destroy a **jīva** (soul or unit of life); (2) never lie or exaggerate; (3) never steal; (4) never be unfaithful to one's spouse or think unchaste thoughts; (5) limit oneself in the accumulation of wealth and give away all extra possessions—for example, contribute to the maintenance of temples or animal hospitals; (6) limit chances of committing transgressions, for example—impose limits on travel; (7) limit the number of personal possessions; (8) guard against unnecessary evils;

This statue, carved from a single piece of stone, represents Jain saint Gommata. (Religious News Service)

Many Jain laypersons make pilgrimages to their temples, sacred places that express the distinctive orientation of the religion. (Government of India Tourist Office)

(9) observe periods of sinless meditation; (10) observe special periods of personal (ascetic) limitation; (11) spend some time living as a monastic; and (12) give alms to a monastic community.

When they feel death approaching, Jains are obligated to take a vow of nonattachment and dispose of their earthly goods. They are even encouraged to starve themselves, for as one might expect in a religion with such an ascetic orientation, starving oneself to death is an ideal.

JAIN LAITY

Jainism evolved from an ascetic's path into a religion of the urban merchant class, of affluent city dwellers. In part this was because Jain lay practitioners chose to become merchants for largely religious reasons. Supported by sympathetic monarchs, the Jain communities built many temples and shrines, some quite magnificent. During the twelfth century, however, a resurgence of Hinduism led to the persecution of Jains, and in the thirteenth century the Muslim conquest of India was followed by persecutions of all faiths other than Islam. Unlike Buddhism, which has all but disappeared from India, Jainism managed to survive in the land of its origin. It even enjoyed a revival under the tolerant Mughal emperor Akbar. Today, the largest number of Jainism's 2 million adherents live in the Bombay area.

JAIN TEMPLES

Since Jainism denies that its saints can help adherents on the path, it offers no cult of relics. Many Jain laypersons do, however, make pilgrimages to the temples, for their temples are sacred places that express the distinctive orientation of the religion. The temples are adorned with the Jain symbol, a swastika

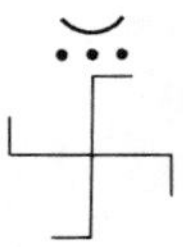

surmounted by three dots and a half-moon. The dots represent the three jewels of Jainism: right faith, right knowledge, and right conduct. The half-moon symbolizes moksha. The arms of the swastika stand for four types of beings: those born in hell; those born as insects, plants, or animals; those born as humans; and those born as spirits of gods or demons.

In the Śvetāmbara temples the images are shown in the meditative seated position with crossed legs; many statues wear loincloths and have glass eyes. In the Digambara temples the ceremonies can be conducted only by a Jain, but the Śvetāmbaras often permit non-Jains to officiate on religious occasions. Though it runs counter to official Jain doctrine, the laity do manage to offer sweetmeats, flowers, and fruits and burn incense lamps and lamps before the images in hopes that the saints might help them traverse the crossing.

SIKHISM

THE WAY OF THE DISCIPLES

Sikhism's primary emphasis is not on prophecy or ritual but on the consciousness of God in human persons. It seeks not an escape from the world but rather spiritual insight during earthly life. The name derives from the Pāli *sikkha,* meaning "disciple." Each disciple is expected to lead a life of prayer and recite or read a prescribed number of hymns each day as well as to serve the religious community. Sikhs define themselves as people who believe in one God, accept the teachings of the first ten guru leaders of the community, and believe in its scripture, the **Adi Granth** ("Original Book").

Today there are more than 17 million Sikhs, about 85 percent of whom live in the Indian state of Punjab. Sikh communities also exist in Malaysia, Singapore, East Africa, England, Canada, and the United States. India's youngest religion, Sikhism underwent two principal developmental stages, the first pacific and the second more militant.

EARLY SIKHISM

Begun in northern India in the fifteenth century C.E. by Guru Nanak, Sikhism sought to harmonize Hinduism and Islam. Reacting to conflicts between Hindus and Muslims, Nanak tried to go beyond contending doctrines and viewpoints to the subject of faith itself. For him the different religious institutions did not matter, only God's word, and he urged his followers to turn away from the outward forms by which humans identify the deity.

His path stresses meditating on the divine name, which is to cleanse humans of impurities and enable them to ascend higher and higher until they achieve union with the eternal One. The path also features worship, which emphasizes adoration without rites of sacrifice or propitiation. In addition, since the path cannot be separated from morality, he encouraged his followers to be courageous and to overcome lust, anger, greed, and egotism. By these means a Sikh can hope to escape from the cycle of birth and rebirth.

THE SANT BACKGROUND AND THE POET KABIR

As stated, Sikhism sought to integrate Hinduism and Islam. To Islam it owes its monotheism: God is held to be the one and true divine being and, as Islam emphasizes, must not be represented in any human form. Despite these debts, the religion is more an offshoot of Hinduism than a true syncretism with Islam.

Sikhism's principle heritage is the Hindu **Sant** devotional movement. Dating from the early thirteenth century, the Sant movement continued even after the founding of Sikhism. The Sant emphasis was on unity rather than duality: human beings would continue to encounter suffering until they attained union with God. The Sants did not identify God with the world; to them he was manifest in creation, especially through his immanence (indwelling) in the human soul.

Sikhism is especially indebted to the Sant poet **Kabir** (1440–1518). This beloved bard rejected the authority of the Hindu Vedas and upanishads and of the Islamic Qur'ān. He was convinced that all human beings were brothers and sisters before the mystery of the divine and that religion without love was empty and powerless. The path of salvation required the invocation of God's name: "Utter the name of God: He extinguishes birth and death. I utter His Name, and whatever I see reminds me of Him; whatever I do becomes His worship."[1]

Kabir had his own telling metaphor for describing the release that is possible through the love of God: God, the true guru, discharged the arrow of his word into the world. The man or woman slain by this word finds true life in a mystical union with God the ineffable.

Visitors approach the Golden Temple at Amritsar. Unlike Hindu shrines, it is open on all four sides, signaling that members of all four principal castes have equal status as disciples. (United Nations)

NANAK'S CAREER

Few details are known for certain about the life of **Nanak** (1469–1539), the founder of Sikhism; critical historical research is only now beginning. His writings are preserved in the Adi Granth. Tradition recounts that he was born to a Hindu family of the warrior caste in Taluandi, a village on the Ravi River about 30 miles from Lahore. He attended a Muslim school, where he was taught elementary Arabic and Persian and learned about Islam. Thus from early in his career the need to integrate the two religions was important.

He married at 19, eventually fathering two sons. During this time he befriended Mardana, a Muslim servant and musician in the home of an important local official. Soon Nanak gathered about him a group of followers who bathed together in a river every day before dawn and met in his home in the evening to sing religious songs he had composed. Mardana accompanied the group on the rebec, a stringed instrument. Thus from the first his constituency was both Muslim and Hindu.

When Nanak was 30 years old, he received what he took to be a divine call. One day he failed to return from his morning bath in the river. His friends, finding his clothes on the riverbank, dragged the waters in a vain attempt to find his body. Three days later Nanak reappeared. At first he gave no explanation for his absence but made only the following cryptic statement: "There is neither Hindu nor Mussulman [Muslim], so whose path shall I choose? I shall follow God's path. God is neither Hindu nor Mussulman and the path which I follow is God's."[2] Later Nanak told them that in a vision he had been carried up to God's presence. God gave Nanak a cup of nectar and then the following message:

> I am with thee. I have given thee happiness, and I shall make happy all who take thy name. Go thou and repeat my Name; cause others to repeat it. Abide unspoiled by the world. Practice charity, perform ablutions, worship and meditate. My name is God, the primal Brahma. Thou art the Holy Guru.[3]

Inspired by his vision and the promise of happiness as well as his special mission to honor the name of God, Nanak began his career as a guru. He expressed his faith in the following statement, which begins the part of the Adi Granth prayed silently each day by all observant Sikhs:

> There is but one God whose name is True, the Creator, devoid of fear and enmity, immortal, unborn, self-existent, great and bountiful. The True One was in the beginning, the True One was in the primal age. The True One is, was, O Nanak, and the True One also shall be.
>
> (Japji 1.1[4])

Nanak's teaching remained in the Hindu Sant tradition. Rejecting the magic spells and divine images of popular religion, he urged his followers that meditation, worshiping God, and singing hymns (especially in the soft light of the morning) would bring about consciousness of the deity.

It is not certain how widely Nanak traveled in India and other lands. Often accompanied by Mardana, Nanak moved from place to place singing and spreading his religious message. During his later career, life in northern India became unsettled. The invasions of central Asian Muslim warriors, led by Babur (1483–1530), plunged India into a prolonged period of violence and bloodshed.

Nanak did not regard his own sons as suited to guide the community, so before his death he appointed Lehna (or Lahina), a member of the warrior caste, as the second guru of the faith. Calling Lehna to him at a public gathering, the old guru placed before his successor a coconut, the symbol of the universe, and five coins, representing air, earth, fire, water, and ether. He then handed over a book of hymns, which represented the message of the new faith, and a woolen string, a symbol of renunciation.

When Nanak died, his body was claimed by both Hindus and Muslims. He had lived in both the Hindu and Muslim worlds, seeking to overcome their respective limitations through a fresh understanding of the deity.

THE FOUNDER'S TEACHING

By meditating on the divine name, human beings are cleansed of impurities and enabled to ascend higher and higher until they achieve union with the eternal One. The process, Nanak said, is comparable to the experience of persons blinded by self-centeredness: awakened from such perversity, they begin to "see" or recognize the presence of God in the surrounding world; they begin to "hear" the voice of God speaking mystically in their souls and thus gain union with God. Having gained such union, human beings become freed from the cycle of birth and rebirth and ultimately pass beyond death into a realm of infinite and eternal bliss.

Nanak used the Hindu word *māyā* to describe the world, but not in its original sense of "illusion." The world is unreal for Nanak only insofar as it is mistaken for something it is not: "delusion" is thus a better translation, which again stresses the role of human error. We are deluded because we misinterpret nature and the purpose of the world, thinking it and the world to be separate from God. Seeing the world delusionally in this way is referred to as *anjan,* a black salve for the eyes and a traditional North Indian symbol of darkness and untruth.

The Concept of God

Besides God there is no other—this is the essence of Nanak's approach to the supreme being. The affirmation is similar to Muḥammad's affirmation "There is no God but Allāh" and Judaism's Shema. In fact, the religion is monotheistic, but not in the same way as Judaism, for it lacks the Jewish sense of history. God's essence can be known only through a personal experience of mystical union, not through the working out of historical events. Nanak was not a prophet but a guru. Moreover, Sikhism does not identify God as immanent within the world in the same way as Hindu monism did in its concept of Brahman. God is beyond all human categories yet is in them. Nanak used the names of other deities as conventional figures to speak of God. "God is Hari, Rām, and Gopāl, and He is also Allāh, Khuda, and Sāhib" (Rāmakali Ast 1.7). Despite his many manifestations, God alone exists; there is no other like him. He is eternal, omniscient, and omnipotent. Yet Nanak did not teach that God had become incarnate, in the same way as Christians speak of Jesus as an incarnation. Such a concept, in the Sikh perspective, would involve God with death, the supreme enemy, as well as with an unstable world.

LATER SIKHISM

From the death of Guru Nanak in 1539 until the death of Guru Gobind Singh in 1708, the teaching of the founder was continued and fostered by his nine successors. Under Ar jan (ruled 1581–1606), the fifth guru, the Sikh community constructed large water reservoirs, began to build the Golden Temple of Amritsar, and enlarged its small pool into an artificial lake. The temple had four doors, signaling that unlike Hindu shrines, it was open on all sides and that members of all four principal castes had equal status as disciples. Guru Ar jan also gathered the hymns of the first four gurus, put them into the Adi Granth, and enshrined the Sikh scripture in the Golden Temple. When he refused to remove from the Adi Granth passages that contradicted Islamic and Hindu orthodoxy, the Mughul emperor had him tortured and executed.

The Sikh struggle against the Mughul empire was intense and protracted. The tenth guru, Gobind Singh (1675–1708), known as "the Lion," reunited the Sikhs in a fellowship of suffering and triumphant devotion. To fend off the Mughals, Gobind Singh founded the **Khalsa**, a militaristic community of the pure. Calling together a gathering of Sikh warriors and reminding them of the dangers of their situation, the guru called for five volunteers to die for the Sikh cause. Claiming that God demanded a blood sacrifice, the leader led five warriors one by one into his tent and emerged four times with a bloody sword. After the fifth man had gone into the tent, Gobind brought out all his warriors alive. A goat had been substituted for the sacrifice of the five men.

Gobind Singh then administered to the five heroes the rite of *pahul,* an initiation by the sword into a new kind of brotherhood of soldier-saints. He gave each man a two-edged dagger and declared that they were henceforth to be known as *singh* ("lion"). A member of the Khalsa was identified by special symbols (the "five K's"): he was not to cut the hair of his head or his beard *(kes);* he was to carry a comb *(kangha);* and he was to wear a steel bracelet *(kara),* a sword *(kirpan),* and short pants *(kacch).* The uncut hair was to be kept in a topknot under a turban, giving Sikh men a distinctive look they retain to this day. Women too could join the Khalsa. They received a single-edged dagger and took the title of *kaur* ("princess"). When the guru opened the Sikh religion to members of all castes, substituting the Khalsa for caste affiliation, naturally many individuals from the lower classes eagerly embraced the faith.

A Sikh pilgrim is seen washing his feet before entering the Golden Temple, the most sacred shrine of the Sikhs. (United Nations)

Gobind Singh's rule was also a watershed with respect to the role of the guru. After all four of his sons were assassinated, he proclaimed that the line of gurus would end with himself. In the future there would be only the Khalsa, the community of Sikhs, and their holy book, the Adi Granth.

Though the militaristic Khalsa is theoretically open to men and women of all castes, its members have come to form an elite within the Sikh community. They are admitted only after an initiation ceremony at which they pledge themselves to an austere code of conduct. They are to bathe daily at dawn and then spend some time in meditation. They are to avoid liquor, tobacco, and narcotics. They pledge loyalty to the teaching of the gurus and the Adi Granth and swear to join the crusade for righteousness in the world.

During the initiation ceremony each candidate comes before the assembly and proclaims: "The Khalsa is of God, the victory is to God." The candidate then is given a drink of nectar, and nectar is also sprinkled on the hair and eyes.

SIKHISM IN THE MODERN ERA

After the death of the last guru, the Sikhs became increasingly rebellious. Members of the Khalsa took refuge in the hill country, coming out at opportune times to challenge Mughul power. In 1799 the Sikhs captured Lahore and made it the capital of a Sikh kingdom ruled by Ranjit Singh (1780–1839). Ranjit Singh's administration also granted religious freedom to Hindus and Muslims.

During the nineteenth century the Sikhs fought valiantly against the British invaders. When the Khalsa was finally crushed in 1849, the Sikh realm was annexed to British India. The British proved to be fair administrators, and the Sikhs remained loyal to them during the Great Mutiny of 1857 and were welcomed into the British army. Sikhs became highly respected soldiers and policemen in Burma, Hong Kong, and other parts of the British Empire.

When independence came to the Indian subcontinent in 1947, the Sikhs were bitterly disappointed at England's decision to partition the Punjab. West Punjab was given to Pakistan, East Punjab to India. Sikhs and Hindus subsequently joined in a bloody war against the Muslims in Pakistan that resulted in over a million deaths. Eventually 2.5 million Sikhs were forced to migrate to East Punjab.

The Sikh demand for a separate state has continued into the late twentieth century. Indian government policy in reply has encouraged division in the Sikh community, at times even supporting a fundamentalist political party. Sikh fundamentalists turned to violence and occupied the Golden Temple in Amritsar. There was bloodshed when it was stormed in 1984 by national troops on orders from India's prime minister, Indira Gāndhi; in reprisal, one of her guards, a Sikh, assassinated her. Violence against the Sikhs became nationwide, and hundreds of innocent persons were killed. The unrest in the Punjab, where the majority of Sikhs still live, has become a threat to secular democracy in India. The conflicts between Hindus and Sikhs have proved difficult if not impossible to control by military force alone. Religious intolerance, protest against which had led to the founding of the religion, continued.

Although Sikhism has been opposed to the caste system since the time of Nanak, caste distinctions still exist among believers to some degree. The largest Sikh caste today is that of the *jats* (farmers). Next come the skilled workers, followed by members of the upper classes.

Sikhs also differ on the matter of eating meat. Some eat beef, and others eat all meat except beef. Still others are vegetarians who do not eat meat, fish, or eggs. At community meals *(langars),* no meat is served.

Since Sikhs regard marriage as a binding contract, it is taken very seriously: there is no child marriage, divorce is discouraged, and adultery is a serious breach. Sikhs are monogamous, and in accordance with the teachings of their founder, men show respect to women. Widows may remarry.

Funerals are usually held on the day after death. Although burial at sea or in the earth is allowed, the Sikhs' accepted method of disposing of the dead, like the Hindus', is cremation.

Sikhs are supposed to visit their local **gudwaras** (sanctuaries) often. The gudwaras vary greatly in size and appearance; some are magnificent temples in the elaborate Mughal style; others are simple buildings. All must have a copy of the Adi Granth inside, and all must fly the *nishan sāhib,* the yellow flag of Sikhism.

In the central room, the Adi Granth is displayed on cushions, usually beneath a canopy. Men and women remove their shoes before entering this area and, out of respect, cover their heads. Any man or woman may read from the holy book. Offerings are made and hymns are sung. As they leave, worshipers walk backward out of the room, never turning their backs on the scripture. There is no priesthood per se. The congregation of each gudwara elects its own officers and votes on all important matters. Women can be present at meetings, but they do not usually participate in the discussion. In recent years some Sikhs have adopted secular habits, though any man who discards the turban and cuts his hair is considered an apostate. Readmission to the community is allowed only after a period of penance.

NOTES

1 John Clark Archer, *Faiths Men Live By* (New York: Ronald Press, 1934), p. 314.

2 W. Owen Cole and Piara Singh Sambhi, *The Sikhs: Their Religious Beliefs and Practices* (London: Routledge & Kegan Paul, 1978), p. 9.

3 Archer, *Faiths Men Live By*, p. 315.

4 M.A. MacAuliff, *The Sikh Religion: Its Gurus, Sacred Writings and Anthems I* (Oxford: Clarendon Press, 1909), p. 35.

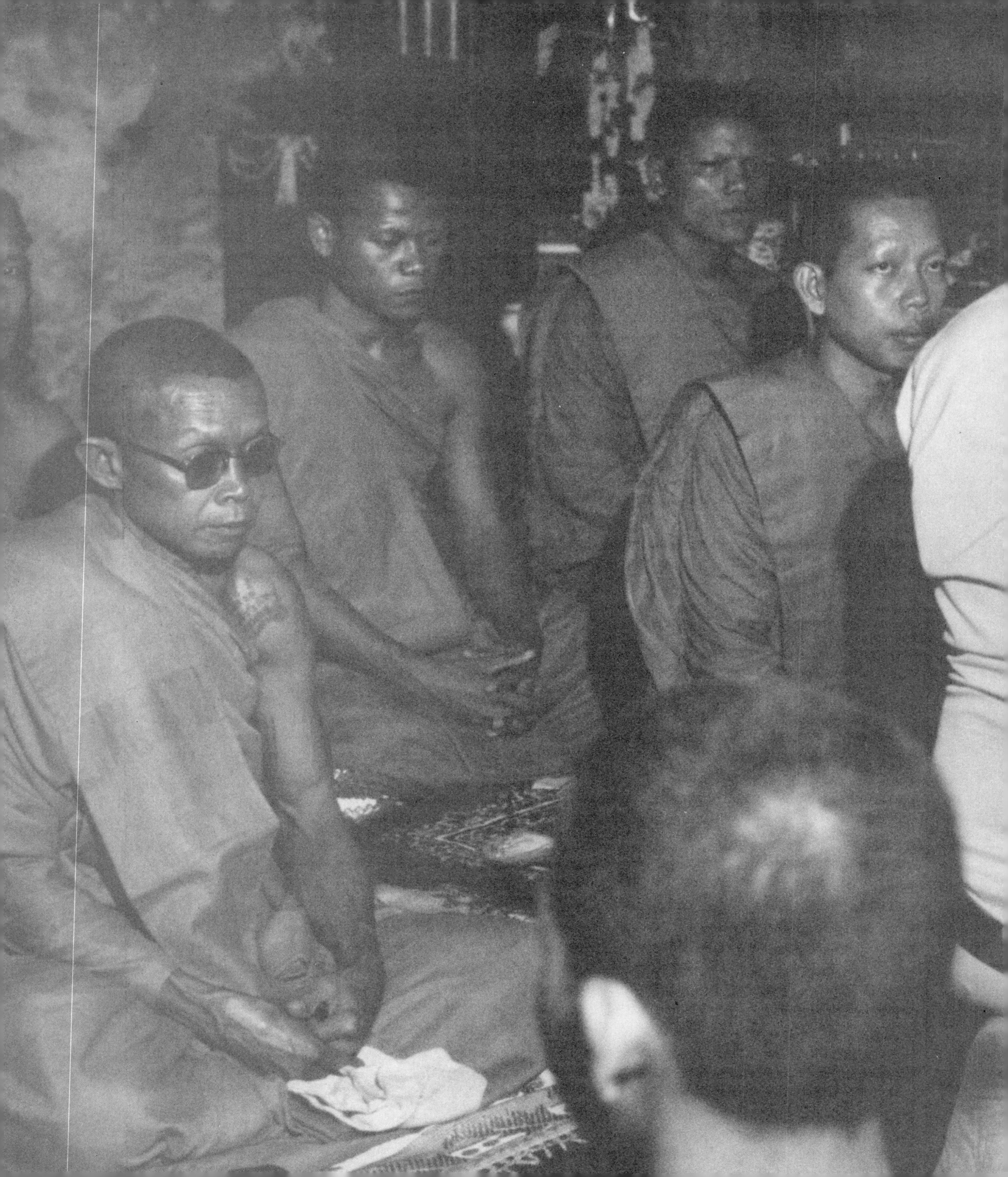

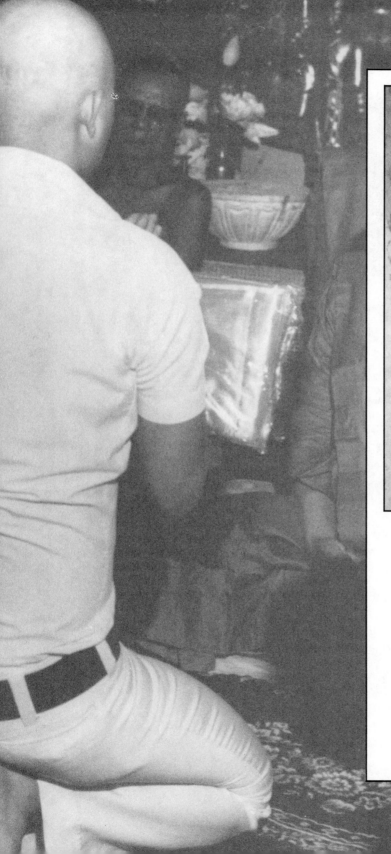

PART TWO

BUDDHISM

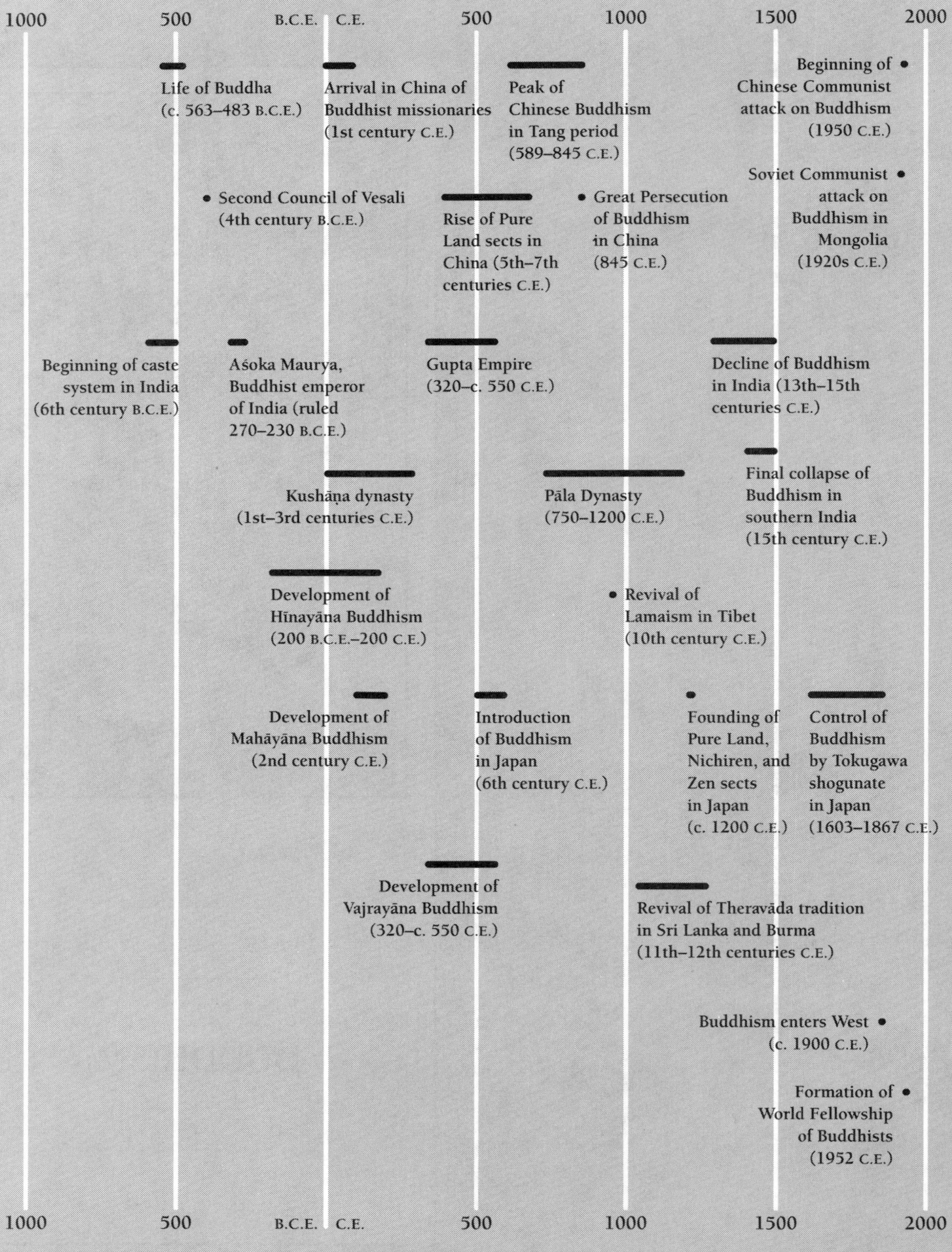
1000
500
B.C.E.
C.E.
500
1000
1500
2000
Life of Buddha
(c. 563–483 B.C.E.)
Arrival in China of
Buddhist missionaries
(1st century C.E.)
Peak of
Chinese Buddhism
in Tang period
(589–845 C.E.)
Beginning of
Chinese Communist
attack on Buddhism
(1950 C.E.)
Second Council of Vesali
(4th century B.C.E.)
Rise of Pure
Land sects in
China (5th–7th
centuries C.E.)
Great Persecution
of Buddhism
in China
(845 C.E.)
Soviet Communist
attack on
Buddhism in
Mongolia
(1920s C.E.)
Beginning of caste
system in India
(6th century B.C.E.)
Aśoka Maurya,
Buddhist emperor
of India (ruled
270–230 B.C.E.)
Gupta Empire
(320–c. 550 C.E.)
Decline of Buddhism
in India (13th–15th
centuries C.E.)
Kushāṇa dynasty
(1st–3rd centuries C.E.)
Pāla Dynasty
(750–1200 C.E.)
Final collapse of
Buddhism in
southern India
(15th century C.E.)
Development of
Hīnayāna Buddhism
(200 B.C.E.–200 C.E.)
Revival of
Lamaism in Tibet
(10th century C.E.)
Development of
Mahāyāna Buddhism
(2nd century C.E.)
Introduction
of Buddhism
in Japan
(6th century C.E.)
Founding of
Pure Land,
Nichiren, and
Zen sects
in Japan
(c. 1200 C.E.)
Control of
Buddhism
by Tokugawa
shogunate
in Japan
(1603–1867 C.E.)
Development of
Vajrayāna Buddhism
(320–c. 550 C.E.)
Revival of Theravāda tradition
in Sri Lanka and Burma
(11th–12th centuries C.E.)
Buddhism enters West
(c. 1900 C.E.)
Formation of
World Fellowship
of Buddhists
(1952 C.E.)
1000
500
B.C.E.
C.E.
500
1000
1500
2000

BUDDHISM TIME LINE

BUDDHISM

CHAPTER 7

THE RISE OF BUDDHISM

Buddhism is based on the life and teachings of Śākyamuni Buddha,* a spiritual master who lived in the fifth century B.C.E. in what is today Nepal and northeastern India. Although the roots of Buddhism are in the Indian subcontinent, so that it shares many of the concerns of the complex of religions known collectively as Hinduism, it seeks to transcend all cultures and traditions and to lead all beings—humans, deities, animals—up to perfect enlightenment and complete liberation from all suffering. Buddhism regards itself as the **Dharma**, the "eternal truth about reality," and it teaches that the Dharma is, over immensely long periods of time, forgotten and then rediscovered by beings who have fully awakened to reality as it is and are therefore called **Buddhas** ("awakened ones"). From this perspective, the so-called historical Buddha, Śākyamuni, is only the latest in a series of Buddhas.

Consistent with its transcultural view, Buddhism is a missionary religion. It has spread throughout Asia and divided into two main forms—Theravāda in Southeast Asia and Mahāyāna in central and eastern Asia. Today it is adapting to life in many countries outside of Asia, especially in Europe and North America.

Buddhism has so many different teachings that it is impossible to fit them into a single, coherent, logical system. They do, however, fit together as therapies or medicine. (In fact, Buddhism is often seen in North America as being closer to psychotherapy than to what is commonly regarded as religion.) Buddhism teaches that beings are sick, and the Buddhas are the physicians. Just as a wise physician has a different cure for each disease, so the Buddhas have different teachings for different beings. And just as medicines do not relate to each other but all lead to health when properly used, so the teachings of the Buddhas are sometimes contradictory, but for the right being at the right time, each can be effective for liberation.

The heart of Buddhism is the Triple Treasure *(triratna)* of the Buddha, the Dharma, and the **Saṅgha**. The Buddha is the teacher, the Dharma is the teaching, and the Saṅgha is the community of those who follow, preserve, and transmit the teaching. We will use the Triple Treasure as the focus of our study of Buddhism.

*In full, Śākyamuni Gautama Siddhārtha, which consists of a title attached to his clan name ("sage of the Śākyas"), followed by his family name or surname ("of the lineage of Gotama") and his given name ("success").

THE LIFE OF THE BUDDHA

Scholars have tried for years to reconstruct the life of Śākyamuni Buddha and his teachings but have not reached a consensus. Even his dates are still debated:

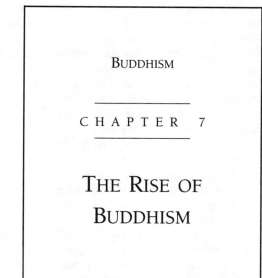

some experts place him around 563–483 B.C.E., others between 448 and 368 B.C.E. However, all agree that the Buddha lived in the northeastern Indian subcontinent during a period of religious and social turmoil. Scholar Charles Drekmeier has coined the expression *tribal trauma* to describe the situation. The older "tribally" oriented social structures were breaking down, and a new, more cosmopolitan society was beginning to develop. From a predominantly pastoral and agricultural society, cities and merchants were beginning to emerge and together were growing increasingly wealthy and powerful. Politically, monarchy was developing, and certain northeastern Indian kings were expanding their domains into other parts of the subcontinent.

In this situation of rapid social and economic change, the older Vedic way of religious life, which had been well suited to an agrarian peasant world, was losing its hold on the loyalties of the people, including the new political and economic elites. This was particularly true in the dynamic northeast, where Vedic influence had never been thoroughly incorporated into the local culture. The result was great anxiety and insecurity, accompanied by exploration into new, more relevant religious patterns.

This is the era of Hinduism's upanishads and the emergence of the Jains and other schools. Many people were leaving their place in ordinary society to take up life in alternative communities made up of wandering ascetics called **śramaṇas**. By the time of the Buddha, there were many such communities, often advocating new kinds of religious beliefs, practices, and patterns of community life. Many were organized around a charismatic leader who taught a doctrine that promised a final salvation through which the problems of life in this world could be totally transcended. The Buddha—who, it is generally agreed, was a member of the nobility (the kshatriya caste)—was one of those persons who gave up worldly life to seek new ways of addressing such problems. After many years of religious experimentation and exploration, he achieved and later taught about a final salvation, the solution to human problems.

Either during his lifetime or very shortly thereafter, the Buddha's followers began to tell stories about his life. In recounting these tales, no effort was made to distinguish between accurate reporting of historical events and mythic elements that expressed the tradition's teachings.

According to the stories, the Buddha was the son of the ruler of the Śākya kingdom in the northeast of the subcontinent. His birth is described as a "descent" from the Tushita heaven, where he had been residing as a result of his good deeds in his previous lives. The birth itself was miraculous and painless and was followed by predictions from the court brāhmans that he would become either a **Cakravartin** (universal monarch) or a Buddha (supremely enlightened sage). Fearful of the prophecy that he might renounce the throne, his father did his best to keep his son happy and contented, surrounded by beauty and insulated from sickness, decay, and death. The young Siddhārtha was given the best possible education and was married to the most beautiful princess, Yaśodharā ("she who radiates brightness or fame"), by whom he had a son. However, he named his son Rāhula, "the fetter"—possibly indicating his or the tradition's ambivalence about the value of married life.

Restless, Siddhārtha wanted to go out of the palace. Wary of earlier predictions that he might become a Buddha, his father ordered all sick and aged persons, all monks, and all funerals banished from the streets of the city while his son passed by. But somehow an old man slipped through the security guards. Siddhārtha was deeply shocked and asked his driver:

> "Good charioteer, who is this man with white hair, supporting himself on the staff in his hand, with his eyes veiled by the brows, and limbs relaxed and bent? Is this some transformation in him, or his original state, or mere chance?"

His driver replied:

> "Old age it is called, that which has broken him down—the murderer of beauty, the ruin of vigour, the birthplace of sorrow, the grave of pleasure, the destroyer of memory, the enemy of the senses.
>
> "For he too sucked milk in his infancy, and later in course of time he crawled on the ground; in the natural order he became a handsome youth and in the same natural order he has now reached old age."

Hearing these words and learning that old age was the fate of everyone who is born, the prince

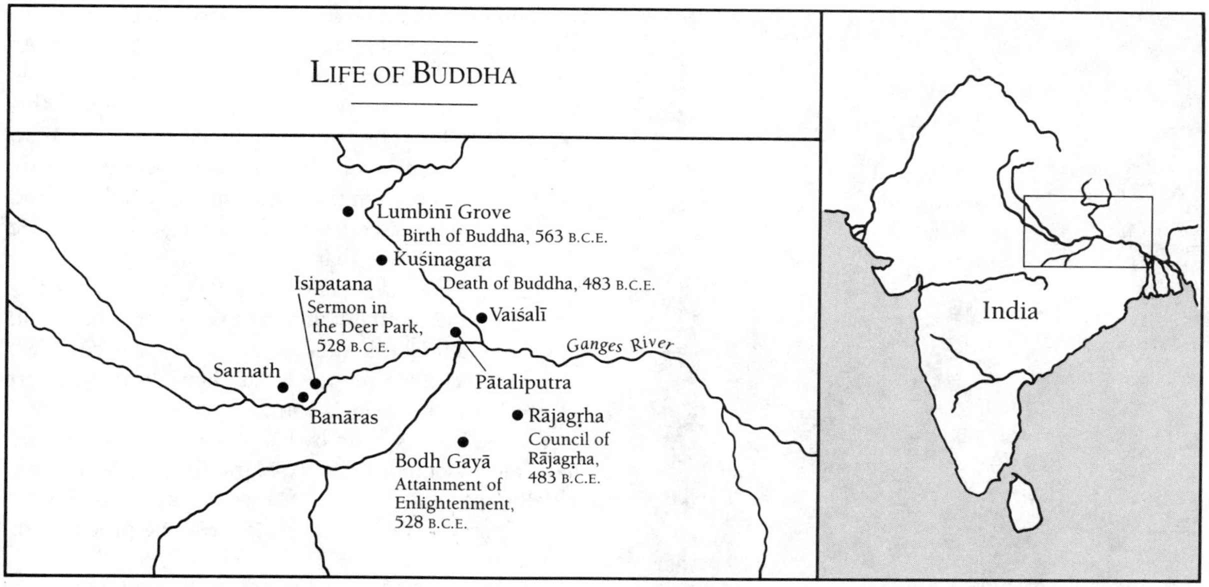

sighed deeply and shook his head; and looking on the festive multitude he uttered these words in his perturbation:

"Thus old age strikes down indiscriminately memory and beauty and valour, and yet with such a sight before its eyes the world is not perturbed.

"This being so, turn back the horses, charioteer; go quickly home again. For how can I take my pleasure in the garden, when the fear of old age rules in my mind?"[1]

So despite all the precautions, Siddhārtha had seen the first of the four things that would cause him to turn away from a life as a worldly ruler. In two further excursions from the palace, he saw a sick man and a corpse. In these three sights the Buddha—and the tradition—recognized the problem of existence, transiency: everything that comes to be ceases to be, whatever we are now we will not be later, and whatever we have we will lose. The situation seemed hopeless. But then Siddhārtha saw the fourth and last sight, a homeless wanderer (sannyāsī) or monk. This man was calm and peaceful; he radiated a serenity that said, wordlessly, "I have found it!" In him the Buddha and the tradition saw the possibility of a life other than that devoted to getting things that are then lost, a life that sought the cause of death.

So one night, leaving Yaśodharā and Rāhula asleep, Siddhārtha left the palace and fled to the forest. There, much as later monks would do, he took off his jewelry, exchanged his robes for simple clothes, dismissed his horse (which, it is said, died of a broken heart and was reborn as a god), and began to live as a sannyāsī, a forest-dwelling ascetic.

In those days the forests of the Indian subcontinent were full of sannyāsīs, and Siddhārtha sought a teacher among them. He found, however, that although there were many who knew how to attain exalted states of consciousness and deeply peaceful ones, none had found the secret of liberation from **saṃsāra**, the cycle of birth, death, and rebirth. Therefore, he abandoned all teachers and sought the truth for himself. He thought that he might be able to free his mind or soul from his body by denying his body—according to the most extreme accounts, he ate only one grain of rice a day, becoming so thin that he could grasp his backbone through his abdomen, and he lost so much weight that if he stood up on a windy day, he would be blown over! At any rate, he seems to have practiced forms of asceticism that despite their severity are not

This temple in Bodh Gayā, India, is said to be erected on the site of the bodhi tree where Siddhārtha withstood the temptations of Māra. (Religious News Service)

unusual among sannyāsīs in the Indian subcontinent even today.

However, the experiment failed, and he was in a quandary. When he had been in the palace, eating, drinking, and sleeping all he wanted, he would become drowsy and confused. Now, hardly eating, drinking, or sleeping at all, he also became drowsy and confused. The only difference was that when he ate he was strong and when he didn't eat he was weak. In neither case was he any nearer to ending the birth-and-death cycle.

Then he remembered a time when as a child he had sat under a tree and allowed his mind to calm down. As his mind calmed, it became clear, and as it became clear it became manageable. He tried to repeat this experience. First he ate something, just enough to build up his strength. Thus he began the tradition's "middle way" between the hedonism of worldly life and the self-denying asceticism of the forest dwellers. He then sat under a tree that would become known as the Bodhi, or "Enlightenment Tree,"* focused and stabilized his mind in meditation, and vowed that he would not move until he had attained perfect and complete enlightenment. Meditation would henceforth be a part of nearly every lineage's path.

At first he was beset by hallucinations of greed and hate and by demons, led by Māra, the god of illusion. Finally, seeing through Māra's trickery, his mind cleared, and as the morning star rose, he proclaimed:

> Through many a birth I wandered in saṃsāra,
> seeking, but not finding, the builder of the house.
> Sorrowful is it to be born again and again.
> House-builder! You are seen. You shall build
> no house again. All your rafters are broken. Your
> ridge-pole is shattered.
> My mind has attained the unconditioned.
> Achieved is the end of craving.
>
> (Dhammapada 153–154)

So saying, he decided to vanish from the phenomenal world, convinced that it would be useless to teach what he had seen. However, one of the deities (who also, according to Buddhism, are trapped in saṃsāra, and therefore wish to know how to end the cycle), told him that if he would but look, he would see that there were many beings "with little dust on their eyes" who would understand him and be helped by what he knew.

Thus began 45 years of traveling in the Ganges basin area, teaching whoever would listen. Many who heard him were so attracted to his words and his way of life that they wished to follow him, and he received them as *bhikshus,* or Buddhist sannyāsīs.

*A descendant of this tree still exists, in the village of Bodh Gayā, Bihar, India, on the spot where the Buddha is supposed to have sat.

During the early years, according to the stories, many ascetics—chief disciples Ānanda and Devadatta among them—became Siddhārtha's followers. But wealthy merchants and powerful administrators too were converted, and by the end of his life even kings and princes were making pilgrimages to his doors. Such stories emphasize the variety of converts to his Saṅgha and the vast range of his appeal, which cut through long-established social and economic barriers.

The Buddha taught into old age. He died after eating some rancid food and, passing into **nirvāṇa** (final release), disappeared from the phenomenal universe. His remains were cremated and memorial mounds, called **stūpas**, were built over portions of his relics, which were distributed throughout the neighboring kingdoms. Although the Buddha had disappeared in person, he could still be contacted through the Triple Treasure he established.

THE TEACHINGS OF THE BUDDHA: THE DHARMA

THE FOUR NOBLE TRUTHS

As it has proved impossible to recover the life of the Buddha with historical accuracy, so it is difficult to say precisely how much of the Dharma comes from the Buddha and how much from his followers. But once again there is agreement among almost all Buddhist lineages. The heart of the Dharma is traditionally contained in the Four Noble Truths set forth in the so-called first sermon of the Buddha at Banāras. They are (1) suffering *(duḥkha)*, (2) the arising of suffering *(samudaya)*, (3) the cessation of suffering *(nirodha)*, and (4) the path leading to the cessation of suffering *(mārga)*.

Suffering

The Four Noble Truths begin with a formulation of the problem that from the Buddha's perspective was the basic human problem, the one that encompassed all of our more specific difficulties and anxieties: suffering. All sentient beings, he contended, live lives in which suffering is an inevitable and ultimately dominant component. Some persons, because of the law of karma, which ensures that good deeds will be rewarded and bad deeds will be punished, have more enjoyment and less suffering than others. Given the law of karma, it is both possible and advisable to perform good deeds in the present in order to maximize future enjoyment and to minimize future suffering. But despite the Buddha's emphasis on the doctrine of karma and the consequent advantages of moral activity, he was steadfast in this: so long as life continues, suffering cannot be avoided.

This emphasis on the pervasiveness of suffering clearly struck a responsive chord among people who had lost their tribal affiliations. All sentient beings are caught up in an ongoing process of continuing birth, suffering, death, and rebirth. Because of the morally structured workings of karma, those who do good deeds in one life can assure themselves of a better condition in their future lives. Every action has a consequence that affects future rebirths. Acts of charity and compassion, for instance, result in a better rebirth; harmful acts and immoral acts lead to a rebirth that involves greater suffering. But even the best kind of life

The great stupa in the Deer Park near Banāras (Varanasi), marking the spot where Buddha delivered his first sermon. (Stephen Borst)

is impermanent and is tinged with the suffering that impermanence brings.

The Cause of Suffering

The analysis of the problem of suffering that constitutes the second of the Four Noble Truths asserts that the cause of suffering is desire and craving *(taṇhā)*. Why does the cycle of rebirth, suffering, death, and rebirth continue? Why is the impermanence of life experienced as suffering? Because craving is an ever present force that drives the life process forward, and in this life process every object of desire that is gained is, because of its inherent impermanence, ultimately lost.

The Cessation of Suffering

The third Noble Truth affirms that a solution to the problem is available—that release from suffering is possible. Though the term *nirvāṇa* is not used in the classical formulations of the Four Noble Truths, later Buddhists recognized that what they had come to call nirvāṇa is the goal to which the Buddha was pointing. Nirvāṇa means literally "blowing out" or "extinguishing," as of the flame of a candle. Here it suggests the extinguishing of all craving and desire and hence all suffering. When the mind no longer grasps and craves what is by nature impermanent, suffering ends. The early texts present this nirvāṇic experience as very positive, analogous to (but more desirable than) the experiences of bliss, joy, heaven, and the like.

The Path Out of Suffering

The fourth and culminating truth affirms that there is a path that releases those who follow it from the realm of suffering, the so-called Noble Eightfold Path—as expressed by the Buddha in his first sermon: right view, right thought, right speech, right action, right livelihood, right effort, right mindfulness, right concentration. As we saw earlier, this path presents a middle way between the overly rigorous asceticism the Buddha first tried and the slothful self-indulgence he saw in most people. The stories about the Buddha himself show that he followed such a middle way in his own quest for enlightenment and throughout his ministry.

CORRELATED BUDDHIST DOCTRINES

If the Four Noble Truths constitute the most famous and most dependable summary of the Buddha's message, the two doctrines that most clearly distinguish his teaching are the closely correlated claims concerning interdependent arising **(pratītya samutpāda)** and no self **(anātman)**. Both of these teachings are sufficiently distinctive and pervasive in the early Buddhist tradition that it is highly probable that they originated in the experience and reflection of the founder himself.

Pratītya Samutpāda: Interdependent Arising

The doctrine of interdependent arising was the Buddha's most sophisticated way of accounting for the existence of the world and individuals, in a way that permitted transcending life's inevitable suffering. Unlike many other religious teachers, the Buddha did not believe in a creator God who creates and continues to sustain individuals and the world. In fact, there is considerable evidence that the Buddha did not reject the belief in gods, demons, and the like. But from his perspective, any gods that might exist were, just like humans, caught up in the suffering-filled round of saṃsāra.

Through the doctrine of interdependent arising, the Buddha sought to describe the entire process in which all beings originate and participate and in so doing suggest how individuals might bring the process to a felicitous end. Though we do not know the exact form in which the doctrine of interdependent arising was originally taught, the early texts set forth both a short formula and a classical summary of the teaching. The short formula is this:

When this is, that is.
This arising, that arises.
When this is not, that is not.
This ceasing, that ceases.

The classical summary explains this obscure formula: all phenomenal reality, both cosmic and personal, comes into being through a process in which 12 constituent elements are continually arising interdependently (that is, dependent on and in conjunction with one another). These 12 constituents are ignorance, karmic predispositions, consciousness, name and form, the five sense organs and the mind, contact, feeling-response, craving, grasping for an object, action toward life, birth, and old age and death.

All reality can be seen as a kind of circular chain, the links of which are these 12 constituent elements. Each one of these elements, and the suffering it involves, therefore depends on each other link, in the same way that each link in the circular chain must remain connected to another link. Therefore, it becomes possible for any individual person at any time to stop his or her involvement in the process by eliminating one or more of the links in the circular chain. Clearly, for the Buddha, the two weak links that are the most susceptible to minimization or elimination—through meditation, behavior changes, or learning the Dharma—are ignorance (which, since it is listed first, seems to be given special importance) and desire or craving.

Anātman: No Self

The other very distinctive doctrine of the Buddha is anātman, the belief that there is no inherently existing self. It meshes neatly with the notion of interdependent arising. At one level the doctrine of anātman serves the same purpose of liberation by denying the existence of any kind of permanent reality behind or within the psychophysical elements that constitute phenomenal reality. But it adds that there is also nothing behind or within our feeling of a sense of self or ātman. Rather, one is really a series of processes that together perceive, categorize, and act. The individual is made up of five psychophysical elements, or *skandhas:* corporeality or physical form (which includes physical objects, the body, and the sense organs); feelings or sensations; ideations, with which we label and understand those feelings; mental formations or dispositions—the likes, dislikes, and impulses we have about those ideas; and consciousness, the awareness of any or all of these elements. By analyzing the person into such constituent elements, the tradition makes more explicit its claim that there is no substantial or inherently existing ātman. And if there is no ātman, there is no essential "I" to protect and fight for. Thus egoistic striving is seen to be delusory, and one's own suffering is reduced. One is also more available to others, for one is freed from one's own agenda. (For a comparison of Buddhist beliefs on salvation with those of other religions of the same region, see the accompanying box.)

EARLY COLLECTED TEACHINGS

During the early centuries of Buddhist history, these and many other teachings attributed to the Buddha were passed down orally; they were supplemented by teachings formulated by members of the community that were often attributed to him, and they were molded into more or less integrated systems of thought and practice. The oral collection of the Buddha's teachings, called *sūtras,* and the collection of monastic regulations **(Vinaya)** were formalized soon after his death. The process of gathering collections of teachings continued for several centuries. Finally, as doctrinal systems started to develop, new types of summaries were gathered into the Abhidharma collections preserved by particular Buddhist traditions. Collectively, the sūtras, Vinaya, and Abhidharma are known as the **Tripiṭaka**, the "Triple Basket," which came to form the core of Buddhist scriptures. Several schools developed, each of which had its own authoritative Tripiṭaka and thus its own rendition of the Buddha's Dharma, or doctrine. Ironically, Buddhism, which began as a rejection of the received traditions of its day, developed a well-defined, though always contested, tradition of its own. In so doing it established its position as one of the several full-fledged religions that were actively competing for the loyalty of the peoples of ancient India.

THE EARLY BUDDHIST COMMUNITY: THE SAṄGHA

The historical Buddha, in addition to being a great teacher, was an extremely effective community organizer. He gathered around him a large number of wandering mendicant followers and lay supporters. He organized a community *(Saṅgha)* of monks and developed a discipline designed to guide their behavior and to regulate the functioning of the community as a whole. At the urging of Ānanda, a leading disciple, he

COMPARISON

Buddhism, Upanishadic Hinduism, and Jainism on Salvation

Roughly simultaneously with early Buddhism and arising out of the same social and religious context, two other religious traditions developed. Like Buddhism, both Jainism and the upanishads of Hinduism both embodied ancient Indian concepts such as saṃsāra (transmigration), karma (law of action), and moksha (enlightenment). And like Buddhism, these two traditions rethought and reworked these ideas, particularly with regard to the goal of the religious life and the most effective means of achieving this goal. The upanishads moved away from the sacrifice-centered Vedic tradition toward a more ascetic, meditational form of religious behavior. The Jains also emphasized ascetic renunciation and self-discipline as the effective method for salvation.

The upanishads were similar to the early Buddhist texts in their criticism of Vedic rituals, which they regarded as superfluous and a hindrance. Emphasizing renunciation and asceticism, both traditions stressed the need for insight and knowledge rather than the "proper" performance of the sacrifice. The upanishads were, however, quite unlike Buddhism in their conception of the ultimate goal of the religious quest. Whereas among Buddhism's central tenets were the doctrine of anātman, which denies the existence of a substantial self, and the doctrine of impermanence, the upanishads maintained that there is an ātman, an essential self that transcends all individuality, limitation, decay, and death.

Furthermore, the upanishads taught that by realizing, through meditation, the funda-

somewhat reluctantly organized a community of nuns along similar lines.

In addition, he took great pains to develop a positive and mutually beneficial relationship between himself and the monks and nuns of the Saṅgha, on the one hand, and his lay supporters on the other. The monastics were expected to provide the lay supporters with models of ideal Buddhist behavior and to offer guidance in the knowledge and practice of the Dharma. For their part, the members of the laity were expected to know and practice the Dharma as best they could, given the constraints of ordinary social life, and to provide the food and other requirements that the monastics needed.

Monasteries began to be established very early, perhaps during the Buddha's own lifetime. They probably started with the mendicant practice of settling in one particular place during the three-month rainy season that inhibited travel. During this three-month period of settled life, close ties between individual monastics and particular lay people could be forged. Soon the Buddhist laity in particular localities began to donate land and buildings to the monastics they knew and respected, so that they could take up permanent residence. Once these lands and buildings were available, many of the mendicants gave up their wandering ways and taught and received support from their local lay communities.

BUDDHIST LIFE STYLES

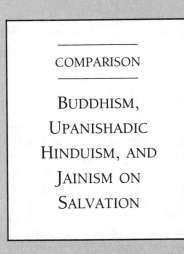

Scholars of Buddhism have often noted the persistence of two different life styles within the Buddhist community, that of the monastics and that of the laity. But as we will see, once the monasteries appeared on the

mental identity between the ultimate Brahman and the individual ātman, liberation from saṃsāra could be obtained. Buddhism rejected such ideas, claiming that all reality was impermanent, and therefore all notions of an essential ātman or an ultimate Brahman were false.

Buddhism is even more similar to Jainism than to the upanishads. Jainism, like Buddhism, had a human founder, Mahāvira, who like the Buddha lived in northeastern India in the sixth and fifth centuries B.C.E. Like Buddhism and the upanishads, the Jains emphasized saṃsāra and the importance of karma. To transcend saṃsāra, the Jains held, one must renounce this world and become an ascetic. Like Buddhism, Jainism stressed meditation and the perfection of acts as techniques leading to insight and liberation.

The early Jain community stressed a severe and often extreme form of renunciation and asceticism, whereas early Buddhism stressed the middle path between extreme asceticism and worldly life. Buddhism also stressed the absolute impermanence of this world and characterized liberation from this world as nirvāṇa, the extinguishing of all sensation. The Jains, in contrast, formulated a system in which the individual soul, or *jīva,* eventually achieves release from saṃsāra, recovers its essential nature, and is reunited with other *siddhas* (perfected beings) at the pinnacle of the universe.

All three traditions—Buddhism, Jainism, and the upanishads—grew out of a common religious and social situation in northern India, borrowing, reformulating, and critiquing many of the same key doctrines. Each at the same time developed new doctrines and practices to meet the needs of its particular community. Over time, as the differences between the various new ideas, practices, and religious ideals deepened, the common core of the three traditions became more and more obscure.

scene, three distinct but nonexclusive life styles developed within the early tradition and are found today throughout much of Theravāda Buddhism. The third we will call forest monks, men who retained the wandering mode of life.

Forest Monks

In the earliest years of the tradition, the forest monks were renunciants who refused to be subjected to the highly regulated and, from their point of view, overly domesticated existence that became increasingly characteristic of life in the monasteries. Unfortunately for scholars, these mendicants were not greatly concerned with the collection and codification of texts from which we might be able to reconstruct the details of their life patterns. We may, however, deduce certain characteristics of their life styles from the texts that we do have and from archaeological and inscriptional materials.

These renunciants lived for the most part in forests and caves and clearly spent a great deal of their time in isolation from other members of the Saṅgha. They were stricter (and often more idiosyncratic) in their asceticism than Buddhists associated with established monasteries. But at the same time they seem to have been less concerned with strict adherence to the Vinaya behavioral rules that were operative in the communal setting. They emphasized the practice of various forms of yoga and tended to value the authority of yogic masters and yogic experience more highly than texts. Some reports reveal among them a special fondness for frequenting the sacred places where stūpas had been established, thus adding to the importance of these sites as pilgrimage destinations.

Exactly how numerous or influential these forest

monks were in the early community we cannot say with certainty, but there are clear traces of their presence. For example, evidence suggests that the Buddha's cousin Devadatta was a rather extreme example of such a monk. Indeed, according to some sources, he may have had sufficient support to challenge the Buddha's leadership and to threaten a schism in the Saṅgha. In many cases the legitimacy of the forest dwellers' style of life was recognized by the Buddha himself. Thus despite the rise of the established monasteries throughout India, forest monks continued to play an important role throughout Buddhism's early years.

Settled Monastics

The second style of life that was evident in the early Buddhist community was that pursued by the more settled monks and nuns who lived in Buddhist monasteries. These monastics tended to place a much stronger emphasis than the forest monks on the detailed rules that the Buddha and his successors had developed to regulate the Saṅgha. They continued to supplement these orally transmitted rules until they were finally written as the Vinaya. These texts spell out in great detail the rules that the Buddha envisioned as the middle way between extreme asceticism and self-indulgence.

For the members of the Saṅgha, the Vinaya prohibits killing, stealing, lying, sexual misconduct, and drunkenness; it also requires celibacy and the renunciation of all material goods except for the four requisites of food, clothing, shelter, and medicine. The Vinaya also requires great decorum in such matters as dress, social behavior, and bodily functions. In good Buddhist fashion, it focuses on intentions as a part of action and relates its rules and interpretations to the goal of rooting out the preeminent Buddhist vices of lust, hatred, and confusion.

The Vinaya also codifies procedures for the Saṅgha's ceremonies and rituals. For example, it establishes procedures for the ordination of new members, offers guidelines for the regular practice of confession and expiation for offenders, regulates the management of communal property, and formulates a quasi-legal framework for the resolution of internal disputes.

The Vinaya code, though relevant to all Buddhist life styles, was clearly oriented toward life in the monasteries. Yet there its rules and procedures were not always strictly followed, though it did foster a more formal, more restrained mode of existence as well as less idiosyncratic forms of behavior and meditational practice. Perhaps most important, great emphasis was placed on mastery of the Buddha's teaching in the form of the transmission and study of textual traditions. It is these texts, first oral and then written, that came to define "standard" Buddhism.

Lay Supporters: Householders

The third life style practiced in the early Buddhist community was developed for and by nonmonastic lay supporters. The Buddha himself was very concerned to attract lay followers and to instruct them in modes of activity that would enable them to practice the Noble Eightfold Path at the same time that they lived and worked as **householders** (people who lead domestic, nonascetic lives). Among his most famous sermons is one addressed to a young householder named Sigala. In this sermon, which some later Buddhists have called a Vinaya for the laity, the Buddha enumerates six preeminent vices, describes the motives that lead to evil actions, warns against six ways of dissipating wealth, and differentiates among kinds of friends. Having noticed that Sigala was in the habit of each day performing a series of rituals honoring the six cosmic regions, the Buddha informs him that he should instead show proper honor and respect to his parents (the east), his teachers (the south), his wife and children (the west), his friends and companions (the north), servants and workmen (the nadir), and religious teachers and brāhmans (the zenith). The Buddha became renowned for such reinterpretations of established religious practices.

Though the Buddha encouraged his followers to show respect to all authentic "religious teachers and brāhmans," from a very early date Buddhist laypersons were especially drawn to venerate the Buddha himself. It is difficult to determine the exact nature or expressions of this veneration during the Buddha's own lifetime. But it is certain that following his death, he was reverently honored by both monastics and lay followers at the pilgrimage sites that marked key events in his life. It is also clear that both monastics and lay supporters performed rituals of veneration at stūpas where his relics were deposited. By the beginning of the Common Era, images of the Buddha were becoming a primary focus for the expression of devotion. Such developments demonstrate that Buddhism was adapting to the needs of a wide social constituency.

Buddhist laypersons also venerated the monastics and gave them gifts to provide for their material support. Some gifts were given to the forest monks (who were often thought to possess special powers that could be tapped to meet lay needs), enabling them to maintain their mendicant life style. Other gifts were given to the settled monastics, permitting them to adhere to their discipline, pursue their studies, and provide local spiritual guidance. Like gifts given symbolically to the Buddha (at stūpas, images, and elsewhere), gifts given to members of the Saṅgha were understood to be prime sources of merit *(puṇya)* that created beneficial karma. Through these gifts, given with a pure heart and without thought of self, the giver could gain a better life in this world and the next and could also advance along a path that would ultimately lead to final release (nirvāṇa).

Early Buddhism and the "New Society"

As noted earlier, Buddhism originated in the northeastern subcontinent during a period when momentous changes were taking place in all areas of life. The Buddha's claim to be the proper focus of religious authority was convincing to many of his contemporaries because his message was relevant to the prevailing social, political, and economic situations of his day. The Buddha's message satisfied the religious needs of many people, and the evidence suggests that large numbers were attracted to his community.

Significantly, most early Buddhists were members of the social, political, and economic elite. The earliest texts depict many very successful encounters between the Buddha and kings and members of their royal courts and between the Buddha and representatives of a rapidly rising class of rich and powerful merchants. There is strong evidence to suggest that although the renunciant orders were open to persons of all castes, a preponderance of those who were actually ordained were either brāhmans (priests) or kshatriyas (rulers, warriors, and administrators). It is also apparent that much of the lay support came from members of the new society who wielded great power and commanded considerable wealth.

These groups had recently lost the moorings of their tribal roots and the associated religious rituals and structures. Like so many city dwellers even today, they faced new questions about the meaning of their lives and the new challenges of a more cosmopolitan life. They experienced a freedom from the personal and emotional controls of the small, tightly knit social groups associated with tribal communities, and at the same time they faced the loss of the sense of participation and place, the security of belonging to such a community.

In contrast to the Vedic tradition, the questions that Buddhists asked and answered were no longer centered primarily on the needs of the group, nor did Buddhism offer a legitimizing rationale for a particular social structure, such as caste. Rather, the Buddha and his early followers addressed the problems of both the individual and society in the new cosmopolitan circumstances.

The Buddha's recommended Eightfold Path emphasized the role of individual responsibility, effort, and intention, each of which found resonance among the self-reliant merchant classes and other city dwellers. His message also responded to the social needs of the time, emphasizing the moral responsibilities of kingship and an ethic of compassion and harmony among competing individuals and groups. His message was universal in that it addressed all men and women regardless of affiliations, it was social in that it set forth new ideals of political and social leadership, and it was individual in that it made each person responsible for his or her own destiny.

Buddhism in the Mauryan Empire

So it is not surprising that the expansion of Buddhism and the spread of the new political and social order occurred in tandem. During the century or two following the Buddha's death, Buddhism became established in many other parts of the subcontinent.

Within this same time span, the area where the Buddha had carried on much of his ministry became the center of a new imperial order, the Mauryan dynasty. This lineage soon came to control and influence the entire subcontinent.

The exact connections between the expansion of Buddhism and the establishment of the Mauryan regime are impossible to trace. However, it is clear that these processes began in the same region at the same time and were linked in a major event in Buddhist history. In the early decades of the third century B.C.E. Aśoka Maurya, the king who completed the Mauryan conquest of the subcontinent, became a supporter of Buddhism. Aśoka's vast empire incorporated virtually all of what is now modern India, and he ruled it for approximately 40 years (c. 270–230 B.C.E.). After his death, he became idealized as a model of Buddhist kingship.

The edicts of this Indian emperor are our oldest Buddhist documents. Inscribed on rocks and pillars, they record that Aśoka honored the Buddha and made pilgrimages to Buddhist shrines; that he espoused and sought to spread a Dharma that, from his point of view at least, was consistent with the Buddha's teachings; that he recommended that certain Buddhist texts be given special attention by his subjects; that he supported the Saṅgha and tried to ensure its unity; and that he dispatched Buddhist missionaries far and wide.

Some analysts have argued that Aśoka was a truly devout Buddhist trying his best to spread Buddhism throughout his empire. Others have argued that, having extended the Mauryan Empire to its natural geographic limits, he adopted a watered-down, quasi-Buddhist version of the Dharma to pacify and unite his empire's many regions and peoples. Either way, his reign marked a major turning point for Buddhism; it became a great religion of Pan-Indian and ultimately Pan-Asian significance.

NOTE

1 E. H. Johnson, *Aśvaghoṣa's Buddhacarita, or Acts of the Buddha* (Delhi: Banarsidass, 1936, 1984), pp. 36–38.

BUDDHISM

CHAPTER 8

THE DEVELOPMENT OF BUDDHISM IN INDIA

During the seven centuries following King Aśoka's death, the so-called post-Aśokan period (c. 200 B.C.E.–500 C.E.), large parts of the subcontinent were ruled by a succession of emperors. Under these empires India enjoyed relative political stability, economic prosperity, and some degree of religious and cultural unity. Hindus during this period developed the religious culture that eventually dominated the land. Simultaneously, Indian Buddhists developed their distinctive religious culture, which also played a significant role in Indian life. They also began in earnest the missionary activities whereby Buddhism came to influence virtually all of Asia.

During the long post-Aśokan period, Buddhism's fortunes rose and fell according to the favor of the reigning sovereign. When the Saṅgha was at peace, due to royal protection and even sponsorship, the monastics had the leisure to reflect on and develop the Dharma. The words of the Buddha, as preserved in the tradition, were memorized, ritually chanted, meditated on in private, debated in public, and made the subject of many commentaries. Although details of this process and its causes have been recovered only in part and remain a topic of scholarly debate, Buddhism emerged during this period as two streams, Theravāda and Mahāyāna, each claiming to be the authentic Dharma.

Theravāda (tradition of the *theras,* or senior monks), or Conservative Buddhism, is best understood as a single lineage based on a comparatively small body of texts preserved in Pāli, a language similar to Sanskrit. It passed into most of South and Southeast Asia, taking on distinctive but clearly related forms in each country, frequently being a major factor in the growth of national identities. Its most characteristic feature is the social visibility of the monastics in their orange or yellow robes and the close symbiotic relationship between the monastics and the lay people. This arrangement was probably very similar to that of the Buddha's own time. Emphasizing rationality, individual effort, and self-discipline, Theravāda promised salvation for a religious elite.

Mahāyāna appears to have begun as a reform movement in the subcontinent around the beginning of the Common Era. In calling itself Mahāyāna, the "Greater Vehicle," it self-consciously distinguished itself from the rest of Buddhism, which it stigmatized as **Hīnayāna**, or the "Inferior Vehicle."* Claiming that Conservative Buddhism had become an elitist profession for monastics, Mahāyāna preached that everyone, whether monastic or lay, had an equal chance of

*When Mahāyāna arose, it branded traditional Buddhism as Hīnayāna, the "Lesser Vehicle," a pejorative term. A significant wing of traditional Buddhism called itself Theravāda, the tradition of the senior monks or elders, but not all of its schools were so named. The scholar Hajime Nakamura refers to this wing by the more neutral term Conservative Buddhism. All names refer broadly to the same traditional wing.

THE YOUNG QUAIL JĀTAKA

Jātakas, stories of acts the Buddha supposedly performed in his previous lifetimes, have been told from Buddhism's earliest days; some may even have been told by the Buddha himself. While in some of these stories the future Buddha was born as a human being or occasionally as a god, in most of the Jātakas—like "The Young Quail Jātaka" recounted here—he appears as an animal. The stories often illustrate a particular point of Buddhist doctrine; in this one both the difficulties in following the Dharma and the power of the adept's discipline are illustrated.

Even fire is powerless against words redolent of truth. One should therefore make a practice of speaking truth.

According to tradition, the Bodhisattva [the future Buddha] was once born as a young quail in the jungle. Some nights after hatching, his tender wings had still to develop, and he was so puny that all the separate parts of his body were clearly discernible. His parents had taken pains to build a nest in a bush well hidden by deep grass. Here he lived together with his numerous siblings. But even in this state he had not lost his sense of what is right, and he was unwilling to eat the living creatures that his parents offered him. Instead he kept himself alive on millet, banyan figs, and other such food as they brought. As a result of this coarse and inadequate diet, his body did not fill out and his wings did not develop properly, while the other little quails, who ate whatever they were given, grew strong and fully fledged. For it is a fact that he who eats anything, without worrying about right or wrong, is happy and prospers, while he who wants to live in harmony with nature and is therefore careful about what he eats has a hard time in this world. (Moreover, the Lord said: "For the shameless crow who is aggressive, bold, and not fastidious, life is easy, though tainted. But for the man who has a sense of shame, who desires only what is pure, who is retiring, diffident, and honest, life on earth is beset with difficulties.)

While they were living like this, a huge forest fire broke out not very far away. The noise it

attaining liberation. It taught that the Buddha had not (as the Theravāda said) disappeared into nirvāṇa but that he could still be contacted in prayer, meditation, and visions. As it developed, Mahāyāna divided into many lineages that can be broadly grouped into two: central Asian forms based on Tibetan texts and East Asian forms based on Chinese texts. Different Mahāyāna schools emphasized mysticism, faith in Buddhas and bodhisattvas, and devotion.

THE BUDDHA

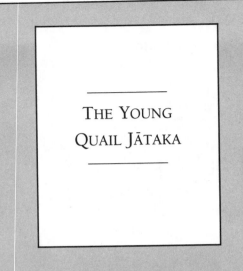

One of the keys to Buddhism's great success during this period was the appeal of the mythology and rituals associated with the Buddha. The Buddha came to seem bigger than life, a man who had both discovered and established the true religion, the great being ***(mahāpurusha)*** who had both attained and transcended the *made was terrifying and incessant; smoke spread in thick clouds, and the advancing line of flames showered sparks. It caused havoc in the depths of the forest and terrified the animals who lived there. Tossed by the wind, its flames outspread like arms, leaping and roaring, with smoky hair wildly disheveled, it seemed to be performing some intricate dance. The animals panicked, and the grass, swaying under the impact of the violent wind, seemed to be fleeing in terror. But the fire pounced on it in fury and scorched it with a shower of glittering sparks. Whole flocks of birds took alarm and flew away in terror. Wild beasts ran around in circles, stricken with panic. Thick smoke enveloped everything, and with the hoarse crackle of flames the forest seemed to be roaring aloud in pain.*

Goaded on by the sharp wind, the fire gradually penetrated the jungle and reached close to the nest. Immediately the young quails, with shrill, discordant shrieks of terror, flew up, without a thought for each other. But the Bodhisattva made no attempt to follow them: his body was too frail, and he was not fully fledged. Yet the Great Being, sure of his own powers, remained unruffled. As the fire approached impetuously, he politely addressed it as follows: "My feet hardly deserve the name of feet, and my wings have not grown. Also, my parents, in awe of you, have taken flight. I have nothing suitable to offer you as a guest. So, Fire, it would be best if you turned back from this spot." This, the plainest truth, was what the Great Being said. And the fire, though fanned by the wind and raging amid deadwood and thickets of parched grass, immediately died down: faced with these words of his, it was as though it had come to a swollen river. To this day, a forest fire, however much its blaze is stirred up by the wind, shrinks back—like a many-headed snake charmed by a spell—smothers its darting flames, and dies down altogether when it reaches that famous spot in the Himalayas.

What, then, does this story illustrate? The saying goes that just as the billowy ocean, with its waves like the hoods of serpents, cannot break its bounds, just as the seeker of the spirit cannot disregard the discipline prescribed by a great sage—so even fire cannot neglect the command of those for whom truth lies at the core of existence. Therefore one should never desert truth.

So, then—even fire is powerless against words redolent of truth. One should therefore make a practice of speaking truth.

Source: Peter Khoroche, *Once the Buddha Was a Monkey* (Chicago: University of Chicago Press, 1989).

qualities associated with universal kingship on the one hand and those of a great **yogī** on the other. What is more, he was perceived as a preeminent exemplar of compassion: merely remembering him or making a pilgrimage to some place associated with him—a stūpa, a reliquary, a site where his footprints were carved in stone—could inspire his devotees and speed them along the path to a better life and ultimately to nirvāṇa.

The stories that were told about the Buddha included not only accounts of his final life as Gautama but also stories, called **Jātakas**, or birth stories of acts he supposedly performed in his previous lives (see the accompanying box, "The Young Quail Jātaka"). Some of the Jātakas are presented as sermons attributed to the Buddha in which he illustrates a point about the effects of karma. Most are folkloric tales in which the future Buddha appears as an animal, a human being, or—very occasionally—a god. Many stories recount how the Buddha cultivated certain virtues, though in many cases the doctrinal points are difficult to discern.

Already by the second century B.C.E., certain Jātakas were being iconographically represented on the great stūpas that were being constructed at the time. By the beginning of the Common Era, collections of Jātaka stories had begun to appear. In one, the *Cariya Pitaka,* a set of relatively short Jātakas are associated with the cultivation of the ten virtues or perfections, held to be characteristic of the Buddha in his final life as Gautama. In certain areas, particularly in northwestern India, individual Jātakas were associated with particular geographic sites where the events that they recount were supposedly performed. Thus the land itself was transformed into a collection of the future Buddha's "traces" and virtues.

As their mythology expanded, Buddhists developed new kinds of visual symbols. For the first five centuries Buddhists did not sculpt images of the Buddha. He was sometimes represented by a relic, an empty throne, a footprint, a stūpa, or some other aniconic symbol. Figurative images, as far as we know, were never used.

Around the beginning of the Common Era, however, for reasons that are not yet clear, images of the Buddha began to appear. These sculptures and paintings portrayed the Buddha as a *mahāpurusha.* He is often depicted as possessing the 32 bodily signs that the Indian tradition identified with the attainment of universal sovereignty. He is shown in a variety of poses and situations, but most often in the midst of his enlightenment experience.

Once the practice of making images and representations began, it very quickly spread throughout the Buddhist world in India and beyond. Even before these iconic representations appeared, Buddhist sculpture and art had begun to play an important role in the life of the Buddhist community, for example, at the sites of the great stūpas that were built during the second and first centuries B.C.E. However, the iconic representations of the Buddha added a new dimension that became central to all later Buddhist traditions. These images taught the often illiterate Buddhists about events in the life of the Buddha. They also came to play a central role in the rituals (pūjā) in and through which the Buddha was venerated. Buddha images were not merely seen as his representations but were believed to make him spiritually present for members of the community.

Ritually, these images came to be used in meditational practices that involved the remembrance and visualization of the Buddha and in devotional practices of veneration of the Buddha. Thus with these sculptures and icons as aids, Buddhism developed its own forms of meditation and worship that enabled it to compete with Hinduism's newly developed theistic forms of meditation and devotion.

Theravāda and Mahāyāna Attitudes toward the Buddha

As Buddhism developed into the two streams that would become Theravāda and Mahāyāna, rival teachings evolved concerning the number of the Buddhas and whether or not they could be contacted in worship and meditation.

Broadly, Theravādins maintained that although there have been many Buddhas in the past and there will be many in the future, only one Buddha appears at a time, and he appears only in the human realm. Having restored and communicated the Dharma, he then disappears into nirvāṇa. Although he can subsequently be *imagined* as present, he can only be contacted through the Dharma and the Saṅgha. Thus, while not worshiping him as actually present, Theravādins concentrated on Gautama, the historical Buddha, whom they remembered in meditation.

Mahāyāna teachers maintained that the departure of the Buddha into nirvāṇa was an expedient means *(upāya)* to assist those who would be paralyzed with fear if they thought that it was necessary to remain in saṃsāra until all beings had been liberated. In fact, said the third-century Lotus Sūtra, not only do Buddhas continue to exist after their apparent deaths, but they have always existed and have always been enlightened. Their becoming Buddhas is a show, an expedient means to inspire unenlightened beings to effort. Many Mahāyāna sūtras also spoke of countless numbers of Buddhas in other worlds and even in the specks of dust of this world. As a consequence, Mahāyānists taught that all Buddhas could be contacted in meditative visualization and in the worship of their properly consecrated images.

One striking result of these new thoughts was that

Around the beginning of the Common Era, Buddhist sculpture and art began to play an important role in the life of the Buddhist community. As sculpture, paintings, and stained glass have been used in many religions and many cultures, reliefs at the great stupas were used to teach people about events in the life of Buddha. Dating from the eighth century C.E., the Borobodur temple in Java includes miles of temple carvings such as those shown here depicting the life history of Buddha. (The Bettmann Archive)

Śākyamuni Buddha, although he always remained important, ceased being central to Mahāyānists. Replacing him, a whole pantheon of Buddhas and bodhisattvas gradually developed. In some contexts these Buddhas and bodhisattvas (some of which seem to have been deities absorbed from other traditions) were organized in a systematic pattern. For example, many Mahāyānists recognized a group of five particular Buddhas, called Dhyāni Buddhas. In this particular formulation—which appears in many sculptures and paintings—one Buddha occupies the cosmic center (Vairocana), one the eastern quarter (Akśobhya), one the southern quarter (Ratnasambhava), one the western quarter (Amitābha), and the fifth the northern quarter (Amoghasiddhi).

In other contexts, particular Buddhas or bodhisattvas emerged as central, becoming quasi-divine figures who were the focal point for particular forms of devotion. One of the earliest examples of this sort was the Buddha Amitābha, who became the focal point of a cult of meditative devotion and visualization. Amitābha, whose name means "immeasurable radiance" or "unlimited light," first appeared around 100 C.E. Faith in Amitābha promised rebirth in a "pure land" that could lead directly to the attainment of release. The bodhisattva Avalokiteśvara ("one who looks down"), who first appeared in the third century, became the embodiment of the Buddhist virtue of compassion and as such a source of comfort and support for many Mahāyāna devotees.

DHARMA

During the post-Aśokan period the earlier collections of sūtras and the Vinaya were extended, more systematic texts were developed, and new items were incorporated. By the beginning of the Common Era the older "texts" that had been transmitted orally and the new texts that were being composed were written down, usually in Sanskrit. Very soon writing came to play a central role in the preservation and dissemination of Buddhist teaching.

Conservative Doctrines: Abhidharma

Conservative Buddhism developed the earliest explanatory or philosophical school, called **Abhidharma** ("advanced Dharma"). This seems to have begun with the attempt to classify the elements of the personality as observed in meditation.

What we perceive as a person initially seems a unity, an inherently existing being. Closer inspection reveals that a person is composed of at least two very different elements—one that is directly evident to the senses and one that can only be inferred on the basis of the sensory data. That which is directly evident is called *rūpa* by Abhidharma; it is broadly similar to what English refers to by the word *matter* or, better, *materiality*. But as a living being a person is clearly more than mere matter. The intangible element, the existence of which can only be inferred, the Abhidharma calls *nāma,* literally "name"; *nāma* is similar to what is called the *mind* or *mentality* in English. On even closer inspection, *nāma* can itself be divided into four groups: sensory input, perceptual categories, habitual reactions, and self-awareness. Together with *nāma,* these four are identified as the five "clusters" *(skandha)* mentioned in Chapter 7. By a similar meditational analysis, Abhidharma identifies 12 bases of sense *(āyatana)*—including the eye and things seen, the body surface and tangible objects, and the mind and cognizable items or *dharmas*—and 18 fields of operation of sense *(dhātu)*—such as the visual, olfactory, and mental fields. The groups of *skandhas, āyatanas,* and *dhātus,* known as *lists,* first suggested around the time of Aśoka, formed the basis of all later schools of Abhidharma, which proposed longer and more detailed lists of elements. Two main schools of Abhidharma survive: the Theravāda school, still employed as a living system; and the Sarvāstivāda school, whose texts, extant only in Tibetan and Chinese, are used by the Mahāyāna for preliminary training in what it calls Hīnayāna.

The intent of the Abhidharma is to provide a kind of owner's manual for the body-mind. Like all such manuals, it is boring and irrelevant when read as literature, but it comes into its own when put to practical meditative use. By understanding and clearly identifying the elements that create and sustain saṃsāra, saṃsāra can be deconstructed and escaped.

Mahāyāna Doctrines: Mādhyamika and Yogācāra

Mahāyāna developed its own sūtras and, based on them, two main explanatory schools, Mādhyamika and Yogācāra. The Mādhyamika school is based on a group of sūtras called *The Perfection of Wisdom.* The oldest text, "The Perfection of Wisdom in Eight Thousand Lines" (c. 100 B.C.E.–100 C.E.), was first subjected to considerable expansion between 100 and 300 C.E. and then, over the next two centuries, to reduction into summaries or "epitomes." The sūtras are sometimes explicitly said to have been spoken by disciples rather than by the Buddha, but adherents regarded them as reliable because the disciples have realized the true nature of the Dharma, so that what the Buddha's disciples teach can be considered as the work of Tathagata, the Buddha himself.

The two best-known sūtras of the *Perfection of Wisdom* group are the Diamond Sūtra and the Heart Sūtra. The Diamond Sūtra, "The Sūtra on the Perfection of Wisdom That Cuts [Ignorance] like a Diamond or Thunderbolt," is a dialogue between Śākyamuni Buddha and his disciple Subhuti that initially sounds more like a dialogue between schizophrenics, for example:

> The Lord [Buddha] continued: "What do you think, Subhuti, can the Tathagata be seen by the possession of his marks?"—Subhuti replied: "No indeed, O Lord. And why? What has been taught by the Tathagata as the possession of marks, that is truly the possession of no-marks." The Lord said: "Wherever there is possession of marks, there is fraud, wherever there is no-possession of no-marks, there is no fraud. Hence the Tathagata is to be seen from no-marks as marks."[1]

The Heart Sūtra, literally "The Sūtra on the Heart of the Perfection of Wisdom," is even more curious. It says that reality is emptiness and that

> in emptiness there is no form, nor feeling, nor perception, nor impulse, nor consciousness; No eye, ear, nose, tongue, body, mind; No forms, sounds, smells, tastes, touchables or objects of mind; No sight-organ element, and so forth, until we come to: No mind-consciousness element.[2]

That is, everything in the Abhidharma lists is nonexistent—rather, it exists, but it does not *ultimately* exist.

These curious *Perfection of Wisdom* texts, which began the movement that became known as the Mahāyāna, were explicitly a protest against what the Mahāyānists regarded as the mistakes of Conservative Buddhism. While accepting the same basic doctrines such as the Four Noble Truths and the doctrines of *pratītya samutpāda* (interdependent arising) and anātman (no self), the *Perfection of Wisdom* writers felt that the Abhidharmists had taken themselves too seriously. Instead of regarding their dharma lists as operational and therapeutic, the Abhidharmists had taken them as absolutes and had hardened them into dogma. Thus, the Mahāyānists claimed, complete liberation was no longer possible through the Abhidharma.* *The Perfection of Wisdom* articulated what the Mahāyānists regarded as the Buddha's original teaching: all entities, whether whole beings or single dharmas, are empty of inherent existence.

This emptiness *(śūnyata),* which can also be called openness or transparency, is stated in *The Perfection of Wisdom* and is argued for in the Mādhyamika school, whose foundation is attributed to Nāgārjuna, a teacher who probably lived in South India in the first century C.E. Nāgārjuna's most frequently employed argument is from absurdity: followed through to its logical conclusion, any view of reality that is taken as absolute, as the one and only view of reality, has absurd consequences and must therefore be abandoned. Only emptiness, he claimed, which was not itself a view but the "purgative" of views, did not result in absurd conclusions. It followed, then, that even the distinction between saṃsāra and nirvāṇa was empty and could not be held to absolutely. Hence reality as it is, the here and now, opened up to liberation, and dogma evaporated.

Whereas the Mādhyamika school focused on logic, dialectic, and debate, the Yogācāra school was more concerned with the nature of perception, which it examined in meditation. Begun in the fourth century C.E. by the brothers Asaṅga and Vasubandhu, Yogācāra was based on the Saṃdhinirmocana Sūtra, "The Sūtra That Unties the Knots." Although it seized on different issues than the Mādhyamika, Yogācāra came to a similar conclusion: reality is empty of inherent existence. Its proof, however, was not logical but experiential: when subject and object are examined closely, with meditative insight, they are seen to have no *absolute* distinction.

While accepting the operational existence of things, Mādhyamika and Yogācāra thinkers both denied the absolute existence of things. The denial of an absolute distinction is called *nonduality*. However, this denial is only a denial: it is not an implied affirmation of the opposite proposition, monism, or "all is one." But it is nothing more than a denial of duality—it is not the denial of everything; it is not nihilism.

SAṄGHA AND COMMUNITY

Taking advantage of the sponsorship of various imperial dynasties during the seven to eight centuries of the post-Aśokan period, Buddhism expanded enormously, both geographically and socially: it established itself not only throughout India but also through much of Asia, not just among the elite but at all strata of the populace.

Forest monks (and perhaps nuns, about whom there is virtually no information) continued to play an important role in the structure and dynamics of Indian Buddhism. Their presence and influence are attested in a variety of texts, as is the awe in which they were often held by other Buddhists. Many of these forest monks were charismatic figures who were believed to have reached high levels of meditational and mystical attainment and to be able to exercise various magical powers. Some monks seem to have operated quite independently of any organized group; others were more closely associated with particular segments of the monastic community. Another group seems to have

*Defenders of Theravādin Abhidharma have responded that it remained operational and did not exhibit the hardening that the Mahāyānists pejoratively attributed to it.

played an important role in the loosely organized communities known as **bodhisattva-gaṇas** ("congregations of future Buddhas") that grew up around certain stūpas.

There were also more settled monastic orders. Both textual and archaeological data indicate that during the post-Aśokan period, monasteries all across the subcontinent proliferated in both towns and countryside, especially along the principal trade routes, where they also served as hostels. Endowing a monastery was one way in which a king or a wealthy person could show devotion and generosity. Some of these monasteries were large, well-endowed establishments that housed substantial monastic populations. Most monasteries were constructed in spacious aboveground compounds. But there were also large monastic complexes—for example, the well-preserved one at Ajantā in central India—located in extensive networks of natural caves. In addition to the major monasteries, there were other smaller monastic complexes of various types.

All Buddhist monasteries of this period provided living quarters for monks and, in a few cases at least, nuns. They usually had a central hall in which the most sacred ceremonies were performed, often in front of some symbol—typically one or more images—of the Buddha or bodhisattvas. Many monasteries were decorated with sophisticated artworks expressing Buddhist devotion. Monasteries often also featured, in a more or less dominant position, a stūpa containing a relic or other "trace" of the Buddha that served as another center for veneration and for making offerings.

The life style in the various monasteries differed greatly. Some establishments possessed great wealth; others were quite modest. Some of the great houses were centers of interactions with monks from all of the Indian subcontinent and other parts of Asia; in others the focus was much more local. Some monasteries strongly emphasized study, meditation, and devotion, whereas in others the monks were more deeply involved in practical affairs. In some the rules of the Vinaya were rigorously followed; in others the regimen was much more lax. But in spite of (or perhaps because of) this diversity, the Buddhist monastic tradition throughout this entire period displayed a remarkable vitality and exerted an extraordinary influence on people of all social levels.

During the post-Aśokan period, settled monastic orders began to appear. In at least some cases, living quarters for nuns existed as well, though little information exists today regarding them. Here modern Chinese nuns are seen at the Nizhong Buddhist Theological Institute in the Sichuan Province. (Eastfoto)

The monasteries that concentrated on study were somewhat like universities, in which one of the main occupations was public debate in order to establish what the Buddha really said and what he really meant. It was this activity that first led to the compilations of authoritative texts and later served as the seedbed of the Mahāyāna as it split off from Conservative Buddhism.

The great flourishing of Buddhist monasticism during the post-Aśokan era was necessarily both the cause and the effect of a rapid expansion of the lay community as well. Buddhism became a favored religion among the Indian rulers and royal courts of the period. Following their Aśokan experience, Buddhists developed their early notions of Buddhist kingship, and a great many Indian monarchs of the time—especially those who had imperial aspirations—identified with one or more of Buddhism's idealized images of royalty. These included the king as Dharmarājan (one who ruled in accordance with Dharma), the king as Cakravartin (a universal sovereign who is a kind of secular counterpart of the Buddha), and the king as the successor of Aśoka, who was taken to have ruled a great Indian empire in accord with dharmic principles. Some kings were even celebrated as mahāpurushas, identified by means of symbolic images and ritual actions as bodhisattvas or even Buddhas.

In addition to kings, queens, and courtiers, many other members of the Indian elite supported the Buddhist cause. These included rich and powerful merchants who, in addition to whatever religious piety they may have had, maintained close business connections with the network of monasteries that extended along the great national and international trade routes. At the same time, other segments of the population also became increasingly involved. In the cities and the villages, many ordinary citizens became members of the Buddhist laity, who supported Buddhist monks and took part in other forms of Buddhist practice. These ordinary people adopted (and adapted) various Buddhist activities, including calendric celebrations, pilgrimages, simple devotional practices, merit rituals for themselves and their ancestors, and exorcistic rites.

Conservative and Mahāyāna Communities

The story of the development of the Buddhist community in the post-Aśokan era is a story of its rapid expansion at various levels. But it is also a story of the development of the community's diverging religious ideals and diverging opinions about the distinctions between the monks and nuns of the Saṅgha and the lay community. These are some of the key issues over which the Theravāda and Mahāyāna traditions split.

The origins of this split are obscure and controversial. From one point of view, the division probably had at least some roots in the differences between two groups that can be identified in earlier Buddhism. Hīnayāna developed in the community centered around the earliest Buddhist monasteries. Mahāyāna evolved from diverse other sources, one of which was the communities of bodhisattva-gaṇas that had grown up around the stūpas. These bodhisattva-gaṇas, which included both forest monks and lay supporters, eventually became organized into monasteries in a process much like the one that had taken place in the very earliest phase of Buddhist history. As this process gained momentum, the Mahāyāna tradition emerged as a serious competitor to the Conservative path.

Conservative Buddhist communities In Conservative Buddhism, as still today in Theravāda, the lay people materially supported the monastics by donating the so-called Four Requisites—food, clothing, shelter, and medicine. In return the monastics, now freed from the need to provide for the present life, concentrated on what pertained to future lives and eventual liberation: study and meditation. Because only the monks and nuns had the time and discipline to meditate and study in earnest, they came to be regarded as spiritually preeminent. As a result, a sharp distinction was made between the monks and nuns of the Saṅgha and the laity.

The possibility of a layperson's gaining nirvāṇa, of course, was not completely denied. Indeed, many members of the Buddhist laity (including Buddhist kings) were considered to hold high positions in the soteriological hierarchy. But the presumption was that although lay people might be able to reach final enlightenment, it was extremely unlikely. Indeed, if they did, one text said, they would die within the week unless they entered the monastic order.

Mahāyāna communities Against the Theravādins' espousal of the privileged status of the monastics, Mahāyānists proposed that the true practice of Buddhism was not a matter of one's ordination into the Saṅgha but of one's attitude. If the heart of Buddhism was compassion, as the Conservatives said, then, the Mahāyānists claimed, whoever had the greatest compassion was the greatest practitioner. And, they went on, compassion can be practiced in any state of life whatever: one had only to repeat a vow that whatever one is about to do is being done with the motive of liberating all beings from all suffering.

A person who takes such a vow the Mahāyānists called a bodhisattva. This was a term used by the Conservatives for Śākyamuni Buddha in his previous lives and for the newly developed objects of devotion such as Amitābha. The Mahāyānists broadened it to

THE MAHĀYĀNIST "THOUGHT OF ENLIGHTENMENT"

Like all the great religions of the world, Buddhism has produced a variety of inspirational works. Śāntideva, a Mādhyamika philosopher of the early eighth century, extolled the religious life of the Mahāyāna in a famous devotional poem called *Entering the Path of Enlightenment.* After praising the thought of enlightenment *(bodhicitta),* Śāntideva confesses the transgressions that have, in the past, kept him in bondage to the phenomenal world of impermanence and suffering. He then launches into a great affirmation of compassion and of the central element in life for all Mahāyāna followers, the act of *bodhicitta-parigraha,* or grasping the thought of enlightenment.

I rejoice in exultation at the goodness, and at the cessation and destruction of sorrow, wrought by all beings. May those who sorrow achieve joy!

I rejoice at the release of embodied beings from the sorrowful wheel of rebirth. I rejoice at the Bodhisattvahood and at the Buddhahood of those who have attained salvation.

I rejoice at the Oceans of Determination (cittotpāda), *the Bearers of Happiness to all beings, the Vehicles of Advantage for all beings, and those who teach.*

With folded hands, I beseech the perfect Buddhas in all places: May they cause the light of the Dharma to shine upon those who, because of confusion, have fallen into sorrow. . . .

Having done all this, let me also be a cause of abatement, by means of whatever good I have achieved, for all of the sorrow of all creatures.

I am medicine for the sick. May I be their physician and their servant, until sickness does not arise again.

With rains of food and drink may I dispel the anguish of hunger and thirst. In the famine of the intermediary aeons between the world cycles (antarakalpa) *may I be food and drink; and may I be an imperishable treasury for needy beings. May I stand in their presence in order to do what is beneficial in every possible way. . . .*

The abandonment of all is Nirvāṇa, and my mind (manas) *seeks Nirvāṇa. If all is to be sacrificed by me, it is best that it be given to beings.*

I deliver this body to the pleasure of all creatures. May they strike! May they revile! May they cover it constantly with refuse!

May they play with my body! May they laugh! And may they be amused! I have given my body to them. What do I care about its misfortune?

May they do whatever deeds bring pleasure to them, but let there never be any misfortune because of having relied on me.

include anyone—monastic or layperson—who was earnestly seeking enlightenment *for the sake of others.* They accused the Conservatives, especially the monastics, of seeking enlightenment for themselves alone.

Connected to this new attitude, the bodhisattva path was made more accessible to the ordinary layperson as well as to the monk and nun (see the accompanying box). New forms of meditation and visualization were developed that allowed practitioners to achieve a special kind of communion with the great Buddhas and bodhisattvas. New rituals were developed in which a man or woman would enter the Mahāyāna path by taking the bodhisattva vows. New devotional practices arose, including praising the Buddha, offering

If their opinion regarding me should be either irritable or pleasant, let it nonetheless be their perpetual means to the complete fulfillment of every aim.

Those who wrong me, and those who accuse me falsely, and those who mock, and others: May they all be sharers in Enlightenment.

I would be a protector for those without protection, a leader for those who journey, and a boat, a bridge, a passage for those desiring the further shore.

For all creatures, I would be a lantern for those desiring a lantern, I would be a bed for those desiring a bed, I would be a slave for those desiring a slave. . . .

So may I be, in various ways, the means of sustenance for the living beings occupying space, for as long a time as all are not satisfied.

As the ancient Buddhas seized the Thought of Enlightenment, and in like manner they followed regularly on the path of Bodhisattva instruction;

Thus also do I cause the Thought of Enlightenment to arise for the welfare of the world, and thus shall I practice these instructions in proper order.

The wise man, having considered serenely the Thought of Enlightenment, should rejoice, for the sake of its growth and its well-being, in the thought:

Today my birth is completed, my human nature is most appropriate; today I have been born into the Buddha-family and I am now a Buddha-son.

It is now for me to behave according to the customary behavior of one's own family, in order that there may be no stain put upon that spotless family.

As a blind man may obtain a jewel in a heap of dust, so, somehow, this Thought of Enlightenment has arisen even within me.

This elixir has originated for the destruction of death in the world. It is the imperishable treasure which alleviates the world's poverty.

It is the uttermost medicine, the abatement of the world's disease. It is a tree of rest for the wearied world journeying on the road of being.

When crossing over hard places, it is the universal bridge for all travelers. It is the risen moon of mind (citta), *the soothing of the world's hot passion* (kleśa).

It is a great sun dispelling the darkness of the world's ignorance. It is fresh butter, surging up from the churning of the milk of the true Dharma.

For the caravan of humanity, moving along the road of being, hungering for the enjoyment of happiness, this happiness banquet is prepared for the complete refreshening of every being who comes to it.

Now I invite the world to Buddhahood, and, incidentally, to happiness. May gods, anti-gods (asuras), *and others, truly rejoice in the presence of all the Protectors.*

Source: Quoted in Marion Matics, *Entering the Path of Enlightenment* (New York: Macmillan, 1970), pp. 153–156.

flowers, confessing transgressions, and cultivating sympathetic delight in the merits of the Buddhas and bodhisattvas. These practices paralleled the Hindu devotional pūjās to their deities.

The new emphasis on the availability of the bodhisattva path to anyone was closely correlated with a new notion of the community: Mahāyānists affirmed a greater parity between the lives of the monk and nun and the layperson. Yet Mahāyānists did not abandon monasticism, and monasteries and temples continued to be the center around which the layperson's life revolved. Indeed, in practice there was often very little difference between Mahāyānists and Conservatives in regard to the relationship between monastics and laity.

High attainment and final liberation, however, were attributed more often to nonmonastic Mahāyāna practitioners.

BUDDHISM AND SOCIETY IN CLASSICAL INDIA

By the end of the post-Aśokan period (c. 550 C.E.), Buddhism had become a major force in Indian life. From one vantage point it was an integral component in the thriving Sanskritic civilization that included other religious components, such as post-Vedic Hinduism. But Buddhism had also developed its own distinctive character.

A number of the large, well-endowed monasteries became cultural institutions of the highest order. They maintained the basic orientation and practices of traditional Buddhist monasticism, but as time went on they became major centers of Indian learning and culture. In many cases these large complexes took on the form of monastic universities, and as such they assumed a primary responsibility for the preservation and transmission of not only the Buddhist tradition but also other aspects of Indian culture: brāhmanic and Hindu approaches and materials as well as the various arts and sciences dealing with such matters as logic, literary studies, astronomy, astrology, and medicine.

Also at the level of the elite, many Indian rulers, both at major centers of imperial power and in more distant parts of the country, performed Buddhist rituals that impressed their subjects and involved many of them. The rituals that these rulers sponsored often included the donation of expensive gifts to Buddhist monasteries and individual monks. By making these gifts, the rulers were able to confirm the legitimacy of their claim to authority; to gain Buddhist-style merit, which enhanced their social prestige; and—what is sometimes forgotten—to support Buddhist institutions and individuals who played an essential role in maintaining and advancing the great Sanskritic traditions of knowledge and culture.

By the end of this period, Buddhists had also established their tradition as a major religiocultural force in the Indian countryside. Many stories were told in which the Buddha chastens or converts local deities such as *yaksas* (often associated with sacred groves) and *nāgas* (serpentlike deities who served as guardian spirits protecting local regions). Other Buddhist stories, including Jātakas, were told in ways that reflected common folkloric themes and often merged with local traditions.

Once Buddhism was established, the village monks, many of whom had been trained in the larger monasteries and monastic universities, became both the spiritual guides for their followers and a primary channel of mediation between Buddhist-oriented Pan-Indian culture and the traditions of local, largely agrarian villages. The Buddha (often represented by an image or a relic that was the focus of a local myth), along with deities supposedly converted to his cause, were venerated at village shrines. The Dharma was reinterpreted by recasting it in terms of the mythology and folklore of this new rural constituency. Similarly, Buddhist rituals involving both monastics and the laity were adapted to suit the traditions and rhythms of the peasantry.

THE APOGEE AND DECLINE OF INDIAN BUDDHISM

As we have seen, Buddhism in the post-Aśokan period expanded in adherents, doctrine, and influence. In the next era, the so-called medieval period in India (c. sixth to eleventh centuries), this pattern changes: Buddhism deteriorates in India yet, paradoxically, achieves some of its most sophisticated and important doctrines, rituals, and techniques, notably in Mahāyāna and in a newly developed "vehicle," Vajrayāna Buddhism. Although these developments were to have great significance for the rest of Asia, they could not staunch the ebbing of Buddhism's lifeblood in India, and after around 1300 Buddhism survived there no longer.

We can see early evidence of Buddhism's decline in the sixth-century destruction of northwestern Buddhist monasteries by Hun invaders. We can also see signs of decline in southern India, where as early as the seventh century a militant and often explicitly anti-Buddhist Hindu Śaivism began to surge to the fore and to gain the support of various southern dynasties. In the centuries that followed, Buddhism's decline continued in these areas and spread to other parts of India as well.

However, in the northeast, the region where Buddhism had originated and where the imperial centers of the Mauryan and Gupta dynasties had been located, the faith continued to flourish for another 500 years. It received strong royal support, first from Harsha Vardhana (c. 605–647), who was able to extend his rule over much of northern India, and then from successive members of the Pāla dynasty, who ruled over most of Bihar and Bengal from 750 until about 1200. With this protection and support, Buddhism displayed a remarkable degree of vitality and creativity. It was here, in the northeast, that Buddhism in India experienced its greatest achievements between the sixth and eleventh centuries.

CONSERVATIVE, MAHĀYĀNA, AND VAJRAYĀNA BUDDHISM

During the medieval period the Conservative tradition continued to hold the loyalty of many Buddhists. Although Theravāda probably remained the majority group, there is little evidence that its leaders offered particularly creative adaptations to the changing circumstances.

From the sixth century on, the dynamism had shifted to other segments of the Indian Saṅgha. The Mahāyānists, for example, continued to develop their understanding of the Buddha, their interpretations of the Dharma, and their structures of communal life. Their pantheon of Buddhas and bodhisattvas was continually extended through both internal developments and an ongoing interaction with classical Hinduism and local traditions. Kings during this period sponsored many debates between Hindus and Buddhists, which further encouraged the development of doctrines and practices. Out of such a dynamic cauldron, Mahāyāna teachings were continually refined and extended. For example, the Mahāyānists expanded their notions of the bodhisattva path to an increasing variety of meditational levels. Śāntideva (early eighth century), for example, described some 15 stages of meditational attainment; in other formulations there were even more. Monasteries also developed new structures and meditation procedures to bolster these new levels of attainment.

The most dynamic and creative developments within Indian Buddhism, however, first emerged not in Mahāyāna monasteries but among the nonmonastic male and female ascetics on the fringes of the Buddhist community. They—or their idealized adepts—came to be known as **siddhas** and began to appear in the north and east of India around the eighth century. From their teachings emerged the third major strand, **Vajrayāna** Buddhism. Its distinctive new character can be seen in the following story.

Sometime during the late eighth century there lived in Orissa, in the east of the subcontinent, a rich brāhman named Saraha. By day he observed the commandments of orthodox Hinduism, but by night he was a Buddhist. And contrary to the rules of both religions, he drank alcohol. Brought to task for this, he plunged his hand into a vat of boiling oil, swearing, "If I am guilty, may my hand burn," and took it out unharmed. But his accusers did not believe him. So in one gulp, Saraha drank a bowl of molten copper. Still, people said, "He *does* drink alcohol!" So Saraha challenged someone to jump into a large tank of water with him, saying, "Whoever sinks is guilty." Saraha floated, and the accuser sank. "Even so," said the people, "he *does* drink alcohol!" However, the king, who had been watching this contest, said "If he has this kind of power, let him drink!"[3]

There are several features to be noted in the story, which is typical of accounts of siddhas.[4] First, by drinking alcohol, he breaks the fifth grave precept of Conservative Buddhism. Second, he breaks the fourth grave precept by lying about it. And third, he is unaffected not only by alcohol but also by boiling oil and molten copper. Consequently, he is recognized as having an unusual kind of power. This power is known as *siddhi,* "achievement," because of which he is called a *siddha.* Siddhis are recorded in many Hindu and Buddhist texts as an occasional by-product of high attainment, but in this case the siddha's consciousness was believed to have "penetrated the seeds of karmic manifestation and altered the usual process of illusory emanation at will."[5]

Vajrayāna Developments of Dharma

This feature of altering the illusion is the most important characteristic of the new form of Buddhism that the siddhas were developing, the vehicle that became known as the Mantrayāna ("mantra vehicle"),

Vajrayāna ("diamond vehicle"), or Tāntric Buddhism.

Because the practices of Vajrayāna are so distinctive, many people have thought of it as a third vehicle in addition to Theravāda and Mahāyāna, but because it differs only in its practices from the latter, it is more properly regarded as a variant of Mahāyāna. For example, Vajrayāna author Saraha wrote:

To a fool who squints
One lamp is as two;
Where seen and seer are not two, ah! the mind
Works on the thingness of them both.[6]

That is, a deluded mind perceives reality as absolutely divided into subject and object. Though subject and object are in fact nondual, a deluded mind reifies their inherent existence. Such a statement might be found in many Mahāyāna texts. The distinctiveness of Vajrayāna is that it advocates living in nonduality in the here and now, in this very body. Vajrayānists called other forms of Buddhism "Path Buddhism" and called their own teachings "Fruit Buddhism." In Path Buddhism one strives to become a Buddha. In Fruit Buddhism one *already is* a Buddha and so acts like one, with all the powers that a Buddha has, such as being unaffected by boiling oil and molten copper.

The teaching that one already is a Buddha might also be found in Mahāyāna writings. But according to Vajrayānists, Mahāyāna generally did not take this teaching seriously: it stated that one was *intrinsically* a Buddha but not *actually* a Buddha. Vajrayānists, however, tried to take seriously the teaching that one already is a Buddha, and maintained a nonduality between their intrinsic and actualized Buddha mind. Vajrayānists said that they worked from a "pure" perspective; that is, they saw reality purely, as the Buddhas see it. Since the rest of us do not see reality like this but live in the illusion of saṃsāra, the Vajrayānists described their path as the vehicle that stops, destroys, or cuts off the illusion we call ordinary reality.

Living Buddhas of Vajrayāna

Vajrayānists' avowals that one already is a Buddha and their emphasis on their siddhas led to a new ideal of religious attainment. In the Theravāda tradition the great models were the arhants, or fully perfected saints; to the Mahāyānists the great heroes were the bodhisattvas, who had postponed their own attainment of nirvāṇa in order to work for the salvation of all beings. In Vajrayāna a third kind of hero emerges, the siddha or guru (master), who had attained both freedom from bondage and magical domination over it. Unlike many Mahāyānists, who held that it would take many lifetimes to become a bodhisattva, Vajrayānists maintained that one could and should become a Buddha much faster. Practitioners with less spiritual maturity might require several additional rebirths—as many as 17, according to some texts. But for those who were more spiritually advanced, the possibility of attaining Buddhahood in this very life was real indeed.

This new affirmation of their religious adepts is also evident in the art of Vajrayāna, which is rich, even voluptuous. Myriads of saints in lush and complex realms were celebrated in vibrantly colorful art. This is seen especially in the Tibetan Vajrayānists' style of painting called *thangka* (Tibetan for "painted picture") in which the Buddhas and other realized beings appear in radiant bodies.

New Vajrayāna Practices

From the Vajrayānists' new perspective, nothing is seen as intrinsically bad, evil, or impure. This means that the passions themselves, which earlier Buddhism had vilified, were now seen as the manifestation of pure mind. In order to work with this new teaching, Vajrayānists developed new practices centering on visualization. First, drawing on general Mahāyāna meditative customs, the practitioner might be asked to visualize the compassionate energy of the Buddha mind as the bodhisattva Avalokiteśvara, seen as a calm, smiling youth. Then, if the teacher judges that the practitioner is ready, he or she is instructed in the visualization of Avalokiteśvara as a fierce, black, scowling, stamping, and roaring man-beast called Mahākāla, the "Great Dark One." If the meditation has been done correctly, the anger of Mahākāla will be found to have eradicated whatever was hindering the compassionate activity of the mind. Other passions may be tapped by visualizing other so-called wrathful deities.

It is at this level, of visualizing passions, that the famous "sexual yoga" was practiced. This is undoubtedly the most misunderstood part of Vajrayāna. It has nothing to do with sex for its own sake, which is, quite simply, saṃsāric involvement in the passions. And it usually has nothing to do with actual copulation. Most commonly, it is a meditation, done while sitting alone, in which compassion, visualized as male energy, and wisdom, visualized as female energy, are imaginatively perceived as uniting sexually. Their union is understood to represent their nonduality. Buddhist sexual yoga is substantially a manipulation of symbols in meditation, and in this respect it is similar to the sexual mysticism found, for example, in Vishṇavite Hinduism and in the bride mysticism of medieval Catholicism.

Two of the most distinctive features of Vajrayāna practice are the maṇḍala and the mantra.

Maṇḍala is a Sanskrit word that means "circle." In Vajrayāna, a **maṇḍala** is the dwelling, or palace, of a pure being such as a Buddha or a bodhisattva. When represented on a flat surface, a maṇḍala looks like a circle inside a square, divided diagonally into four segments. Such a representation, however, is only a plan or blueprint used as a teaching aid in the initiation into the liturgy of the maṇḍala. When visualized properly, it becomes a three-dimensional palace, a cube or sphere of such gigantic proportions that it overwhelms the calculating mind and is seen as the structure of the entire universe.

The **mantra** is understood in the Vajrayāna as a way of bringing out pure mind through speech. Most Buddhas and bodhisattvas have, according to Vajrayāna, their own *bīja-mantras* ("seed sounds"). For example, the bodhisattva Avalokiteśvara's bīja-mantra is *"Oṃ maṇi padme hūṃ."* These syllables are the manifestation in sound of the compassionate mind that manifests visually as the bodhisattva Avalokiteśvara. By repeating this expression over and over, Vajrayāna claims, the compassionate energy of one's Buddha mind is nourished.

Vajrayānists extended this understanding of the importance of sacred sounds. In certain circumstances the entire universe was seen—or better, heard—as a vast concatenation of sacred sounds and syllables. Furthermore, just as each of the various deities in the pantheon was believed to have its bīja-mantra, each of the psychic components within an individual was also associated with a particular bīja-mantra. Thus to know and manipulate the appropriate sounds makes it possible to bring the psychic as well as cosmic forces under control and to achieve the various levels of attainment.

The Vajrayāna Saṅgha

The various Vajrayāna masters, together with their disciplines, constituted the core of the fully developed Vajrayāna community. Some of these masters were forest monks who followed, in somewhat modified form, the rather unorthodox life style that had been characteristic of the early siddhas. Some combined more traditional monastic behavior patterns (including adherence to the Vinaya and the study of texts) with more specifically Vajrayāna patterns. These life styles were not mutually exclusive, and many Vajrayāna practitioners moved back and forth between the two.

Considerable evidence suggests that certain Vajrayāna masters were closely associated with the Pāla court in northeastern India (eighth to twelfth centuries), and these masters probably took the lead in developing Buddhist Tāntric liturgies that were specially designed for the use of kings. These included rituals performed in part for the purpose of enhancing the Buddhist status of the kings, perhaps even to consecrate them as bodhisattvas or living Buddhas. They also included rituals designed to protect the ruler and his kingdom against the intrusion of evil forces that might threaten their well-being.

There are also good reasons to suspect that Vajrayānists helped in maintaining the loyalty of the lay community. Both the religious and the intellectual attainments of the siddhas were well known, and their magical powers were widely respected. Many Western scholars have maintained that the Buddhist appropriation of Tāntric elements was a cause of the Buddhist loss of popular support in India. In fact, the new vitality that the Vajrayāna practitioners introduced into Indian Buddhism probably enabled it to retain popular support much longer than it would otherwise have done.

THE DECLINE OF BUDDHISM IN INDIA

We have observed that despite the great medieval efflorescence of Buddhism in the northeast, Indian Buddhism as a whole suffered a long series of devastating setbacks. By the eleventh century the decline of Buddhism that had already occurred elsewhere in India began to be seriously felt in the northeast as well. By the middle of the thirteenth century, Buddhism as a living religious and cultural force in India had ceased to exist.

Though scholars have debated the causes for this decline for many years, no adequate explanation has been put forward. However, it is possible to identify four factors that help to account for Buddhism's fate. These four factors were interrelated, though their relative importance varied from time to time and from region to region.

Socioeconomic considerations The first factor was associated with Buddhism's social stature. In its early years, Buddhism had the greatest appeal to people in the upper echelons of the social, political, and economic hierarchy. Even during its heyday, it was very much a high-culture tradition that received strong support from the political and economic elite. This does not mean that Buddhism cut itself off from the lower classes or failed to establish itself in the villages where the great majority of Indians lived. It does mean, however, that the penetration into the grassroots of society was not as extensive or as deep as the penetration achieved by Hinduism. Thus Buddhism was especially vulnerable to the forces of political and economic change.

Monks versus laity A second closely related factor in the decline of Buddhism in India was the development of a widening gap between the monastic communities and the lay populations with which they were supposedly associated. According to the Buddhist ideal, they were interdependent: the monks were to provide the religious ideal and dharmic teaching, and the lay community was to provide material support such as food, robes, and housing. However, as the monasteries became well-endowed, landowning institutions, the monks stopped needing to cultivate lay support; as a result, their day-to-day interactions with the people diminished.

Hinduism's vitality These internal characteristics and developments made the Buddhist communities vulnerable to challenges from without. The third important factor in the decline of Indian Buddhism was the increasing vitality (and in some cases the increasing militancy) of new and dynamic forms of post-Vedic Hinduism. The new theistic traditions of Vaishṇavism and Śaivism that began to take form during the centuries approaching the year 1000 shared, from that time forward, the support of Indian kings and the rest of the Indian elite. They took very deep root among virtually all other segments of the population as well.

With the passage of time, the Hindu traditions gained in strength, appropriating many aspects of Buddhist teaching and institutional life. For example, Śaṅkara, the great Hindu leader who lived in the ninth century, developed a Hindu philosophy that incorporated many Buddhist insights; he also played a major role in establishing a network of Hindu monasteries that followed the Buddhist model. In South India, Hindu traditions gained the upper hand before the millennium—well before any major incursions from outside forces.

Foreign invasions A fourth factor that played a crucial role in the demise of Buddhism in the north was invasion by foreign forces. Over a period of seven centuries, invasions into northern India gradually destroyed the political regimes and monastic institutions on which Buddhism had come to depend.

Already toward the end of the Gupta period, the invasions had begun with a first wave of Huns coming into the northwest from their earlier homelands in central Asia. Chinese pilgrims who subsequently visited the area reported widespread destruction of Buddhist monasteries. In the eighth century, Muslim Arabs arrived at the mouth of the Indus River and established a relatively benign Muslim regime in the northwest. Later, however, Muslim Turks arrived on the scene, and the process of destruction gained momentum. Gradually, the Turks extended their raids farther and farther to the east. By the end of the twelfth century, the famed Buddhist monastic university at Nālandā had been sacked and largely destroyed, and early in the thirteenth century, the great sister institution of Vikramaśīlā suffered a similar fate.

By the middle of the thirteenth century, Buddhism

in India was, except for a few pockets in eastern Bengal and South India, a thing of the past. In the very subcontinent where Buddhism had originated and come into its own as a great religion, the descendants of the Buddhist population were absorbed into the ranks of Hinduism and Islam. Only the monuments remained, and many of them were abandoned or transformed. For the Buddhist world that now extended across virtually all of Asia, the ancient center had collapsed.

NOTES

1 Edward Conze, trans., *Buddhist Wisdom Books* (London: Allen & Unwin, 1958–), p. 28.

2 Ibid., p. 89.

3 After Keith Dowman, *Masters of Mahāmudrā* (Albany: State University of New York Press, 1985), pp. 66–68.

4 See Herbert V. Gunther, trans., *The Royal Song of Saraha* (Berkeley, Calif.: Shambala, 1973).

5 Dowman, *Masters of Mahāmudrā,* p. 69.

6 Gunther, *Royal Song,* p. 63.

BUDDHISM

CHAPTER 9

BUDDHISM AS A WORLD RELIGION

BUDDHIST EXPANSION

The same missionary outreach that led to Buddhism's original growth and expansion within India carried the tradition into many other parts of Asia as well. The earliest known effort to introduce the Dharma beyond the Indian subcontinent took place during the reign of Emperor Aśoka in the third century B.C.E. According to the edicts and later chronicles, Aśoka sent Buddhist emissaries to the Himalayan regions in the north and northwest, to Suvannabhumi (the "Land of Gold") in the southeast, and to Sri Lanka in the far south. Buddhism soon took root both in the northwest and in Sri Lanka.

During the following centuries, Buddhism spread from northwestern India all along the central Asian trade routes that led to the cities of northwestern China. By the early centuries of the Common Era, Buddhist communities in central Asia and northern China were well established. By the sixth century, several Buddhist kingdoms were thriving in Southeast Asia along major trade routes, and Buddhism was spreading rapidly through China and entering Korea and Vietnam. Around that time Buddhism was also introduced into Japan, where it quickly put down roots and assumed an important role in Japanese life. It was established in Tibet by the year 800. Thus by the time that Buddhism died out in India in the thirteenth century, it had spread throughout virtually all of southeastern, central, and eastern Asia, where it has maintained a continuous presence ever since.

Patterns in the Spread of Buddhism

Without making absolute generalizations, we can note a definite pattern in Buddhism's spread. First, the central beliefs and modes of practice stayed close to what they were in India. Emphasis remained on the historical Buddha and a glorification of his life, and both the practice of relic veneration and the building and worshiping of stūpas continued. Monastic institutions were established in the new areas, modeled on their Indian counterparts.

Second, there was a close correlation between the Buddhist vehicle that was on the rise in India at the time of each phase of expansion and the tradition that ultimately became dominant in each new area. Thus when Buddhism was introduced into Sri Lanka and Southeast Asia, Indian Buddhism was basically Conservative, and the Theravāda form came to be dominant there. When Buddhism entered East Asia, Mahāyāna had come to the fore, and it continues to attract the greatest number of adherents in China, Korea, Vietnam, and Japan. Vajrayāna was beginning to emerge in India when Buddhism entered Tibet, and so that is the vehicle that became dominant there.

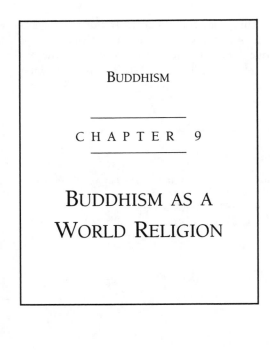

BUDDHISM IN "GREATER INDIA"

The history of Buddhism in Sri Lanka and Southeast Asia falls rather clearly into three periods. The first began with the introduction of Buddhism into Sri Lanka (and probably Southeast Asia as well) during or close to the reign of Emperor Aśoka. The Theravāda reform that took shape in the eleventh and twelfth centuries began the second period. The third phase occurred when British and French colonialism entered the picture in the nineteenth century.

During the first period, Sri Lanka and Southeast Asia were part of an area that some scholars have called "Greater India." Though this designation is not completely accurate, it does make it clear that many of the religious and political developments that took place in Sri Lanka and Southeast Asia were intimately linked with occurrences in India itself, especially specifically Buddhist developments.

Literary and archaeological evidence indicates that from the time of the Aśokan mission, Buddhism has had a more or less continuous history in Sri Lanka. According to much later Sinhalese (Sri Lankan) chronicles, the Sinhalese king was converted by Aśoka's son, and the famous Mahāvihāra monastery was established in the capital city of Anuradhapura. By the first century B.C.E., Buddhism had become an integral part of Sri Lankan life. A Sinhalese mythology soon developed that claimed that the Buddha and the Sinhalese kings shared a common lineage, that the Buddha had visited Sri Lanka and prepared the country for the reception of his religion, and that important relics of the Buddha (including the famous Tooth Relic) had miraculously come of their own volition from India to Sri Lanka. By the fourth or fifth century of the Common Era, Sinhalese texts were claiming that Sri Lanka was singled out to become the *Dhammadipa* ("island where the Dharma prevails").

Mythology developed claiming that the Buddha had visited Sri Lanka and that important relics of the Buddha had miraculously come of their own volition from India to Sri Lanka. Here, drummers parade before the temple housing the famous Buddha tooth relic in Kandy, Sri Lanka. (Ceylon [Sri Lanka] Tourist Board)

During the early centuries of the first millennium C.E., Conservative Buddhism was dominant in Sri Lanka, and it probably also retained more influence there than in most areas of the subcontinent itself. Mahāyāna traditions, however, became firmly established in the largest and most influential Buddhist monastery (Abhayagiri), and from at least the eighth century onward, Sri Lanka was a major center of Vajrayāna learning and practice.

In contrast to those in Sri Lanka, Buddhist kingdoms in lower Burma, in central Thailand, and at the tip of the Indochina peninsula were set up only in the Common Era. Archaeological evidence and reports by Chinese travelers suggest that Conservative traditions were the first to be established and that they persisted most strongly in Burma and Thailand. After about 500 C.E., the Mahāyāna and Vajrayāna traditions gained vigor in these areas and completely dominated Buddhist life between 500 and 1000 in Malaysia, Indonesia, and Cambodia.

GROWTH AND CONSOLIDATION OF THERAVĀDA TRADITIONS

Though the history of Buddhism in Greater India closely parallels the history of Buddhism in the subcontinent, distinctive new developments did take place. The most important occurrence was the growth and expansion, within the Conservative tradition, of a Theravāda

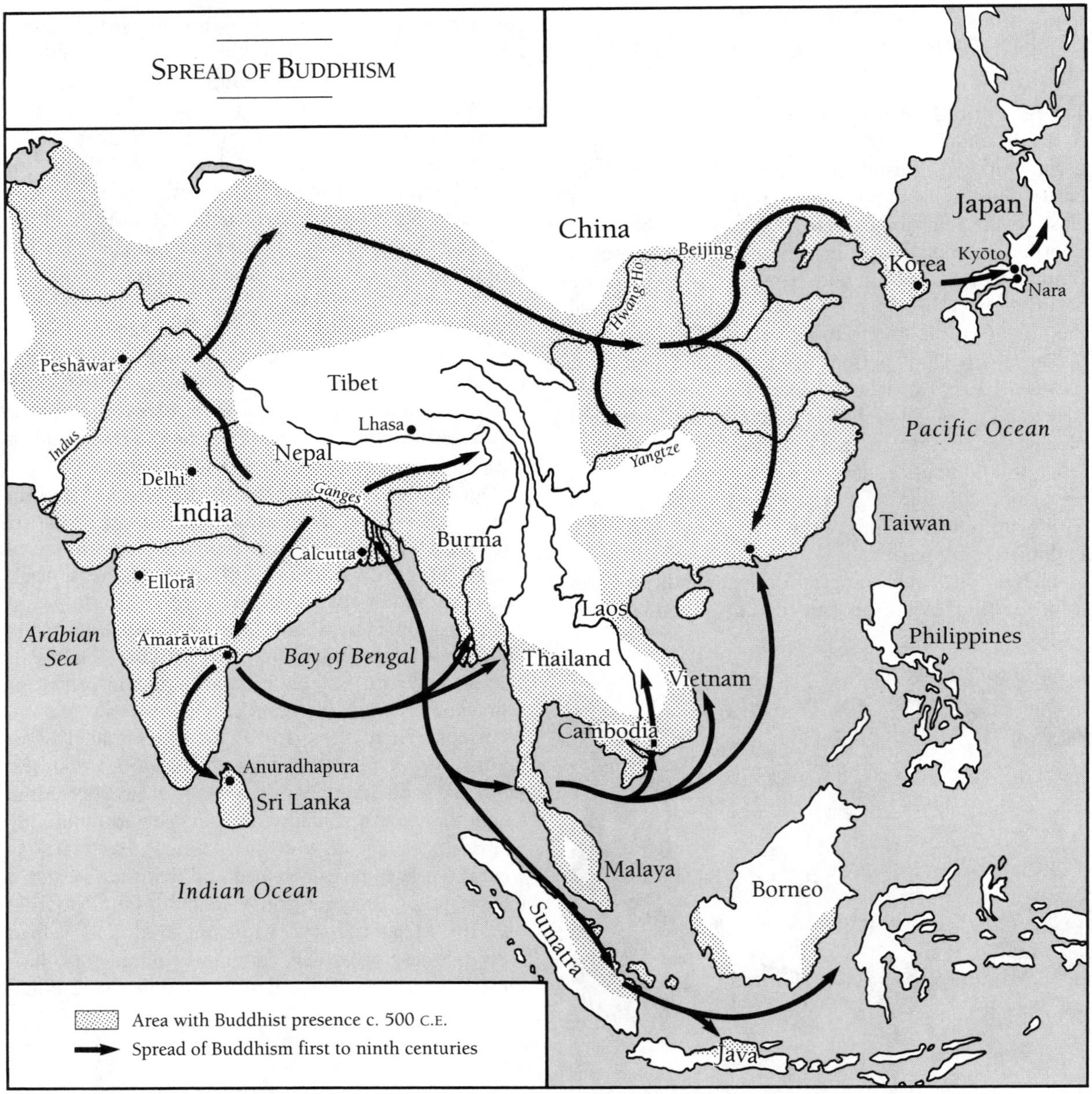

school that used Pāli rather than Sanskrit as its sacred language. These Theravādins tended to emphasize the central importance of the historical Gautama and to represent him as a mahāpurusha (great person) who had in the course of his many lives achieved liberation through his own efforts. They recognized the existence of other Buddhas, but among these only the future Buddha Maitreya played a significant role.

At the level of the Dhamma (the Pāli name for the Sanskrit *Dharma*), the Theravādins had their own version of the Tipiṭaka (Sanskrit, *Tripiṭaka*), written in Pāli, which they considered the language of the

Buddha himself. A major turning point in the evolution of the Theravāda tradition occurred in the fifth and sixth centuries C.E. when a series of great scholars generated a large body of commentary texts in Pāli that became a basic resource for later Theravāda practitioners. The key figure in this process was Buddhaghoṣa, a monk from India or lower Burma who translated many commentaries on the Tipiṭaka from Sinhalese into Pāli and wrote an extremely influential summary of Theravāda doctrine, *The Path of Purification*.

In Sri Lanka and Southeast Asia, some Theravāda Buddhists produced an esoteric interpretation of the Pāli texts and adopted various forms of Vajrayāna ritual. Some of these practices were associated with extreme forms of asceticism; others were oriented toward the laity. In many cases, these practices were designed to generate a permanent *dhammakāya* ("Dharma body") symbolized by a "crystal globe" that would appear in the center of the body near the navel. In other cases, rituals that involved a symbolic return to the womb were presented as a means to the immediate attainment of nirvāṇa. The significance of these Vajrayāna expressions of the Theravāda tradition has been recognized only recently.

The Theravāda community involved forest monks and other practitioners of yogic meditation who lived on the fringes of society. It also included monks who lived in settled monasteries such as the great Mahāvihāra in Sri Lanka, heavily endowed institutions deeply involved in local intellectual and economic life. Its lay supporters and practitioners included kings, nobles, and commoners. However, prior to the Theravāda-oriented reforms that took place in the twelfth century, probably the majority of the laypersons who supported the Theravādins also supported other Buddhist schools and in some cases Hindu shrines and practitioners as well.

ROYAL TRADITIONS IN SOUTHEAST ASIA

A second Buddhist development that occurred in Greater India was the extension of the Indian tradition of Buddhist kingship. This development—carried to its furthest extent in Southeast Asia—involved an evolution of Indian patterns whereby notions of the Buddha, the Dharma, and the Saṅgha were closely correlated with notions of kingship, the principles of social order, and the state. Unfortunately, no Southeast Asian texts from this period have survived, but it does seem that there was an intimate link between the king and the Saṅgha: the king was generally the official sponsor and protector of the Saṅgha; he was its most important patron and was responsible for the building of many large monasteries and Buddhist monuments, some of which are the most impressive religious monuments ever constructed.

Buddhist Religious Monuments

One of the most interesting examples of Buddhist royal architecture in Southeast Asia has been unearthed at sites associated with Dvaravati, a kingdom in central and northeastern Thailand during the late first millennium. Heavily influenced by Conservative traditions that used both Sanskrit and Pāli, the Dvaravati kingdom encompassed numerous cities and villages. Many such places had, at their center, Buddhist stūpas constructed of brick.

At about the same time, a powerful king who reigned in central Java was sponsoring the construction of what many Buddhologists and art historians consider the most magnificent Buddhist monument ever built. Constructed over a natural hill, Barabuḍur is a massive stūpa. Its extensive and sophisticated sculptured surface is decorated with complex Mahāyāna and Vajrayāna imagery.

Although the details are unclear, it is generally agreed that Dvaravati and Barabuḍur were designed to integrate three kinds of reality: (1) the great cosmic Buddha and the dharmically ordered cosmos he ruled, (2) the traditional ancestral spirit of the mountain and the spirit realm he ruled, and (3) the king who sponsored the construction and the great dharmic order of the kingdom he ruled.

A variation on this theme was seen in the thirteenth-century Cambodian temple-city of Angkor Thom, constructed by King Jayavarman VII. Jayavarman consolidated and helped to legitimize his rule by building a magnificent new city that would be an architectural embodiment of the cosmos. In contrast to most of his predecessors at Angkor, who were Hindus, Jayavarman VII was a Mahāyāna Buddhist; thus he built his city as an embodiment of a dharmically ordered cosmos conceived in Mahāyāna terms.

Jayavarman's city included a great central temple constructed in the form of a sacred mountain, the Bayon. The impressive tower that rose above the center of the temple had four sides on each of which an identical royal face was engraved. This face—presented as that of the bodhisattva Avalokiteśvara, the guardian spirit of the Angkor kingdom, and Jayavarman VII—looks out over the four quarters of the temple, the city, and the kingdom in the four cosmic directions. Below the great central tower, the main mass of the Bayon is decorated with extensive sculptures that depict, as an integral part of the dharmically ordered kingdom, elements and activities associated with the various provinces over which Jayavarman VII ruled.

Our evidence does not tell us how deeply Buddhism penetrated the lower echelons of Southeast Asian Buddhist societies. The great effort and expense that were invested in building Buddhist monuments and their high level of sophistication demonstrate that Buddhism was at certain times and places a major religious, political, and cultural force. Clearly, rulers and commoners alike were followers of Buddhism. Yet equally clearly, almost everywhere that Buddhism flourished, it coexisted with forms of Hinduism and with indigenous beliefs and practices.

THERAVĀDA CULTURE IN SRI LANKA AND SOUTHEAST ASIA

The decline of Buddhism that was in full swing on the Indian subcontinent by the early second millennium extended to much of Greater India as well. In some areas, especially in Malaysia and Indonesia, Buddhism lost its hold, while Hindu theism and Tāntrism gained strength. In later centuries successful Muslim traders gradually converted local rulers and their subjects to Islam. Well before the intrusion of European colonialism, Islam had spread throughout the previously Indianized areas in Malaysia, Sumatra, and Java. Buddhist institutions (and Hindu ones) were almost completely supplanted by Islamic successors.

In Sri Lanka and in mainland Southeast Asia, the collapse of Buddhism in the Indian subcontinent had a very different effect. In these areas, the cessation of Indian influences coincided with the emergence of a series of powerful reform movements that succeeded in establishing Theravāda Buddhism as the dominant local religious force.

The first of these movements occurred in the eleventh century, when kings in northern Burma and Sri Lanka both instituted Theravāda patterns that had been preserved among the Mon peoples in lower Burma. The most important Theravāda reform occurred in twelfth-century Sri Lanka. It was organized by a very successful Sinhalese king, Parakkamabahu (1153–1186), who worked with a group of reform-minded forest monks associated with the Mahāvihāra monastery. They were able to create a unified structure for the Sri Lankan Saṅgha and raise the Theravāda tradition to preeminence.

These reforms also stimulated a burst of literary creativity and promoted Theravāda Buddhism as a popular religion. The Theravāda monks composed new commentaries and other texts in Pāli and Sinhalese, some highlighting Buddhist devotion and others teaching meditational techniques. This new flurry of vernacular writing was part of a general movement whereby Theravāda Buddhism penetrated into virtually every area of Sinhalese life and culture. Just as pilgrimage had become an important Buddhist practice in India, Sri Lankan Buddhists developed their own pilgrimage sites. Places that had long been considered sacred by the indigenous traditions, such as mountain peaks, were incorporated into Buddhist practice. The Buddhists developed their own calendar rites, their own festivals honoring various Buddhas and bodhisattvas, and their own funeral rights.

The Sri Lankan Theravāda reforms quickly spread to Southeast Asia, where they melded with reforms that had already begun in Burma. By the end of the fifteenth century, the reformed Sri Lankan Theravāda tradition was firmly established at the various Burmese royal courts. Farther to the east, the Theravāda tradition was adopted by the Thai kings and peoples. In Cambodia, the Theravāda tradition became preeminent at Angkor, which had once been a Hindu-Mahāyāna empire.

Like the reform-oriented Sri Lankans, the Theravādins of Southeast Asia carried their teaching and practice far beyond the boundaries of the political and cultural elite, reaching out to most of the local ethnic groups. Though earlier Buddhist and Hindu traditions that had been established in various regions remained at least partly intact, the Theravāda reformers gradually extended their own influence.

The thirteenth-century C.E. Cambodian temple-city of Angkor Thom, constructed by King Jayavarman VII, was built as an architectural embodiment of the cosmos. The city includes a great central temple constructed in the form of a sacred mountain, the Bayon. The temple city is often called the "eighth wonder of the world." (Tass from Sovfoto)

By the time the first Europeans arrived in the area in the sixteenth and seventeenth centuries, Theravāda had become the dominant and pervasive religious force in the central rice-growing areas of Burma, Thailand, Laos, and Cambodia. Buddhist beliefs and stories had merged with regional and local traditions; Theravāda rituals had become embedded in the cycle of agricultural rites performed at the royal courts and in the villages. Theravāda ideals of community life, both monastic and lay, had become firmly established among both the elite and the populace as a whole.

RELIGIOUS TRENDS IN THERAVĀDA CULTURE

Theravāda Buddhism served as an international religious culture throughout Sri Lanka and Southeast Asia. Theravāda Buddhists shared a common sacred language, Pāli, a sense of common religious identity, common ideals of religious salvation and sainthood, and common norms of monastic and lay behavior, all of which continuously interacted.

Developments of Buddhology

Gautama Buddha (along with the future Buddha Maitreya) was always the primary focus in Theravāda. However, in each area, the veneration of Gautama Buddha was closely correlated with local traditions. Legends were told of his visits to the local area, and relics and images came to be associated with local sites and practices. Among the famous regional symbols of the Buddha's presence were his footprint, venerated on a sacred mountain in Sri Lanka; the Tooth Relic, the center of an important royal cult in the Sinhalese capital of Kandy; the Mahāmuni ("great sage") image in Burma; and the Prabang image, which gave its name to the Laotian capital, Luang Prabang.

Wherever Theravāda prevailed, alongside or below Gautama Buddha came Hindu-related or indigenous deities, venerated or propitiated in accordance with local practices. In Sri Lanka, the Buddha himself headed a pantheon of deities, each associated with certain sacred sites. In Burma, the old Vedic god Indra, who came to occupy one of the important heavens in the traditional Theravāda cosmology, was identified with a powerful *nat* (local guardian deity) who headed a pantheon of lesser nats that resided on a famous mountain. In Laos, Theravāda rituals performed at the great stūpa in the old capital of Luang Prabang included the reenactment of the process whereby the Laotian ancestral deities had purportedly created the natural and social order within which the Laotian peoples lived.

Extensions of Dharma

In all the various Theravāda countries, the primary source of Dharma was a common tradition of Pāli texts that included the Tripiṭaka and its corpus of commentaries. There were, however, many other Pāli texts of more limited distribution that took a very distinctive form in each of the major Theravāda kingdoms in Southeast Asia. Some Pāli texts contained Vajrayāna ideas and practices.

A corpus of vernacular texts that played a very important role in forming and expressing the local tradition was written in the regional languages of Burma, Thailand, Cambodia, and Laos. One classic example is *The Three Worlds of King Ruang,* a fourteenth-century Thai-language cosmology that exerted a major influence in central Thailand's religion, culture, and society.

Saṅgha and Community Life

Similar patterns of commonality and difference can be observed across the premodern Theravāda world. The ancient forest monk tradition continued in all Theravāda countries. This tradition was particularly influential in the areas along the northern and northeastern perimeters of Theravāda religious culture—northern Burma, northern and northeastern Thailand, Laos, and Cambodia. The forest monks were most active in promoting the Vajrayāna in these peripheral areas.

As a part of the unifying reforms that were initiated in twelfth-century Sri Lanka, the Theravādins developed a new kind of relationship between the religio-social hierarchy and the monastic community. The king, who was now recognized as a bodhisattva, headed a hierarchically structured social order that acknowledged the spiritual authority of the monks. The monastic order was set up as a parallel hierarchy; it was headed by a *saṅgharājā* ("Saṅgha king") who was usually appointed or confirmed by the king. These two hierarchically structured orders, each headed by its respective king, worked in tandem to constitute Theravāda Buddhist society.

This Sri Lankan pattern was adopted as an ideal by the religious and political elite in many Southeast Asian kingdoms. However, it was implemented much more effectively in some countries than in others. It was most successful in kingdoms, such as the Ayuddhia kingdom in central Thailand, where there were a strong centralized power and long periods of relative political stability. It was least effective in places and times of political and social disruption, such as Sri Lanka in the seventeenth and early eighteenth centuries.

Relationships between Theravāda monks and their lay supporters were often close, particularly in small towns and villages with local monasteries. The monks provided religious services, spiritual guidance, and educational training to the local lay community, and the laity contributed moral and material support, supplying food and robes, building shelters, and contributing to the upkeep of the monasteries. The closeness of the relationships that actually developed between the monks and the laity was, however, deeply affected by differences in local customs. In Sri Lanka, the degree of mutual involvement was somewhat limited by the fact that entrance into the Saṅgha generally implied a lifetime commitment to the monastic way. In many areas of Burma, in contrast, every young boy was expected to spend a certain time as a novice within the monastic community. In central Thailand, temporary ordination was regularly practiced; every young Thai man would spend at least one three-month rainy season as a fully ordained monk. Thai men of all social classes, from peasants to kings, were also commonly reordained for periods lasting from days to years. Such practices inevitably strengthened the bonds between lay people and monks by partly integrating the two very different life styles.

BUDDHISM IN CENTRAL ASIA, CHINA, AND JAPAN

The spread of Buddhism from India to central Asia and on into the very different civilizations of East Asia is a stunning testimony to the universality and vitality of its message and institutions. In contrast to the Buddhist expansion into Sri Lanka and Southeast Asia, which continued Indian Buddhism's central motifs and ideals, expansion into central Asia, China, and Japan took the faith far beyond its original Indian context and implanted it in a radically different religious and cultural milieu.

The history of Buddhism in central and eastern Asia can be divided into two overlapping periods: a first during which Indian influences were strong and a second in which China (later supplemented by Japan) replaced India as Buddhism's main center. The first period began with the expansion of Buddhism into central Asia and China around the beginning of the Common Era and drew to a close toward the early decades of the ninth century. The second period began in the fifth and sixth centuries and continued until the massive intrusions of European power in the nineteenth century.

NORTHWESTERN INDIA AND CENTRAL ASIA

The Buddhist missions dispatched from the Aśokan court included one that was sent to the area that is now Pakistan, and by the first century B.C.E. Buddhism was well established there. During the first and second centuries C.E., three important developments occurred. First, the Kushāṇa dynasty, of central Asian origin, with its capital in northwestern India, came to rule an empire that extended from deep in central Asia far into the Indian subcontinent. Second, major trade routes expanded; these—the famous Silk Roads—extended from northwestern India through the now-pacified Kushāṇa domains in central Asia on into China. Third, Kushāṇa kings and many of their subjects were converted to Buddhism.

Buddhism spread to China along the Silk Roads through the deserts of central Asia. Many of the merchants who organized the caravans were Buddhist supporters, and Buddhist monks who joined the caravans settled in various localities to help to establish monasteries that served as hostels for weary traders and travelers. Many of the local rulers became supporters of the Buddhist cause, and significant numbers of their subjects followed their lead.

During the early centuries of the first millennium, the dominant Buddhist traditions in northwestern India and central Asia were Conservative. Over time, however, Mahāyāna Buddhism gained strength. Some scholars believe that many Mahāyāna developments originated in this area. For example, it is often claimed that Buddhists in northwestern India or western central Asia modeled the mythology of Amitābha Buddha on the Iranian god Mithra. This Buddha became the focus of Pure Land Buddhism, which grew into the most popular form of East Asian Buddhism. Some scholars have even suggested that certain important Mahāyāna texts, such as the famous Lotus Sūtra, were composed in central Asia.

Although during the middle centuries of the first millennium travel along the Silk Roads sometimes

This Chinese translation of a Buddhist work was found at Tun-huang and dates from 868 C.E. Buddha is shown addressing Subhuti, an aged disciple.
(The Granger Collection)

became difficult, it never ceased. Many different religious traditions spread along these routes, including Zoroastrianism, Manichaeism, Christianity, and Islam. In this multireligious environment, Buddhism—both Conservative and Mahāyāna—maintained an important presence at many points along the way.

The southern caravan route entered China at Dunhuang (Tun-huang), at the western end of the Great Wall. Dunhuang is an extraordinary city of elaborately carved and painted cave temples. In one of these temples, around 1035 C.E., an unknown person concealed thousands of manuscripts on Buddhism and other subjects written in Chinese, Tibetan, and Uighur. These remained hidden until an itinerant monk rediscovered them in the early twentieth century. Still incompletely studied, the Dunhuang material is one of the richest sources of Mahāyāna texts and iconography.[1]

After the sixth century, traveling the Silk Roads became increasingly precarious. Marauders often made the routes virtually impassable. The prosperous oasis kingdoms were devastated, and Islam became dominant in many areas. By the 900s, the central Asian links that had for centuries connected the Buddhists of India and China had been severed, and the once-thriving centers of Buddhist learning and practices, so crucial in the development of Buddhism, had become virtually extinct.

CHINA

The Golden Age from Han to Tang

The establishment and spread of Buddhism in China marks a remarkable breakthrough. To this point, we have been discussing Buddhism as it developed in its homeland and in other areas where it was one of the first religions with a tradition based on written texts and institutional ideals correlated with large-scale patterns of political and social organization. In China, by contrast, Buddhism interacted with a culture that had its own highly sophisticated texts and political and social patterns.

China had developed two interrelated and complementary systems, generally known in the West as Confucianism and Daoism (Chapter 10). Confucianism was primarily concerned with personal relationships, politics, and society, and secondarily with more cosmic matters such as the place of humans in the universe. Daoism focused on cosmic matters and only secondarily on politics and society. Buddhism supported and criticized both systems.

Confucianism, centered on the family and the state, regards the stability of both as of supreme importance. Buddhism allied itself with Confucianism by stressing kindness and generosity, especially to one's parents, and its elaborate funeral services appealed to the Confucian reverence for the ancestors. However, it struck at the heart of the Confucian system with its notion of rebirth, according to which one's sacred ancestor might have been reborn as a dog. In addition, a son or a daughter who became a Buddhist monk or nun had to take a vow of celibacy, going against Confucianism by imperiling the continuity of the family line. And since initiation into the Buddhist monastic order involves the shaving of the head, Confucians could claim that, for all its talk of kindness to parents, Buddhism was in fact insultingly unfilial, for the *Book of Filial Piety (Xiao Jing)* says: "Seeing that our body, with hair and skin, is derived from our parents, we should not allow it to be injured in any way. This is the beginning of filiality."[2] Further, Buddhist monastics followed the Indian custom of regarding themselves as superior to the sovereign and refused—until a compromise was worked out—to follow the Chinese convention of kowtowing to the emperor, whom Confucianism regarded as the Son of Heaven.

In general, Buddhism attempted to nurture the Confucian emphasis on kindness and then extend it to nonhuman forms of life and to offer sons and daughters an alternative to marriage and the continuation of the family.

Buddhism sided with Daoism against Confucianism in regarding matters of state as subsidiary to cosmic harmony and immortality. Indeed, the Chinese at first mistook Buddhism for a variety of Daoism and supposed that the Buddha had been a student of Lao-zi, Daoism's legendary founder. It seemed that perhaps Buddhism had a recipe for immortality that might be superior to that of Daoism in that it did not require the ingestion of a somewhat toxic elixir, that the Daoists recommended. But Buddhism wished to go beyond Daoism as much as beyond Confucianism. When the

Indian Buddhist missionary Bodhiruci was asked if Buddhism had any recipes for immortality that compared to those of Daoism, he spat on the ground and replied:

> What do you mean? How can you compare the two? Where in this land [of China] could you find the formula for immortality? Even if you should remain young and live forever, you would still be within the realm of saṃsāra![3]

The point here is that Daoism seeks to prolong life and prevent death, whereas Buddhism seeks to end what it regards as an indefinitely long cycle of lives and deaths.[4]

The beginning of Buddhism in China is ascribed to a dream in which Emperor Ming (58–75 C.E.) of the Han dynasty saw a golden, flying deity. His advisers interpreted this as a vision of the Buddha who, they said, was an Indian who had attained the Dao, the Way, and could fly. Impressed, the emperor dispatched envoys to the Indian subcontinent to gain more information. They brought back the *Sūtra in Forty-two Sections,* a collection of sayings of Śākyamuni Buddha modeled on the *Analects* of Confucius. Whatever the truth of this legend, it is certain that Buddhism penetrated China from the top down.

After the collapse of the Han dynasty and therefore of Confucian control, Buddhism was able to make some headway. Its progress was quite different in the north and the south of the Chinese subcontinent. The north was ruled by the leaders of nomadic tribes, mostly Huns and Turks, who had broken through the Great Wall and established a series of kingdoms. Many of these rulers and their followers became supporters of the Buddhist cause and ardent practitioners of Buddhist rituals that promised worldly benefits.

The old Han aristocracy had fled south to escape the invaders who had taken over the north. Buddhists took advantage of the fact that the recent defeats had lowered the prestige of the ancient Confucian and Daoist traditions. Many members of the old elite were converted to Buddhism, and they soon developed a distinctive "gentry Buddhism" that placed a strong emphasis on philosophical reflection and refinement. Sophisticated Indian philosophical texts were translated into Chinese, thus laying the foundations for the development of distinctively Chinese versions of Buddhist doctrine that became established among the elite.

During the golden age of Buddhist influence in China, rulers sponsored temples and monasteries, giving them great wealth. Here a gilded roof ornament in the shape of a dragon head is part of the decoration of one monastery. (Eastfoto)

During the fourth through sixth centuries, however, both in the north and in the south, Buddhism spread far beyond the ruling elite. Buddhist monks, acting both as teachers of the Dharma and as experts in magical practices, converted large numbers of people in town and countryside. Monasteries were established, pagodas (Chinese stūpas) were constructed, and devotional cults spread broadly among the people.

When the Sui and Tang dynasties (sixth through

tenth centuries) unified China, they turned to Buddhism as a religion that could help them engender geographic and social unity. For more than 250 years (589–845), its golden age, Buddhism enjoyed substantial support from the imperial power, the aristocracy, and the common folk. Buddhist texts were translated from Indian and central Asian languages, producing a Chinese Buddhist Tripiṭaka, a compendium of Conservative, Mahāyāna, and Vajrayāna texts. Many Buddhist schools flourished, including several distinctively Chinese schools that influenced all of East Asia. Buddhist influences were felt in every aspect of Chinese culture and art, from architecture and sculpture to painting and literature.

Throughout this golden age, Buddhist institutions and ritual practices flourished. Temples were sponsored by the rulers; others were privately endowed, and many received lavish donations that gave them great wealth and control over vast estates. The chanting of Buddhist sūtras, or spells, and the performance of all sorts of merit-making acts became ubiquitous, both at the royal court and among ordinary people. Festivals such as the celebration of the birthday of Śākyamuni Buddha and pilgrimages to sacred mountains associated with Buddhas and bodhisattvas were participated in by large numbers of people from most segments of society.

Notwithstanding its great success in its first eight centuries, Buddhism was never able to overcome completely the sense that it was a foreign religion, nor was it able to neutralize completely the accusation that its monastic order (which became increasingly wealthy and therefore increasingly vulnerable to criticism) was a threat to family life and a drag on the economy. Thus anti-Buddhist movements were able periodically to challenge Buddhism's favorable position in the Chinese court and in Chinese life.

Finally, in the middle of the ninth century, these anti-Buddhist feelings became the catalyst for a violent attack that brought the golden age of Buddhism in China to an end. In 845, Emperor Wuzong mounted a massive anti-Buddhist persecution that resulted in the destruction of thousands of Buddhist temples, the appropriation of their lands, and the defrocking of more than 200,000 monks and nuns. Even though this persecution was short-lived, the monasteries suffered a serious economic and cultural blow from which they never completely recovered.

From Tang to the Present

The persecution of 845 C.E. took away much of the institutional independence of Chinese Buddhism. Subsequently, Buddhism became more a part of than an exotic addition to Chinese culture.

Pure Land Buddhism, with its emphasis on recitation of the name of Amitābha Buddha, a practice that could be carried out in the midst of one's daily work, became popular with the laity. In the monasteries, recitation of the name of Amitābha Buddha was combined with formal periods of Chan (Zen) sitting. Between 1280 and 1368, the Mongols brought in a Tibetan form of Vajrayāna. Chinese Buddhism as we find it today is a combination of Pure Land and Chan practice on a theoretical base of the more technical schools that flourished until the Tang, with occasional Vajrayāna elements.

Philosophically, Buddhist doctrines and practices were incorporated into Neo-Confucianism. Practically, the Chinese tended to turn to the Buddhists for funeral ceremonies.

During the Communist revolution of Mao Zedong, Buddhism, along with Confucianism and Daoism, underwent a further major persecution, but there is evidence that it is again recovering (Chapter 12).

KOREA AND VIETNAM

East Asian studies in the Western academic establishment have concentrated on China and Japan and have neglected Korea and Vietnam. Some Western scholars are now working with Korean materials, and we are beginning to glimpse the rich contributions of Koreans to the history of Buddhism. Vietnamese Buddhism still remains largely unstudied.

It is traditionally held that Buddhism was introduced to Korea by the Chinese monk Shun-dao in 372 C.E. On the basis of Chinese forms, Koreans developed five native lineages, of which the most important was the Dharma Essence *(Popsong)*, founded by Wonhyo (617–686). This was the first attempt to unify all teachings in one lineage, a characteristic feature of Korean Buddhism. Chinul (1158–1210), whose work has just become available in English, showed how the wordlessness of *Sŏn* (Zen) could be seen as compatible with the wordiness of intensive study.[5] In 1916, Venerable Sotaesan founded Won Buddhism, which, under the slogan "Develop our spiritual morality while the material civilization is being developed," preaches a universalist message uniting all religions, and all Buddhist lineages, in the naturally enlightened mind, symbolized by an empty circle.

Vietnam received Theravāda, apparently via the sea route, about the first century C.E. and various forms of Mahāyāna by land from China between the sixth and seventeenth centuries. It produced its own version of Zen (called *Thiền*) and, as in China and Korea, blended it with Pure Land practice. All lineages were combined into the Unified Buddhist Church of Vietnam in 1963. Buddhism has played an important part in various Vietnamese patriotic uprisings, and, during the so-called Vietnam War, was highlighted by the international press for its resistance to the United States.

JAPAN

The first known introduction of Buddhism into Japan took place in the mid-sixth century, when Buddhist images and scriptures were brought by a diplomatic mission from Korea. The new religion quickly gained support, and within a few decades the prince regent, Shōtoku Taishi (574–622), became a Buddhist and chose to model his ideal centralized government after the pattern of China's Buddhist-oriented Sui and Tang dynasties. Seeing China as the source of both high civilization and true Buddhism, Japanese monks made pilgrimages to the continent and, on their return, established Japanese lineages. Two of the most famous of these pilgrims were Saichō (762–822) and Kūkai (774–835).

Saichō established the Tendai lineage on Mount Hiei, just to the northeast of Kyōto. The temples on Mount Hiei multiplied and grew in strength to become a kind of monastic fortress overlooking what was then the capital of Japan. The government, feeling threatened, sent forces against it in 1570 and reduced its approximately 3,000 temples to 125. From the religious standpoint, Tendai, as a compendious lineage encompassing, as it claimed, all of the teachings of the Buddha, both Hīnayāna and Mahāyāna, became the seedbed for later lineages. During the Kamakura period, as imperial power waned in favor of the military junta, it began to break up. The most important progeny of Tendai were Japanese forms of Chan (Zen) and Pure Land Buddhism and a native lineage called the Lotus Lineage *(Hokke-shū)*.

Japan, unlike China, Korea, and Vietnam, made, as much as it could, a firm institutional distinction not only between Zen and Pure Land Buddhism but also among the many sublineages that developed on the archipelago.[6] It counts at least two major forms of Zen and two of Pure Land. Rinzai Zen, established by Eisai (1141–1215), is a vigorous form emphasizing alarming techniques such as shouting and beating and the posing of apparently impossible riddles *(kōan)* to awaken the student's innate Buddha mind. Sōtō Zen, which is more popular with the common people, is a quieter form relying on "just sitting" *(shikandaza)* until the student's Buddha mind manifests itself. The Pure Land Buddhism of Hōnen (1133–1212), known as Jōdo-shū ("Pure Land Lineage"), recommends the recitation of the name of Amitābha Buddha as often as possible in order to draw his wisdom and compassion into the defiled mind of the believer. The reform of his disciple Shinran (1173–1262), known as Jōdo Shinshū ("True Pure Land Lineage"), became the dominant form of Buddhism in Japan. Jōdo Shinshū simply surrenders to the power of Amitābha, which it finds already present and operative in the believer's mind.

The Lotus Lineage was founded by Nichiren (1222–1282), an extraordinarily outspoken Tendai monk who claimed that only his form of Buddhism was the true one. Indeed, followers held, it alone could save Japan from the invasion that the Mongols were then planning. Nichiren was condemned to die, but, it is said, just as the executioner raised his sword, there was a bolt of lightning, and his sentence was commuted to exile.

Kūkai returned from China with the plans of two great maṇḍalas from two different streams of Chinese Vajrayāna, from which he innovatively formed the distinctively Japanese Vajrayāna lineage known as Shingon-shū ("Mantra Lineage"). The mysterious rituals of Shingon, known as *mikkyō*, "esoteric teaching," appealed to the heart of Japan in a way that Tendai did not, for they resonated with the indigenous cult of the mountain shaman or *hijiri*, with which Kūkai became identified.* Kūkai attempted to unify the Sinified city

*Elements of *mikkyō* are also found in Tendai, but they are not so prominent.

culture with the native Japanese rural culture by establishing both Tōji, a city temple near Kyōto, and Kongōbuji, a somewhat inaccessible country temple on Mount Kōya. He also used his two maṇḍalas to develop a synthesis of Shintō and Buddhism and is traditionally credited with developing the Japanese syllabic writing system *(kana)* to ensure the proper pronunciation of the Shingon mantras. Mount Kōya became an important national cemetery, with the graves of Japanese notables lining the path leading to Kūkai's resting place, where, legend says, he is not dead but resting in deep samādhi from which, at the proper time, he will arise to lead the people.

During the Tokugawa period (1603–1867) the government kept all religions under tight control, and Buddhism was largely reduced to the status of a funerary cult, from which it has had difficulty recovering. Much of the religious power in present-day Japan is in the hands of the newer sects, primarily reformed versions of Shintō.

BUDDHIST TRENDS IN EAST ASIA

Throughout its long and eventful history in East Asia, Buddhism remained remarkably faithful to its Indian and central Asian origins. At the same time, however, Chinese, Vietnamese, Korean, and Japanese Buddhists made important selections, adaptations, and additions. When compared to other Buddhists, such as in Sri Lanka, the Buddhists of East Asia tended to emphasize the unity between the ultimate and the relative. Affirming the sacredness of this-worldly phenomena, their religious practices were designed to lead to a realization of this unity of the religious and the secular and to a positive view of the religious value of the natural world. At the level of community life, they tended to develop patterns of organization that reduced the differentiation between the Saṅgha and the laity.

New Roles for Buddhas and Bodhisattvas

The full range of Buddhas and bodhisattvas of India and central Asia was gradually introduced into East Asia, although inevitable changes gave the pantheon an East Asian cast. For example, in China, where bureaucratic modes of thought were pervasive, it took on a rather bureaucratic form. The various Buddhas and bodhisattvas were given East Asian mythologies and iconographies, and many indigenous deities were incorporated.

In China, the historical Śākyamuni Buddha's life story came to resemble the biographies of the traditional Chinese sages, and social virtues such as filial piety were emphasized. Popular stories connected many of the great Buddhas and bodhisattvas with life in China. In addition, various Buddhas and bodhisattvas were associated with Chinese pilgrimage sites and were endowed with many attributes and functions borrowed from native deities.

In Japan, the process of adaptation was carried on by identifying the Buddhas and bodhisattvas with indigenous deities and spirits known as *kami.* For example, the Shingon sect identified the Buddha Vairocana with the greatest of the Shintō kami, the sun goddess. Other Buddhas and bodhisattvas were identified with kami associated with various sacred locales.

In East Asia, Śākyamuni retained an important and often central position and continued to be a major focus of interest and veneration in many of the indigenous schools such as Tiantai (Tendai), Chan (Zen), and Nichiren. But in other East Asian traditions, Śākyamuni was almost totally eclipsed. In the Pure Land sects, Amitābha Buddha was the principal figure, and in the East Asian Vajrayāna tradition, Vairocana—though a far less compelling and less popular figure than Amitābha—was recognized as the primal manifestation of the enlightened mind.

There were also changes in the character of the great bodhisattvas. During the early period of Buddhist development in East Asia, Maitreya, for example, was the central figure in one of the major traditions. Over time he gradually lost his role as a focus of Buddhist practice, but he assumed two other quite different identities. In one strand of the tradition, he retained his identification as the future Buddha and became a central figure in a series of revolutionary peasant rebellions.

The second transformation of Maitreya was less important but more surprising. At a certain point in the history of Chinese Buddhism, Maitreya was in certain circles identified with an eccentric tenth-century Chinese monk named Budai and subsequently came to be represented as a potbellied, innocuous figure known as the "laughing Buddha." In this form he became one of the most ubiquitous figures in the popular pantheon of East Asian Buddhas and bodhisattvas. His image, situated at the entrance of Chinese monasteries, is revered primarily by laypersons seeking health, wealth, and happiness.

Another example of the process of adaptation is the transformation of the bodhisattva Avalokiteśvara. In India and central Asia, this great exemplar of compassion had typically been a male bodhisattva and remained so during the early phases of Chinese Buddhist history. But by the second millennium, Avalokiteśvara was commonly portrayed as a female figure resembling an ancient Daoist deity known as the Queen of Heaven. In this new form, Avalokiteśvara (in China, Guanyin, and in Japan, Kannon) became an extremely popular deity who was especially revered as the patroness of women and of childbirth.

Dharma: The Great Synthetic Schools

During the centuries when East Asians were first appropriating Buddhism, they established direct counterparts of various Indian schools. Thus the Conservative tradition was represented by several Chinese and Japanese schools that were the direct descendants of their Indian and central Asian predecessors. The Mādhyamika tradition was also represented by Chinese and Japanese schools, as was (at a much later date) the Yogācāra tradition. The Buddhists in East Asia, however, soon began to create different and more influential Mahāyāna and Vajrayāna schools that were distinctively their own. These new schools can be divided into two groups: the first consisted of those with more universalist or "catholic" orientations, namely, Tiantai (in Japan, Tendai), Huayan (Kegon), and the esoteric school known as Chenyan in China and Shingon in Japan. The second group, Mahāyāna schools with a more elitist or focused perspective, included the Chan (in Japan, Zen) school, various Pure Land groups, and the uniquely Japanese Nichiren sect. Each of the three universalist schools of Buddhism in East Asia had its own way of classifying the vast corpus of Buddhist texts and doctrines, as well as its own way of interpreting the Dharma.

Tiantai/Tendai The Tiantai system, formulated during the sixth century, classified the various strands of the tradition according to five different phases in Śākyamuni Buddha's ministry. During the first, it said, the Buddha preached the Avataṃsaka Sūtra, a long text presenting a variety of sophisticated Mahāyāna stories and doctrines. When the Buddha realized that this sūtra was too profound and complex for his uninitiated hearers to understand, he devoted the next three phases of his ministry to preaching sermons with a simpler, more straightforward content. These included such collections as the Conservatives' *Piṭakas* and the Mahāyānists' *Great Perfection of Wisdom.* Finally, they said, the Buddha revealed the ultimate truth by preaching the Lotus Sūtra. Evaluating the phenomenal world highly, the Tiantai taught that all beings have an inherent Buddha nature that could be brought out through Buddhist practices. Tiantai exerted a major influence on most later East Asian Buddhist schools.

Huayan/Kegon The Huayan school, which remained a philosophy and never developed into a practiced lineage, originated in the sixth century. According to the Huayan teachers, the Huayan (Avataṃsaka) Sūtra rather than the Lotus Sūtra provided the fullest and most complete expression of the Buddhist Dharma. In regard to doctrine, the Huayan teachers extended the Tiantai teaching on the identity of the absolute Buddha nature with each phenomenon by emphasizing the complete harmony and interpenetration among the phenomena themselves. Thus they also affirmed a positive understanding of reality that had a great appeal to the this-worldly sensibilities of the Chinese. This emphasis on the interconnectedness of all aspects of reality was also used by rulers as a way of reaffirming the need to maintain a stable, unified, and harmonious state.

Chenyan/Shingon The Vajrayāna (*Chenyan* in China, *Shingon* in Japan) was brought to China in the eighth century by a series of famous Indian missionaries. Initially a failure in Japan, it succeeded there when reintroduced by Kūkai. Shingon is most distinctive for its modes of iconographic representation, visualization, and ritual practices. The East Asian Vajrayāna schools shared with their Indian and Tibetan counterparts a strong emphasis on symbolic representation both to express the nature of reality and to aid in religious practices. Shingon used two maṇḍalas, one to represent the indestructible, immutable aspect of the enlightened mind and the other to reflect its dynamic manifestation in and through all phenomena. By properly meditating on these two maṇḍalas, the practitioner can realize nonduality.

Dharma: Other East Asian Schools

Despite the great contributions of the comprehensive Tiantai, Huayan, and Chenyan schools, they did not remain the dominant Buddhist traditions in East Asia. The most popular schools to develop were those of Chan (Zen) and Pure Land, both of which had a more focused perspective.

Chan/Zen According to legend, the **Chan** school was established in China by a famous Indian missionary named Bodhidharma (c. 500) who popularized the practice of formless—neither visualizing nor intellectualizing—meditation. The Chinese Chan masters concentrated on evoking a direct insight into the **Buddha nature**. This Buddha nature was identified with the true self, cleansed of all attachments and distortions, and with the natural world, which was thought to exhibit the Buddha nature in a pure and unspoiled way. This is stated in the Sūtra of Hui Neng:

> Within our Essence of Mind these Trikaya [three bodies] of the Buddha are to be found, and they are common to everybody. Because the mind [of an ordinary man] labours under delusions, he knows not his own inner nature. . . . But should we be fortunate enough to find learned and pious teachers to make known to us the Orthodox Dharma, then we may with our own efforts do away with ignorance and delusion, so that we are enlightened both within and without, and the [true nature] of all things manifests itself within our Essence of Mind.[7]

Many Chan masters went so far as to challenge the usefulness of scriptures, images, and other elements traditionally associated with Buddhist belief and practice.

The "sudden enlightenment" school, known as Linji in China and Rinzai in Japan, emphasized the discipline of grappling with enigmatic riddles (in Chinese, *gongan;* in Japanese, *kōan*). The more popular "gradual enlightenment" school, known as Caodong in China and Sōtō in Japan, emphasized the practice of meditational sitting devoid of any object or goal. One simply recognized that since one was already Buddha, there was nothing else to be done.

The Chan/Zen tradition also placed a positive value on manual work, the cultivation of the arts (for example, gardening, painting, and the tea ceremony), and the practice of military skills.

Pure Land The other focused perspective, the Pure Land schools that developed in China, traced their lineage to patriarchs of the fifth and sixth centuries. According to the Pure Land tradition, the process began when Huiyuan (334–416) introduced a visualization and devotional practice centering on the Buddha Amitābha and promising rebirth in his realm, the Pure Land. Then, during the first half of the sixth century, Tanluan (476–542)—who had reportedly received the Pure Land Sūtras directly from an Indian missionary—succeeded in establishing a full-fledged Pure Land school. In Japan, in the twelfth and thirteenth centuries, related but distinctively new Pure Land sects were formed out of the Tendai and Shingon schools that had for several centuries dominated the Japanese Buddhist scene.

Proponents of the Pure Land tradition maintained that the world was in a state of decline and that the epoch in which they lived was thoroughly degenerate. In this situation, easier methods of salvation were needed. These easier methods involved a dependence on the "other power" of the Buddha Amitābha (in Japan, Amida) together with the very simplest form of practice, the repetition of Amitābha's name, a practice called *nienfo* in Chinese and *nembutsu* in Japanese. In the Japanese Jōdo Shinshū (True Pure Land) school founded by Shinran, the emphasis on faith in Amida and his grace became so exclusive that even the usefulness of such recitation was called into question. In many East Asian Pure Land traditions, the older Buddhist goal of attaining nirvāṇa was completely replaced: Pure Land adherents now sought rebirth in a heavenly paradise.

Nichiren Although the Nichiren school had much in common with the Japanese Pure Land groups, it displayed a character all its own. Nichiren adherents shared much of Nichiren's own militantly prophetic spirit and followed his lead in accepting the authority of the Lotus Sūtra. Along with religious devotion, they advocated the recitation of a sacred formula, *Namu myō hō renge kyō* ("Hail to the Sūtra of the Lotus of the True Dharma"), which was believed to be more reliable than the repetition of Amida's name. Their goal, however, was not limited to rebirth in a heavenly paradise; it included the purification of the Japanese nation and the establishment of Japan itself as a "land of the Buddha."

Saṅgha: Patterns of Communal Life

Like Buddhism in southern, southeastern, and central Asia, Buddhism in East Asia maintained the ancient forest monk traditions associated with itinerant wandering and radical forms of asceticism. In China, for example, an imported notion of the great saints, which had been developed in some Indian Buddhist contexts, soon became associated with indigenous traditions of the hermit's life and ascetic discipline. Thus there developed in Chinese Buddhism an ideal of Buddhist *lohans* or saints, who were similar in many respects to the important *xian* (immortals) of popular Daoism.

In Japan, there were two different types of Buddhist forest monks. The first type were sophisticated monastics who gave up settled Saṅgha life to wander the countryside. Many of these highly cultured wanderers quite self-consciously practiced a distinctively Japanese "way of poetry," composing marvelous poems that expressed a distinctively Japanese Buddhist view of the beauty and sacredness of the natural world. The second type is represented by the *yamabushi* (mountain ascetics) and other miracle workers who were associated with the more shamanic aspects of the indigenous kami tradition.

Early patterns of East Asian mainstream monastic life remained similar to the Indian model. But as Buddhist monasticism interacted with its new environment, several changes were made. The community soon began to revise its heritage in a way more in line with the historical and biographical modes of thinking characteristic of East Asia. During the fourth and fifth centuries, Indian and central Asian sources were used to reconstruct the history of the transmission of the Dharma in India to the first Chinese patriarch. During the Song period in China, Tiantai monks produced a treatise listing nine of its early patriarchs, and the Chan community produced its own genealogical literature, including the famous *Records of the Transmission of the Lamp*.

The Saṅgha gradually adapted itself to China's emphasis on the primacy of family and state. Buddhists justified the monks' and nuns' vocations primarily in terms of their contribution to the moral and social order, as well as the merit they accumulated for their parents and ancestors. Institutionally, the Saṅgha was made subordinate to state authority, both symbolically and in fact. Generally speaking, the monks accepted state control over such matters as the ordination, registration, and unfrocking of members of the Saṅgha. In Japan, the Chinese tradition of state control was quickly adopted by the authorities. By Tokugawa times, the Japanese shōguns had thoroughly subordinated the ecclesiastical structure to the purposes of state.

A different kind of East Asian Saṅgha adaptation involved relaxing the prohibitions against "mundane" activities. In the Chan/Zen tradition, for example, the rule against performing manual or agricultural work was rejected, and Zen monastics were required to earn their living by tilling the soil (hence the Zen maxim, "One day no work, one day no food"). Certain proponents of this requirement went even further by maintaining that such work, if performed with proper intent, could help one to attain enlightenment.

The Vinaya rule of celibacy for monks was also relaxed in Japan. A major turning point came in the thirteenth century when Shinran, founder of the Jōdo Shinshū sect, popularized the practice of clerical marriage. Along with the customs concerning inheritance that it fostered, a married clergy soon came to be accepted not only in Shinran's lineage but in other groups as well. Thus many Japanese Buddhist temples became family-dominated institutions that were passed on from one generation to the next.

Saṅgha: The Laity

In East Asia, as elsewhere in the Buddhist world, the laity has always played a significant role in the Buddhist community. As early as the fifth century, many East Asian rulers assumed the roles of the great Buddhas and bodhisattvas. At about the same time, lay members of the Chinese aristocracy in southern China developed a lay-oriented form of "gentry Buddhism" that placed a special emphasis on the Vimalakirti Sūtra, in which the protagonist is a lay bodhisattva. In Japan, the samurai (warrior) caste generated its own forms of lay practice associated with intense self-discipline and cultivation of the martial arts. In each particular East Asian area, laypersons of social rank from king to peasant provided support for the monastic community and adapted traditional Buddhist teachings and practices to their own local needs and concerns.

Later, the increasingly worldly orientation of the

Part of a mural painting in the 1,300-year-old Potala Palace in Lhasa, Tibet, is seen here. The palace was the residence of the Dalai Lama until his exile under the Communist Chinese conquest of Tibet. (Eastfoto)

Saṅgha (along with its submission to state control) was countered by the appearance of new, predominantly lay organizations and movements. In China in the seventeenth and eighteenth centuries, many Buddhist lay people formed organizations that were committed to the serious practice of basic Buddhist morality and meditation. In Japan, a number of laypersons formed anticlerical groups and assumed responsibility for their own initiations, communal rites, and programs of religious instruction. During the final centuries of the premodern period in East Asia, these lay movements enlivened Buddhist traditions that were otherwise rather stagnant and uncreative.

Buddhism in Tibet

Though Buddhism had been established from the early centuries of the Common Era in various areas around the high and remote Himalayan region of Tibet, it did not actually penetrate into the Tibetan plateau until the seventh or eighth century. Once Buddhism was entrenched in this harsh and rather desolate environment, it was adapted to its new context, and a distinctive form gradually took shape. Tibetan Buddhism was the direct successor of the Vajrayāna tradition that developed in the Indian subcontinent during the Pāla period (750–c. 1200). But Tibetan Buddhism has also, throughout its history, been profoundly influenced by the particularities and dynamics of Tibetan culture, politics, and religion.

This Tibetan tradition, with its esoteric teachings, its rich iconography, its complex and colorful liturgies, its shamanic and exorcistic practices, and its highly accomplished and venerated leaders called **lamas** (gurus), has held great fascination for westerners, both scholars and spiritual seekers. Other Western observers, however, particularly those better acquainted with Theravāda Buddhism, have sometimes been shocked by the strong emphasis that the tradition has placed on esoteric rituals that are reputed to employ sexual techniques, seemingly mechanistic ritual performances, and magic. Still others have been put off by the extensive political and economic involvement of the lamas in a theocratically organized feudalistic society. The distinctiveness of Tibetan Buddhism, however, is due mainly to the pervasive presence of

Vajrayāna elements, with which these observers were unfamiliar.

THE ESTABLISHMENT OF BUDDHISM IN TIBET

The history of Buddhism in Tibet is sometimes divided into three periods—the establishment of Buddhism in Tibet, its reestablishment after persecution, and the period of the dominance of the Dalai Lamas.

In the first period, King Songtsengempo (c. 620–649) established a central government and is credited with introducing Buddhism through two wives, one from Nepal and the other from China. This report, whose historicity is in doubt, symbolizes that Tibetan Buddhism, like Tibetan culture, is at the meeting point of Indian and Chinese influences, although at the so-called Lhasa Debate (c. 792—its historicity is also disputed), Tibetans decided to emphasize Indian forms of Buddhism over Chinese. During the reign of Songtsengempo a Tibetan script, adapted from an Indian model, was invented, and a form of literary Tibetan was developed specifically for the translation of Buddhist texts.

The first effective missionary was Padmasambhava, who arrived around 779. His life is surrounded by mystery and enlivened by miracles. He is said to have converted Tibet by first converting the local deities: arriving in a village, he would challenge the deity to a contest in magic. The deity would do its best, but Padmasambhava would do better. The deity would submit to Padmasambhava and be appointed a "protector of Buddhism." The human inhabitants of the village would then follow their deity's example and take refuge in the Three Jewels. Padmasambhava's school of Buddhism is known as Nyingmapa ("Ancient Ones") and has a heavy emphasis on Vajrayāna, which it sees as divided into three outer and three inner Tāntras.

About 836, King Langdarma succeeded to the throne and began a vigorous suppression of Buddhism. He was assassinated in 842 by a man wearing a black cloak and riding a black horse. His black cloak, however, had a white lining, and the horse was actually white but painted with a dye that washed off in water. Riding his horse through a river and then reversing his cloak, the assassin made good his escape.

THE REESTABLISHMENT OF BUDDHISM

For some time there was no central authority in Tibet, but Buddhism made a slow comeback. Rinchen Zangbo (958–1055) began a retranslation of the Buddhist texts, initiating what came to be known collectively as the Sarma ("New") translation schools, in contrast to the Nyingma ("Old") translation schools.

Atīśa (982–1054) came to Tibet from India in 1042 and founded the Kadampa, a school that is respected by all the Sarma lineages, especially for its practical advice,[8] as in the Seven Points of Mind Training, teaching how the ups and downs of everyday life can be regarded as aids on the path to enlightenment.

Marpa (1012–1096), a married man known as the Translator, is credited with the founding of the Kagyupa school. His most famous pupil was Milarepa (1040–1123), who gave his teaching in songs that are known and loved by Tibetans of all lineages.

The Sakyapa school was founded by Könchog Gyelbo (1034–1102). It has a distinctive teaching on the unity of the sūtra (exoteric) and Tāntra (esoteric) practices, which it calls Path and Fruit, respectively. In the thirteenth century, after Tibet submitted to Chingiz Khan but had managed to convert Kublai Khan to Buddhism, Sakyapa lamas became advisers to the court of the Great Khan and were established as rulers of Tibet.

THE GELUKPA REFORM

Dzongaba (1357–1419) was deeply concerned at what he regarded as the corruption of Buddhism in Tibet in his day. A man of prodigious learning, he fearlessly challenged the greatest teachers to public debates and soundly defeated them. His reform, known as the Gelukpa ("Virtuous Ones") school,* restored the tradition of monastic celibacy and attempted a comprehensive presentation of all the Sarma schools. In the spirit of their founder, the Gelukpa emphasize learning and debate as means to enlightenment. Monastic

*During certain rituals, Gelukpa monks wear large, gold-colored headgear. This so impressed early Western observers that they dubbed the monks "Yellow Hats." This unhelpful term is still occasionally used.

debate sometimes lasts far into the night and is cheered and jeered like a sport.

In 1578, Altan Khan bestowed the title of Dalai Lama (Mongolian for "Great Ocean" and understood to imply great wisdom) on the Gelukpa teacher Sönam Gyatso. He was subsequently identified as the *third* Dalai Lama, and, until the Chinese invasion in 1950, the Dalai Lamas, regarded as rebirths of themselves, were the effective political rulers of Tibet; their Gelukpa order became the dominant, and sometimes the only authorized, Buddhist teaching.

RELIGIOUS TRENDS

From Tibetan Buddhism's earliest stages, the Vajrayāna tradition was the most distinctive formative influence. However, the Tibetans—and later the Mongols—gradually created their own version of this tradition, their own way of understanding and expressing the Dharma, and their own patterns of religious authority and social organization.

Buddhas and Bodhisattvas

Tibetan Buddhism shares with Theravāda a reverence for the importance of Śākyamuni as the historical Buddha, but as a Mahāyāna tradition it expands its focus to include other Buddhas and bodhisattvas in other world systems.

Dividing the Dharma into three levels of teaching, it recognizes three different manifestations of Buddhas and bodhisattvas—human forms for the elementary or Hīnayāna teaching, divine forms for the intermediate or Mahāyāna teaching, and transdivine or ultimate forms for the Vajrayāna teaching. The Buddhas and bodhisattvas manifest themselves at the lower levels as peaceful entities and at the higher levels as fierce entities whose pure, egoless energy compassionately destroys all obstacles to enlightenment.

In addition, at the Vajrayāna level, refuge is taken in many nonhuman, spiritual guides such as the protectors and female ministers. The most popular objects of worship are Jenrayzee, the Tibetan form of Avalokiteśvara (who, in contrast to the Far East, appears in Tibet only as a male), and Tārā, a motherly manifestation of the compassionate mind, who is said to have taken a vow to become a Buddha without (as is the rule) being reborn as a male.

The Dharma

Tibetan Buddhism divides the Dharma into three levels or "vehicles" (*yāna*).* The Hīnayāna is the path of negation (no harm) and self-improvement, the Mahāyāna is the positive path of compassion and assistance extended to all sentient beings, and the Vajrayāna cuts off ordinary appearance (the delusion of saṃsāra).

These vehicles are to be practiced in order, and it is a distinctive feature of the Tibetan Dharma that it has a "graded path" of a set sequence of courses, inherited from the great Indian Buddhist universities. Only after having attained some internal peace (through the practice of Hīnayāna) can we help others (through the practice of Mahāyāna) without projecting our problems onto them. But only when altruistic action has become second nature are we ready to practice the Vajrayāna, in which we live no longer in saṃsāra but in the reality of Buddha consciousness.

Tibetans translated and assembled their own collection of scriptures, dividing the hundreds of volumes broadly into two groups—the Kanjur, or "Translation of the Buddha Word," and the Tenjur, or "Translation of the Teachings," or commentaries.

The Saṅgha and Society: Continuity and Enrichment

The Vajrayāna tradition in Tibet was characterized by a tension between its more restrained and more uninhibited forms. The more restrained practice was represented by the Kadampa and the later Gelukpa schools, which recognized the importance of the Vinaya and the sūtras as well as the Tāntras. Schools advocating the more uninhibited approach focused on oral traditions and the Tāntric manuals. These schools tended to be more lax in their enforcement of the monastic rules, particularly those prohibiting marriage and the consumption of alcoholic beverages, and also to be more skeptical of the value of intellectual pursuits. In some cases they encouraged extreme forms of ascetic activity.

Despite the schools' differing degrees of conservatism, the various segments of Tibetan Buddhism all drew on native traditions to acquire both worldly and

*The Nyingmapa teaches nine vehicles, by subdividing the Hīnayāna into two and the Vajrayāna into six.

mundane powers. These contributed to the advancement of beliefs concerning human consciousness and of rituals designed to promote healing in this life or a better rebirth in the next.

Although not a Buddhist text per se, the Tibetan *Book of the Dead,* which claimed to be a guide through the various states and opportunities encountered between death and rebirth, was probably recited in this kind of ritual context. In addition, dramatic and colorful rituals accompanied both traditional monastic practices and community liturgies and festivals.

One form of indigenous belief recognized the existence of demons who were capable of invading individuals. To expel these demons, the monks performed elaborate rituals, involving the chanting of Buddhist mantras and texts, the performance of often comic dramas, and the ritual feeding and expulsion of the invading demons. These were public events for an entire village. The demons can be regarded as having either an objective or a subjective existence, depending on the level of the Buddhist teaching. Thus their ritual exorcism can be considered a form of meditation.

AUTHORITY IN THE TIBETAN TRADITION

The affinity between Indian and Tibetan Buddhism is apparent in matters of community life. The forest monk tradition was continued by wanderers and hermits who maintained and extended the typically Vajrayāna emphasis on extreme and often idiosyncratic forms of religious asceticism. These wanderers and hermits were in many cases renowned practitioners of various forms of black and white magic; as a result, they were both highly respected and greatly feared.

Tibetan Buddhist monasteries often operated as universities, like their Indian counterparts, maintaining high standards of intellectual life and carrying on the great traditions of study and debate. Within their massive walls, the Indian arts and sciences were cultivated and transmitted. In addition, small monasteries dotted the country, many functioning as local temples.

Over time, Tibetans generated their own distinctive patterns of leadership. The most obvious example was the emergence of the lama as a primary locus of religious prestige and authority. *Lama* is a translation of the Sanskrit word *guru* and is used in Tibet to refer to one's spiritual teacher. Only certain teachers are called lamas, and they may be lay people or monastics of either sex.* The new emphasis on the lama can be seen in the Tibetan formula of refuge:

> *I take refuge in the lama.*
> *I take refuge in the Buddhas.*
> *I take refuge in the Dharma.*
> *I take refuge in the Saṅgha.*

Although the lama is added as a fourth *phrase* to the Triple Refuge, he or she is not a fourth *refuge* but rather the human being who is believed to manifest the Triple Jewel most clearly. A lama is chosen with great care. Only after extensive testing of a person whom one thinks might possibly be one's lama is the commitment made.

As the office of lama became the typically Tibetan institution concerned with personal guidance, so the *tulku* became associated with public authority. *Tulku* is Tibetan for *Nirmāṇa-kāya,* the human manifestation of a Buddha, within the system of the three bodies of a Buddha or bodhisattva. Although belief in rebirth is common to all Buddhist traditions, Tibetan Buddhism is the only form that regularly identifies particular persons as tulkus of particular Buddhas or bodhisattvas.

The institution of the tulku was emphasized by the Gelukpas after they rose to power. Since they maintained celibacy, they could not follow the custom of passing on high office from parent to child. So they developed the teaching that certain important persons succeed themselves, so to speak. After a tulku dies, his or her rebirth is sought according to strict and elaborate rules, and after thorough testing, the rebirth is recognized and reinstated.[9] Many tulkus, such as the Dalai Lama (regarded as a manifestation of Jenrayzee), the tulku who is most widely known, have held and continue to hold considerable political power.

BUDDHISM IN THE MODERN ERA

During the nineteenth and twentieth centuries, Buddhists of every tradition and geographic region have

*Early Western observers incorrectly coined the misleading word *Lamaism* to refer to Tibetan Buddhism.

faced unprecedented challenges and opportunities. At the ideological level, they have confronted powerful intrusive forces, such as Christianity, Western rationalism, scientific and industrial technology, democracy, and communism. At the institutional level, they have had to deal with political and economic domination by Western powers that had little understanding of or sympathy for Buddhism. They have had to endure the disruption of the traditional social and economic patterns in which Buddhism had played a role. In addition, Asian Buddhists have had to cope with local movements committed to limiting or even eliminating Buddhist influence.

The Buddhist response has varied from conservative resistance to reform to bold new initiatives, and the results have varied. In some areas the tradition has been severely disrupted; in others it has been maintained with differing degrees of vitality; and in some parts of the world new Buddhist communities have become established.

REFORM MOVEMENTS

Attempts to maintain and revitalize Buddhism in this age of rapid change have brought important innovations. Buddhists who were influenced by modern modes of thought and social forces began to devise new ways of appropriating and presenting the tradition. They introduced new interpretations of the Buddha, new ways of understanding his teachings, and new approaches to the life and organization of the Buddhist community.

Buddha

Modern reformers' interpretations of the Buddha have underscored his humanity and the rationality of his approach to the problem of human suffering. They have written new biographies removing the most problematic features of the traditional accounts. Some of these biographies have presented him as a social reformer carrying on a crusade against the Hindu caste system; others have emphasized his achievements as a master of meditation and his role as spiritual therapist; still others responded to modern needs by presenting him as the teacher of a rationally grounded ethic.

Dharma

New interpretations of Buddhist teaching have been made in sophisticated philosophical terms and in a more popular vein as well. Many Buddhists have related Buddhist thought to Christianity, to Western philosophical perspectives, and to scientific modes of thinking. In Japan, this has been done for two centuries by sophisticated scholars, especially those of the so-called Kyoto School of philosophy. Strong Buddhist apologists have begun to appear in the past century in the Theravāda countries as well: in Sri Lanka, for example, Gunapala Dhammasiri has mounted a very sharp and pointed Buddhist polemic against Christianity, and in Thailand, Bhikkhu Buddhadasa has formulated an equally sophisticated but more conciliatory approach.

At the same time, many have stressed the relevance of Buddhist teachings for social and ethical issues, highlighting distinctively Buddhist traditions of social responsibility. Some Buddhist apologists have maintained that Buddhism can be the basis for a truly democratic society; some have contended that Buddhism and Marxism can be creatively synthesized; and some have insisted that Buddhism, as a nontheistic religion, can provide a foundation for world peace. In the 1930s, a Buddhist message of social activism was strongly set forth by a famous Chinese Buddhist reformer, Abbott Taixu. In more recent times, a similar message has been dramatically promulgated by Thich Nhat Hanh, a Vietnamese monk who emerged as an internationally known Buddhist leader during the Vietnam War.

Saṅgha

On the community level, Buddhist reformers have tried to "purify" the monastic order and to redirect its activities to make them more relevant to modern conditions. They have tried to discourage monastic activities that have little immediate practical value while requiring an extensive investment of resources. They have introduced new kinds of education designed to train monks for nontraditional religious and social roles that they consider more relevant in the modern world. They have encouraged monks to assist in providing secular education at the popular level and to perform such social services as aiding the poor and caring for orphans. In some countries, including Thailand and Myanmar (Burma), monks have been trained to carry on missionary activities among non-Buddhists (particularly among minority ethnic groups) and to participate in government-sponsored programs of national development.

Laypersons have been encouraged to study the Buddhist scriptures and to practice forms of meditation particularly suited to their distinctive needs and situations. Lay associations have become influential in virtually every Buddhist country; they sponsor a variety of Buddhist programs, defend the cause of Buddhism in national affairs, and provide the leadership for Buddhist ecumenical movements.

The laity in various Asian countries has also supported the Mahābodhi Society, organized in the late nineteenth century to reclaim and restore the sacred sites and monuments of Buddhist India. Lay leaders took the initiative in organizing the celebrations of the 2,500-year anniversary of Buddhism held in the 1950s in various parts of the Buddhist world. Lay activity was especially prominent in Burma, where a major Buddhist council (the sixth according to the Burmese reckoning) was convened. Lay leadership was also essential to the formation, in 1952, of the World Fellowship of Buddhists, which has met every four years since then.

THE COMMUNIST CHALLENGE

Despite the remarkable continuity in Buddhist reformist trends during the modern era, the fates of various Buddhist communities have been very different. In the Communist-dominated regions of the Asian mainland, including Inner and Outer Mongolia, North Korea, China, Tibet, and Indochina, where for centuries the majority of the world's Buddhist population has been concentrated, the vitality of Buddhism has been seriously undermined. In some of the non-Communist areas, such as Sri Lanka, Southeast Asia, Taiwan, South Korea, and Japan, Buddhist communities have been able to maintain their basic integrity and continue their activity. In addition, distinctively new Buddhist communities have been established in both Asia and the Western world.

The basic pattern of Communist dealings with Buddhism has been evident since the Bolshevik takeover in Russia and the establishment of the Soviet-inspired Mongolian People's Republic in the early 1920s. The Communist governments moved as quickly as possible to replace Buddhist teachings with Communist ideology, to weaken and then eliminate the economic privileges and powers of the monasteries, and to isolate and discredit the monastic leadership. In this way they were able, within a few decades, to divest the Mongolian monastics and their followers of any real power or influence. However, with the recent breakup of the Soviet Union, Mongolian Buddhism has experienced a significant revival.

In China, the Communist rise to power came much later. It was preceded by a long period of Buddhist adjustment to Western and modern influences during which many intellectual and social reforms were attempted. However, these reforms did not succeed in breaking the close and long-standing ties between Buddhism and traditional Chinese society. When the Communists took over, Buddhism—like many other aspects of Chinese life—suffered severe setbacks. The traditional rights and privileges of the monasteries were rescinded. Large numbers of monks were defrocked and forced into materially productive occupations. The buildings were taken over and made into museums or used for government purposes, and the Buddhist associations that had been organized by the earlier reformers were unified and brought under strict government supervision.

The state-dominated Chinese Buddhist Association was founded to foster Chinese relations with Buddhist countries but was given little opportunity to advance the Buddhist cause within China itself. During the late 1950s and the early 1960s, the already weakened tradition was further undermined by the antitraditionalist campaigns mounted during the Cultural Revolution. Since the death of Mao Zedong in 1976, however, there have been increasing indications that the government is adopting a more moderate policy toward all religions, including Buddhism.

After the Chinese conquest of Tibet in 1959, Tibetan Buddhism came under an even stronger attack than the Maoist regime had mounted against Buddhism in China itself. Tibet's traditional isolation left it unprepared for the new situation. The Dalai Lama was forced to flee, along with thousands of others.

The Chinese unleashed a brutal repression, including the persecution of the monks who had remained. This policy has continued to the present time. Yet

Rare pieces of art, such as this seventeenth-century spiral silk wall decoration, have been smuggled out of Tibet by fleeing monks. The refugees have presented the pieces to the Dalai Lama in India, where they join him in exile. (UPI/Bettmann)

much evidence exists that the policies of the Chinese invaders have failed to break the Buddhist hold on the loyalty of the Tibetan people. The exiled Dalai Lama continues to command the respect of large segments of the Tibetan population and the world; he was awarded the Nobel Peace Prize in 1989 for his efforts to free his nation.

The Communist takeover in Indochina is so recent that its long-range effects are difficult to predict. At first, government policies in Vietnam, Laos, and Kampuchea (Cambodia) were similar to those employed by Communist regimes elsewhere in Asia. Buddhist teachings were disparaged, Buddhist practices were discouraged or prohibited, the privileges enjoyed by Buddhist monasteries were eliminated, and the influence of Buddhist institutions was eroded. In Kampuchea, when the Pol Pot government was in control (1975–1979), Buddhist leaders and institutions were the special objects of a persecution pursued with unprecedented violence and intensity.

In recent years, however, there has been a significant change. In Vietnam, there are signs of a small-scale Buddhist revival that is not being repressed by the government. In Kampuchea, Buddhism has made a significant comeback and is once again playing a role in many aspects of national life. And in Laos, where the repression of Buddhism was never as severe as it was in other areas of Indochina, Buddhism seems to have retained the loyalty of much of the populace and to be slowly regaining at least grudging recognition from the government.

BUDDHISM IN NON-COMMUNIST ASIA

Outside the Communist orbit, Buddhism has fared better. For example, in Sri Lanka, Myanmar (Burma), and Thailand, Theravāda Buddhists have been able to retain both a dominant religious position and a strong political and social influence. The groundwork for the continued preeminence of Buddhism in these three countries was laid during the colonial period in the late nineteenth and early twentieth centuries. At that time, an intimate bond was forged between the local Theravāda traditions and an emerging sense of national identity and destiny. In Sri Lanka and Myanmar, this bond was established in the context of resistance to British rule. In Thailand, it was cultivated by an indigenous elite engaged in a successful struggle to maintain Thai independence.

In Sri Lanka and Myanmar, the strong association between Buddhism and a militant, ethnically oriented nationalism has led to Buddhist involvement in intense and bitter conflicts with non-Buddhist minority groups. In Sri Lanka, Buddhism has become associated with the Sinhalese side in the brutal struggle between the Sinhalese majority and the Hindu (Tamil) minority. In Myanmar, Buddhism has become associated with the government side in the seemingly endless struggle between the government and the minority groups that live in the hills. In Thailand, where

Buddhism's position as a state religion has never been seriously threatened, the government and the various ethnic groups have avoided major conflicts.

The most interesting and dynamic developments have occurred in Japan. The modern period in Japan began with the Meiji Restoration (1868), which brought with it the elimination of the special privileges Buddhism had enjoyed under the Tokugawa shōgunate. State Shintō became the national religion until the Japanese defeat in World War II, when Japan became a secular state. Nevertheless, despite the loss of the special position it once held, Buddhism has remained a significant part of Japanese life. Japanese Buddhists have retained many of their ancient beliefs, practices, and patterns of communal organization; at the same time, they have adapted to the changing conditions.

During the modern period, several important Buddhist-oriented "new religions" have appeared. The most dynamic of these—for example, Reiyūkai (Association of the Friends of the Spirit), Risshō Kōsei Kai (Society for the Establishment of Righteousness and Friendly Relations), and Sōka Gakkai (Value Creation Society)—have their roots in Nichiren Buddhism and popular folk traditions. They are lay movements that focus on attaining practical goals such as health and material well-being. Appealing originally to the lower and middle classes, they have made many millions of converts and currently exert a significant influence, not only on the religious life of the country but also on its economic and political life.

EXPANSION IN INDONESIA AND INDIA

Buddhism's survival and activity in the modern world can also be seen in the distinctively new Buddhist communities that have been established in other areas of Asia, especially in Indonesia and India. In Indonesia, the Buddhist revival has been rather limited. But the revival in India represents a major development in contemporary Buddhist history.

The first stirrings of new Buddhist life in India began in the early decades of the twentieth century, when several Buddhist societies were formed by small groups of intellectuals. The members of these societies discovered in Buddhism a form of spirituality that they could reconcile with both their newly acquired rationalistic attitudes and their reformist ideals of social equality. Since the late 1950s, several communities of Tibetan refugees, including one headed by the Dalai Lama, have established an additional Buddhist presence in India.

By far the most interesting and important aspect of the Buddhist resurgence in India has been the mass conversion of members of the lowly "scheduled" castes. This has taken place primarily in Maharashtra state, of which Bombay is the capital. The conversion process was initiated in 1956 by Dr. B. K. Ambedkar, the leader of the Mahar people. Ambedkar publicly adopted Buddhism on the grounds that it was the religion best suited to the spiritual, social, and economic well-being of his followers. Initially, some 800,000 persons were involved in the new Buddhist movement, and the number of adherents has more than doubled during the past 35 years.

EXPANSION IN THE WEST

Buddhism had never seriously penetrated into the West prior to the modern period. But since the late nineteenth century, Buddhists have established a religious and social presence in practically all parts of the Western world, particularly the United States. The primary impetus for the spread of Buddhism to the West was the establishment of immigrant communities from China and Japan. These communities have continued to grow and to develop new forms of Buddhist life suitable for the Western environment. Currently, Buddhist communities composed of Asian-Americans are firmly implanted in Hawaii, California, and many other states. Some are identified with traditional schools such as Pure Land and Zen; others represent new Buddhist movements such as Risshō Kōsei Kai and Sōka Gakkai. More recently, the population of Asian-American Buddhists has been significantly expanded by the arrival of Theravāda Buddhists from Southeast Asia and of Tibetan Buddhists.

The penetration of Buddhism into the West has not been limited to immigrant communities. Beginning in the 1890s, Buddhist societies have been founded in various European countries, Australia, and the United States. The leaders of these societies have included

Buddhism in the West has not been limited to immigrant communities, but has been the object of widespread popular interest. Here worshipers gather at a Buddhist monastery in Woodstock, New York. (Maggie Hopp)

scholars of Buddhism as well as spiritual seekers drawn to the religions and philosophies of the East. More recently, Buddhism has also become the object of widespread popular interest, particularly in the so-called counterculture that flourished in the 1960s and 1970s. This interest has been stimulated and nurtured through the writings and activities of Asian missionaries such as the great Japanese scholar D. T. Suzuki, Tibetan exiles such as Tarthang Tulku, and native enthusiasts such as Philip Kapleau. Buddhist influences also appeared in the works of avant-garde literary figures of the 1950s and 1960s such as Jack Kerouac and Gary Snyder. The surge of interest in Buddhism during the 1960s and early 1970s encouraged the establishment of a network of Buddhist organizations and meditation centers across the United States, from Honolulu and San Francisco to Vermont.

BUDDHISM AND THE FUTURE

Will the Buddhist communities that stretch from southern Russia through China to Southeast Asia be able to regain their strength despite the effects of devastating attacks by Communist rulers? Will the Buddhist communities in the fringe areas of southern and eastern Asia continue to enjoy the kind of government support or toleration that they now receive? If so, will they be able to achieve the delicate balance between conservatism and reform that will be needed if they are to maintain their vigor and relevance? Will the fledgling Buddhist groups in Indonesia, India, and the West be able to sustain their dynamism and become permanently established in their new environments? Only time will tell.

NOTES

1 The mystery and romance of Dunhuang is well captured in the novel *Tun-huang* by Yasushi Inoue, translated by Jean Oda Moy (Tokyo and New York: Kodansha International, 1978), and the album *Tunhuang* by Kitaro on Canyon Records (© 1981).

2 Mary Lelia Makra, *The Hsiao Ching* (New York: St. John's University Press, 1961), p. 3.

3 *Taishō Shinshū Daizōkyō,* vol. 50, p. 470.

4 For a selection of texts defending Buddhism against Confucian

and Daoist criticisms, see Chapter 5 in William Theodore de Bary, ed., *The Buddhist Tradition in India, China, and Japan* (New York: Modern Library, 1969).

5 Robert E. Buswell, Jr., *The Korean Approach to Zen: The Collected Works of Chinul* (Honolulu: University of Hawaii Press, 1983); Robert E. Buswell, Jr., *Tracing Back the Radiance: Chinul's Korean Way of Zen* (Honolulu: University of Hawaii Press, 1992).

6 *Japanese Religion: A Survey by the Agency for Cultural Affairs* (Tokyo: Kodansha International, 1972) lists many hundreds of lineages.

7 A. F. Price and Wong Mou-Lam, trans., *The Diamond Sutra and the Sutra of Hui Neng* (Boulder, Colo.: Shambhala, 1969), pp. 54–55.

8 For a selection of this advice, along with a representative anthology of texts from the other major Tibetan Buddhist schools, see Stephen Batchelor, ed., *The Jewel in the Lotus: A Guide to the Buddhist Traditions of Tibet* (London: Wisdom Publications, 1987).

9 In accordance with the Buddhist teaching of the lack of an inherently existing self (anātman), the rebirth is neither identical with nor entirely different from the former incarnation. An intriguing account of a Spanish child who has been identified as the rebirth of a famous Tibetan tulku is Vicki MacKenzie, *The Boy Lama* (San Francisco: HarperCollins, 1988).

PART THREE

RELIGIONS OF CHINA AND JAPAN

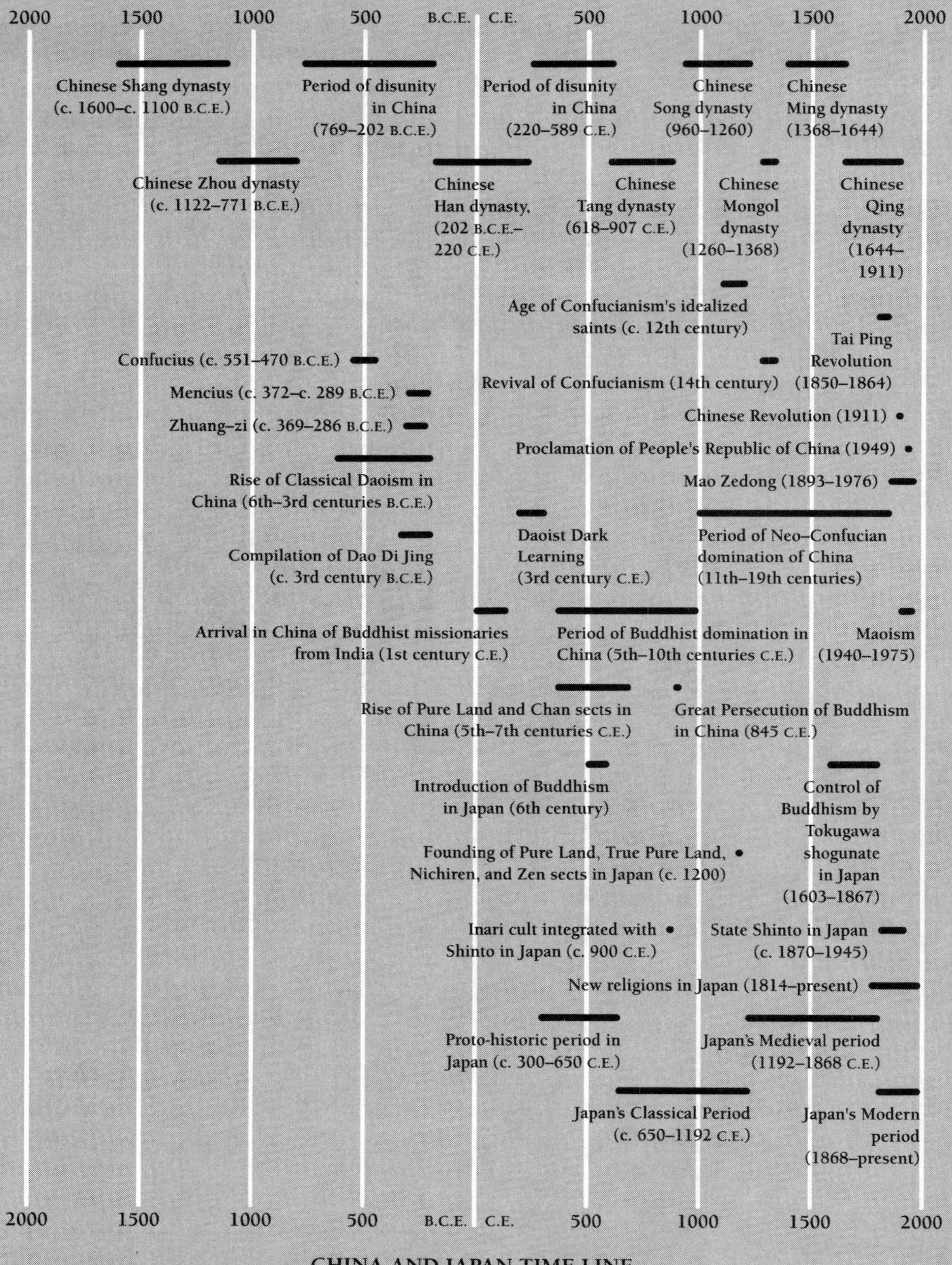
2000
1500
1000
500
B.C.E.
C.E.
500
1000
1500
2000
Chinese Shang dynasty (c. 1600–c. 1100 B.C.E.)
Period of disunity in China (769–202 B.C.E.)
Period of disunity in China (220–589 C.E.)
Chinese Song dynasty (960–1260)
Chinese Ming dynasty (1368–1644)
Chinese Zhou dynasty (c. 1122–771 B.C.E.)
Chinese Han dynasty, (202 B.C.E.–220 C.E.)
Chinese Tang dynasty (618–907 C.E.)
Chinese Mongol dynasty (1260–1368)
Chinese Qing dynasty (1644–1911)
Age of Confucianism's idealized saints (c. 12th century)
Tai Ping Revolution (1850–1864)
Confucius (c. 551–470 B.C.E.)
Revival of Confucianism (14th century)
Mencius (c. 372–c. 289 B.C.E.)
Zhuang-zi (c. 369–286 B.C.E.)
Chinese Revolution (1911)
Proclamation of People's Republic of China (1949)
Rise of Classical Daoism in China (6th–3rd centuries B.C.E.)
Mao Zedong (1893–1976)
Compilation of Dao Di Jing (c. 3rd century B.C.E.)
Daoist Dark Learning (3rd century C.E.)
Period of Neo-Confucian domination of China (11th–19th centuries)
Arrival in China of Buddhist missionaries from India (1st century C.E.)
Period of Buddhist domination in China (5th–10th centuries C.E.)
Maoism (1940–1975)
Rise of Pure Land and Chan sects in China (5th–7th centuries C.E.)
Great Persecution of Buddhism in China (845 C.E.)
Introduction of Buddhism in Japan (6th century)
Control of Buddhism by Tokugawa shogunate in Japan (1603–1867)
Founding of Pure Land, True Pure Land, Nichiren, and Zen sects in Japan (c. 1200)
Inari cult integrated with Shinto in Japan (c. 900 C.E.)
State Shinto in Japan (c. 1870–1945)
New religions in Japan (1814–present)
Proto-historic period in Japan (c. 300–650 C.E.)
Japan's Medieval period (1192–1868 C.E.)
Japan's Classical Period (c. 650–1192 C.E.)
Japan's Modern period (1868–present)
2000
1500
1000
500
B.C.E.
C.E.
500
1000
1500
2000

CHINA AND JAPAN TIME LINE

RELIGIONS OF CHINA

CHAPTER 10

ROOTS OF RELIGION IN CHINA

Chinese religions share not a common founding figure but a common geographic home. Even so, we will see a leitmotif running through all of them, for the faiths of China, perhaps more than those of any other region, have shown a profound continuity in worldview, goals, and patterns of behavior. Despite their 4,000 years of history, Chinese religions remain, at heart, one.

The leitmotiv we will see is an emphasis on harmony. In this traditional view, what is most important is not an individual person, thing, or power but rather the nature and quality of their interrelationships. These interconnections are between nature and human society. Commitment to this ideal of universal harmony has led many religious leaders to formulate methods and programs by which it can be brought about and preserved.

This is not to say that the evolution of China's religions has been without drama. On the contrary, these religions have a long and complex history, centering on the rise of two contending ways of life, Confucianism and Daoism, and interactions between them. Both had appeared by the beginning of the fourth century B.C.E. By roughly 200 B.C.E., Confucianism had become an organized entity, serving the religious needs of China's elite ruling class: adopted as the state orthodoxy, it remained so for some 400 years. At about the beginning of the Common Era, Daoism rose to the fore, appealing especially to the disenfranchised peasants and the common people; it continued to offer them hope, meaning, and solace for 2,000 years. In the second century B.C.E. Buddhism entered as a third player on the field, brought by missionaries from India by way of central Asia. A century later, when Confucianism became discredited following the collapse of its patron, the Han dynasty, both Daoism and Buddhism grew rapidly at all levels of society. After reaching their zenith of influence in the Tang dynasty (600s–800s C.E.), both Buddhism and Daoism gradually gave way to a rejuvenated Confucianism, now called Neo-Confucianism, which dominated the religious and cultural life of China until the start of the twentieth century.

But we must never forget that this drama unfolded over a background of values, attitudes, and expectations that have, over the ages, changed little. One

On Transcribing and Pronouncing Chinese

Chinese names can be rendered in English according to two systems of transliteration, pinyin and the older Wade-Giles. Because it is easier to sound out accurately, pinyin is becoming the preferred system and the one that we use in this text, but where a name is commonly known in its Wade-Giles transliteration, that spelling is given in parentheses.

Pinyin is pronounced as it looks, with the following exceptions: *ong* at the end of a word is pronounced "ung"; thus *Song,* a dynasty, rhymes with *hung*. The letter *x* is pronounced like "sh," but with the tongue placed against the front teeth. And *q* is pronounced "ch"; hence *Qin,* the dynasty from which the country's English name derives, is pronounced "chin."

metaphor used to describe China's religious tradition is that of a great tree with common roots and trunk but many branches. The root attitudes, which emphasize the harmonious interrelatedness of all things, have remained largely intact, changing slowly if at all over time; the three isms constitute the main branches, each of which has produced many twigs and flowers. We will first explore the substratum of belief that is common to Chinese religions, discerning its earliest manifestations and connections, and then explore some of the blossoming branches.

The Unity of Chinese Religions

The goal of life, according to most Chinese religions, is the establishment, maintenance, and enjoyment of harmony in this world. This means that this world has at least the potential to fulfill the deepest needs and highest ideals of human life. It also means that orderliness is vital to the good life: all things, natural as well as human, must have a proper place and function within the whole.

This need for an overriding order may ultimately derive from the ancient Chinese people's long struggle to survive along the middle reaches of the Yellow River. The inland climate was harsh: its summers were hot and its winters cold. Although the silt the river deposited renewed the fertility of the soil, periodic floods presented a constant danger. To the north lay vast steppes inhabited by tribes of seminomadic herders and hunters, the feared northern barbarians, whose way of life was alien and whose propensity to wage war was feared. As a defense, the earliest Chinese built fortified towns that grew eventually into cities. The same threat led a millennium later to the construction of the Great Wall. Such large projects demanded that power be centralized in the hands of a strong aristocracy that was then able to organize the people for military defense and large-scale irrigation and agricultural projects. Thus the need for an overarching order and a harmonious society was probably felt in China from its very earliest days—indeed, long before the first written records (dating from around 1500 B.C.E.) found on bones and bronze castings. By that time, the first historical dynasty, the Shang, was well established, along with an entrenched hierarchical structure and a corresponding emphasis on order and harmony.

Even though life was to be fulfilled in this world rather than in an other-worldly heaven, the Chinese, like many other peoples, nevertheless believed in an afterlife. At physical death people were thought to enter a shadowy, nonphysical mode of existence that permitted them, now as "ancestors," a limited interaction with the world of ordinary life. The Chinese neither held out the promise of heavenly bliss nor feared hellish punishment but rather sought a this-worldly salvation.

The quest for harmony in this world takes several directions. One is the pursuit of social, political, and intellectual control. Rules of behavior—what we might think of as etiquette or formal behavior—became especially important as the primary means of regulating both human-to-human and human-to-nature interactions. If everyone knows how one is expected to act in every situation, no one will disrupt the order of life. This leads to a highly formalized, even ritualized pattern of living—the emphasis especially of Confucianism. In a related way, harmony will be enhanced if the individual is submerged in the group. Traditionally, the Chinese boy or girl is socialized through an elaborate set of decorum rules that regulate behavior in part by insisting on adherence to a strict social hierarchy. This emphasis on conformity to social norms leads to another key Chinese notion: in any given situation, everything and everyone has a single proper place ("a place for everything, and everything in its place"). This attitude gives Chinese society a distinctively personal character in that all things, both natural and human, are viewed through this model of interpersonal relations. For example, one conducts government, business, or family affairs based not on objective laws or rules applicable to all equally but on the exchange of gifts or personal favors: one seeks to establish a personal relationship with the people or powers on whom success depends. Thus various rites of hospitality, such as gift giving and sharing of meals, characterize not just more intimate family interactions but all of life, including religious activities.

The quest for harmony goes beyond family and government to encompass the physical, natural realm. The architecture of ancient China reflected this interest in order, harmony, and proper place. For example, the

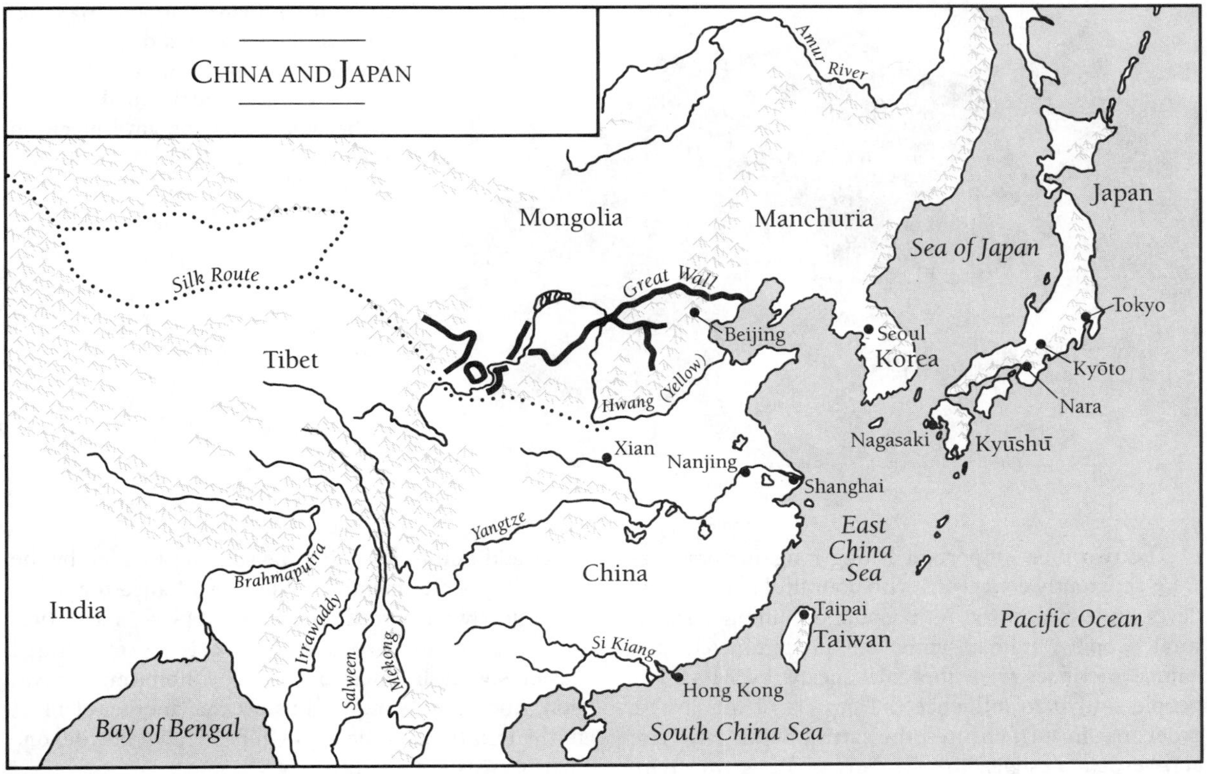

CHINA AND JAPAN

walled compound of a local feudal lord was commonly rectangular; the gates that pierced each of the four sides were aligned with the four cardinal directions. Inside, the lord's residence and ancestral hall were placed at the center; the mound of earth sacred to the "god of the soil," the chief agricultural deity, was always to the south, its "proper" direction. When large cities were built, their architects employed the same precise pattern. This arrangement both symbolized the hierarchical order of the human world and reflected a more fundamental harmony with the powers of earth and sky. Such architecture, in turn, helped to reinforce the emphasis on place and order. When the feudal lords—and later princes, kings, and emperors—performed rituals, they sought to ensure, through gifts (sacrifices) and praise (prayers), a cosmic harmony. They felt that the survival of human life depended on harmony and order. We can get a clearer sense of this substratum of common belief if we look at China's earliest religions, for they exhibit these patterns clearly.

CHINA'S EARLY RELIGIOUS HISTORY

THE SHANG DYNASTY

China's most ancient artifacts date from the Shang dynasty (1500s–1100s B.C.E.). Settled around the Yellow River in north central China, the Shang were an agricultural people who built large fortified towns, probably to protect themselves from invaders from the north. Although our data are incomplete, we can say that their society was highly stratified. It was probably dominated by a ruling class of warriors, perhaps descendants of a once-distinct group that had conquered an agricultural people. Their main source of wealth was grain crops like wheat and millet. The male aristocrats probably spent most of their time making war, hunting, and cultivating the arts. We know little of women's activities.

The Hall of Supreme Harmony was the location of the emperor's dragon throne. The quest for harmony was central to Chinese religion and life, going beyond family and government to encompass the physical, natural realm. (Shashinka Photo Library)

The two most important Shang religious practices were apparently concerned with bountiful harvests and devotion to ancestors. As is common among agricultural peoples, animal symbolism predominated, and animal sacrifices were the chief means by which the people sought to influence the powers of the cosmic order that in turn ensured the earth's bounty. Dragon and serpent designs, the symbols of life-giving rain, clouds, and mist—and thus also of abundant harvests and of the mysterious life-giving power of the earth—were also frequent and have been found even on pre-Shang pottery from the region.

Shang rites showed that human beings, animals, and plants were seen as participating in the great cosmic processes of planting, growth, and harvest. The rituals suggest that survival was acknowledged as being dependent on a smooth relationship with this cosmic process.

The hidden world of the ancestors played a part in this cosmic scheme. The Shang believed that at death, a person joined the ancestors. More powerful than in life, an ancestor could influence his or her descendants' future and the natural world. Shang-di ("Supreme Ruler"), the most important deity, was the divine ancestor of the ruling family; his envoy, the wind, was the ruler of the spirit powers. An ancestor would reward or punish the behavior of the living just as the various gods and goddesses could. To ensure that the ancestors would be well disposed, survivors who could afford to do so provided elaborate grave furnishings and made offerings of food and clothing.

In addition to lessening the sense of loss felt by the surviving family members, the rites of ancestor reverence clearly reinforced the notion of place. These rites also tended to associate the society's established customs with the ancestors, thereby inhibiting innovation. Ancestor reverence thus became another element in the traditional pattern of Chinese religious life, one that persists even to this day.

The quest for order and harmony apparently also encouraged the important Shang practice of divination. In divination one consults with spirit beings to interpret natural phenomena and predict future events. The Shang's favorite method was to inscribe a yes-or-no question on a tortoise shell or a piece of animal bone. Then they would scratch the words *yes* and *no* randomly on the object, which was then roasted over the fire. Cracks that appeared near a *yes* or a *no* were taken to be answers from the spirits. Typical questions were "Will the harvest be good?" "Will I live a long life?" and "Will we be successful in war?"

THE ZHOU DYNASTY

The patterns of traditional Chinese religion can also be seen in the next major period, that of the Zhou (Chou) dynasty (1122–771 B.C.E.). The Zhou, who overthrew the Shang rulers, had been a farming people living about 300 miles southwest of the Shang kingdom. Once they wrested power from the Shang, they ruled through a pyramidal feudal system in which each lower member owed allegiance to the higher members. But the prestige of the Shang remained so awesome that the Zhou preserved much of their previous culture, even adopting many of the Shang's religious practices and laws. In fact, they even saw to it that sacrifices to the ancestors of the deposed Shang rulers were continued.

The most important continuity was that, though they expressed it in their own way, the Zhou embraced the Shang concern for order and harmony. This can be seen in the Zhou ancestral cult, as we have it from their *Book of Songs,* from which comes most of our knowledge of this early period. The main celebrations renewing ties to the ancestors occurred in conjunction with their spring and autumn rituals. The activities centered around a rite of hospitality. The ancestors were invited as honored guests to the house, where they were treated to an elaborate ceremonial meal. The ancestral souls were called forth by pouring libations on the ground and by burning food. Prior to this summoning, the eldest son of the family entered a period of mourning and purification. Usually, a grandson or another kinsman of the most recently deceased male was selected to be "possessed" by the dead during the banquet. Thus as the ancestors were experienced as actually present, enjoying the food and gifts, the assembled family gained access to them and their blessings. When, at the end of the ritual, they asked the ancestors if they were pleased with the gifts, the people could be assured that they could look forward to continued harmony and blessings.

Like so much of Chinese popular religion, Zhou rites were directed toward the goals of abundant life, good harvests, and avoidance of calamities. A more subtle function of these rites undoubtedly was to heighten the sense of the meaningful order of all life by ritually showing that each family member belonged to a biologically and socially enduring stream of life. The living must have seen themselves as part of a larger community that included the dead and must have felt an increased obligation to live up to their forbears' idealized behavior.

Zhou Deities and the Dao

Among the ancestral figures that came to assume a more distinct identity as a deity was **Hou Ji**, the god of millet and first ancestor of the ruling Zhou family, who was thought to have discovered agriculture. He gave his descendants the first millet and other seeds and taught them the secrets of cultivation. According to the myth preserved in the *Book of Songs,* a goddess became pregnant as the result of "stepping on the footprints" of the high god Shang-di. After giving birth to Hou Ji, she performed the ceremony of placing the child upon the earth, thus acquainting him with the site of his future labor. Hou Ji's divine parentage thus provided everyday agricultural activities with divine significance. In addition, planting and harvest rites in his honor served to ensure that these activities remained in harmony with the larger cosmic order.

Another important deity unique to the Zhou was **Tian** (T'ien), usually translated as Heaven. It may seem odd to call heaven a deity, but the Zhou people thought of the vault of the sky not as a place but as a force, for it was the original source of natural and moral order. Indeed, Tian was originally the supreme Zhou deity; though eventually identified with Shang-di, Tian was always more vaguely defined and less personal. The Zhou rulers never claimed Tian as their ancestor. When the ruler came to be called the Son of Heaven, this was understood to signify a status relationship, not descent. In later times, emperors were thought to continue as rulers only because their behavior accorded with the norms of morality and ritual correctness and not because of hereditary right; this was known as the Mandate of Heaven (Tian-ming).

Just as the lands occupied by the Zhou people were thought of as the center of the world, so the king's palace in the capital city was its focus, the center of the entire heavenly realm. The king himself was identified with the stationary North Star, around which the heavenly canopy revolved—one more display of a cosmic harmony integrated with humanity.

The ordering principle that made such cosmic harmony possible was called **Dao** *(Tao),* a key concept in Chinese religions. The most basic meaning of the word *Dao* is "road" or "path," especially with reference to the stars' celestial paths and by extension the whole orderly procession of heavenly bodies. Other regular patterns were also associated with this term, especially the seasonal cycles of cold and hot, wet and dry, and dormancy, growth, and harvest. Early calendars were essentially descriptions of Dao in that they integrated all these elements.

In the concept of Dao the Chinese emphasized that order and harmony were matters not only of space but

COMPARISON

Social Order and Natural Order

Many cultures understand their social patterns to be on a continuum with natural and supernatural phenomena. For example, the Vedic people conceived of their societal obligations in terms of *ṛita,* a term that they also applied to the order followed by natural phenomena. To act according to ṛita was, for them, like going with the harmonious flow of a world that is forever changing. Later Hindus conceived of their social roles and duties in terms of *dharma,* a principle of right that was rooted also in the universe, but a universe that was firm, steady, and unchanging. Thus society's rules, too, would be unlikely to change; indeed, once texts like Manu's had laid out the particulars of dharma, they remained nearly unchanged for centuries.

The Chinese conceived of their world in terms of the *Dao,* a term originally signifying the stars' celestial paths and hence the whole procession of stars, planets, and other heavenly bodies. Humans, spirit beings, weather patterns, and other natural phenomena all followed the same Dao. Because they conceived of it temporally, from very early days the Chinese were driven to write careful histories, trying to detail how natural patterns correlated with human ones.

In detail these notions differ, but they share a sense that human processes are associated with the natural order and that there is a close relationship between human obligation and natural forces.

also of time. Just as there is but one proper time to plant or harvest, so there was but one Dao for all activities; there was but one proper pattern for human life. The natural and the social—both were manifestations of this ultimate Dao (see the accompanying box).

The assumption that the natural and human realms reflect each other led to the practice at the king's court of appointing a so-called grand recorder. It is thanks to such officials—part astronomer, part historian, and part astrologer—that we have early records. These men and their aides were charged with carefully observing and recording any unusual events, celestial or terrestrial, in the natural or human realm, so that their meanings might be read. Histories came to be kept so as to record patterns in the past; similar patterns in the present might then be used to predict the future. All these unusual events were indicators of the Dao; to discern them was to know the Dao. Then, too, some events were disruptive of the cosmic and human order: they were against the Dao and were sometimes accompanied by terrible consequences. The worst of these, from the point of view of the king and his court, was the withdrawal of the Mandate of Heaven, which meant the destruction of the dynasty.

Yin and Yang

Closely related to the idea of the cosmic Way were the twin notions of **yin** and **yang.** These were the names given to the two opposite but complementary forces or tendencies inherent in all things by which it was possible to understand the nature of the dynamism or changeableness of things. After all, the cosmic order, Dao, was not a changeless, timeless reality; rather it pointed to a pattern of orderly and to some extent predictable change. Probably *yin* originally meant "covered as by clouds," hence dark, secret, and cool;

yang meant something bright and shiny, hence light, open, and warm. Each thing's nature and its changes resulted from the mixture of these two principles.

Scholars have proposed that these twin notions arose in early China as a reflection of seasonal rhythms, climate, growing seasons, and the division of labor between the sexes. The summer, when it was warm and the rains would fall, was the time to plant, harvest, and fatten the herds. This work fell to men, often at some distance from the family hearth. During the cold winter season, indoor work became dominant, especially the weaving of cloth. These labors fell to women. Thus human activities, and maleness and femaleness, were correlated with the rhythms of nature. Summer eventually came to be correlated with male work, maleness itself, and thus yang; winter meant women's work, femaleness, and finally yin. Neither yang nor yin was considered inherently good or bad. Both were necessary components in the world's proper operation. Good was the proper mixture of both; bad was an excess of either.

Ultimacy

Our recognition of a sense of ultimacy in this common substratum of Chinese religion leads us to several conclusions. First, ultimacy was encountered in ordinary things and events of this world. Human life was not in conflict with ultimacy in part because the ultimate was perceived not as transcendent but as immanent, found in everyday life and within the individual. Second, certain things and certain persons were thought to be more sacred than others. Especially sacred were the forces of nature, the gods and goddesses thought to control these forces, the revered ancestors, and living persons of high status, such as kings and emperors. Third, ultimacy was experienced not so much as a personal, direct relationship to a deity or an ancestor (on a vertical or transcendent axis) but rather in the net of relationships that included all things (horizontal or immanent within the pattern of life). The great sage Confucius articulated this well in teaching that participation in the rituals that establish and reinforce the lived web of interrelationships is at least as important as the individual elements within them.

THE AGE OF THE HUNDRED PHILOSOPHERS

During most of the Zhou dynasty, the feudal political structure remained relatively stable. This began to change dramatically in the eighth century B.C.E. As the old feudal structure of Zhou society slowly disintegrated, barbarous tribes invaded from the west. In 769

As this set of bronze sacrificial vessels shows, both the Shang and their successors, the Zhou, were expert metalworkers. (The Metropolitan Museum of Art, Munsey Bequest, 1924)

B.C.E. an army of dissidents sacked the capital, killing the Zhou emperor. China was soon carved into a number of independent states, each headed by a ruler who hoped to unify China under a new dynasty. The period became one of constant warfare.

Such warfare brought in its wake serious political and economic disruption. This was especially troubling to the Chinese people, for whom harmony and order held such importance. Not surprisingly, many thoughtful individuals attempted to discern the causes of the disharmony and the meaning of human existence and to find new solutions to the problems ravaging people's lives—so many, in fact, that the sixth century B.C.E. became known as the age of the hundred philosophers. It was during this unsettled time that the two main players in the drama of Chinese religion, Confucianism and Daoism, emerged. Both came to address the needs of this period for a new way to understand and bring about harmony, and both tapped the roots of Chinese beliefs to do so. Far from rejecting custom, they sought to articulate and clarify the wisdom hidden within it.

CONFUCIUS: THE RITUALIZATION OF LIFE

During this period of strife and philosophical speculation, the great moral philosopher and teacher Kong zi (formerly known as Kung Fu-tzu, romanized as Confucius; 551–470 B.C.E.) was born. According to tradition, Confucius came from an impoverished family of the lower nobility. He became a petty government bureaucrat, but possibly because of his reputation for speaking his mind, he never rose to a position of high responsibility. He continued to criticize government policies and made a modest living as a teacher. In his later years he is said to have devoted himself to editing the classical books of history now known as the *Wu Jing* ("Five Classics"). Teachings attributed to him were collected as the *Analects (Lun Yu)*.

For the past 2,000 years the teachings of Confucius have had a great influence on the thought, government institutions, literature, arts, and social customs of China. Confucianism has also been influential in Japan, Korea, and Vietnam. Many people consider it primarily a social and moral philosophy, yet as practiced by the educated upper classes, Confucianism had definite religious dimensions.

Li *and Social Order*

Confucius saw the answer to his era's problems in the ritualization of life, which was found in the practice of **li**. *Li* was the most important term in Confucius's thought. It encompassed a number of ideas conveyed in English by separate words, such as *ritual, custom, propriety,* and *manners.* That li was applied to so many human activities is itself significant because li was thought to be the means by which life should be ordered and the proper harmony established. A person of li was thus good and virtuous; a state ordered by li was harmonious and peaceful.

The oldest meaning of *li* referred to the sacred rites of hospitality, particularly the important ancestral rituals. Indeed, for the early Chinese the term *li* was nearly synonymous with religion. Confucius took this core idea—of activity specifically pertaining to ultimate things—and enlarged it so that all activities could be viewed as ultimate. On the one hand, this meant that every act took on an aura of mystery and seriousness hitherto reserved for ancestral rites and solemn sacrifices to the gods. On the other hand, it also meant that specifically religious rites themselves were judged by Confucian society as relatively less important. As Confucius himself put it, "Devote yourself earnestly to the duties due to men, and respect spiritual beings, but keep them at a distance" (*Analects* 6.20). This distancing of spiritual beings, which included the ancestors, was both a sign of respect for their power and a refocusing of religious concern onto human affairs. Confucius and his followers continued to perform the ancient rites, but their main goal was to make the attitudes and sense of order appropriate to these rites pervade all the affairs of life. For this, li was essential.

The first step in the Confucian program to establish the proper order of things (Dao) among human beings was to reform government. Confucius himself briefly held a position in the administration of his native state of Lu (modern Shandong). His pupils, however, were much more successful as office seekers, and much of the discussion between master and pupil recorded in the *Analects* pertained to the proper conduct of state affairs. By the time China was reunified in the late third century B.C.E., Confucian scholars dominated the bureaucracy that ran the imperial government.

Far from favoring an egalitarian and democratic ideal, the assumed direction of influence in the

Confucian view of the state was from the top down. Confucius believed that if the leaders could be changed, the people would also "rectify" themselves by correcting their behavior. The *Analects* put it this way:

> Lead the people with legal measures and regulate them by punishment, and they will avoid wrong-doing but will have no sense of honor and shame. Lead them with the power of virtuous example *(de)* and regulate them by the rules of *li,* and they will have a sense of shame and will thus rectify themselves. (2.3)

In the phrase "regulate them by the rules of *li,*" the term translated rather abstractly as "to regulate" had the very revealing concrete and primitive meaning of kernels of wheat filling the ear evenly. This simple yet powerful image conveyed the Confucian emphasis on order in a single and concise image: kernels regularly and predictably filling their assigned space in an assigned pattern, over and over. The image conveyed regularity, predictability, and continuity—all the cornerstones of order—as well as a sense of each thing fitting in its proper place. The goodness and abundance of this order was also found in the image of a good harvest.

To act according to li was thus to do what was right in the proper manner at the proper time—that is, to follow the Dao. This exemplification of the Dao could not help but be imitated by the people. Coercion, therefore, would not only be unnecessary but would also indicate a falling away from the Dao. The ideal was neither to coerce people nor to give them anarchic freedom but rather to lead them to participate voluntarily in the rhythm of li and, in effect, the social structure.

The use to which Confucius sought to put li might be called a form of social engineering, although such an idea would have been alien to him because it implies *arbitrary* manipulation. He sought to create an environment in which people would naturally be harmonious and thus virtuous, but he believed that there was only one right way, the Way, to do it. Harmony was an unavoidable consequence of the shaping power of li because li was the perfect reflection of cosmic order, Dao, as applied to human society. A land whose people acted according to li was a civilized country; one whose people did not follow li was not civilized, and its people were not fully human in the sense that they had no means of realizing their potential as human beings.

This etching represents Kong zi (romanized as Confucius). Confucius was a great moral philosopher and teacher and redirected Chinese religion to a concern about human affairs. (The Granger Collection)

As Confucius said in the *Analects:* "Respectfulness without li becomes laborious bustle; carefulness without li becomes timidity; boldness without li becomes insubordination; straightforwardness without li becomes rudeness" (8.2).

Ren *and Humaneness*

We all have the potential to become people of **ren**, of humanity or humaneness. To embody this quality of humaneness was the goal of Confucius's followers. But ren was more than humanity in the external sense; it was the measure of individual character and, as such, the goal of self-cultivation. Self-cultivation could be attained just by conforming to li; ren is the human quality that results from acting according to li. Li and ren are thus two sides of the same coin. But when Confucius spoke of ren, he emphasized in the following question the individual effort required in the proper performance of li: "If a man is not humane [*ren*], what has he to do with ceremonies [*li*]?" (3.3). This individual effort was thought of as self-control or self-mastery. As Confucius said, "To master or control the self and return to li, that is ren" (12.1).

The psychological aspects of this doctrine, which later became important in China when psychologically sensitive Buddhism came to the fore, were never fully clarified by the Confucians themselves. Some thought of the road to ren as the control of individual impulses and desires, an effort of the will aided by social pressure. This tended to make Confucianism a rather rigid set of uniform social rules. But others, notably the Neo-Confucian schools of thought that developed much later, saw ren as a quality of an individual's inner being: the self had been mastered in the sense that it had been transformed under the impact of li. A famous autobiographical statement by Confucius in the *Analects* supports this later view:

> At fifteen, my mind sought learning. At thirty, my character was firmly set. At forty, my doubts were at an end. At fifty, I knew the will of Heaven. At sixty, I could hear the truth with equanimity. At seventy, I unerringly desired what was right. (2.4)

Thus Confucianism contained within it a degree of differentiation from the Chinese substratum described earlier. Individualism, though still very much in the service of the whole, has crept in to this hierarchical system.

The Confucian Sage and the Glorification of the Past

Confucius did not see himself as an innovator, though in some respects his doctrines were quite new. As we have seen, he made li, the ancient ritual pattern, into an all-encompassing style of life, a significant reinterpretation. Yet he claimed and probably himself believed that he was only trying to return to the original and proper way of the ancient **sages**. Confucius idealized these figures as holy men who embodied perfect wisdom. Their very presence in the world was enough to bring about a golden age. They were perfect beings, possessing powers of knowledge, insight, and virtue far beyond those of ordinary people. Four sages are mentioned in the *Analects:* Yao and Shun were legendary kings of remotest antiquity and models of the perfect ruler; Yu the Great was part divine protector of agriculture and part irrigation engineer who tamed the floods of the Yellow River; and the duke of Zhou was the brother of the dynasty's founder. Confucius especially revered the duke of Zhou as the ideal scholar-administrator that Confucius himself aspired to become and into which he sought to turn his students.

The most important quality such sages exhibited was **de** (*te,* virtue), best understood as a sacred personal force, something akin to charisma, inherent in a sage's very presence. De had the power to change the course of history by bringing about a harmonious order during the sage's lifetime. The virtue of the ancient sage-kings and hence their connection with the Dao was so great that they could rule by "inactivity." As Confucius put it in the *Analects,* "He who exercises government by means of his virtue [*de*] may be compared to the north pole star, which keeps its place and all the stars turn toward it" (2.1), a reference to an ancient Zhou image. Later Confucian masters taught that all humans could and should aspire to a sage's de.

Confucius used the image of the ancient sages and their de as the inspiration for proper conduct. To emulate the great sages of antiquity, one first had to study the ancient books to learn their Way. Thus study and imitation of the sages became part of the Confucian way. "Most exalted is [the sage] who is born with knowledge; but next is the man who learns through study" (16.9). It was this more modest goal to which Confucius aspired and to which he urged his disciples. Not daring to rank himself among the sages, Confucius said of himself: "I strive to become such without satiety, and teach others without weariness" (7.3).

The Ideal Man and the Ideal Woman

Confucius struggled against the entrenched privileges of the feudal hereditary aristocracy of his day. Its members used political power to indulge their own pleasures and protect their own wealth and status. To him this was a gross distortion of the proper order as embodied in the Way of the ancients. The ideal that Confucius taught was called **zhunzi** *(chün-tzu),* usually translated now as "superior man" or "true gentleman." Confucius altered the meaning of the term from a person born to a position of wealth and privilege to one honored for individual merit. What mattered was character, not background. To build character meant to study and learn the Way of the ancients and scrupulously to follow li.

Confucius's superior man was similar in many ways to the gentleman of Victorian England. He was cultured and reserved. He was expected to exhibit a thorough knowledge of manners (li) and to care more for his own integrity and inner development than for wealth. Specifically, the superior man had the following qualities:

1. *He was above egoism.* He looked at the humane impulses within himself, and if all were well there, he did not worry about his relations with others. He served the common good, which was the reason he sought public office. Even in his official duties as adviser or administrator, he did not argue or contend; he simply stated the truth without concern for the consequences to himself.

2. *He was not narrow.* The superior man's function, his role in the world, was not to carry out any technical occupations or specific arts or crafts. As Confucius explained, "The superior man is not an implement" (*Analects* 2.12). His usefulness lay in the transforming power of his character. When his disciple Fan Ch'ih asked to be taught husbandry, Confucius answered:

> "I am not so good for that as an old husbandman." . . . Fan Ch'ih having gone out, the master said, "A small man, indeed, is Fan. If a superior man love li, the people will not dare not to be reverent. If he love good faith, the people will not dare not to submit to his example. If he love good faith, people will not dare not to be sincere. Now, when these things obtain, the people from all quarters will come to him, bearing their children on their backs—what need has he of a knowledge of husbandry?" (13.4)

3. *Above all, he was a man of ren.* In the context of the zhunzi, ren is best rendered as "altruism," since it included empathy for all and concern for their well-being. But such altruism should not be expressed indiscriminately; the goal was not an egalitarian society but an orderly, harmonious hierarchy of persons and things. Through the structure imposed by li, one was concerned with justice—that is, with seeing to it that all persons were treated as befitting their station in life. Confucius advised his students to requite good with good and evil with justice and to love what is good and hate what is evil. His was not a universal ethic of love but an ethic ordered by li.

Although the Confucian ideals were defined primarily in terms of male standards, the tradition also defined a parallel set of standards for its women. In the cosmic principles of yin and yang, Confucians found the model for both male and female gender roles. As yang was seen as active and strong, men were supposed to initiate strong actions. Yin, in contrast, was identified with earth: inferior to heaven, yielding, passive, and weak. Women's proper behavior was understood as upholding and reflecting this necessary complement to the dominant role of heaven/yang/man. In her roles—defined as a daughter, wife, and mother—she was to be obedient to the appropriate dominant male, namely, her father, husband, and son or sons, in that order.

This ideal of passive servitude, however, required more of women than helpless inactivity. At marriage a woman joined her husband's family; since her life was dedicated exclusively to maintaining order and contentment in that family, the ideal Confucian woman exhibited a great deal of courage and personal strength. In later thought she was held responsible not only for her own "wifely way" virtue but for the moral character of her husband as well.

MENCIUS, DISCIPLE OF CONFUCIUS

For more than two centuries after Confucius died, progress toward the peaceful and harmonious way of life he advocated was slow. Contending states still made war on one another. The government still remained in the hands of military men and the old aristocracy. Yet increasingly, Confucianism made its mark on China, especially on its intellectuals. Indeed, by the fourth century B.C.E., most of the kings had gathered communities of scholars or philosophers to adorn their capital cities with a glow of high culture.

Among these was a brilliant Confucian scholar called Meng-zi (romanized as Mencius, c. 372–289 B.C.E.). True to his master's teaching, Mencius urged the rulers of the various states to adopt Confucian principles. He taught that rulers were given the Mandate of Heaven on the basis of the Confucian ideal of virtue; the ruler who was himself without virtue and was unconcerned for the welfare of his people would lose the Mandate. Mencius even taught that if a ruler is unjust and lacking in virtue, and thus without the Mandate, his subjects have the right to revolt. In doing so, they become the instrument of heaven, exercising its natural tendency toward return to the proper world order.

Mencius venerated Confucius, and at one point he is said to have exclaimed, "There never has been another Confucius since man first appeared on earth."[1] Mencius not only accepted his master's teachings but, being a creative thinker himself, also amplified them and added to them. While he accepted Confucius's vision of a cosmic order regulated by li, Mencius sought to develop a more systematic ethical system for the zhunzi. He grounded ethics in human nature: humans were essentially and originally good, and all else followed naturally from this inborn tendency. The basis of this goodness was the quality of ren, which needed only to be nurtured and channeled into appropriate paths as described by li. Thus not only was the order of harmony of the world visible in the regular patterns of nature and the perfect society, but it could also be experienced in the depths of human instinctual goodness. "Can it be that any man's mind naturally lacks Humanity [*ren*] and Justice? If he loses his sense of the good, then he loses it as [a] mountain [loses] its trees."[2] Just as trees grow naturally on a mountain, so does goodness flow naturally from the human heart. Human actions not in accord with the Way and those that result from the inevitable bustle of daily activities obscure this inner correctness. Yet one's true nature always remains; it can be known "in the still air of the early hours."

Mencius never lived to see a ruler institute his principles. But some 1,500 years later his thought became central to Neo-Confucianism. Two of his ideas came to be especially appreciated: his belief that sagehood was inherent in all human beings so that, if properly nurtured, it could grow in this world and his efforts to discover the inner life of the human mind.

LAO-ZI AND THE BEGINNINGS OF DAOISM

The disruption and anxieties of the period of warring states produced another body of thought, Daoism. Although this new religion had its roots in the common substratum of Chinese thought, it viewed the world very differently from Confucianism. More important, it proposed very different solutions to the problems of disharmony raised during the era of constant warfare.

Daoism earned its name from the central importance it gave to the concept of Dao, the Way. Its founder is traditionally said to have been Lao-zi (Lao-tzu), supposedly an elder contemporary of Confucius. Although today few scholars believe that any such person lived, it is still convenient to speak of Lao-zi as the author of the obscure but fascinating *Dao De Jing* (*Tao Te Ching*, "Classic of the Way and Its Power"). This text—combining religion, philosophy, poetry, and mysticism—dates from the beginning of the third century B.C.E. It has exerted a great influence on Chinese thought and attitudes and was eventually adopted by the popular Dao sects as their most important scripture.

Like Confucius, Lao-zi sought harmony in this world, but he located ultimacy not in social life but in nature itself. This he symbolized with the term *Dao*. If one could achieve a direct experience of the Dao, he said, its power would transform the individual, who would come to embody the Dao. Since it is ultimate reality and by nature harmonious and orderly, contact with it will transform a person, melting away problems and anxieties. No Confucian-style preaching of virtue, no reverent imitation of the ancients, no scrupulous attention to ritual, is necessary. Indeed, these things are quite dangerous—part of the problem, not of the solution. Because they are human rather than natural products, they derive from selfish human ambitions and not from the Dao, which is purely natural and spontaneous.

For Lao-zi, the Dao—and, indeed, human existence—was far more mysterious than it was for Confucius. Again and again, the *Dao De Jing* sounds the theme of the unknowableness of ultimate reality:

The Dao that can be told of is not the real Dao;
The name that can be named is not the real name.

This bronze piece, dating from the Song dynasty, depicts Lao-zi riding a water buffalo. Today few scholars believe that any such person lived, but it is still convenient to speak of him as the author of the *Dao De Jing*. (Worcester Art Museum)

This nameless thing is the origin of heaven and
earth;
One may call it the Mother of all things.

(*Dao De Jing* 1)[3]

The mysteriousness of the Dao meant that one cannot adequately describe or conceptualize it. It exceeds human grasp both intellectually and practically. Beyond human possession or control, no words or thoughts can capture it:

One who knows does not speak;
One who speaks does not know.

(*Dao De Jing* 56)[4]

Nonetheless, this Dao is not a transcendent ultimate, removed from the world, but is immanent, found in the world. It is in fact active and present in all things, including human beings. One can for this reason encounter the Dao directly as ultimate power and mystery, in a mystical experience beyond concepts and reason. Through such experiences one can learn to yield to the Dao and live within its peace and harmony, for it is harmony itself. Thus Daoism recasts the common Chinese emphasis on harmony and the Way by focusing on the mystical experience of it.

To experience the Dao requires no Confucian ritualistic guidance. The Daoist sage was thought to be truly free to act without forethought or ritual plan. The sage could act spontaneously and do so without anxiety because the basis of his or her actions was the experience of the Dao itself.

One result of the *Dao De Jing*'s mystical emphasis is that, like many mystical texts around the world, its language and imagery are deeply paradoxical: one learns to be without learning; one acts without action. The truth, like the Dao, is hidden and unexpected. What is weakness to ordinary people is seen as strength; the apparently weak will eventually triumph over the seemingly strong. Only fools try to impose their will through force. Real strength is not like stone but like water:

There is nothing softer and weaker than water,
And yet there is nothing better for attacking hard
and strong things.

(*Dao De Jing* 78)[5]

Other paradoxical images abound: to be active, one must be passive, like the traditional Chinese woman, who was able to accomplish her ends by attracting a willing man. The wise should be like an uncarved block of wood: pure, unpretentious, and without ego or artifice.

Naturalness

Just as the most obvious and accessible aspect of the Dao is the reality of nature that one can see, smell, and touch, so the most important characteristic of the Dao is **naturalness** *(ziran),* the quality of a thing's just being itself, spontaneously and without deception or calculation. A tree that has been shaped by wind and climate is natural; one that has been pruned into the shape of a swan is not. A person who is in tune with the Dao is spontaneous; one who is concerned to act a part or impose his or her will on others is not.

Daoism thus seeks a goal similar to that of Confucianism, harmony, but conceives of it and pursues it differently. Unlike Confucius, who emphasized trying to act in conformity with ritualized li, Lao-zi emphasized acting naturally. Only then will one be in perfect harmony; no ritualized behavior patterns are needed.

Daoism would also object to other societies, not just Confucian ones: compared to the natural world, almost any human society would be unnatural. When humans begin to think, they also begin to scheme and calculate for selfish ends. Not knowing the truly good—the Dao—we make false distinctions between good and evil that merely serve our own petty ends. Indeed, every doctrine of virtue is itself a sign that the proclaimer has lost the Dao, for the true sage would have no need for doctrines, concepts, or self-conscious concerns for virtue. This leads Lao-zi to a vision of a utopian society (*Dao De Jing* 80). Disdaining all artificiality, people in the utopian land will forgo the use of eating utensils; needing only natural simplicity, they may even give up writing. Content in themselves, they will not be curious to gossip about their neighbors.

The natural person forgets the self. To show how, Lao-zi distinguishes between action *(wei)* and nonaction **(wu-wei)**. Wei is willful, selfish action; it is always harmful because it is not in harmony with the Dao. Proper action is thus paradoxically called *nonaction;* since the sage's actions merely reflect the Dao, he does not act; the Dao acts through him.* We might say that the Daoist sage seeks harmony within himself and in the process loses himself to the Dao, whereas the ideal Confucian zhunzi seeks it outside himself and in the process loses himself to ritual. Virtue for Lao-zi became a mysterious internal power of the Dao itself, not a social program flowing out of the cultivation of character. For Lao-zi, the wise are to turn inward, not outward, to find the ultimate. Only when this way of life became general would the world achieve harmony.

ZHUANG-ZI AND THE DAOIST LIFE

The book that tradition ascribes to Zhuang-zi (Chuang-tzu; c. 369–286 B.C.E.) and bears his name is often paired with the *Dao De Jing* as the other of the two basic books of classical Daoism. It dates from the same era as its more famous companion and articulates a very similar view of the Dao. Whereas Lao-zi wrote as a poet, delighting in ambiguity and multiple meanings, Zhuang-zi wrote as a philosopher who turned the analytical and logical tools of philosophy against thinkers who describe reality in words. While Lao-zi played with paradoxical images, Zhuang-zi played with paradoxical arguments. He made fun of the Confucian conceptual framework, and Confucius himself often appears here as an ironic figure, uttering outrageously un-Confucian statements.

Unlike Lao-zi, Zhuang-zi sought to describe the practical procedures and consequences of a Daoist life. He often used parables, harnessing everyday events to illustrate his points. A famous example titled "Mastering Life" tells the story of a woodworker named Qing who won praise for making a bell stand so perfect that it seemed fashioned by supernatural powers. Qing modestly denied any real artistry and apologized for his technique:

> When I am going to make a bell stand, I never let it wear out my energy. I always fast in order to still my mind. When I have fasted for three days, I no longer have any thought of congratulations

*Although a sage could be male or female, Lao-zi, like many Chinese, employed the male pronoun when referring to sages. But to reach the ultimate stage, a sage would have to transcend social and gender limitations.

> or rewards, of titles or stipends. When I have fasted for five days, I no longer have any thought of praise or blame, of skill or clumsiness. And when I have fasted for seven days, I am so still that I forget I have four limbs and a form and body. By that time, the ruler and his court no longer exist for me. My skill is concentrated and all outside distractions fade away. After that, I go into the mountain forest and examine the Heavenly nature of the trees. If I find one of superlative form, and I can see a bell stand there, I put my hand to the job of carving; if not, I let it go. This way I am simply matching up "Heaven" with "Heaven."
>
> (*Zhuang-zi* 19)[6]

Here we see the practice of fasting used as a meditative technique for calming the mind and turning the attention away from external, egoistic things and toward the inner, immanent Dao. Other techniques such as breath control and physical exercises, Zhuang-zi suggests elsewhere, may also help to open one to the experience of the Dao. When it comes, quite unexpectedly, its power flows into the person to accomplish great things, spontaneously and effortlessly.

Zhuang-zi also echoes Lao-zi's austere view of the Dao: not only is the Dao, like the sage, without compassion, without humaneness, but the true sage should joyously embrace this impersonal pattern of change. All things are a part of the Dao and thus subject to endless transformation. While we live, we should playfully "ride upon the Dao." When it comes time for us to die and face the great transformation, we should not foolishly cling to what we have been:

> Suddenly Master Lai grew ill. Gasping and wheezing, he lay at the point of death. His wife and children gathered round in a circle and began to cry. Master Li, who had come to ask how he was, said, "Shoo! Get back! Don't disturb the process of change!"
>
> Then he leaned against the doorway and talked to Master Lai. "How marvelous the Creator is! What is [it] going to make out of you next? Where is [it] going to send you? Will [it] make you into a rat's liver? Will [it] make you into a bug's arm?"
>
> (*Zhuang-zi* 6)[7]

If one is properly attuned to the Dao, one has no anxiety. The sage had learned to forget knowledge, to forget the distinctions of life and death, good and evil, on which the value systems of the ordinary world are based. He could see things as they really are—all part of a single organic whole, the ultimate harmony of the Dao.

Zhuang-zi's name for this exalted state of mind was *wu-nian,* literally "no thought" or "no mind," a term later appropriated by the Chan (Zen) Buddhists to describe the state of enlightenment within the world. The sage's state of "no thought" was a state of self-forgetfulness, a state of tranquil acceptance of all things, a state of mind beyond the feelings of sorrow and joy that accompany ordinary life. Paradoxically, this state is described as accompanied by a higher kind of joy that takes delight in all things equally. This transcendent, mystical state makes ultimacy available in this world as a lived experience of the profound harmony of the Dao. No adversity can touch such a person; no anxiety can disturb such a mind.

NOTES

1 W. A. C. H. Dobson, *Mencius* (Toronto: University of Toronto Press, 1963), p. 88.

2 Ibid., p. 141.

3 Wing-tsit Chan, trans. and comp., *A Source Book in Chinese Philosophy* (Princeton, N.J.: Princeton University Press, 1963), p. 139.

4 Ibid., p. 166.

5 Ibid., p. 174.

6 Burton Watson, trans., *Chuang Tzu; Basic Writings* (New York: Columbia University Press, 1964), p. 127.

7 Ibid., p. 81.

Religions of China

CHAPTER 11

Three Visions of Harmony: Confucian, Daoist, Buddhist

Toward the end of the third century B.C.E., the armies of the northern Chinese state of Qin conquered the last rival state and established the first truly centralized government for the whole of China (221–207 B.C.E.). The victorious prince proclaimed himself emperor with the grand title Shi Huang-di ("first sovereign ruler-god") and declared the founding of the new Qin dynasty. To eliminate opposition to his new regime, the emperor ordered the destruction of all nonpractical and nontechnical books, including Confucius's sayings. Fortunately, scholars—especially Confucians—hid many of the texts and were able later to reconstruct much of the traditional classical literature. For our purposes, the most important legacy of the Qin dynasty was the establishment of the pattern of imperial rule that was to last for more than 2,000 years. Thus we enter the period known as classical China. Not only was the imperial structure permeated with religious values and practices, but the rulers also saw themselves as the regulators of the religious lives of their subjects.

THE HAN DYNASTY (202 B.C.E.–220 C.E.)

The ruthless and inhumane methods of control and exploitation of the Qin dynasty led to its overthrow after only a few years. Its successor, the Han dynasty, brought several centuries of political stability, economic prosperity, and cultural flowering. With it the stimulating but dangerous period of the hundred philosophers was over. Instead, the Han Chinese sought not innovation but consolidation of past gains. For example, editions of the Confucian literary classics were prepared, and a national library and university were founded.

Religious events and trends, as always, were tied to the cultural and social patterns of the period. For example, a new social class arose during this period: the literati, or scholar-officials. These highly trained civil servants took an increasingly larger responsibility for the operations of the government. The literati were drawn from a new kind of landowning gentry, the so-called *hundred families*. Their wealth made it possible for their sons to pursue the lengthy process of education (daughters were permitted no schooling). And in an attempt to institutionalize the Confucian rule of merit, education at this time became the gateway to government service and social prestige.

The practical goal of education was to prepare a young man for the difficult **civil service examinations,** which were required for a government career. The content of the exams was overwhelmingly Confucian, consisting of the Five Classics and their Confucian commentaries: the *Chun Jiu* (Spring and Autumn Annals), attributed, probably erroneously, to Confucius; the *Yi Jing* (Book of Changes); and the *Shu Jing*

(Book of History). The members of the ruling class, the cultured elite, were therefore steeped in Confucian learning, values, and attitudes.

Because the zhunzi, or true gentleman, was expected to exercise authority and to bring harmony to the people in his care by moral example and by ritual observance more than by enforcement of law or by coercion, the Confucian bureaucrats were not prepared by their education to be experts in any technical area. As Confucius had hoped, they were schooled in the "arts of living," what we would call the arts and the humanities; anything else could be learned in the process of administration or delegated to underlings. Moreover, the official duties of the government officeholder included many ceremonial activities such as participating in local or imperial rituals of the state cult. There was no independent priesthood; hence, inevitably, officeholders' duties took on religious overtones.

Confucianism triumphed as the imperial ideology in part because it offered a religious way of ensuring cultural harmony and unity without requiring the harsh methods seen in the Qin period. By reviving court ceremonies and emphasizing the role of the emperor as a mediator between heaven and earth, Confucianism supported the throne and its rule with an air of ultimacy and legitimacy. In addition, since the literati largely controlled the government, they were often able to thwart the ambitions of aristocratic or military adventurers and to blunt the arbitrariness and self-indulgence that often accompany imperial rule.

The Confucian interest in ritual as a means of promoting wider social harmony often coincided with the imperial concern to solidify its temporal and spiritual power. This can be seen in the phenomenon of the Ming Tang, or calendar house. Confucians had long admired the western Zhou period for the purity of its ritual observances. Based on their reading of the ancient texts, the Han scholars reconstructed an idealized building in which the Son of Heaven would imitate the path of the sun through the zodiac and perform many of the rites intended to ensure the abundance of crops and the peace and harmony of the empire. This graphically shows that the Confucians used ritual to ensure that the harmony inherent in the natural world would be transferred to the human world and also to establish that the emperor is the representative of all humanity in these rituals.

Such an understanding—that the natural world and social harmony are related and are centered in the rule of the emperor and the other authorities—is expressed by Dong Zhonshu (second century B.C.E.), the Han period's greatest Confucian thinker. By combining the Confucian concern for ritual and the virtue of the zhunzi with the ancient notion of yin and yang, Dong sought to relate the recurring patterns of natural and social order to the pattern of historical events. Yin and yang, he taught, give rise to five "elements" or agents: wood, fire, earth, metal, and water. All phenomena (for example, colors, tones, directions, seasons) result from the combination of these elements, and they succeed each other with regularity and predictability. Just like natural phenomena, historical events and eras are dominated by these various agents. Furthermore, all historical events flow naturally from previous events in a historical pattern that is the mirror of the cosmic pattern. Thus just as the five agents have a natural sequence, so do the various dynasties naturally succeed one another in a predictable fashion.

These correspondences were designed to explain everything and therefore to provide a framework of meaning in which all events could be seen as part of a cosmic pattern and process. To people of the Han period—at least the Confucian elite—this cosmic and historical harmony was a necessary part of a meaningful world. Even disasters like the fall of dynasties or earthquakes made sense as parts of a well-functioning system that was, in the long run, benevolently disposed toward humanity. Such a view also gave new significance to the old idea of the Mandate of Heaven, which was made known through the harmony and prosperity of a reign; the removal of the Mandate would be recognized by the absence of these indicators. Thus the old folk wisdom was reinforced that the government take note of any usual occurrences that might signal the will of Heaven. This theory also supported the widespread belief in omens and divination, for the natural and human worlds are interconnected.

POPULAR RELIGION DURING THE HAN

The Confucian attitude toward the religious yearnings and practices of the common people was one of either limited affirmation or hostility. The government affirmed the family cult of ancestor reverence and filial piety by building it into its own system of ritual and hierarchical social relationships. It also supported some of the many popular cults of local mountain and agricultural deities and others by awarding their temples and shrines imperial grants and titles. In this way the Confucian government not only enlisted these deities in the promotion of the prosperity and harmony of the state but also increased the loyalty of these cults' followers.

Among the popular beliefs and practices of the Han period were various techniques aimed at producing a long life or, sometimes, magical powers, such as the ability to levitate. Loosely connected to such beliefs was devotion to the **immortals** *(xian),* mysterious and capricious figures who were thought to have achieved immortality and great magical power through a combination of alchemy, asceticism, meditation, and good deeds. This belief in the immortals was sometimes embraced also by the elite: one of the great military leaders of China, Emperor Wu Di (141–87 B.C.E.), sent a group of explorers into the East China Sea with instructions to find the home of the immortals and bring back the elixir of eternal life.

Beyond this, the Confucian elite largely ignored the beliefs of the people except when they threatened the power of that elite. For example, Daoism was becoming an important influence among the common people, and in recognition of this in 164 C.E. the emperor had a temple to Lao-zi built in the capital, using in it rituals based on the official sacrifices to Heaven. However, when, in the second half of the Han period, Daoism became powerful enough to threaten the Confucian elite, the government forcibly suppressed it.

Popular Daoism

The new religion that became such a threat to the authorities, called popular Daoism, must be viewed against the social, economic, and religious frustrations of the common people. As the Han elite appropriated more and more of the wealth and shielded it from taxation, the burden of financing the government was shifted more and more onto the small landholders and tenant farmers. These people had the least stake in the status quo and were not drawn to the lofty idealism of the zhunzi or interested in the great rituals of cosmic harmony. Nor did they have the leisure or the education necessary to study the classics. Thwarted of any realistic hope of sharing social or economic power, the powerless and poor came to seek remedies through armed uprisings and religious fervor.

The popular religion was centered first in rituals asking the gods and goddesses for a share in the good life and second in an ultimate Dao that was mysterious yet also accessible to human appeal through powerful magical rituals. Popular tales of immortals and other adepts with amazing powers to overcome the limitations of ordinary human life gave credence to the hopes of the people, especially when charismatic leaders arose who claimed to know the secrets of these powers.

Two major Daoist sects were active during the second half of the Han dynasty, and although their political ambitions were eventually crushed, they continued to exist throughout the period of disunity after the fall of the Han (third through sixth centuries). The first was the Celestial Masters group, which was formed in about the middle of the second century in western China, where it carved out an autonomous theocratic state. The second was the Yellow Turbans group, which began in the northeastern peninsula (Shandong province) and eventually controlled eight provinces before it was put down in bloody battles at the end of the second century. Both sects emphasized the art of healing, the confession of sins, and magical rituals, and both were led by charismatic leaders who functioned as magical healers as well as military leaders.

They also shared an essentially utopian vision of life, which held that once the Confucian state had been overthrown, there would be a time of peace, prosperity, and harmony. This hope was held most fervently by the Yellow Turbans, who called themselves the followers of the *Tai Ping Dao* (Way of the Grand Peace). They believed that they could achieve this blessed state through purification rites and rituals expressing the harmony inherent in the nature of things.

These two Daoist sects focused on healing, both of the individual and of the group. The individual sought to be healed of physical and mental disease. According to the Chinese popular worldview, disease was closely tied to the various divine powers—some malevolent, others benevolent—that were thought to control the phenomena of the world. Individuals seeking to be healed or protected had to bring about a state of harmony between themselves and these largely unseen powers. This would in turn help to make their relationships with both spirits and other humans function smoothly. Thus a healthy individual required a healthy group. To enhance the health of the group, parishes were organized around a priesthood and a regular set of congregational (group performance) rituals. Daoist priests healed both by serving as ritual intermediaries to the spirits and by administering magic potions and formulas.

The concern for healing also bound together other elements of organized Daoism. For example, morality was cast in its light. In addition to traditional values such as honesty, filial piety, and respect to various deities and spirits, now moral prohibitions against injury to living beings were added, probably under the influence of Buddhism. To fail to live up to the moral code was regarded as a major cause of suffering and disease. Confession of one's transgressions and asking for forgiveness thus became a new feature of Daoist ritual life. It was often seen as a prerequisite to healing. In the Celestial Masters sect, for example, misdeeds and repentances were written on three pieces of paper; the first paper was buried, the second was placed on a mountaintop, and the third was thrown into a river. The purpose of this ritual was to inform all the cosmic powers of one's repentance and thus encourage them to restore one's health.

During this period the ancient quest for a long life and even for immortality also became associated with the popular Daoist sects. The cult of the immortals and the practice of alchemy were now incorporated into organized Daoism. Individuals themselves could become adept at such practices or use the powers of experts. They might also seek the elixir of immortality or some other means of prolonging their lives.

There were many techniques for achieving a long life. Some used **alchemy**, which combined ritual and meditative preparations in a rite of purification. Daoists also elaborated rituals of purification into a meditative, even ecstatic discipline, thus taking a major step beyond what was hinted at by Lao-zi and Zhuang-zi. Henceforth a direct and ecstatic experience of the Dao not only was a result of disciplined withdrawal from a hostile social and economic environment but was seen as a method by which one could overcome the limitations of ordinary life while still immersed in it.

Daoist meditation techniques were just as much based on the popular notions of healing as they were on Lao-zi's ideas of the Dao. Lao-zi had formulated the belief that the microcosm (an individual human being) and the macrocosm (the world of nature and the Dao that lay behind it) could be brought into harmony. Popular Daoism's meditation techniques took this idea much further by assuming a very detailed set of correspondences between what might be called the inner and the outer worlds.

The deeper the Daoist mystics probed, however, the more preoccupied they became with appropriating the sacred powers of the many popular deities. While meditating, people could apprehend these divine powers inside themselves and experience themselves as internally identical with the divine powers of the cosmos. Purification rites and meditation became viewed as a way to live in perfect harmony with these powers, which were regarded as the manifestation of the Dao in the inner world.

This popular form of Daoism represented a departure from Chinese religious tradition. Heretofore the people of China had participated in religious activity according to their membership in different kinds of groups, such as the family, the village, or the scholarly profession. These new Daoist sects were voluntary organizations that cut across earlier organizational lines and forged a new kind of group loyalty.

RELIGION IN THE PERIOD OF DISUNITY (220–589)

Early in the third century, the Han dynasty collapsed, and China was plunged into a long period of political disunity and instability, marked by wars and social upheaval. As often happens in such periods of dramatic social turmoil, the religions also changed. First of all, the failure of the dynasty served to destroy the Confucian government and generally to discredit Confucianism both as a philosophy of government and as a way of life for the cultured and educated elite. Many among this group turned instead to the Daoist tradition of Lao-zi and Zhuang-zi. They did not simply embrace this old religion, however, but adapted it to suit their new outlook. The result was a form of Daoism known as the **Dark Learning**, which combined elements of both elite Daoism and Confucianism. At the same time, among the common people, the popular forms of Daoism already developed in the late Han times continued to flourish. In addition, Buddhism, brought at this time by missionaries, began to take root in Chinese soil, particularly among certain intellectuals.

The Retired Intellectuals

Daoism as a way of life was explored by disappointed scholars and court officials who fled the corrupt petty states of the fragmented empire in search of a simple life far from the political world. Daoism provided not only a basis for rigorous philosophizing but also a justification for casual gatherings of "retired" intellectuals, referred to as the Pure Conversation movement. Scholars, poets, and painters who disdained official positions would meet to discuss their respective pursuits and to enjoy one another's company. Daoism provided them with a sense of participation in the mysterious and dark life of the cosmos, and no doubt it helped to compensate them for the loss of their influence in the political world. At the same time, these intellectuals were unconsciously forming a pattern of behavior and a life style that would henceforth become available to educated persons who went into retirement either voluntarily or involuntarily. As time went on, Buddhism—especially the Chan sect, known as Zen in Japan—would adopt this pattern.

THE BUDDHIST CONTRIBUTION TO CHINESE LIFE AND CULTURE

Buddhism began to enter China around the beginning of the Common Era when it was still a strong, vital religion in India. Missionaries followed the trade routes across central Asia during the Han dynasty and soon founded centers of Buddhist learning in northern China. After the fall of the Han, Buddhism flourished under the patronage of some of the various petty states established by the non-Chinese conquerors of northern China. But the common people knew little of this exotic foreign religion; even Chinese intellectual circles had at first only a distorted picture. Many saw Buddhism, with its elaborate rituals, meditation, complex philosophies, and withdrawal from the world, as a variant of Daoism. The tendency to identify Daoism with Buddhism during this period eventually led to considerable borrowing between the two groups. Buddhism thereby lost much of its foreign flavor, and Daoism was enriched by assimilating foreign ideas.

The first Buddhist enclaves in China were centers of learning whose primary function was to translate into Chinese the vast and abstruse Buddhist literature of India. But soon the most exotic feature of the new religion became known: the organization of its adherents into monasteries and convents. The monastic institution was not only the heart of early Chinese Buddhism, but in many ways this presented the greatest obstacle to its acceptance. As we have seen, devotion to family values and filial piety were deeply ingrained at all levels of Chinese society. Yet here was an institution that, symbolically at least, required its members to turn their backs on the world, abstaining from not only its pleasures but also its family responsibilities. Buddhist monks and nuns, because they were celibate, could not carry on the family line. In the monasteries and convents they lived in new "families," and their duty was no longer to their parents or to human society.

Despite this handicap, Buddhism did gain adherents, especially among the young educated gentry, many of whom found in the monastery's quiet, contemplative atmosphere a haven from the uncertainties of official life. There both women and men were freed from their strictly defined Confucian social and religious roles and could cultivate scholarly, meditative, and aesthetic pursuits while moving always toward the experience of nirvāṇa (enlightenment). For the Buddhists, the final goal of nirvāṇa required the experience in meditation of the truth of oneself—or, as they often put it, detachment from the false notion of self.

Buddhism, with its monastic system, seems to have struck a chord among many Daoists of that day, as it reinforced the Daoist aversion to the artificiality of the ritualized and hierarchical Confucian life. Consequently, the Daoists began to build their own monasteries and convents. The already well established Daoist tendency to produce hermits adapted readily to the Buddhist example: Daoists seeking individual religious experiences and enlightenment came to live together as "communal hermits."

CULTURAL FLOWERING IN THE TANG DYNASTY (618–907)

After the more than three centuries of internal weakness and foreign domination, China again achieved political unity and stability. The Tang dynasty was an especially prosperous period marked by creativity in literature and the arts and an unusual degree of cosmopolitanism. Caravans crossing central Asia linked the markets of India and the Mediterranean ports with the Chinese capital of Changan (modern Xian), which became a center of foreign ideas as well as foreign goods. An increasingly international China became home to Christian missionaries, Jewish communities, and Tibetan monks of the Vajrayāna Buddhist lineage.

With Confucianism still weak, Daoism flourished during this time, although it was overshadowed by Buddhism, which dominated Tang intellectual and artistic life. For some time Buddhism received the enthusiastic official support of the emperors. Its adherents were from all classes of Chinese society, and thousands of Chinese men and women retired to monasteries and convents to meditate and learn the Buddhist Dharma.

The Buddhism of the Tang dynasty was divided into a number of schools or denominations, each with its own teacher lineage, monasteries, and even preferred script. The most important division was between **universalist ("catholic") schools**, which tried to be inclusive of all Buddhist scriptures and practices (most notably the Huayan and Tiantai schools), and **exclusivist sects**, which gave exclusive attention to a single strand of the tradition (the Pure Land schools) or put nearly exclusive emphasis on a single practice (the Chan schools). The universalist schools were by far the more politically active and the wealthier of the two and were much more involved in the high culture of art and literature. Thus they largely assumed the functions of the old Confucian literati in Tang society. They emphasized elaborate and costly ritual performances—a kind of Buddhist li—and made effective use of the arts of painting, sculpture, and architecture to enhance the impact of these rituals and to reinforce their role as culture bearers. They expanded and

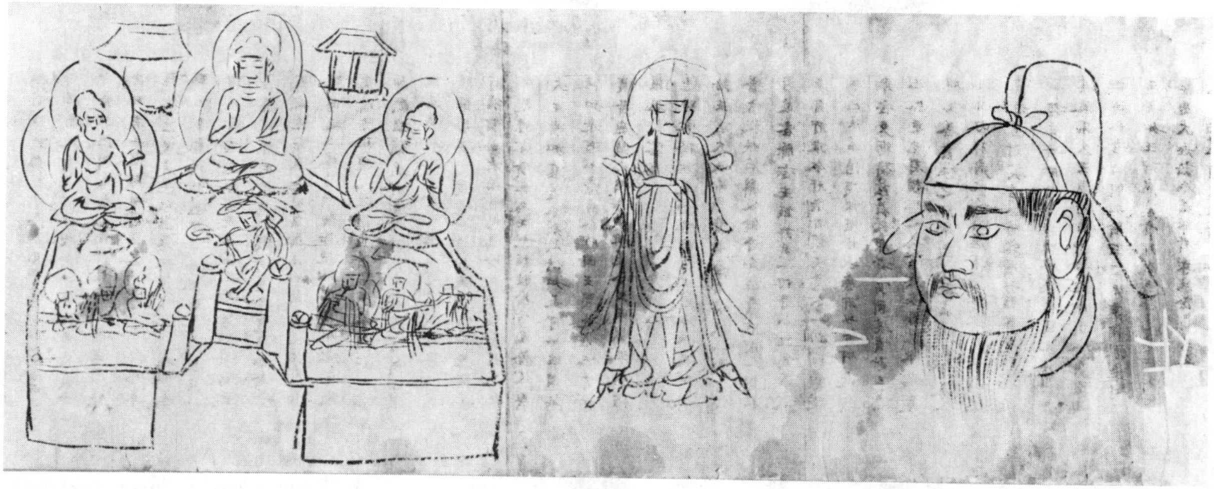

These sketches were drawn by an anonymous artist on the back of a sutra fragment, a hand scroll dating from the ninth or tenth century C.E. By the end of the Tang dynasty, religion powerfully influenced all aspects of Chinese cultural life, including artistic creation. (William Rockhill Nelson Gallery of Art—Atkins Museum of Fine Arts)

mastered the increasingly Buddhist philosophy, which gave them a claim to intellectual leadership.

Among the exclusivist sects, by far the largest were the Pure Land sects. Though based on three texts translated from Sanskrit, the Chinese transformed Pure Land practice from the elite, monastic meditation technique it had been in India to a simple devotional practice suitable to the poorest and least educated layperson. Anyone could chant the **nienfo** (*nembutsu* in Japan), the words "Namo Omito Fo." To chant it was to invoke the name of the Buddha Amitābha, who, it was believed, would enable the chanter to be reborn in his other-worldly paradise, the Pure Land. One could therefore live in this life, enjoying its pleasures and enduring its pain, while at the same time working toward a more pleasant life after death.

The other influential exclusivist school was Chan. The word *chan* means "meditation" (derived from Sanskrit *dhyāna,* "meditation"), and as its name implies, the Chan school emphasized meditation as its central practice. It claimed with some justification that this was true to the original intention of the Buddha himself. Also, Chan remained strongly dedicated to monasticism as providing the best environment for meditation. But its meditative practices developed in a manner unique to China. For example, the enigmatic riddles used as meditation objects *(kōan)* seem to owe more to the classical Daoist love of paradox and mystery than to the more coldly logical Prajñāpāramitā literature of India. And whereas Indian Buddhists clearly knew of a realm of mind beyond the rational, the Chan rejection of any philosophical system appears to owe more to Lao-zi's poetic declaration, "The Dao that can be told of is not the real Dao / The Name that can be named is not the real Name." The austere simplicity of Chan monastic life also echoes Lao-zi's admonition to live naturally and without desire or ceremony. Finally, it is significant that Chan poetry and painting show a love of nature not characteristic of Indian Buddhism but markedly shared with the Daoists, who saw in nature the manifestation of the Dao's simplicity and naturalness as an outward reflection of the inward harmony of enlightenment.

The worldly success of Chinese Buddhism also led to its downfall. The more dominant Buddhism became, the more it came to be resented by many Confucians and Daoists at the court, who increasingly spoke out against what they regarded as its foreign values and way of life. Its monasteries, they noted, had become wealthy, and its communities represented an organized

This seated Buddha dates from the eighth century C.E., the Tang dynasty, during which time Buddhism dominated intellectual and artistic life. (The Metropolitan Museum of Art, Rogers Fund, 1943)

body independent of state control. By imperial order in 845, thousands of monasteries were forcibly closed, and tens of thousands of monks and nuns were compelled to resume their lay lives.

The purge was successful. Never again would Buddhism exercise significant political or economic power in China. Moreover, the intellectual and cultural ascendancy of Buddhism was also seriously undercut, making possible the reemergence of Confucianism in the following Song period. An important, if unintended, result of the persecution of the ninth century was that from the Song dynasty onward, the Pure Land schools dominated Chinese Buddhism at all levels. These schools were less affected than the universalist schools in part because their religious practices were simpler and required much less economic and political involvement with the world. In addition, these schools represented a far greater degree of accommodation to Chinese values, being largely the product of the Chinese mind acting on the received Buddhist tradition.

After the persecution, Chinese Buddhism increasingly merged with folk religion. By the fourteenth-century Ming period and continuing into modern times, many Chinese had come to believe in karmic retribution, reincarnation, multiple hells and heavens, and a number of Buddhas and bodhisattvas—all derived from Buddhism. Yet they had little sense of themselves as Buddhists. Instead, they practiced their unorganized folk religion within the family or at the local temple without concern for the quest for enlightenment that preoccupied Buddhist monks. Further, Pure Land Buddhism largely lost its independent existence; most of its monasteries became places where both Chan and Pure Land practices were carried out. At the same time, temples that were not monastic centers usually used Pure Land devotional practices. Of these, devotion to the bodhisattva Guan Yin became especially popular. Evolving from the remote male Avalokiteśvara of Indian conception, who "looks down" with compassion on suffering beings, the female Guan Yin intercedes in the ordinary problems of faithful men and women.

Beginning in the Tang and completing the process in the Song dynasty, Confucianism slowly regained its old position of prominence. Yet Chinese Buddhism had made such a lasting contribution to Chinese religious life that even Confucianism was significantly influenced by the long centuries of Buddhist domination.

Religions of China

CHAPTER 12

Neo-Confucianism: From the Classical Era to Modern Times

THE REVIVAL OF CONFUCIANISM

The dominant religious, philosophical, and political force in China from the Song dynasty of the tenth century until the end of the imperial system in the early twentieth was Neo-Confucianism. After the fall of the Tang, the first Song ruler called on the reemerging Confucian literati to help him bring stability to the administration. On their recommendations, the conservative emperor dropped the Daoist and Buddhist texts from the school curriculum and reinstated the Confucian classics. Although most Chinese continued to follow popular religious cults that included elements of Daoism and Buddhism, members of the official and scholarly classes turned back to the Confucian classics; writing new commentaries, they developed workable new theories of government, insight into the human condition, and a satisfying and meaningful way of life. Neo-Confucianism thus became the religion of the ruling elite.

Although Neo-Confucianism had been launched in official circles somewhat earlier, its cause was greatly advanced by highly respected commentaries on the Confucian classics written by two philosopher brothers, Cheng Hao (1032–1085) and Cheng Yi (1033–1107). Some time later two other philosophers gained prominence: Ju Xi (1130–1200) consolidated the earlier writings, prepared a standard commentary on the classics, and drew up a compendium of Confucian philosophy, and Wang Yangming (1472–1529) was greatly influenced by Buddhist thought.

Neo-Confucianism blended the old Confucian way with Buddhism. From old Confucianism it derived an emphasis on moral principles: Neo-Confucians sought properly ordered, harmonious human relationships, reflected in rule-governed behavior. But they recast this orientation in a very Buddhist light, teaching that all thought, ordinary experience, and performance of ritual are based on a single absolute, ultimate reality. Just like the Buddha nature, this absolute was thought to be the one principle essential to both gaining and organizing knowledge, and it could be directly encountered in an experience that would be ultimately transforming. It was the goal of a properly ordered life. The Neo-Confucians called this absolute **Li**. Though pronounced the same, this a different word from the *li* (ritual) discussed earlier. This *Li* means "reason, principle, order." The Confucian classics had used this idea merely to refer to the orderliness of things that li (ritual) had established. But to the Neo-Confucians, Li became a metaphysical entity, reality itself.

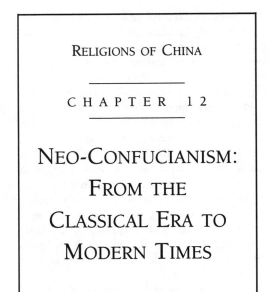

Cheng Yi spoke of this Li with the same tone of awe and celebration with which the Buddhists had spoken of the Buddha nature, and with very nearly the same words. It is emptiness: "Empty and tranquil, and without any sign, and yet all things are luxuriantly present."[1] Ju Xi later said of Li, "The Great Ultimate is nothing other than Principle [Li]."[2] Even heaven and earth existed by means of Principle, and that Principle was even before them. By its means yin and yang were generated.

Although Neo-Confucianism placed a high value on ritual as the pattern of properly ordered, harmonious human relationships, proper behavior had its origin in a purely ideal, absolute realm of Li. In Li all relationships exist virtually or potentially; outward observance only exemplifies these absolutes. This ideal realm, though immanent in all things, was approachable primarily by means of inward experience in meditation. Thus Neo-Confucians, unlike their Confucian predecessors, were concerned to probe the human mind for insight into its mechanisms. For example, one seeming paradox they pondered was how the mind in the ideal state might be both tranquil and, while working in the everyday world, active. The Buddhists had wrestled with this problem when attempting to understand the mind of the bodhisattva. The Neo-Confucians' answer was similar to the Chan Buddhists': both sought a state of tranquillity in activity.

This psychological concern also thrust the Confucian notion of the sage again into the foreground. In the thought of Confucius, the sages were all powerful men in the distant past. Neo-Confucian sagehood, however, was closer to the Mahāyāna Buddhist bodhisattva—it was a state of being to which the religiously gifted could aspire here and now. The sage would achieve a state of **enlightenment** that would set him or her apart from ordinary humans. This enlightenment was sometimes understood as a powerful mystical experience that transformed the personality. Further, both the sage and the bodhisattva were expected to engage in activities in the world for the benefit of others. Yet there were differences too: unlike the bodhisattva, the sage, though able in periods of meditation to regain his or her essential and original tranquillity, was not thought capable of maintaining such a state while active. Further, when active the sage would exhibit a typical Confucian array of virtues and attitudes, including some very non-Buddhist emotions. Ju Xi says:

> [Man's] original nature is pure and tranquil. Before it is aroused, the five moral principles of his nature, called humanity, righteousness, propriety, wisdom and faithfulness, are complete. As his physical form appears, it comes into contact with external things and is aroused from within. As it is aroused from within, the seven feelings, called pleasure, anger, sorrow, joy, love, hate, and desire, ensue. As feelings become strong and increasingly reckless, his nature becomes damaged. For this reason the enlightened person controls his feelings so that they will be in accord with the Mean. He rectifies his mind and nourishes his nature.[3]

Thus the great Confucian virtues, here called the five moral principles, are present eternally in the ideal and absolute realm of pure Principle. They constitute essential human nature, the original nature. Emotions are grounded in Li, the absolute, Principle, and are aroused by the activities of everyday affairs. In themselves, emotions—even anger and hate—are not considered bad. But when the emotions become overstimulated, a disparity may appear between one's inner, essential nature and one's outer, conscious life. Then one's actions, guided by overly active emotions, will no longer be in accord with Principle, and a return to Principle in a meditative experience of renewal is required.

This new emphasis on controlling emotions had a notable impact on the new orthodoxy's view of women. Males remained the focus of Neo-Confucian thought, and the primary threat to their emotional quietude was often associated with women. Rather than taking this as a call to males' self-control, Neo-Confucianists emphasized the need for a strict standard of chastity for women, so as to free men from the possibility of harmful emotional involvement. This emphasis transformed the moral code for women from a restrictive but balanced combination of virtue, personal cleanliness, and domestic work to an almost obsessive preoccupation with chastity. This was particularly significant for widows, whose chaste devotion to their husbands was to continue, sometimes leading to the ultimate act of devotion, suicide.

In addition to its emphasis on emotional control and female chastity, Neo-Confucianism retained an old Confucian political and moral stance. It continued to emphasize the regulation of public and private lives, keeping everything in its proper place, and ritualized social patterns. Yet it also offered its constituents the fulfillment of religious needs hitherto available only in Buddhism or Daoism. Accompanying a well-regulated social life was inner harmony and the direct experience of the ultimate, Li.

The School of Mind

This inner experience was especially vivid and dramatic in the Neo-Confucian School of Mind. An extraordinary biography of the Ming period philosopher and statesman Wang Yangming, its traditional founder, has been preserved. It shows in detail how much Neo-Confucianism owes to Buddhism and Daoism, while at the same time remaining loyal to old Confucianism. In his youthful quest for religious fulfillment, Wang immersed himself in both Buddhism and Daoism. Although he eventually gave them up, his thought, both in its content and in the dramatic way he discovered it, is strongly reminiscent of Buddhism. During a period in which he was temporarily out of favor at court, he went into retreat with a few disciples. Living the life of a Chan monk, he meditated on life and death, humbly chopping wood and carrying water for his students. He was plagued by the question of what a sage was, and he devoted himself to becoming one.

> One night it suddenly dawned upon him in the midnight watches what the sage meant by "investigating things for the purpose of extending knowledge to the utmost." Unconsciously he called out, got up and danced about the room. All his followers were alarmed; but the Teacher, now for the first time understanding the doctrine of the sage, said, "My nature is, of course, sufficient. I was wrong in looking for Principle in things and affairs."[4]

Wang was thus "enlightened" about his own nature, in which he discovered nothing less than Principle itself. That is, he had solved his and Neo-Confucianism's most fundamental problem, how to reconcile within his own life and experience the old Confucian concern for external things and affairs with the Buddhist concern for the inner life and inner experience. In a dramatic, Buddhist-like experience of enlightenment, he found the truth of Confucian principle. This set him on an intellectual course in which he identified Principle with Chan's "original mind" and insisted that for the sage there can be no disparity between thought and action.

Toward the end of the Ming period (fourteenth through seventeenth centuries) there lived Gao Panlong, another Neo-Confucian philosopher-statesman. Though from another school, Gao's autobiographical writings are similar to the School of Mind. As a young man, Gao set out to become a sage, by which he meant a perfected human being who, through deep insight into his own nature, perfectly exemplified the Confucian virtues of humaneness (ren), righteousness, decorum (Li), and wisdom. Gazing at a beautiful panorama, Gao asked himself how he could have remained unmoved by meditation on such a setting and concluded that his efforts so far had been a failure. Dividing his time between study of the classics and disciplined meditation, Gao's efforts culminated in a powerful enlightenment experience of the sort often referred to as "oceanic trance." He described it thus:

> Suddenly it was as if a load of a hundred pounds had fallen to the ground in an instant. It was as if a flash of lightning had penetrated the body and pierced the intelligence. Subsequently I was merged with the Great Transformation until there was no differentiation.[5]

Gao not only described his own experience but also wrote several short pieces on meditation technique and described a special meditation house he had built for himself in tranquil surroundings, the effect of which was for him profound and lasting; it established for him a lifelong meditative regime of re-creative self-cultivation.

TRADITIONAL CHINA UNDER CONFUCIANISM

China's social and religious structure changed astonishingly little from the eleventh century through the nineteenth. It was dominated by Neo-Confucianism; even the Mongol invasion and dynasty (1260–1368) hardly affected its dominance of the elite. Confucians continued to promote their religious values and curbed Buddhism and Daoism by monopolizing and controlling the governmental bureaucracy. This led it to clear domination of the intellectual life of the nation. Yet Confucianism, for all its power, never tried to root out other religious practices or institutions. This is partly because Confucianism was always an elite tradition and did not appeal to the masses. Its stress on scholarship, government service, and the maintenance of a rigidly hierarchical social structure kept any popular Confucianism from developing. The zhunzi ideal of the exemplary figure was itself elitist, inasmuch as it saw the masses as the passive recipients of a harmony imposed from above and fully lived only by the few. Thus the Confucian attitude toward Daoist, Buddhist, and folk religious practices was one of bemused toleration, ripening into active persecution only if these groups threatened political stability or the Confucians' special position.

Thus Confucianism promoted its own religious values by reinforcing ritual, moral codes, and legitimization of authority within such institutions as the family, the village, the occupational guild, and the state. This has meant that for many, and not just Confucians, religion in China has been an expression of a quality felt to be inherent in all human endeavors rather than a specialized activity more or less insulated from the rest of life. Perhaps nowhere in Chinese life beyond the government has Confucianism exerted more influence than on the family, especially the literati and merchant families of comfortable means. The hierarchical Chinese family, with its ritualistic system of unequal but supposedly mutually beneficial relationships, was seen not only as the foundation of human society but also as the model for government. Just as the parents nurtured their children, the emperor nurtured his subjects; and just as the children were expected to revere their parents, the nation was expected to revere its emperor.

Even though we have been referring to Neo-Confucianism monolithically, in fact it had different effects at various levels of society. We shall examine the several layers of the imperial or official level, the popular level, the family, and the Buddhist and Daoist sects.

The Imperial or Official Level

During this period there were three elements at the imperial, or official, level of religion in China.

The Imperial Cult The set of religious activities under the direct control of the court was known as the imperial cult. Rituals included the seasonal sacrifices in which the emperor himself played a central, priestly role. Here the division of religious labor inherent in the hierarchical principle was exemplified to the most extreme degree: the people were not permitted even to witness the rituals that were carried out on their behalf and most clearly expressed the common identity of the Chinese nation. The emperor was the people's representative to their deities.

The most important imperial ritual of the year was the worship of Heaven and the imperial ancestors at the time of the winter solstice. A large, open mound of earth composed of three circular terraces still stands south of the imperial palace in Beijing where the emperor, acting as chief priest, conducted this rite. After purifying himself, he mounted the terrace, and at various levels he would kneel and pray before tablets inscribed with the names of the celestial and spiritual powers, such as the sun and moon and the spirits of specific stars thought to constitute a kind of heavenly bureaucracy. Other tablets bore the names of the imperial ancestors and the ultimate power, Sovereign Heaven, Supreme Deity. One nineteenth-century observer described this solemn occasion thus:

> The service opens by peals of music. The Emperor in his robes of azure ascends the altar by the steps on the south, and advances to his place at the center of the round altar in front of the tablet to Heaven. . . . There he stands while the whole burnt offering is consumed in the furnace southeast of the altar. The "three kneelings and nine prostrations"—three prostrations with the head to the pavement at each kneeling—are now performed before the tablet to Heaven and before each of the tablets to his Ancestors. The libations are presented, and the written prayer is read.[6]

The Educated Elite The literati, composed of the powerful bureaucrats who ran the government offices, would-be officeholders, and members of the rich gentry class, practiced Confucian rituals. Twice a year in towns and cities, local officials offered prayers, incense, and food at the temples of Confucius and his ancestors. Instrumental music, the singing of hymns extolling Confucian virtues, and stylized dancing also accompanied these commemorative rites. These rituals reinforced both the literati's loyalty to the state and their sense of responsibility as culture bearers whose very way of life was the model of civilized behavior.

Local Officials In county seats the magistrates presided at many rituals throughout the year. They

The Imperial Palaces still stand today in Beijing. Walls and a moat surround what is actually a group of palaces, the home of Chinese emperors for over five hundred years. During this time, the emperor acted as the people's representative to their deities, carrying out elaborate rituals in and near the palaces. (Eastfoto)

regularly offered prayers to Confucius, to gods of war and of literature, to the local city god, to agricultural deities, and, incorporating some popular elements of Buddhism, to "Father Buddha" and certain bodhisattvas.

The Popular Level

An intermediate level of popular religion flourished; it mixed Confucian components with Buddhist, Daoist, and folk elements. It consisted of village or neighborhood ceremonies celebrated throughout the year, usually on the birthdays of the gods being honored. Many of these deities were the same as those included in the official cult, but many local deities were also celebrated. Typically these rites would draw people from the countryside to the temple located in the town. A parade of such pilgrims, carrying banners identifying their home village and accompanied by music and fireworks, would snake through the streets to the temple, where each village group would make offerings and pray for the deities' boons. Often fortunetellers and diviners would join the festivities, offering their services to the devout. Sometimes one or two of them might even become possessed by the spirit of a deity, thereby providing direct communication with him or her.

Also at this popular level were other individual religious activities not carried out within the family group: personal petitions to local shrines, campaigns for personal moral rectification, and individual participation in meditation and physical exercises thought to promote health and long life.

The Family Level

At the family level, the ancestral cult held pride of place. The ancestors received the most solemn and most regular attention; all important family events were ritually announced to them, and marriages were performed in their presence. The great ancestral remembrances were occasions for the many branches of a family to gather, so they strengthened the authority of the head family and its patriarch. Filial piety kept alive this feeling of solidarity, and all family members felt responsible for the family's wealth and honor. In addition, such worship must have brought a sense of connection to a timeless realm of the sacred dead. It represented a repeated experience of ultimacy, transcendent in that the dead were godlike in their power and wisdom and immanent in that one's own destiny was someday to join in that awesome company.

Specifically Religious Institutions

Given that the dominant political group was the Confucians, it is not surprising that Buddhism and Daoism were both waning and, from the ninth century on, periodically oppressed. The Buddhist Saṅgha was persecuted with the most zeal. It had a tightly knit organization, marked by impressive initiation rituals for monks and nuns. Its adherents wore unusual clothes and hairstyles, which differentiated them from the ordinary people. Some monasteries owned land, making them economically independent. Above all, the loyalty of these monks and nuns to the Saṅgha was known to weaken their commitment to the distant imperial establishment. Despite the Buddhists' denials of political aspirations, these features made them a threat in the Confucians' eyes. And indeed, lay Buddhist secret societies, which followed a quasi-monastic pattern of initiation and rituals, did sometimes express religious and political protest.

China in a Period of Revolutionary Change

CONTACT WITH THE WEST

The events and movements of religious significance in recent centuries in China have come largely as a response to contacts with the Western world. The story is complex, involving not only religion but also politics, economics, and technology—the entire cultural spectrum. In general, it is a story of the clash of cultures during which Chinese indifference gave way to curiosity, which was in turn replaced by growing anger and fear and finally culminated in the twentieth century in what might be called a passionate ambivalence. Many Chinese, especially among the elite, have hated the West for its threat to traditional (primarily Confucian) values, and many at all levels of society have grown angry at Western colonization and economic exploitation. But the West has also been loved, especially by the less powerful and also the more liberal segments, because it offered a previously unknown degree of political, economic, and religious freedom and material progress.

Although the adventures of Marco Polo in the thirteenth century sparked the European imagination, the first important contacts came when the Spanish and Portuguese expanded their empires into East Asia in the sixteenth century. At first the Chinese court regarded these few "Western barbarians" with scant interest. This attitude is understandable. The very sophistication of Chinese culture, its customs, thought, and values, had always helped it to maintain its historical and cultural continuity against other cultures. Foreigners they viewed as barbarians, and barbarians had nothing to offer the civilized. But with the coming of the Jesuit missionaries, things began to change. From the first the Jesuits adopted a policy of deemphasizing their strangeness. They learned Chinese, studied the Confucian classics, and impressed the literati by entering into their philosophical discussions and praising Confucian morality and love of learning. The Chinese literati perceived Christianity mainly as a moral system consistent with Confucianism. They also admired the missionaries' useful disciplines of mathematics and astronomy. So successful were these missionaries that some were even given official posts.

But the very policy of deemphasizing differences and seeking harmony by accommodating to Chinese ways, which had served the Jesuits so well, ultimately proved to be their undoing. The Jesuit missionaries had allowed Chinese Christians to continue to participate in the state cult and ancestor veneration, classifying these practices as nonreligious "civil ceremonies." This changed in 1706, when the church hierarchy barred Chinese Christians from such ceremonies, effectively stopping them from participating in a practice that the Manchu emperor regarded as essential. This sparked the famous Rites Controversy, for the angry emperor demanded that the more permissive Jesuit practices again be followed. When the church again refused, the Christian missionaries were expelled from China. Christianity had come into conflict not only with the deeply held attitudes of the

Chinese people but also with the power of the emperor and his Confucian literati.

CULTURAL AND RELIGIOUS CRISES IN THE NINETEENTH AND TWENTIETH CENTURIES

The restless and, some would say, reckless creativity of the West had produced by the middle of the nineteenth century not only superior armaments and economic exploitation through colonialism but also intellectual and religious movements of far-reaching consequences. The secular scientific worldview had developed, and new ideologies such as socialism and communism were being formulated. China could no longer maintain its aloof isolationism now that the world had, uninvited, forced its way in. And the world was itself in a state of agitation.

The Confucian elite attempted to keep the West's intellectual influence at a distance, just as the imperial government tried to do in the economic and military spheres. One of the most persuasive spokesmen for the traditionalists was the government official and Confucian scholar Feng Guifen (1809–1874). Feng coined the term *ziqiang* (**"self-strengthening"**) as the proper attitude of the Chinese toward the Western threat: Western science and technology had much to offer, and in fact, he proposed, translation centers should be set up and the best students sent there to learn Western mathematics, physics, and medicine. But the Chinese must be very selective in their borrowings: according to Feng, "What we then have to learn from the barbarians is only the one thing, solid ships and effective guns." Apart from this, the West had little to offer: "Those [books] which expound the doctrine of Jesus are generally vulgar, not worth mentioning." In 1860 Feng clearly set down the formula that was to dominate Chinese thinking until the end of the century:

> If we let Chinese ethics and famous [Confucian] teachings serve as an original foundation, and let them be supplemented by the methods used by the various nations for the attainment of prosperity and strength, would it not be the best of all procedures?[7]

This attempt to accept but limit change exhibits China's ambivalence: earlier it could be Westernized in such a way that these foreign elements could be harmonized with a traditional Chinese framework of values and attitudes. But it was not to be, since technology came embedded in a foreign culture with alien values and beliefs that increasingly sang a siren song to Chinese of all social strata. It was a question not just of finding a place in the Chinese order for things Western but of which order would prevail.

By 1898 China had fought and lost short wars with Britain, France, and Japan and had lost political and economic control of portions of its own territory to Russia, Japan, Germany, France, and Britain. With the increased economic and military penetration of China by the Western powers came a renewal of Christian missionary activity. This time it was predominantly British and American Protestant denominations. Especially through their schools, orphanages, and hospitals, Christianity had a noticeable impact. Some Chinese observers were nonetheless optimistic about this Western incursion. If the Confucian essence were truly strong, such secondary problems would disappear by themselves. After all, it had worked before with Buddhism.

The Tai Ping Rebellion

While the literati were wrestling with the impact of Western learning, a synthesis of East and West was being formulated on the popular level out of elements of Christian and Chinese religiosity. Instead of the aesthetic and detached humanism of early Confucian flirtations with Christianity, it was the popular culture that was most affected. This led to the **Tai Ping Rebellion**, which devastated China and almost toppled the Manchu dynasty.

Ironically, *tai ping* means "great peace," and it harks back to the popular Daoist movements that had sought to overthrow the Han dynasty. The leaders of this revolt believed that the Daoist utopian vision of harmony and simplicity would be established on earth as the biblical kingdom of the Christian God. Furthermore, without being restrained by the tradition of interpretation of Christian teachings and a culture based partly on them, the Tai Ping leaders applied Christian concepts to their own society with revolutionary zeal.

The splendor of the imperial court (above) contrasts sharply with the bare existence of the common people like this shopkeeper's family. Dissatisfaction with this inequality led first to the Tai Ping Rebellion and culminated in the Communist victory in 1949. (Religious News Service)

They tried to establish their religious utopia by military force, and they very nearly succeeded.

The founder of the Tai Ping movement was Hong Xiuchuan (1814–1864). As a young man he had taken the civil service examinations, only to fail twice. After an extended period of nervous collapse, he recalled a vision of divine beings and heaven. Eventually he encountered some Christian missionaries and, after reading some of their religious tracts, interpreted his visions as showing that he was Jesus's younger brother, now called on to complete Jesus's work as a second messiah. Hong taught that the great evil in the world was Confucian teaching, and having successfully struggled against Confucius and the various demons in heaven, he had been sent down to earth again with a sacred sword to restore Christ's true teaching. Thus Hong came to view the religion of the threatening West as having been originally Chinese.

The Tai Ping vision of a heavenly kingdom on earth was derived as much from centuries-old peasant frustrations as from the Christian gospel. Its leaders sought racial egalitarian social structures: all people would be equal, including women; the old hierarchical system would be abandoned, and property would be held in common; and all would be members of the same family. Confucian notions of the world as a family were mingled with Christian millennialism and folk religious ideas of a struggle against demonic forces. The form of organization of the old Buddhist secret society was given a Christian content: instead of the future Buddha (Maitreya) who would renew the Dharma and thereby inaugurate a new golden age, a new messiah would appear—in fact had already appeared in the person of Hong—who would establish a permanent reign of justice and plenty.

Curiously, the barbarian demons against whom Hong's sword was sent were not the westerners but the Manchu rulers who had taken China from the Chinese and thus perverted God's heavenly kingdom. The Great Peace (Tai Ping) and God's universal kingdom would come with the overthrow of the Manchus.

From 1850 to 1864 Hong and his generals were at constant war with the Manchu regime. It was a double irony that native Chinese troops under native Chinese leadership finally stopped the Tai Ping advances after the Manchu troops had failed and that the intervention of the "Christian" powers of the West, notably Britain, led to the rebels' ultimate destruction. The great dream of peace had brought death to an estimated 20 million people.

CHINA IN THE TWENTIETH CENTURY

The dissatisfactions of the peasantry that had led to the Tai Ping Rebellion had not died with them. Their frustrations and the brittleness of the old Chinese system led to progressively weaker governments and civil war, culminating in the Communist victory in 1949. During this period one event stands out as most significant to later Chinese history: the emergence of Mao Zedong (Mao Tse-tung, 1893–1976) as the leader of the Communists in the famous **Long March** of 1934. The national government under Jiang Jieshi (Chiang Kai-shek, 1887–1975) began its notorious "bandit extermination" campaigns against the Communists in 1927, eventually surrounding the Communist guerrilla bases in southern China. The Communists managed to break out and escape to the north; although thousands died on this exhausting 6,000-mile Long March, the result was a strengthening of the Communist movement. In their survival, the peasants, frustrated by the centuries of domination by a small elite, saw the hope of salvation. After Japan's defeat in World War II, the Communist armies were able to sweep Jiang's forces out of the mainland and into exile on the island of Taiwan. In October 1949, before cheering throngs in Beijing, Mao Zedong proclaimed the People's Republic of China.

Religion under the Communist Regime

The official attitude of the Communist government toward traditional religion should come as no surprise. Karl Marx wrote in the nineteenth century that religion was the opiate of the masses, an instrument used by oppressive regimes to divert the attention of the people from their true enemies and even to enlist them in the willing service of their own exploiters. Therefore, religion should not exist in a truly communist society and should at best be only tolerated.

Indeed, it has survived to the extent that the rulers of the new China have made freedom of religion a part of their constitution; yet the government has mounted a number of campaigns against citizens who practice it. Sometimes these campaigns have been verbal: Confucianism is identified with a repressive "feudal" system; the people should "struggle against Confucius." Some campaigns have gone further, denouncing and prohibiting many popular Buddhist, Daoist, and folk religious practices as superstition. Often religious institutions have been closed, churches and temples destroyed or confiscated, and priests and ministers sent to forced-labor camps. But most telling is the fact that former monasteries are now shoe factories, and temples have been abandoned or converted into showpieces to bolster national pride and increase tourism. To the Communists, fossils of religion are useful only in teaching the masses about the evils of the past.

Religious Aspects of Maoism

For some time scholars have pointed out that any modern ideology functions much like a traditional religion. Thus an ideology like Marxism provides a world of meaning and a way of life for its followers: it organizes their energies, defines what is worth doing, constructs a mythology of struggle and saintly heroism, and establishes rituals designed to reinforce these values. For this reason, many scholars have called Marxism a pseudoreligion. Like traditional religions, Marxism attempts to transform people into its own image of perfection. When it is successful, it engenders a sense of awe and reverence, of exhilaration or guilt, in the presence of what it holds to be sacred and of ultimate value. We will consider the evidence that the Maoist form of Marxism is an enemy of traditional religions partly because it appropriates many of the functions of religion.

From the Maoist point of view, the traditional religions of China were not wrong in presenting descriptions of the structure, order, and harmony inherent in reality. The religions' error was in the specific content of their vision. For example, Confucianism advocated social and economic inequality, believing that such inequality was part of the very fabric of reality. The error of Buddhism and Daoism was that their monastic life styles harnessed the labor of others to support the monks. Moreover, Daoism believed in a transcendent reality that was ultimate

This photo shows the National Day Parade, October 1, 1950. Workers celebrated the first anniversary of the founding of the People's Republic of China, marching with posters of their leader, Mao Zedong. There is much evidence that Maoism became an enemy of traditional religions partly because it appropriated many of the functions of religion. (Eastfoto)

both in the sense of "mysterious and undefinable" and in the sense of "most important." No one could capture this ultimate Dao in words, and no other value could take precedence over it. But Maoism sought to apply the sense of ultimacy to its *own* values by inducing a powerful personal experience of Marxism and associating its values with this experience.

The values and goals that Marxism proclaims are liberation of the masses from the capitalist yoke, unlimited material progress, and creation of a classless society. In its Chinese version, it should be seen as the inheritor of many of the fundamental values of China that we have repeatedly encountered. The state was to be one in which everyone had a valued place and would be supported in that place. Its society was to be absolutely democratic, and everyone's place was to be regarded as equally valued and rewarded. This utopian society would be of such natural harmony that the state itself would eventually cease to exist. But this meant that all self-centered tendencies toward individual privilege and pride must be quashed. Here Maoism was in accord with the old Confucian and Daoist emphasis on selfless performance, though its aggressive methods of bringing this about—thought control and brainwashing—were new.

Other features of Maoism also point to its quasi-religious character. It cherished and often recited its "holy history." The Moses-like figure of Mao is portrayed as leading the Communist armies on the Long March. They encounter many difficulties along the way, with enemies on all sides. Many holy martyrs fall during this period of "salvation history," but finally the victory is won. The foreign devils (imperialists) are thrown out of China, and the domestic demons (landlords and capitalists) are punished.

Also like many religions, Maoism has its holy book.

The famous "little red book" containing the thoughts of Chairman Mao held all wisdom and was to replace all philosophies, theologies, and scriptures. In every spare moment, people were expected to read, memorize, and ponder his thoughts. The People's Liberation Army, which "had the deepest love for Chairman Mao and constantly studied his works," helped to organize family study sessions on the holy book. Typically, families held regular meetings to study and implement Mao's teachings and "make self-criticisms and criticisms of each other."[8] One possible result of all this is described in ritual terms: a meal was prepared of wild herbs and ordinary food, the former to represent the past and the latter "as a token of our present happiness." Then the family stood before Mao's picture and pledged renewed allegiance to him.

Maoism and the Transformation of Culture

Holiness, or ultimate value, was found not only in the person and works of Chairman Mao but also in the Chinese masses. It was the people, especially the peasants, who instinctively knew the correct doctrine and who felt the need for communism long before the actual organizers and leaders of the movement emerged. And it was to these same people that the leaders, including Mao himself, always had to return. As Mao once stated:

> Our god is none other than the masses of the Chinese people. . . . When we say, "We are the Sons of the People," China understands it as she understood the phrase "Son of Heaven." The People have taken the place of the ancestors."[9]

Though freedom of religion is a part of the constitution, the Communist regime mounted a number of campaigns against citizens who practice it. During the 1980s, however, a cautious rapprochement with Confucianism was seen. This photo is of dancers performing the ancient "Liu Yi" dance as part of a memorial ceremony for Confucius. (Eastfoto)

Like the ancestors, the people provided the fundamental direction to life and shaped social values.

This view has had far-reaching consequences for modern China, and the Maoist vision of cultural transformation took its first step here: culture begins with the masses; what is correct comes from the masses. But they are inarticulate, so Mao must interpret for them. Furthermore, no amount of mere study of words or abstract ideas can substitute for actual experience. Intellectuals and urban youths must be sent to the countryside and live the life of a rural peasant in order to grasp and internalize the true mass perspective. The so-called **May Seventh schools** attempted to do just this with study sessions at school alternating with periods of agricultural work.

The ongoing task of each generation, then, is the transformation of the individual's personal, selfish, and urban outlook to the peasant's collective, self-sacrificing attitude. Even artistic and literary activity must show this peasant attitude; it too must be socially relevant and "correct."

Maoism's quest for purity of attitude was sometimes resisted, even within the ranks of the faithful. For example, the strengthening of the nation demanded the development of a strong military and a powerful economy. This in turn required the development of a modern industrial base, applying modern technology and management skills. But the need for expertise in these modern skills could and often did run counter to the desire for revolutionary purity. The usual way of discussing this problem was to distinguish between being "red" (politically correct) and "expert" (expert at a modern skill). Since 1949 China has oscillated between these two poles, emphasizing now one and now the other.

The most zealous, emotional, and disruptive period of emphasis on ideological purity ("redness") was during the Cultural Revolution. During this time (from 1966 to the early 1970s), the production of goods was allowed to suffer greatly in the service of purity. Purges not only of intellectuals and managers but also of Communist party bureaucrats were carried out on an immense scale by roving bands of youths known as the Red Guards. Clearly, to be red was of supreme importance, and all had to be sacrificed for it. This chaotic rite of purification stopped only when the army finally stepped in to restore order.

By the time Mao Zedong died in 1976, Maoism had spent its crusading zeal. The emphasis of the Cultural Revolution on red at the expense of expert had already begun to wane, and the late 1970s saw a further shift away from the emphasis on ideological purity.

The Present Situation

The 1980s and early 1990s have seen an increase in China's willingness to open itself to the world, especially to the West. Although some private enterprise is now possible, and the press is a little freer, the specter of the red-versus-expert dichotomy still broods over China. The leadership tentatively experiments with increased individual freedom while at the same time attempting to maintain state and ideological control. A particularly shocking example of this may be seen in the government's response to the student protests that erupted in the spring of 1989. Refusing to attend classes, thousands of university students held mass meetings in several major cities. At first it appeared that their demands for greater individual freedom, political democracy, and an end to official corruption might in some way be met. But the slaughter of hundreds of protesters on June 3–4 in Tiananmen Square in Beijing quickly put an end to such hopes. Many since have been arrested and some reportedly put to death. University students must now spend many hours in studies designed to engender ideological purity and to purge them of Western liberal ideas.

Maoism is for the moment quiescent—even a limited amount of criticism of Mao has been permitted, and his birthplace, once a busy pilgrimage destination, is now largely deserted. There is some speculation, however, that among the peasants, if not government leaders, Mao still lives in the hearts of many. In the present climate of cautious toleration, the government has relaxed restraints sufficiently to allow Christians once again to practice their faith openly, although severe restrictions still prevail, and the number of functioning congregations is limited. Daoism, except for the most elementary folk beliefs and a small monastic community, has been all but destroyed. Buddhism is still a presence: some temples have been allowed to reopen, and perhaps with help from abroad the monastic tradition, now in utter ruin, may be rebuilt not just in form but also in practice.

As for the future, the collapse of Maoist idealism has left many Chinese with a hunger for values that some observers interpret as an expression of deep, unmet religious needs. Some Chinese scholars have even suggested that traditional religion is important to the stability of even a socialist society. This is apparently the thinking behind a cautious rapprochement with Confucianism as witnessed by an academic conference held in 1987 with government acquiescence in the hometown of Confucius. Some more adventuresome Chinese scholars have suggested that parts of the old teaching may still have relevance as a replacement for the discredited ideology of Marxism. If connection to what is believed to be ultimate is a part of every viable society and every fulfilled human life, then the Chinese, cut off from their traditional access to ultimacy, are facing a spiritual malaise far deeper than that of the West. In the modern West, despite its secular framework, religions continue to flourish, providing meaning and value to many, both as individuals and as part of voluntary religious communities. In China, however, the people face not only a public but also a private spiritual vacuum.

NOTES

1 Attributed to Cheng Yi by Ju Xi in *Chin-ssu Lu (Reflections on Things at Hand)* 1.32, in *A Source Book in Chinese Philosophy*, trans. and comp. Wing-tsit Chan (Princeton, N.J.: Princeton University Press, 1963).

2 Ibid., 48:8b–9a.

3 Ibid., 2.3.

4 Frederick Goodrich Henke, trans., *The Philosophy of Wang Yang-ming* (La Salle, Ill.: Open Court, 1916), p. 13.

5 Rodney L. Taylor, trans., *The Cultivation of Sagehood as a Religious Goal in Neo-Confucianism* (Missoula, Mont.: Scholars Press, 1978), p. 128.

6 Henry Blodgett, "The Worship of Heaven and Earth by the Emperor of China," *Journal of the American Oriental Society* 29 (1899): 65–66.

7 Ssu-yu Teng et al., *China's Response to the West* (Cambridge, Mass.: Harvard University Press, 1954), pp. 53, 52.

8 Donald E. MacInnis, ed., *Religious Policy and Practice in Communist China* (New York: Macmillan, 1982), p. 341.

9 Ibid., pp. 16–17.

Religions of Japan

CHAPTER 13

Japan's Religions: From Prehistory to Modern Times

THE JAPANESE RELIGIOUS CHARACTER

As we trace the history of religion in Japan, we will come to see many similarities to religion in China. We will see, in fact, that Japan has borrowed many religious ideas and practices from the Chinese. Yet we will also become aware of sometimes subtle differences. Like the Chinese, the Japanese have valued harmony in nature and in human society. But while the Chinese have viewed the world as a naturally orderly and thus harmonious place susceptible to disruption by ill-considered human actions, the Japanese have regarded the world as a place of natural and enduring tension: forces tending toward order and harmony contend with forces tending toward disorder and disharmony. Thus the native Japanese deities **(kami)** themselves were characterized by a degree of freedom, even caprice, not envisioned by the Chinese. To the Chinese, both nature and human society resulted from the dynamic interplay of yin and yang; these were in turn governed by the mysterious and ultimate harmony, Dao. But to the Japanese, nature and society resulted from the interplay of ultimately unpredictable kami. Moral categories apply to these deities and hence to the world only imperfectly. The kami—and humans by extension—are neither good nor bad but, depending on the situation, a mixture of both. Some kami may even be predominantly destructive.

The readiness to live with dynamic tension may also be seen in the way Japan has adopted foreign elements. When it welcomed Chinese ideas—Confucianism, Buddhism—and later Western technology and culture, it never adopted any in their entirety. For example, elements of Confucianism and Buddhism were allowed to remain side by side with indigenous Japanese elements, especially Shintō, their inconsistencies and tensions unresolved.

Both the Chinese and the Japanese have valued ritual, but in different orientations. Whereas Confucian ritual seeks to embody and celebrate a harmony that already exists, Shintō ritual seeks to create a temporary island of harmony within a chaotic and dangerous world. Thus the Japanese may perform a ritual to ask a destructive deity to leave the area or to invoke protective kami to ward off destructive ones.

Also, mystical experience has been put to a different use in Japan. In a trance state, the Japanese shaman does not seek a permanent transformation of personality or personal salvation. This contrasts with the Daoist mystic, who sought a permanent loss of self so as perfectly to embody the ultimate Dao. The Shintō shaman sought (temporary) loss of self in order to be possessed by the capricious kami so that their unique messages could be transmitted to humans. Their goal, like so much of Japanese religion, was to protect this world from unpredictable dangers.

OVERVIEW OF JAPANESE RELIGIOUS HISTORY

Japanese history can be divided into four periods. First is the protohistoric period from around the third century C.E. through the middle of the seventh. Our knowledge of it is fragmentary and based largely on myths and legends preserved for many decades only in memory. During most of this time, when the people of the relatively isolated Japanese islands knew no writing system, what came to be called the Shintō religion was taking form, as were many of Japan's folk religious beliefs and practices.

A legend from the seventh century tells of the gift from a Korean king of the first Buddhist artifacts. These images and texts opened Japan to the richness of Chinese civilization, with its writing system and vast literature of poetry, history, philosophy, and religion. That embracing of things Chinese was the key feature of the second period, the classical (mid-seventh through twelfth centuries). It was characterized by the rapid assimilation of Chinese ideas and the tension that resulted from the only partly successful attempt to restructure Japanese society after Chinese models. At first these "modern" ideas and practices, including Buddhism and Confucianism, affected only the top echelon of society, the aristocrats who clustered around the imperial court, but by the end of the period, they had reached the ordinary villagers. Also during this period, Shintō became a recognizable religion and achieved official sanction at court; many of its myths and rituals were written down for use by government-supported priests. Indeed, the religious landscape of the time contained elements of Confucianism, Buddhism, and Shintō scattered about in what often seems bewildering confusion. In short, the classical period witnessed a melding of foreign and indigenous religious traditions.

The third, or medieval, period (thirteenth through eighteenth centuries) saw the triumph of Buddhism in the rise of new and popular sects that tended to subordinate Shintō. Pure Land Buddhism came to dominate the common people, while Zen was especially popular among the upper classes. At the same time, Confucianism became so intimately incorporated into both Buddhist and Shintō practices that it ceased to exist as an independent tradition. But it once again became a serious subject of study toward the end of the period, first among Zen monks and later among government-supported scholars who thought of themselves as Neo-Confucians. Shintō also enjoyed a revival during the later medieval period, first among **national scholars** who modeled themselves on the Confucians and then among the people themselves, who made frequent pilgrimages to Shintō shrines.

The modern period (nineteenth and twentieth centuries) has been a time of rapid cultural and religious change during which Japan evolved from a decentralized, isolated, feudal society to a self-consciously modernizing nation that successfully assimilated Western technology, economic organization, and political power. Socially and religiously, the modern period has been characterized by disruption of traditional patterns of life and consequent confusion and uncertainty. This situation has led not only to changes in the relative importance of older religious groups but also to the formation of numerous "new religions."

In general, the Japanese have sought to preserve old values while at the same time assimilating foreign elements, sometimes with painful results. Confucianism and Buddhism, dominant at the end of the medieval period, quickly gave way to a rejuvenated Shintō, which was increasingly molded by the government into a civil cult of patriotism. With the destruction of that artificially created edifice after World War II, contemporary Japan can be described as existing in an uneasy equilibrium made up of contending religious sects, especially the very visible new religions; a noticeable show of secularism; and an underlying and often unconscious attachment to customary religious observance involving elements of folk religion, Shintō, and Buddhism.

THE SHINTŌ SUBSTRATUM OF JAPANESE RELIGIOSITY

Just as we argued for a substratum of commonly held religious ideas in China, so we will present a set of religious ideas and attitudes that form the foundation of much of the religious behavior of the Japanese. Although we will call this substratum *Shintō,* it includes the vaguely defined and disorganized Japa-

Japanese women are seen here coming to pray for the well-being of their families at the Shintō shrine Mitsumine Jinja, as their ancestors have done for nearly two thousand years. (Religious News Service)

nese folk beliefs and customs as well as the more articulate later "official" myths and rituals. Examination of the central concept of *kami,* together with the myths and rituals associated with it, will help us to form a picture of the Japanese religious character.

SHINTŌ AS A "LITTLE TRADITION"

Even today, Shintō, along with Buddhism, enjoys the allegiance of most Japanese. Rather than a system of dogmatic beliefs or a definite code of ethics, Shintō is a diverse set of traditional rituals and ceremonies. It has no founder; no all-powerful deity; no inclusive, canonical scripture; and no organized system of theology. Moreover, Shintō has incorporated many folk religious customs. It has also been influenced by Confucianism, Daoism, Buddhism, and, in modern times, Christianity. Nevertheless, certain attitudes and practices have persisted from the earliest times to the present, and these form much of the substratum of Japanese religiosity.

No written documents survive from before the seventh century, Shintō's most important formative period. Historians have had to draw on later folklore, archaeological findings, and oral traditions written down long after their original formation. Even in more recent periods, the development of Shintō has been difficult to ascertain beyond vague outlines. This is due to the very nature of Shintō, which has been for much of its existence what some scholars call a "little tradition," a set of customary activities lived by the common folk rather than a body of thought and practice carried by the learned and powerful.

This does not mean that Shintō has no structure or internal coherence: there are many common assumptions about the nature of the world and human life and destiny. These assumptions and the Shintō they influenced became, so to speak, the vessel into which everything else was poured. They thereby bestowed a peculiar Japanese shape onto all of its contents.

THE NATURE OF THE KAMI

The term *Shintō,* sometimes called *kami no michi,* means "the way of the gods." Some scholars derive the term *kami* from a word meaning "above, high, lifted up"; by extension, it means something unusual, special, and powerful; finally, it can also connote something august, awe-inspiring, mysterious, divine. The kami constitute an immanent ultimate, found within all things. It is similar to the notion of *mana* on other Pacific islands—an undifferentiated power inherent in all things that gives each its peculiar nature, efficacy, and attributes. The undifferentiated character of kami may be seen in the fact that many local shrines house kami whose names are not known and about whom no myths exist. Such shrines are merely local places of reverence rather than evidence of attempts to establish a relationship with a particular deity.

When this undifferentiated power becomes concentrated, however, it sometimes manifests itself as a sac-red object, an event, or, especially, a person, with a name and a distinct personality. Thus myths, legends, and folk tales sprang up around the kami, and *matsuri* (festivals) were celebrated in their honor. These kami are similar to the gods of Greek or Hindu polytheism. Usually well disposed toward humanity, many kami are thought of as protective spirits. Yet, as noted earlier, there are also disruptive and destructive kami who have to be placated and kept at a distance. Indeed, any kami can become dangerous if good relations are not maintained through ritual activities. Japanese folk religion views the world as an often unpredictable interplay of dangerous and beneficial forces.

There are three main types of kami: deified powers of nature or abstract mental attributes, clan ancestors, and souls of the celebrated dead.

Deified Abstract Powers To the early Japanese, the kami were primarily the superhuman powers that animated the world around them. Most kami are associated with nature; they include the deities of heaven, earth, the seas, and the underworld. Their names suggest that they were deifications of natural or human forces. **Amaterasu**, the most important kami, whose name means "heavenly shining one," is in part a manifestation of the sun. Myths tell of "creative" kami who are identified with the power of growth and reproduction, "straightening" kami who are responsible for setting things right, "bending" kami who bring misfortune, and "thought-combining" kami who confer wisdom. Other kami are associated with such natural objects as heaven and earth, the stars, mountains, rivers, fields, seas, rain, animals, plants, and minerals.

Clan Ancestors These kami are also sometimes thought of as nature kami but are revered primarily as the first ancestors of family lines. For aristocratic families (the great clans), these were probably the most important kami, for their existence reflected and legitimized the clans' claims to social and political preeminence. The most famous of the ancestral kami is Amaterasu, the sun goddess, the founder of Japan's ruling family. For many centuries Amaterasu was served at her primary cult site at Ise by a priestess who was an imperial princess. Originally each clan preserved its own myths about its clan ancestor and maintained a shrine at which this kami was regularly worshiped. Usually these kami had their primary shrines at the local center of clan power, though a powerful clan might move its shrine to an important political center. (This suggests the political importance of such shrines.)

Souls of the Dead Humans venerated for their high office, extraordinary personality, or great deeds (either constructive or destructive) might also be honored as kami. All the deceased emperors and many war heroes are kami, as the elaborate imperial tombs and numerous shrines testify. In Tokyo today, the Yasukuni shrine is famous as a place where the people go to revere the war dead. Potentially this type of kami can arise when anyone has died in forlorn circumstances, that is, when the spirit of the dead has some reason for being troubled and unfulfilled. Other such kami have more benign origins; for example, a saintly religious person might be enshrined and become a means by which the person's "kami power" may be tapped for human benefit.

SHINTŌ MYTHOLOGY

A rich source for enlarging our understanding of the Japanese religious character is the myth collections assembled at imperial command early in the eighth century. Inspired by Chinese historical writings, Shintō scholars collected their oral myths and historical traditions into two important official "histories," the *Kojiki* ("Records of Ancient Matters"), which appeared in 712, and the *Nihon-shoki* ("Chronicles of Japan"), published in 720. Many myths were woven together in these texts in such a way that religion buttressed the political legitimacy of the Japanese state. In addition, the state conferred on Shintō the status of a great tradition through ideological and financial support. Shintō's position was later overshadowed by Buddhism, but the Shintō revival carried out by Japanese intellectuals in the Tokugawa period (1600–1868) once again gave Shintō, and especially its myths, a dominant position among Japan's religions.

A Creation Myth: The Primordial Parents

The dynamic tension in Japanese religions is seen in a major theme in these myths: creativity. The myths tell of the creation of the world out of chaos. Such creation took many forms: sexual union from which kami were born, cutting up or subdividing existing kami, and releasing the blood of kami. Each drop of this sacred life fluid was believed to have the power to generate new kami and thus new phenomena, things, and powers. Certainly a sense of *mana* is overwhelming in these early myths, in which even a kami's most casual activity produced new deities. Three of the major Shintō divinities were created as the result of ritual performance, in this case a rite of purification.

To explore the Shintō sense of the world's dynamic tension, let us look at the myth of the Primordial Parents. It holds that the first kami arose from the primordial chaos and dwelt on the high plain of heaven. Next were created the kami of birth and growth. Finally, the original parents—**Izanagi**, the male principle, and **Izanami**, the female principle—descended from heaven along a rainbow bridge. Standing on the tip of this bridge, Izanagi thrust his jewellike spear into the ooze below. When an island emerged, the two kami stepped down to it, mated, and produced the eight great islands of Japan. Many kami were born to the couple, but when the fire kami was born to Izanami, she was killed by the flames. Izanami thus went to Yomi, the land of the dead beneath the earth, and in his grief Izanagi followed his wife. Despite the warning of Izanami, whose body was now corrupt, he could not keep himself from looking at her. They quarreled, and Izanagi fled back to the upper world, pursued by the polluting forces of decay, disease, and death. These forces turned into the thunder demons, kami who bring disease and death to humanity. Seeking to repair the harm he had inadvertently caused, Izanagi vowed to create life even faster than the thunder demons could destroy it. Thus was established the tenuous balance between death and life.

In this tale, the tension between male and female is used to reinforce the tension between creativity and destruction. The union of husband and wife in love leads to both birth and death, and love turns to hate when the death taboo is broken. What is achieved is a kind of balance between the positive and negative forces: life dominates death but can never be wholly victorious. Such tensions—between life and death, male and female, chaos and order—are part of the structure of reality and can never be resolved entirely. Both sides are necessary for the world to function properly. They exist in a state of dynamic tension.

This dualism of cosmic forces, like the yin and yang of China, influenced Japanese differentiation of gender roles. As the Shintō myths show, women were associated with blood (particularly birth blood), death, chaos, and other polluting, negative forces. Men, by contrast, were identified with purity, life, and order. In one respect, this dichotomy suggested that women were a source of pollution to men and should be kept under the strict control of males (as fathers, husbands, and sons). Thus social and political power belonged exclusively to men, and women's activities were confined to the domestic sphere. In this context, Japanese culture imposed on women extreme standards of chastity like those of Neo-Confucian China. Yet women's association with mysterious phenomena like birth and death also rendered them religiously essential, and they became shamans capable of communicating with venerated dead ancestors and kami.

SHINTŌ RITUAL

The Japanese, like the pre-Buddhist Chinese, apparently had no notion of an afterlife as a place of reward or punishment. Certainly, the ancestors were honored as the source of family life, and among aristocrats the

The Great Torii (gates) of Itsukushima shrine. The gate to this shrine, dedicated to the three daughters of the Shintō god Susano-ō, stands offshore the sacred Miyajima Island. At high tide, the gate is surrounded by water; at low tide, it can be reached on foot. (Consulate General of Japan)

first ancestor was celebrated in myth as a great kami. But death and the land of the dead were regarded as the primary source of pollution, and contact with the dead required ritual cleansing before one could recommence social or religious activities. The reward for a significant life was a cult established in one's honor in this world, not a happy state in the next. Moreover, there was no concept of the perfectability of humanity, nothing like enlightenment or the Confucian sage. Shintō cultic activity was directed solely toward ensuring a viable existence in this world of dynamic, delicately balanced, and often unpredictable forces.

Matsuri

Shintō knows two distinct types of ritual action. Both seek communication with the kami who order and animate the world. The first and more common type is called **matsuri**, or celebrations. Matsuri are usually scheduled according to a regular ritual calendar of yearly and monthly rites. Priests preside at the services, which seek basically to ensure continued order in the cosmos. Humans wish to influence the sacred powers so as to keep the world favorable to human life and prosperity. Matsuri are basically rites of hospitality, analogous to inviting honored guests to one's home. Kami are entertained, offered food and drink, and praised or flattered, and promises are made to them.

A matsuri typically has five parts. The shrine area is considered a sacred space, established by its characteristic *torii,* or gates. The kami are thought to have descended to the shrine buildings, which are therefore never entered, not even for ritual purposes. First, the priests undergo purification rituals like bathing, eating special foods, and abstaining from sexual intercourse to prepare themselves for the presence of the kami. Then the kami, who dwell in heaven, must be called down to the ceremony. Once present, they are given offerings of food and drink, such as rice, sake, or fish. Music, dancing, and praises are also offered. Next the priest dips a branch of the sacred *sakaki* tree, a kind of evergreen, in holy water and waves it over the assembly, sprinkling all with the kami's blessings. Finally, a meal of the food offered to the kami is eaten by the priests and others.

The relationship between humans and kami is one-way: we are dependent on them as children are on their parents. Thus the communication of these rituals is also one-way: from the human priests to the kami. The gestures and order of these rituals are fixed; innovation and spontaneity are strongly discouraged.

One might perform a matsuri for specific purposes: to usher in the new year, to guard the spring planting, or perhaps to ensure a generally harmonious relationship with these powerful beings. In other matsuri gifts are offered in the hope of driving away destructive kami, thus creating a temporary oasis of order and safety.

Shamanic Rituals

The second type of Shintō ritual is shamanic, involving communicating with the kami by falling into a trance. The kami is considered to possess the shaman, or **miko**, and to animate her body, speaking through her mouth. (Although men can also become kami-possessed, from earliest times professional miko have been women.) Communication in shamanism is primarily from kami to human, although an interpreter is usually present in order to question the kami when it "descends." This kind of ritual is often used in what we might call crisis situations—special, nonroutine circumstances when the will of the kami seems unclear but important. In ancient times, when shamanism was practiced by the elite levels of Japanese society, such a situation might be a decision about war or an attempt to understand the cause of a natural disaster such as an epidemic or an earthquake.

There is evidence that prior to the eighth century, the empress herself often served as miko for important matters of state. According to the *Nihon-shoki,* Empress Jingū acted as the miko when the emperor sought the will of the kami in his plans to punish unruly subjects in border areas. The emperor played the *koto,* a stringed instrument, to call down a kami who took possession of the empress and identified herself as Amaterasu. The kami told the emperor instead to mount an expedition against Korea, where riches were to be had. But because the emperor refused to believe and act on the kami's words, he soon met an untimely death, and the shaman empress came to rule in his stead. The story as recorded stood as a clear warning to anyone who might be tempted to disobey the commands of the kami.

Among the common people, shamanic rituals are still performed. In rural areas, people might seek out the miko to ask the kami for advice on important decisions, such as the choice of a marriage partner, or to determine the cause of a disease or other misfortune. Answers to such questions often state that someone has offended one or another kami through an improper ritual performance or simply neglect, thus reminding us of the kami's unruly character.

Religion and Society in Early Japan

Having surveyed the Shintō religious substratum, we can begin to understand the events of Japanese religious history. The social structure of early Japan was dominated by the heads of the great clans. These clans held most of the land by hereditary right, giving it to the cultivation of peasants who were themselves bound to their tasks by heredity. Certain families of peasants, called *be,* were attached to the land and thus to the landholders. Just as members of the aristocratic clans were born to their position, so were the members of the be. There were also be of artisans, such as potters and metalworkers. Even shrines had their be of priests. Everything in this early feudal society was tied by the twin cords of heredity and place.

The religion of the clans was a form of Shintō centered on a family shrine. The deities worshiped there seem to have been partly the clan's ancestral kami and partly agricultural kami of the place itself. In the earliest times, a chieftain probably oversaw the clan in a paternalistic way, supervising the clan's affairs and rewarding and punishing individuals and subclans. Although the chieftain probably had priestly duties within the ancestral shrine, his wife appears to have been the principal religious figure. Serving the kami directly as priestess and sometimes as shaman, she perhaps oversaw subordinate priestesses. As shaman she would have had considerable influence in clan affairs, since she spoke for the kami.

The clan heads, their immediate families, and their more closely related cousins formed the aristocracy, the more important members of which gathered around the emperor at his palace. Indeed, the imperial family was but another clan, one that had inherited, along with land and be, the right to rule and to perform Shintō rituals for the benefit not only of its own clan—the usual pattern—but also for the nation as a whole. The aristocracy seems to have paid little attention to the common people, so long as their labor resulted in wealth for the clan. The religious practices and beliefs of the common people have not been recorded except in distorted form as folklore; they seem to have followed practices similar to those of the aristocrats.

Sometime during the sixth century, Chinese forms of Buddhism were introduced into Japan by way of Korea. Eventually, Buddhism brought with it the splendors of Tang dynasty Chinese civilization, including a system of writing that opened the gates of Chinese literature, Confucian theories of government and ethics, and Daoist lore. For the most part, the Japanese aristocrats were dazzled by things Chinese, which were regarded as being of utmost value and

Matsuri (celebrations) are one type of Shintō ritual. They include music and dance, as seen in this procession that dates from the Heian era (794–1185). These rituals are fixed; innovation and spontaneity are strongly discouraged. (Shashinka Photo Library)

prestige. The elite wrote their poetry and official government documents in Chinese. This also allowed the Japanese entry into the greater Asian cultural sphere, since China was at its center. The common people, however, were for some time quite unaffected by these developments among the elite, further distancing the aristocracy from the rest of the people.

RELIGION IN THE CLASSICAL PERIOD

Confucianism, which was a part of the package of Chinese civilization, made itself felt especially in the political arena. Confucianism promoted the centralization of power on the Chinese model of a bureaucratic state with the emperor at its head, leaving little or no place for the old clan-centered aristocracy. Had this been fully implemented in Japan, it would have destroyed the power of the clans by centralizing power in the hands of the imperial court. In fact, a system of provincial administration did officially replace the old clan structures, although neither the clans nor their traditional Shintō cults were abolished. Instead, the clans became unofficial organizations whose internal loyalties and cohesion kept them at odds with the central authority. Confucianism even indirectly enhanced the prestige of Shintō since the development of an official mythology that focused on the imperial court served the Confucian goal of the centralization of national life.

The centralized government also required a capitol to house the large bureaucracy and to symbolize the new order. The emperor in 710 built a splendid palace at Nara, which became in the Confucian way the symbolic pivot around which the rest of the universe revolved. Both Nara and the later capital at Heian (present-day Kyōto) were laid out in the Chinese fashion in a grid pattern oriented to the four compass points. The palace was situated at the northern end of the city, and clustered around the palace were the houses of the aristocracy. The courtiers, increasingly separated from the land and their old clan seats, became the bearers and cocreators of the new culture. Much of the flowering of poetry, pottery, weaving, architecture, gardening, elegant dress, and court ritual characteristic of the classical period was the result of this Confucian influence. Although the Confucians tried to impose the Chinese sense of harmony, the Japanese never adopted it completely. Rather than bringing an overarching order to Japanese society, its bureaucracy simply became one more element in Japan's dynamic and complex structure.

THE CONFLUENCE OF SHINTŌ, BUDDHISM, CONFUCIANISM, AND DAOISM

By the end of the ninth century, the pattern of classical Japan had become well established. There was considerable religious diversity, especially among the elite under the patronage of the court and noble families. This diversity was manifested not just as religious sects contending for the exclusive loyalty of individuals; rather, these loyalties contended within each individual. Virtually no one felt that worship at a Shintō shrine precluded devotion to a Buddhist deity or practice of Confucian filial piety. And this was true almost as much of religious professionals—Buddhist monks and nuns and Shintō priests—as it was of anyone else. No aristocrat of this time would think of dealing with illness only with medicine: Buddhist priests were always called to chant the sūtras as powerful means of exorcising disease-causing spirits. And funerals were invariably conducted by Buddhist priests. Yet no one would neglect duties toward one's ancestors or toward the traditional Shintō clan kami.

The ritual calendar of that time reveals many Shintō, Buddhist, and Confucian festivals and even a few Daoist ones. Despite the practice of Buddhist rites by many aristocrats and emperors, rituals performed at the palace were predominantly Shintō. Though supported by the court, Buddhist rites were usually conducted not in the palace but at various temples around the city and in distant shrines in the provinces. Yet Buddhism grew ever more powerful. In both Nara and Kyōto, Shintō shrines had to share space with Buddhist temples and monastic houses. Pious emperors and wealthy aristocrats endowed monastic centers both in the capital and in the provinces. The government established and regulated a national Buddhist hierarchy of priests and supported many Buddhist temples.

Buddhism was part of the Chinese cultural heritage that Japan borrowed and adapted to its own ends. This meant that, in the Confucian way, Buddhism needed to be carefully regulated and restricted by the government. Leaders saw Buddhism as a powerful civilizing force that would bring education and the literary arts to Japan, as well as direct benefits such as effective intervention with the sacred powers. To serve these ends, in the mid-eighth century the government built official Buddhist temples in each province throughout the nation. The eighth-century Buddhist center at Nara became an especially important center of political, intellectual, and artistic life. Its arresting Tōdai-ji temple housed the Daibutsu (Great Buddha), a 45-foot statue of the Vairocana Buddha, the great sun Buddha (a reminder, perhaps, of the imperial family's claimed descent from the sun goddess, Amaterasu), which may be seen and worshiped there even today.

The main work of these temples was the same as that of those in the capital: the preservation of the nation — its peacefulness, its harvests, and its emperors. Monks and nuns appointed by the government offered prayers day and night. In addition, many Buddhist temples served as centers of Chinese, not just Buddhist, learning. Moving beyond its appeal to the elite, Buddhism, like other Chinese cultural and religious elements, was slowly adopted by the common people. It was included in official policy, and its temples, monasteries, and art were intended in part to support the centralizing of the elite culture.

Perhaps the most revealing document from the beginning of the classical period is the seventh-century Seventeen-Article Constitution. Not really a constitution in the legal sense, this brief edict set forth a fundamentally Confucianist philosophy of life. Indeed, it was basically a Japanese adaptation of the zhunzi ideal — a handbook for producing the ideal government bureaucrat. It was written by Prince Regent Shōtoku, who is still revered today as the first great champion of Buddhism in Japan. Yet of the 17 articles, only one is devoted to Buddhism (it urges support of the Buddha, Dharma, and Saṅgha), and only one even alludes obliquely to Shintō. In fact, this is the first clear statement of what may be called the prevailing spirit of the classical age: the compartmentalization of religious and cultural elements into more or less separate, specialized spheres of life. Shōtoku was typical of his era in assuming that these religions were not incompatible. Each represented a valuable specialty and could contribute something to Japan's dynamic conglomeration of elements. Confucianism encouraged loyalty to the government and an ethic of family cooperation. Buddhism protected the future of the individual in the next world and could wield great ritual power to ensure the stability of the state in this world. Shintō offered the best means of placating natural forces, thus ensuring plentiful harvests and a minimum of natural disasters.

The common people adopted Chinese elements much more slowly. There is evidence that the imperial court even sought to prevent Buddhist elements from reaching the peasants for fear that its religious powers might be used against the central authority. Nonetheless, by the end of the classical period in the late twelfth century, more practical elements of both Buddhism and Daoism had filtered down to the peasants. But here, too, the native Japanese tradition continued to shape religious life: foreign elements tended to be molded into a Shintō shape and were often considered simply to add force to the already established practices. For example, practitioners of Daoist divination used a Shintō miko to communicate with the native kami and sought to deal with the same spiritual problems as Shintō. The Buddhist chant invoking the name of Amitābha (in Japanese, Amida) was used in a similar way to cure ills and to ensure the chances of a good harvest.

SHINTŌ-BUDDHIST SYNCRETISM

The impact of all this Buddhist activity in and around Nara and Kyōto, especially on the aristocracy, was tremendous. But since few people saw religions as exclusive, Shintō continued to flourish, with many Buddhist elements. The mixture of Shintō and Buddhism proceeded along several paths. In this process it is clear that despite inherent tensions, devout Buddhists continued sincerely to believe in the reality and power of the Shintō kami.

The Jingū-ji System

As early as the middle of the eighth century, an emperor had built a shrine to the local kami within the precincts of the Buddhist Tōdai-ji temple in order to pacify the local spiritual powers. This eventually became common practice in Buddhist temples. It recognized the prior claim of the kami to the land and to the allegiance of the people; the Buddhists were rather like guests of the kami.

The reverse attitude was also present: the Shintō kami were thought to need the Buddhist Dharma, like any other sentient being. The kami should be taught the way to enlightenment, just like humans. To this end, Buddhist sūtras were chanted at Shintō shrines, and eventually it became a common practice to establish a small Buddhist temple within Shintō shrines. Typically nothing was lost and nothing thrown away; the old was supplemented by the new in this ***jingū-ji*** ("shrine-temple") **system**.

From this position it was a small step to the idea that the kami were already enlightened and were in fact disguised manifestations of the various Buddha and bodhisattva figures mentioned in the sūtras. This notion of identity or equivalence was easy and even natural at the folk level, since kami were known more for their location than for their theological definition. Since even the names of the kami enshrined at a particular spot might not be known or agreed on, they might easily be thought of by Buddhist names. Some were thought to be bodhisattvas who had intentionally disguised themselves to bring about people's conversion or enlightenment.

This statue of Buddha is the largest in Japan. Located in Kamakura near Tokyo, the twelfth-century statue stands 11.5 meters high (over 37 feet). People from all over Japan travel to see and worship at the statue. (Tass from Sovfoto)

Tendai Saichō (Dengyō Daishi, 762–822) sought to make his new Tendai sect the national form of Buddhism. It would unify the nation under a single sect closely allied with the imperial court; all others would be assimilated into it. Although he never accomplished this goal, Tendai did become the most important Buddhist denomination, a position it maintained until the end of the classical period. It attempted to include all Buddhist ideas, texts, and practices, unified under the leadership of the Lotus Sūtra, which it viewed as the culmination of Buddhist thought. The Lotus Sūtra greatly emphasized the notion of *upāya* (expedient means) by which the Buddha had taught that there were many ways or vehicles to salvation. All were useful and in a relative sense "true." But the text also presented the ultimate, absolute truth, which was the central way of Tendai.

Perhaps the most important idea stressed by Saichō and subsequent Tendai masters was the bodhisattva. The Lotus Sūtra taught that all Buddhas were in fact bodhisattvas; none had actually gone to nirvāṇa; all remained active in the world, leading all beings to nirvāṇa rather than selfishly enjoying nirvāṇa alone. This image of active bodhisattvas tirelessly working in the world for the benefit of all beings helped to make Tendai appealing to the Japanese court. The government awarded subsidies for training "bodhisattva monks" who would not only penetrate to the abstruse secrets of the Lotus Sūtra doctrines and achieve enlightenment but also become teachers of the nation as a whole. They would study not only Buddhism but the Confucian classics as well. Not only would they study and practice religion in its narrow sense, but, out of compassion for all, they would become engineers, craftsmen, and laborers in the service of the state. Cheerfully putting their hands to the construction of schools, roads, bridges, irrigation systems, and other useful things, they would at the same time bear witness to the truth of the Lotus Sūtra and of Buddhism. Saichō even equated the bodhisattva monk with the Confucian zhunzi, the true gentleman or ideal government bureaucrat!

Shingon Kūkai (Kōbō Daishi, 774–835) had similar ambitions for his Shingon Buddhism, which, rather than basing itself on the Lotus Sūtra, was grounded in Tāntric or Vajrayāna Buddhism. Shingon centered on elaborate rituals and meditations focused on visualizations of maṇḍalas, complicated paintings of the Buddhas, bodhisattvas, helpers, and demons that populate not only the external realms but also the inner psychological and spiritual realms.

Shingon's elaborate rituals appealed to all levels of society, since all could participate, even if only as spectators. Indeed, Tendai Buddhism found room for many of these esoteric practices within its broad, inclusivist philosophy. Although to more sophisticated Tendai and Shingon monks and nuns these practices were often understood to be forms of meditation leading to ultimate religious experience, to the popular mind they held the power to affect the external world in useful, this-worldly ways. Salvation in the ultimate sense of personal transformation was of less concern to them than immediate utility. Such a reorientation is again reminiscent of Shintō, which had always stressed ritual and had never had an unworldly, personal notion of salvation.

The Medieval Period

After the relatively stable classical period, dominated by the emperor and several powerful clans, medieval Japan was tumultuous. The dominant groups were military: samurai warriors led by their shōguns (generals). These military groups were actually clans of lower rank, sometimes distant cousins of the various emperors. As military men are wont to do, they fought frequent and bloody battles for power, though there were several long periods of relative stability during the early medieval period.

With struggles so frequent, these were difficult times for most of the Japanese people. The aristocracy was impoverished and politically irrelevant. At the same time, the common people were at the mercy of the samurai, who ruled by force, exacting high taxes from them and enlisting them also in the fighting.

THE RISE OF NEW BUDDHIST SECTS

Despite—or perhaps because of—the political instability and social and economic disorder, this period was one of vitality for Buddhism. Under these circumstances, at all levels of society a sense of insecurity and helplessness seems to have overtaken people. Many people came to agree with Buddhism that ordinary life was caught in an all but endless cycle of impermanence and suffering. And by now the common people too had accepted the Buddhist ideas of karma and reincarnation.

The commoners had neither the leisure nor the education to follow the Buddhist monastic regimens. The samurai, however, did have the time and the skills. And despite their new power and prestige, they felt the relevance of the Buddhist teachings. Impermanence and suffering were part of their constant experience because as warriors they must be ever ready to face the horrors of wars. Insecurity and a sense of helplessness were also theirs because, despite their power as a class, as individuals they were bound by ties of loyalty to superiors who could, at any moment, ask of them their lives.

New religious movements arose in the early medieval period to meet these new religious needs. Three new types of Buddhism took form: Pure Land Buddhism, which emphasized devotion to the Buddha Amida; Nichiren, which regarded the Buddhist monk Nichiren as an incarnation of a bodhisattva; and the highly disciplined, monastic Zen. The first two sects became popular movements that adapted monastic practices for use by the laity, allowing them to continue their life in the world while performing rites that offered them hope for salvation from their sufferings. Faith became the new key to salvation.

Pure Land Buddhism This sect was of course not new to Japan. Devotion to Kannon (in Chinese, Guanyin) and to Amida had been mentioned in the

Lotus Sūtra. Indeed, devotion to Amida had long been an important practice among Tendai monks. But now the texts devoted exclusively to Amida seemed increasingly relevant, for they described in detail the paradisiacal Pure Land into which the fortunate might be reborn. Moreover, commentaries written in China emphasized that in degenerate times and for people with little merit or spiritual ability, entrance into this happy land could be gained through the *nembutsu* chant or prayer. This was no more than the simple repetition—aloud, under the breath, or mentally—of Amida's name, in the formula *Namu Amida Butsu* ("Hail to the Buddha Amitābha").

The Tendai monk Hōnen, late in the classical era, began popularizing this devotional practice among the laity as a means to ensure rebirth in the Pure Land. His disciple Shinran (1173–1262) became an especially persuasive preacher of this practice. Eventually new and independent Buddhist sects grew up among people who traced their religious lineage to one or the other of these two men. The Jōdo (Pure Land) sect, following Hōnen, emphasized both good works (merit) and the *nembutsu* chant as a means of salvation. The more radical *Jōdo Shin* (True Pure Land) sect, following Shinran, disparaged merit and even the nembutsu as a means, arguing that ordinary people were *absolutely* dependent on the power of Amida. Even the chanting of the nembutsu did not lead to salvation because the impulse to chant it itself came from Amida. Faith alone was required.

Nichiren The much less numerous Nichiren sect, though similar in many ways to Pure Land, bore the stamp of the unusual personality of an ex-Tendai monk, Nichiren (1222–1282). This charismatic and eccentric man became convinced that he was the reincarnation of one of the bodhisattvas described in the Lotus Sūtra. As such he was empowered to impart the true meaning of the sūtra. This alone was the way to salvation. Abandoning the idea of upāya and the toleration and syncretism it implied, he declared that all other forms of religious practice, including Buddhist forms, were evil. His practice borrowed from Pure Land forms in that he required his followers to chant the formula *Namu myō hō renge kyō* ("Hail to the Sūtra of the Lotus of the True Dharma") as a way of achieving both enlightenment and this-worldly benefits such as wealth, health, and safety. His followers hoped that they could convert all of the Japanese people, thus making the nation into a Buddhist utopia, a Pure Land on earth.

With this era's pessimistic outlook, the dynamic tension so characteristic of Japanese religiosity throughout the classical period apparently reached nearly intolerable intensity. There were several reasons for this. First, the old, relatively optimistic appraisal of life in this world could not be maintained in the face of such hardship and uncertainty. Second, the classical Japanese had assumed a unified world, a kind of harmony that subsumed the tensions and thus kept them at a tolerable level, but in medieval times it was difficult to accept such an overarching harmony. Thus the proliferation of Buddhist sects at this time indicates both earnest attempts to solve the religious problems and at the same time symptoms of the failure to do so completely. Separate sects sought in their own ways to overcome this tension and allay the sufferings of the people. But each fragmented the religious world even more and moved further away from a unified worldview. Pure Land emphasized almost exclusively the next life, leaving this life to mere custom, a void that folk Shintō and Nichiren Buddhism tended to fill. Nichiren Buddhism increasingly specialized in the healing arts to minister to that dimension of the practical life. Moreover, even within their own specialized spheres, these sects were only partly successful. Ironically, even as Pure Land Buddhism sought to allay the anxiety of the masses about the future life, new forms of uncertainty and tension emerged within this religious movement itself. For example, when Shinran, the founder of the True Pure Land sect, took off his monastic robes and married, he declared the monastic life to be useless in the quest for salvation. Only the great compassion of Amida could save such a wretch as he. Such desperation and extreme humility was characteristic of many of his followers. He taught that one had only truly and with utter earnestness to cast oneself on the mercy of Amida to be assured of rebirth in paradise. Yet how could one be sure of one's earnestness? And how could one achieve utter humility if one did not entirely feel it at every moment? Anxiety on such points continued to trouble many.

Zen Zen (in Chinese, Chan) was the last Buddhist sect founded in the early medieval period, and unlike the other new sects, it was transplanted directly

These are the hands of a Zen Buddhist monk at a monastery of the Sōtō sect in Japan. In this posture of "Kyosakku," or "awakening spirit," the long stick is often held for hours. (Paolo Koch/Photo Researchers)

from China. A form of Zen had been known earlier but had been seen merely as an optional emphasis within a crowded field of Buddhist monastic practices. Clearly, conditions were only now favorable for it to take root in Japan as an independent sect. Zen established itself primarily as a monastic movement, and as in China, the monks came from all segments of society. But in addition, in Japan, Zen's austere meditative disciplines appealed particularly to the new elite, the samurai class. Two forms were transmitted directly from China, the Rinzai form by Eisai (1141–1215) and the Sōtō form by Dōgen (1200–1253). Both emphasized simplicity and practical guidance toward enlightenment *(satori)* here and now.

The Zen monastery became a place of intense effort in meditation, and although some samurai actually became monks, many more spent temporary retreats at monasteries or engaged monks as private tutors. They wished especially to learn the techniques of concentration and self-forgetfulness that could reinforce their ideals of loyalty and service to their military superiors. For good reason, they increasingly came to believe that Zen concentration could make them superior in battle: to lose the sense of self was at the same time to lose the fear of death; to increase concentration could enhance archery and swordsmanship skills by disengaging the mind from any inhibiting fear of failure or attempts consciously to control the body. Just as Zen monks sought the spontaneity of egoless enlightenment, the samurai sought the spontaneity of the egoless exercise of fighting skills. The dynamic tension characteristic of Japanese religiosity is especially striking here, for the samurai used the techniques of Mahāyāna Buddhism—the way of the bodhisattva dedicated to an enlightenment suffused with compassion—to kill more efficiently in the loyal service of their samurai master.

Like the common people, the samurai were subject to feelings of peril, suffering, and impermanence. But whereas the common people often felt helpless and became passive in the face of adversity, the samurai used Zen to enhance direct action and self-control. These attitudes, together with their warrior ethic of loyalty and determination, were approaches to life that had won them their high station.

Zen, through its success as the preferred religious practice of the new elite, also came to exercise tremendous influence in the arts. Indeed, despite the troubled times, a new flowering of culture came about. The arts of Nō drama, *haiku* poetry, and the tea ceremony all emerged through Zen, and a new Zen-inspired emphasis on simplicity, asymmetry, and naturalness came to dominate such older arts as painting, architecture, and landscape gardening.

THE REUNIFICATION OF JAPAN

Toward the end of the sixteenth century, Japan experienced a series of wars that eventually resulted in the establishment of a strong central government, though still under samurai control. The many small power centers were gradually consolidated by force and alliance until 1603, when the Tokugawa clan emerged victorious in a final battle. From the fortress at Edo (modern Tokyo), the Tokugawa clan led the nation through a long period of armed peace that lasted until just before the restoration of imperial rule in 1868.

The Tokugawa period was a time of religious consolidation and even routinization rather than creativity. The shōgunate sought to unify the nation by promoting Neo-Confucianism as the justification of its rule and the organizing principle of society. The goal of unity, so hard won on the battlefield, was to be preserved by establishing a Confucian-style harmony. The shōgun was the head of the nation, understood as a single family with a hierarchical organization and strong ties of loyalty and obedience. On the basis of this model, the peasants were for the first time bound to the land, and rigid class distinctions among the samurai, farmers, and merchants were established. Everyone was to have a place as established by law, and that law was enforced by Tokugawa swords.

The Tokugawa period also brought the first contacts with the West. First to appear were Spanish and Portuguese traders and Jesuit missionaries. The Japanese were at first quite interested in trade and in European firearms and medicine. Christianity, seen by some as a symbol of technological and cultural advancement, gained a small but loyal following in some areas. Indeed, during the wars of unification, some samurai leaders actually promoted Christianity as a counterpoise to the politically powerful Buddhist sects. But by the end of the sixteenth century, rumors of Western imperialistic intentions had reached the Japanese leaders. As early as 1587, the most powerful *daimyō* (feudal lord) issued an edict prohibiting foreign missionaries from operating in his domains and "interfering" with Shintō and Buddhist teachings. Little effort was made to enforce this until 1597, when 26 Japanese and European Franciscans were crucified at Nagasaki. Then in 1614 the Tokugawa regime, in an attempt to tighten its grip on the reins of power, issued an edict banning the practice of Christianity. This led eventually to a Christian uprising in Kyūshū, where several Christian daimyō had constructed strongholds. In 1639 the Christian forces were defeated, and the shōgun closed Japan to virtually all foreign contacts. Japanese Christians were hunted down and forced to recant or suffer martyrdom.

Effects of the Closing of Japan

The closing of the nation to foreign trade and ideas only served to make the social, political, and economic structure more rigid. Confucian ideas were used to strengthen loyalty to superiors and family ties. Moreover, Buddhism was used as an arm of the state to keep watch on the people through a "parochial system" in which every household was ordered to affiliate with a particular Buddhist temple. By government order, every Japanese became a Buddhist at a single stroke.

The effect of this extraordinary policy was at first mixed. Even Shintō priests had to become Buddhists, and some chose to leave the priesthood altogether.

Another result of making Buddhism the state religion was a proliferation of Buddhist temples and new academies. Yet in the long run Buddhism suffered greatly from this deceptive windfall. Buddhist religious life tended to become hollow and formalistic; many priests were attracted to their profession not by piety or zeal but by its financial security. As a result, the prestige of Buddhism steadily declined. Among the elite, Buddhism was seen as inferior to Confucianism; the common people turned increasingly to Shintō.

Among the educated classes, however, the study of Confucian philosophy eventually had an additional and unexpected result: it reawakened an interest in classical literature and history, at first the Confucian classics but later works that came to be considered classics of Japanese history, culture, thought, and religion. Shintō was increasingly seen as the bearer of the ancient and therefore classical Japanese value system and way of life. Thus the stage was set for a Shintō revival.

The National Scholar Movement

In 1728 a priest of the Inari shrine in Kyōto submitted a petition to the Tokugawa rulers in which he pleaded for patronage to establish a school of "national learning" *(kokugaku)* for the study of Japanese classical literature. This was the beginning of a renewal movement that sought to strip Shintō of its foreign (that is, Chinese) elements and establish it as an intellectual force rivaling the dominant Buddhist and Confucian schools of the time. Although in the beginning the movement was concerned only with religious and philosophical matters, it later became a political cause as well. National scholars Motoori Norinaga (1730–1801) and Hirata Atsutane (1776–1843) established a set of texts as a basis for Shintō theory and produced commentaries on such Japanese classics as the *Manyōshū,* the *Kojiki,* and the eleventh-century novel of Japanese court life, *Genji monogatari*

("Tale of Genji"). These works were presented as sacred scriptures to the newly awakened Shintō intellectuals.

An early work by Motoori called *Tama kushige* ("Precious Comb Box") became the manifesto of the movement. In it Motoori attached special importance to the descent of the imperial prince in the myth that established the descendants of the sun goddess as Japan's emperors:

> In the Goddess' mandate to the Prince at that time it was stated that his dynasty should be coeval with Heaven and Earth. It is this mandate which is the very origin and basis of the Way. Thus, all the principles of the world and the way of humankind are represented in the different stages of the Age of Kami. Those who seek to know the Right Way must therefore pay careful attention to the stages of the Age of Kami and learn the truths of existence.[1]

Hirata made even stronger claims for nationalism, and his views on the uniqueness and superiority of the Japanese national spirit ***(kokutai)*** were later made the basis for the ultranationalist ideology of the 1930s. In 1811 he wrote *Kodō taii* ("Summary of the Ancient Way"), in which he asserted:

> People all over the world refer to Japan as the Land of Kami, and call us the descendants of the kami. Indeed, it is exactly as they say: our country, as a special mark of favor from the heavenly kami, was begotten by them, and there is thus so immense a difference between Japan and all other countries of the world as to defy comparison. . . . We, down to the most humble man and woman, are the descendants of the kami.[2]

During the Tokugawa period, when this statement was written, the emperor, as the standard-bearer of the old tradition and direct descendant of Amaterasu, was an obscure figure living in seclusion in Kyōto; the real seat of government was 400 miles away at Edo in the hands of samurai. To express such ideas at that time was not only religiously innovative but also possibly politically dangerous. It was no accident that in the nineteenth century the leaders of the Meiji Restoration, who swept away the feudal regime, did so in the name of this same ***kokutai,*** which implicitly supported the emperor as the only legitimate ruler of Japan.

The Modern Period

By the middle of the nineteenth century, the disparity between official ideology and the realities of social, political, economic, and religious life in Japan had seriously weakened and discredited the Tokugawa regime. Many people recognized the need for change, and when an American naval flotilla sailed into Tokyo Bay in 1853 demanding diplomatic and trade relations, it was a sufficient catalyst to bring about radical change. Military rule was ended, and direct imperial rule was restored in 1868. Like the early classical period, the modern period was a time of cultural disruption and innovation brought about by the rapid assimilation of foreign elements, this time from Western rather than Chinese civilization.

Once again the Japanese embraced the new while cleaving to the old. Again they borrowed selectively and experienced a dynamic state of cultural and religious tension. To be sure, this period of rapid change was not accomplished without pain, especially the pain of disorientation in social structure and religious values. Even so, by the standards of the age, Japan rose to the challenge with amazing energy: by the early years of the twentieth century, the nation had gone far toward transforming itself into a technologically advanced industrial nation with great military power and extensive colonial possessions, and by the century's end it had become a technological and economic marvel.

Seeking both to dissociate itself from the discredited Tokugawa regime and to build a new basis for national unity and identity, the new government soon launched an attack on Buddhism while at the same time promoting Shintō. In the reform edict of 1868, Shintō shrines were required to purge themselves of all Buddhist influences. Buddhist priests attached to Shintō shrines were forced to return to lay life. The Shintō-Buddhist priesthood had to choose one or the other religion, and in 1872 it became illegal for Buddhists to teach that kami were manifestations of Buddhist figures. The people blamed Buddhism for many of the evils of the past, and in their reformist anger they destroyed many Buddhist temples.

But as always, it was not easy to forge a new cultural synthesis out of disparate elements in so short a time.

The quest for a viable national identity that was both modern and continuous with tradition proved especially difficult. To gain the respect of the world, it was necessary to embrace both religious freedom and democratic government; yet to remain true to Japanese tradition, both had to be modified. The modifications actually wrought led to a new emphasis on Shintō traditions and values.

In the new state ideology, the emperor, as the direct descendant of Amaterasu, was promoted as a divine person who symbolized Japan's national origins and unity. His religious status meant that he could not rule directly, participating in everyday political affairs, for this would jeopardize his sacred dignity. Yet a parliament, as a deliberative body, could hardly be thought of as being able to perceive the imperial will. Thus the constitution drawn up in 1889 provided for both an emperor and a parliament but gave real power to neither. Rather, real power was held by a small group of men operating behind the scenes and without legal standing or accountability. Japan wanted ultimate religious sanction in political affairs but bought it at the price of a government unresponsive to the people and sometimes arbitrary in its exercise of power.

A similar dilemma existed more directly in the realm of religious affairs. Just as the new rulers of Japan wanted religious sanction in politics, they also wanted religion to serve political ends. Shintō had in effect been made the national religion, although the constitution guaranteed religious freedom. The problem was "solved" by separating what was now termed state Shintō from sectarian Shintō. The former was declared to be nonreligious and the duty of every loyal citizen. The latter was organized into several sects that did not receive government patronage. Reverence for the emperor and respect for his authority, as well as reverence for many national heroes and the mythic kami, was required of every Japanese and was taught in the government schools under the guise of state Shintō.

The success of this educational policy can be seen by noting that the Japanese people, by 1941, had been molded into a powerful technological and military force. Embued with a sense of great national purpose, most were amenable to almost any policy that their leaders, wrapped in the cloak of sacred, imperial authority, initiated. Most impressive of all, perhaps, is the fact that the leaders themselves seemed to have genuinely believed that they were carrying out the will of the emperor and expressing the Japanese *kokutai*, or national essence. It is significant that when the nation lay in ruins in 1945 with the war lost, the leaders of Japan feverishly tried to negotiate a peace that would respect that same mysterious and sacred principle of national identity and significance.

State Shintō

We have seen that the official position of the Japanese government from early in the Meiji period to 1945 was that state Shintō was not a religion. However, this so-called civil cult retained its religious character. It became a system in which the ultimate values of the ancient religion of Japan were harnessed by the central authority to promote loyalty to itself, social solidarity, and patriotism. It was a powerful tool in the hands of those who in the nineteenth century had undertaken the difficult task of creating a modern nation out of the feudal domains of the Tokugawa period. By the twentieth century, it had become the tool of militarists who brought the nation to ruin in World War II.

JAPAN'S NEW RELIGIONS

During the nineteenth and twentieth centuries, many new religious groups sprang up in Japan and organized themselves as independent religious bodies. These so-called new religions began as closely knit sectarian groups, many hundreds of which still exist. Most continue to emphasize group solidarity, and many combine Shintō, Buddhist, Confucian, Daoist, and even Christian and other Western elements, though most may be classified as primarily Shintō or Buddhist. They undoubtedly represent in part a religious response to the tensions inherent in the rapidly changing cultural and political situation.

In general, perhaps the single most important characteristic of such cultural transformation is the feeling of having been cut off from one's religion and thus from the source of life's meaning. This absence of continuity is particularly dangerous for ritual, which depends heavily on past models that are repeated, imitated, and celebrated. In Japan, as elsewhere, one response to the destruction of traditional models has been to establish new ones. But no parliament or

Shintō priests at Mitsumine Jinja. The Allied military occupation of 1945–1952 sought to put an American stamp on postwar Japan. As part of this attempt, the Shintō Directive of 1946 disestablished state Shintō, converting the many shrines into independent, private religious institutions. Because certain aspects of Shintō are felt to be an essential part of the Japanese identity, many people believe that these aspects should be declared not religious, thereby circumventing the religion-state separation directive. (Religious News Service)

executive decree could suffice to gain the allegiance of the people. The religious category for innovation and devising new models is revelation, and the model must have sacred origins. In the Japanese case, the Shintō pattern of communication with the sacred kami was employed by many new sects, most often in the form of shamanic possession.

One of the most dramatic examples of modern shamanic possession in the service of new revelation comes from Tenrikyō ("religion of divine wisdom"). Its founder, Nakayama Miki (1798–1887), was possessed by Tentaishōgun and nine other kami, who proclaimed through her:

> Miki's mind and body will be accepted by us as a divine shrine, and we desire to save this [seen and unseen] world through this divine body. Otherwise, and if you all refuse our desire, the Nakayama family shall completely cease to exist.[3]

Among Miki's most impressive achievements are the many poems she composed under the inspiration of the kami. Taken together, they constitute a new mythology, a new understanding of the origins and meaning of the cosmos.

Although hundreds of new religions have appeared, especially since the defeat of 1945, they all have similar characteristics regardless of whether they are of primarily Shintō or Buddhist origin. Besides their dependence on shamanic revelation, they include an emphasis on healing the ills of body and mind, a dependence on myth rather than philosophy as the locus of meaning, an appeal to the nonintellectual and lower socioeconomic levels of society, a propensity for congregational worship and other group activities unusual in older forms of Japanese religion, and a strong allegiance to a single founder or to later charismatic leaders.

The largest and most highly visible of the new religions is Sōka Gakkai ("value-creation society"). Also known as Nichiren Shōshū because of its later affiliation with the medieval Nichiren sect of Buddhism, this group claims millions of followers, both in Japan and abroad. Its political party, the Kōmeitō ("clean government party"), has managed to elect several members to the Japanese Diet. Along with an authoritarian internal organization and militant conversion tactics, Sōka Gakkai has a utopian scheme to convert Japan into a Buddhaland. It is particularly noted for its practice of chanting the name of the Lotus Sūtra as a means of gaining power to achieve whatever goals the individual may have. Its ultimate goal it calls happiness in this life, which it believes to be the true meaning of nirvāṇa.

The appeal of the new religions, especially apparent in the case of Sōka Gakkai, stems in large measure from their genius in providing a sense of belonging to a supportive group and a mutually reinforced sense of meaning through structured ritual, ethical, and social behavior. In a world increasingly typified by the breakdown of traditional family and community ties in the face of urbanization and industrialization, this ability to give the individual a sense of belonging is clearly important. The Japanese, so recently deprived of the supportive environment of a very traditional society with its unquestioned loyalties and highly structured life and troubled by questions of identity of self and nation as a result of their defeat in war, are obviously attracted by such religious movements. Individuals can find in the new religions the reinforcement of like-minded people who together create a small world of their own, a world in which each person has a role and a meaning in relation both to the kami or other deities and to the community as a whole. This small world of order, predictability, and support then allows the individual to cope with the larger world of change and unpredictability, of work and family, of international threat and economic vulnerability. These two worlds again exhibit the old pattern of dynamic tension by which the Japanese have sought religiously to come to terms with life.

Yet another significant characteristic of many of the new religions of contemporary Japan is the importance of women in their creation. We have already mentioned Tenrikyō and its founder, Nakayama Miki. Other examples from the Shintō-oriented new religions include Ōmotokyō ("teaching of the great origin"), jointly founded by a husband and wife. Jiyūkyō ("freedom religion") was founded by a woman who announced that she was the incarnation of Amaterasu. Another prominent female religious figure is Kitamura Sayo (born 1900), founder of the Kōtai Jingū sect, a revitalized Shintō group with a feminist slant.

JAPANESE RELIGION SINCE WORLD WAR II

Perhaps a dozen of the hundreds of new religions, both Shintō and Buddhist, have dominated Japan since the war, and they are noted for their missionary zeal and vitality. Even so, a number of traditional religious groups claim significant memberships. In addition to shrine Shintō, there are traditional Buddhist groups that make up various branches of Tendai, Shingon, Nichiren, Pure Land, and Zen Buddhism. Yet it must be admitted that the primary function of many of the priests of these groups is to conduct funerals. Religious activities include regular rituals and the social and spiritual support functions common to neighborhood religious establishments everywhere. A number of Zen monasteries continue rigorous meditative discipline in the training of new priests, and some even cater to lay retreats where nonpriests can for a few days live the life of a monk. Moreover, a number of Western Zen masters have been trained in Japan to serve as missionaries in North America, where Zen centers have sprung up in recent decades. Still, Japanese Buddhism is known internationally today more for the outstanding quality of its historical scholarship than for the rigor of its practice.

Shrine Shintō

Among all the religions of Japan, Shintō was the most directly affected by defeat in war. The Allied military occupation, which lasted from 1945 to 1952, sought to put an American stamp on postwar Japanese society. The constitution that took effect in 1947 tried to make Japan a bastion of democracy and individual freedom in the Western pattern. War was made unconstitutional; so were armed forces for any purpose but self-defense. As a part of this policy, the Shintō Directive of 1946 disestablished state Shintō in a sweep, converting the many shrines into independent, private religious institutions relying solely on private and voluntary contributions for their continued existence. Public officials were prohibited from participating in religious ceremonies in their official capacities, and the emperor was made publicly to deny his divinity.

Events since 1952 have frequently reminded both government and citizens of the special relationship between Shintō and the Japanese national identity. The imposition of the American insistence on strict separation of religion and state has been a problematic source of tension for the Japanese nation and for Shintō leaders. For example, to this day, the position of the emperor and the meaning of the imperial institution have resisted clarification because the traditional Japanese conception of the emperor and of national identity clearly run counter to the American scheme. To pretend that the emperor is not a religious figure or that he exercises his religious functions purely as a private person is as misleading as it would be to pretend (like the prewar government of Japan) that shrine Shintō is not religious.

Yet shrine Shintō has shown considerable vitality in spite of its difficult position. Soon after the issuance of the Shintō Directive in 1946, the Association of Shintō Shrines was formed to coordinate the programs of the newly independent shrines. This group has been active in setting up education programs, raising money, and providing an effective united voice for shrine Shintō. The association managed to prevent the destruction of the Yasukuni shrine in 1946, and it even helped to arrange for the emperor and empress to be present at ceremonies there in 1952. It has attempted again and again to reestablish the great Shintō shrines at Ise and Yasukuni as national shrines. The association has also tried to have the constitution rewritten in order to safeguard the position of the emperor as the head of state and to have the imperial household rites recognized as national religious ceremonies. It has been successful in litigation to permit the performance of Shintō ceremonies at the various traditional points in the construction of government buildings. And the association has induced the government to underwrite the maintenance of certain Shintō ceremonies as important "cultural properties." What cannot be done in the name of religion can sometimes be accomplished in the name of culture.

With the death of Hirohito, the Shōwa emperor, in January 1989, a new era, Heisei ("achieving peace"), was inaugurated, and a new emperor reigns. The funeral of the old emperor and the official ceremonies of accession of the new emperor, held in November 1990, again brought about heated argument in the Japanese press regarding the issue of religion-state separation. As a way out of this dilemma, even today there are people who favor the old formula of a governmental declaration that certain aspects of Shintō are not religious because they are felt to be such an essential part of the Japanese identity.

NOTES

1 Ryusaku Tsunoda, William T. de Bary, and Donald Keene, *Sources of Japanese Tradition* (New York: Columbia University Press, 1964), vol. 2, pp. 16–18.

2 Ibid., p. 39.

3 Hori Ichirō, *Folk Religion in Japan* (Chicago: University of Chicago Press, 1968), p. 237.

Glossary

Abhidharma name of a Theravādin Buddhist school and its series of seven scholastic works (the *Abhidharma Piṭaka*). Well-known for enumerating mental and physical constituents of the experienced world.

adhvaryu A priest in the Vedic sacrificial ritual who performed manual jobs in the ceremony, including the offering and pouring of oblations.

Adi Granth The principal Sikh scripture, assembled by Guru Arjan (1581–1606), preserving the writings of Guru Nanak (1469–1539), the founder of Sikhism.

ahimsā Noninjury and nonviolence toward any living being, emphasized by Jains and Buddhists.

alchemy In popular Daoism, the partly chemical art of concocting the elixir of immortality. As presented in the work of Go Hong, it consists of making a compound of gold and mercury to be taken as a pill and is to be accompanied by good deeds and meditation.

Amaterasu The Shintō sun goddess from whom the Japanese emperors are purported to be descended.

anātman No self; no soul; in early Buddhism, the denial of the existence of an ultimate substantial soul.

ancestor Any of the deceased persons of one's family, generally of honorable social standing, who are venerated for having set moral precedents or laid the foundations of culture. In Chinese religions, ancestors are venerated in themselves.

Aryas An Indo-European people who from the middle of the second millennium B.C.E. dominated northern India. Developed the Vedas.

Ārya Samāj ("Aryan Society") Society founded by Dayananda in 1875 that undertook to reform Hinduism by rejecting all post-Vedic scriptures and their ideas.

āśrama Hindu stage of life. Traditional āśramas for males were brahmacārin (student), gṛihastha (householder, during which one worked and raised a family), vānaprastha (forest dweller), and sannyāsa (which see). A woman's āśramas involved moving from being the responsibility of her father to that of her husband and then of her sons.

Atharvans In the Vedic age, an ancient order of shamans who performed curative and protective rituals in Aryan homes. In time they won a role in performance of the aristocratic śrauta sacrifices.

Atharvaveda Vedic text produced by the Atharvans containing 565 metrical and prose hymns in 19 books. It includes both magical and ritual elements and systematic speculations on the meaning of the Vedic ritual.

ātman In Hinduism, the ultimate essence of a person, conceived of as an immaterial reality that provides consciousness.

avatar In Vaishṇava thinking, a form assumed by the supreme being to undergo descent and birth on earth, to do deeds for the benefit of humanity. For example, Kṛishṇa is held to be an avatar of Vishṇu.

Bhagavadgītā The oldest scripture created by the Hindu Bhāgavatas, who worshiped Kṛishṇa Vāsudeva, a poem of 18 cantos preserved in the Hindu epic known as the Mahābhārata.

bhakti A spirit in Hindu interpersonal relations characterized by warm devotion and affectionate sharing.

bodhisattva-gaṇas In Buddhism, "congregations of future Buddhas" that grew up around certain stūpas. These loosely organized communities of monks and lay people played a significant role in the development of Buddhism.

Brahman In the upanishads, the all-controlling power and single unifying essence of the universe.

brāhman The priestly caste, highest of Hindu society's four varṇas. Originally responsible for performing the Vedic sacrifices, the brāhmans later became teachers and performers of rituals.

brāhmaṇa A document belonging to the second phase of the historical development of Vedic scriptures, recording comments on the collection of hymns.

brahmasūtras A series of aphoristic Hindu texts on Brahman, the earliest of which dates from around 200 C.E.

Brāhmo Samāj ("Society of Believers in Brahman") A nineteenth-century organization for the reform of Hinduism by purging it of polytheism and social discrimination on the basis of caste, founded by Ram Mohan Roy in 1828. It was a powerful influence for change for nearly a century.

Buddha ("Awakened One") Name given to Śākyamuni, Gautama Siddhārtha, a spiritual master of the fifth century B.C.E. in northeastern India. The name came to be applied to all humans believed to have experienced and rediscovered the eternal truth (Dharma).

Buddha nature Late Buddhist doctrine that all sentient beings have within them something of the Buddha, inherently pure but apparently in an obscured and tainted state. Enlightenment lies in removing the taints, often through meditation and other ascetic techniques, to allow this inherently pure nature to shine forth. Characteristic especially of Chan (Zen) Buddhism.

buddhi In the traditional Hindu analysis of the psyche, a mental faculty that confers on an individual a personal self-consciousness and an intellectual ability to ponder information, make decisions, and formulate commands.

Cakravartin ("Turner of the Wheel") In Buddhism, a great, universal ruler.

Chan Any of several Buddhist sects emphasizing meditation, well known for their use of riddles, paradox, humor, and the rejection of any explicit philosophical system. Chan appealed especially to an urban elite. Known as *Zen* in Japan.

Chenyan East Asian Vajrayāna school that emphasized symbolic representation, the use of maṇḍalas, and the realization of the indestructible and immutable aspect of the enlightened mind. Known as *Shingon* in Japan.

civil service examinations Long and difficult tests in the Confucian classics, first instituted in the Han dynasty, used to determine opportunities for social standing and economic prosperity in the Confucian state. They were required for literati status and a position in the government bureaucracy and sought to institutionalize the Confucian rule of merit.

cosmogonic myths Myths accounting for the coming into being of the world or the universe.

cosmogony An account of the creation or origin of the universe.

cosmology An account of the character of the universe as a totality, often seeking to explain the processes of nature and the relationships among the various parts of the universe.

Dao ("Way") The true, proper, and natural course of events. In Confucianism, the true way of life embodied in the teachings of Confucius; in Daoism, ultimate reality as well as the proper natural way of life humans must follow.

Dark Learning Philosophical side of Daoism popular among the literati during the period of Chinese disunity that emphasized the mysterious "dark" life of the cosmos and the immanent and transcendent aspects of the ultimate Dao.

de Sacred personal force, a kind of charisma or power by which some leaders attract devoted followers. Among Confucians, virtue, or the power of moral example; among Daoists, the mysterious power of the Dao.

deva Any deity of Hindu polytheism, conceived of as a radiant being dwelling in the sky, in the atmosphere, or on earth.

dharma In post-Vedic thinking, the cosmic principle of right behavior, expressed in codes of religious law. One's dharma is one's duty, the pattern of actions prescribed by sacred codes.

Dharma In Buddhist teaching, the eternal truth about reality. Over the centuries, Dharma came to encompass the principal doctrines of the three main schools of Buddhism.

dharmaśāstras Scriptures that record Hindu religious law in verse form, largely replacing the dharmasūtras.

dharmasūtras Prose works discussing Hindu social morality that began appearing in the fifth century B.C.E.

Digambaras The stricter party of the Jain religion whose "sky-clad" ascetics practiced nudity as part of their spiritual path.

divination Seeking to know about the divine or spirit realm, particularly with respect to present and future actions.

Durgā In Hindu Śaivite mythology, a favorite personal form of the *śākti* (female aspect) of Śiva. Durgā is known particularly for having destroyed a demon named Mahisha.

enlightenment Freedom from ignorance; perceiving the ultimate truth about the nature of reality—the highest goal of many Daoist, Buddhist, and Hindu sects. Typically conceived of as a life devoid of selfishness and egocentrism and often described as a combination of a tranquil mind, deep insight, and action for the benefit of others.

exclusivist sects Buddhist denominations that flourished in the Tang dynasty and thereafter became the dominant forms of Buddhism in China. The Pure Land schools offered a simple way to salvation that appealed especially to the laity; it postponed enlightenment *(nirvāṇa)* to the afterlife. Chan (Zen) emphasized an austere life dedicated to meditation within a monastery and enlightenment in this life.

gender roles Assignments of purportedly appropriate actions, feelings, and accomplishments depending on one's sex. These assignments differ among religions and cultures and are instilled in various, usually subtle ways.

Gopāla ("Cowherd") Epithet applied to the young and rambunctious Kṛishṇa, who spent his childhood among rural cowherds to escape the malice of a hostile king, to differentiate him from the knightly Kṛishṇa of the Bhagavadgītā.

gṛihyasūtras Hindu texts defining rites and procedures for domestic *(gṛihya)* rituals as well as the principles of social and religious practices in general.

gudwara ("gate of the guru") A Sikh temple or sanctuary housing a copy of the Adi Granth.

guru A Hindu spiritual teacher selected by an aspirant, deemed to be an expert in mystical disciplines and an effective guide to the life of introspection.

haoma A plant whose juice provides a potent drink used in ritual. See also *soma*.

Hou Ji God of millet among the Chinese Zhou people and the first ancestor of the Zhou ruling house. Myths told of his discovery of agriculture and his gift of this knowledge to humans.

householders People in the second of the Hindu āśramas, who work, marry, and raise a family.

Huayan A sixth-century Chinese philosophical school of Buddhism that emphasized the harmony and interrelatedness of all phenomena. Known as *Kegon* in Japan.

immortals (*xian*) Wizardlike saints of popular Daoism known for their eccentric behavior and superhuman powers. They were humans who by good deeds and the arts of alchemy and meditation, and sometimes luck, achieved immortality.

Indo-Europeans People from around the Caspian Sea area assumed to have migrated both east and west starting around 2000 B.C.E. Because they had mastered bronze-tipped weapon making and the horse and chariot, they conquered many local peoples. They thus influenced many cultures in Asia and Europe, playing important formative roles in India, Iran, Greece, Rome, and northern Europe.

Indra A major deity of the Ṛigvedic pantheon; the ancient war god of the Aryas and in India also a champion against powers that withhold rain.

Indus civilization The civilization flourishing in northwestern India near the Indus River before the Aryan invasion (pre-1700 B.C.E.). Renowned for their highly consistent and well-organized cities. Main sites include Harappā and Mohenjo-Dāro.

initiation A ritual that marks a transition between physical states, coupled with a change in social status. Often a time when the esoteric meaning of religious myths, rituals, and symbols is revealed.

Izanagi With Izanami, one of the primordial parents in Shintō mythology. Their actions illustrate the dynamic tension characteristic of Japanese religiosity.

Izanami See *Izanagi*.

Jātakas Folkloric stories of acts that the Buddha supposedly performed in his previous lives, in which the Buddha appears as an animal, a human being, or a deity. Jātaka collections began appearing around the start of the Common Era.

jātis Castes; groups bound to a hereditary occupation in the traditional Hindu social order.

Jina ("Victor") Name given to Nataputta Vardhamana (c. 599–527 B.C.E.), who gave Jainism its present form, held to have victoriously crossed the river of life, overcoming human misery. From this title Jainism derives its name.

***jingū-ji* system** "Shrine-temple" system whereby in the classical period most Shintō shrines also enclosed a Buddhist temple and vice versa.

jīva Life, soul, all that is living. Jains hold that jīvas mingle with particles of karma to determine an individual's destiny and character; when the jīva is freed from karma, liberation occurs, and the soul rises to the zenith of the universe, remaining motionless and free from suffering forever.

Kabir Sant poet (1440–1518), teacher of Sikhism's founder, Guru Nanak.

Kālī A goddess of mercurial and often violent disposition, representing the uncertainties of nature in an agricultural land; loosely integrated into Hinduism as a consort of Śiva.

kami Sacred spirits or deities believed to dwell in Shintō shrines.

karma ("action") A social or ritual act that is morally significant by virtue of being part of one's dharma or religious duty. Also, a dangerous or beneficent energy generated by the performance of such acts. One's karma will inevitably bring appropriate retribution.

karmic matter Particles of karma, thought by Jains to mix with the soul (*jīva*) to determine an individual's destiny and character.

Kegon See *Huayan*.

Khalsa ("Pure") The militaristic wing of Sikhism, begun by Gobind Singh (1675–1708). Members pledge themselves to an austere code of conduct, to wear special symbols, and to protect the religion. All members take the name Singh, "lion."

Kokutai "National Essence," the name given by the Japanese National Scholars to the unity of political and religious structure; also interpreted to mean the unique character of "Japaneseness."

Kṛishṇa Vāsudeva The Supreme Lord of the Hindu Bhāgavatas.

kshatriyas Members of the Vedic second varṇa, or warrior class; later, members of any of various military castes within the second varṇa.

lamas Religious leaders in Tibetan Buddhism.

li Ritual, decorum, propriety; one of the building blocks of Confucius's thought and the key to achieving universal harmony. All life should be regulated by it. Externally, it brings about a smoothly working society; internally, it manifests itself in *ren*.

Li Principle, a key term in Neo-Confucianism, in which it stood for ultimate reality, immanent in all things. Mystical experience of Li was the basis of the sage's enlightenment.

liṅgam In the iconography of Śaivism, the short, round-topped pillar that is the principal emblem of Śiva. Vaguely in the form of the male organ, it suggests to worshipers the generative power of Śiva in the creation of the universe.

Long March The 6,000-mile retreat of the Chinese Communist guerrillas in the 1930s that became the principal "salvation history" for the Maoist movement. Many exemplary Communist martyrs were made during this march.

Mahābhārata A vast Hindu epic containing the Bhagavadgītā.

mahāpurusha ("great man") Name Buddhists applied to Buddha and an enlightened bodhisattva. Comes to be applied to any great man.

Mahāvira ("Great Hero") Name given to Nataputta Vardhamana (c. 599–527 B.C.E.), the twenty-fourth and last Tīrthaṃkara, or ford finder; first practitioner of ascetic nudity and organizer of Jainism.

Mahāyāna One of the three main early schools of Indian Buddhism, today found primarily in Japan, Korea, and China.

manas In Hindu thought, the lower mind. As used in Vedic texts, it is thought to include aspects of both mind and emotion.

maṇḍala ("circle") In Buddhism, a circular symbol, often enclosed in a square. Buddhist stūpas were maṇḍalas. The maṇḍala was especially important in Vajrayāna Buddhism, where it signified the dwelling or palace of a pure being such as a Buddha.

mantra A sacred sound; originally a hymn of the Vedas, in Hinduism it came to signify the sound, often a one- or two-syllable word, used as the focus of meditation. In Vajrayāna Buddhism, Buddhas and bodhisattvas were thought to have their own seed mantras, their manifestation in sound; meditation on a seed mantra could intensify the figure's characteristics in the mind.

matsuri Ritual celebrations held at Shintō shrines by priests on a regular basis. Most matsuri are public and include prayers, blessings, and a meal.

May Seventh schools Schools of the Maoist period in China, named for the date (May 7, 1966) of the directive that established them, requiring that all students devote six months to classroom study and six months to purifying labor in the countryside each year.

māyā The power of creation and illusion in Hindu philosophy. In the teaching of Śaṅkara, a deluding agency of mysterious nature that causes the human consciousness to perceive a universe of many persons and things, whereas the unity of all is the revealed truth.

miko Japanese female shamans who by entering a trance are able to be possessed by kami and other spiritual beings. When in the trance, their words are taken to be those of the kami.

moksha Enlightenment, release, liberation, from the retributions ordinarily entailed by one's past deeds and thus from the necessity of further deaths and rebirths in the world. For most Hindus such liberation is the highest blessedness, salvation itself.

Nanak Founder of Sikhism (1469–1539), who emphasized the unity between Islam and Hinduism and urged the contemplation of God and the singing of hymns.

National Scholars A group of intellectuals who in the late medieval period revived Japanese classical learning and instituted a Shintō renewal.

naturalness The proper way of life in Daoism. To be in harmony with the Dao, one had to learn to act spontaneously as a straightforward reflection of the Dao rather than as motivated by the promise of personal gain. See also *wu-wei.*

Nembutsu See *Nienfo.*

Nichiren A Japanese Tendai monk (1222–1282) whose name is also applied to the "Lotus lineage" school of Buddhism he founded. Militaristic and nationalistic, Nichiren emphasized devotion, the authority of the Lotus Sūtra, and the recitation of a sacred formula.

Nienfo The chant *"Namo Omito Fo"* ("Hail to the Buddha Amitābha") used in Pure Land Buddhism. Many lay people have thought it the only practice necessary to ensure rebirth in the Pure Land of Amitābha, just short of nirvāṇa. Known as *Nembutsu* in Japan.

nirvāṇa Enlightenment (literally, blowing out). The state gained by Buddha and by any being who is able to extinguish all attachments and defilements. Though gained in and through meditation, affects all of one's life. Said to be indescribable, though wonderful. At death, one who has gained nirvāṇa does not become reborn.

outcastes In the Hindu social system, the caste not included in the four main varṇas. Its members handled polluting things, such as corpses and dirt.

Pārśva An early Jain teacher (872–772 B.C.E.) held to be the twenty-third Tīrthaṃkara, or ford finder.

polytheism The belief in or worship of many gods, typical of Egyptian, Vedic, Hindu, Greek, Native American, and other religious systems. Often these gods are considered to have powers over particular aspects of reality and to reflect a deeper underlying principle or essence.

prāṇa ("breath") The internal current of air that Hindus believe to be the fundamental animating principle of a living being.

pratītya samutpāda The doctrine of interdependent origination taught by the Buddha, holding that all elements of reality arise in conjunction with one another.

primordial beings Mythic creatures who came into being at the beginning of creation. Often ambiguous in shape, they have the power to change forms and to defy other rules of time and space that are part of the natural order that became established after them.

pūjā A post-Vedic style of ritual, adapted to the worship of devas who have consented to dwell on earth in images or other material objects.

Pure Land Any of several Buddhist sects emphasizing faith and devotion to the Buddha Amitābha, leading to rebirth in his other-worldly paradise, the Pure Land. Begun in India, Pure Land became influential in rural China, where it centered on invoking the name of Amitābha (see *Nienfo*).

rājanyas Vedic name for the kshatriyas, or members of the warrior caste, who came to be the rulers of India.

Rāmāyana An epic poem composed by Valmiki around the fourth century B.C.E. about the career of Rāmacandra of Ayodhya. Any book on that theme can be called a Rāmāyana, however. One such is the great Hindi poem composed in the decade following 1574 C.E. by Tulsi Dās, which he titled the *Rāmcaritmānas* ("Pool of the Deeds of Rāma").

ren Humaneness, a basic building block of Confucius's thought; for a Confucian gentleman *(zhunzi),* love for humanity and a sense of obligation toward society, exercised primarily through *li.*

Ṛigveda The largest and ritually most important of the four Vedas, containing 1,028 hymns used in the Aryas' sacrificial rituals.

ṛita In the cosmology of the Vedas, the impersonal principle of righteousness and harmony that is operative in both the actions of virtuous human beings and the regularity of the movements of natural bodies.

rite of passage A ritual that effects a change in social status, as from youth to adulthood. Generally has three stages: separation from society, a transition or liminal phase, and reintegration into society as a member with a new status. Often plays on the theme of death and rebirth.

sacrifice The act of making an offering to a deity or spiritual being, often through the death of a victim on behalf of the sacrificers.

sage The ideal embodiment of the Dao. In old Confucianism, an impossibly high status reached by only a few ancient kings and other worthies. In classical Daoism, the perfect example of a person living naturally, in harmony with the Dao. In popular Daoism, the equivalent of an immortal *(xian),* a practitioner of alchemy and discoverer of immortality. Among Neo-Confucians, a realizable ideal that tended to replace the *zhunzi* as a goal of religious practice.

Śaivas Post-Vedic Hindu monotheists who believe that Śiva is the one Lord of the Universe.

Śāktas Hindus whose worship is directed toward one of the personifications of Śiva's *śākti,* or feminine aspect.

śākti The feminine aspect of Śiva, which created and controls the world, often personified as a mythical consort of Śiva, such as Durgā or Kālī.

samādhi A condition of intense mental concentration without awareness of thoughts or sensations, the culminating trance in Hinduism or Buddhism in which the saving insight is revealed.

Sāmaveda One of the four Vedas, a collection of songs of the sāmans, the cantors of Aryan sacrificial ceremonies, taken primarily from the ninth book of the Ṛigveda.

saṃsāra The cyclical world, characterized by the cycle of birth, life, death, and rebirth.

saṃskāras Hindu rites of the round of life. These ceremonies, usually performed in the home, mark important transitions among members of the three highest castes, including birth, initiation, marriage, and death.

sandhyās Personal Hindu meditations performed at daily solar transitions such as dawn, noon, and dusk.

Saṅgha ("Group") The order of Buddhist monks; the Buddhist clergy collectively.

sannyāsa In Hinduism, renunciation of desires or of worldly gains or worldly life itself. In this last sense, *sannyāsa* can entail a ritual departure from home and entry into the fourth āśrama of life, that of the *sannyāsī.*

sannyāsī A Hindu who has renounced worldly life.

Sant A Hindu devotional movement that influenced early Sikhism.

satī ("true one") A widow who carries out the medieval Hindu rite of immolating herself on the funeral pyre of her deceased husband; also, the practice of this rite.

satyāgraha ("holding on to truth") Mahātma Gāndhī's principle for the nonviolent attainment of social justice.

self-strengthening A nineteenth-century theory promoted by Confucian bureaucrats that sought to borrow Western technology without Western cultural or religious values. Technology would strengthen China to resist foreign values.

shahāda The fundamental creed of Islam, the first and most important of the Five Pillars: "There is no god but God, and Muḥammad is his apostle."

shaman A priest-doctor who uses religious and magical techniques to cure the sick and reveal the hidden. Often uses trance-inducing techniques to "travel" to the spirit world to seek guidance in human affairs. Also called *medicine man.*

Shingon See *Chenyan* and *Vajrayāna.*

siddha A sage in Hinduism or Vajrayāna Buddhism, often believed to be endowed with *siddhis,* or supernormal powers, such as levitation.

Śiva A high deity in post-Vedic Hinduism. To some polytheists he was the special god of destruction, but to montheists he became the one Lord of the Universe.

smṛiti ("remembered") A Hindu scripture that is deemed to be of second rank because of its post-Vedic human authorship and yet of much authority because it is believed reliably to reexpress the message of the Vedas.

soma An exhilarating drink poured as a libation in Vedic sacrifices and drunk by the priestly sacrificers. See also *haoma.*

śramana Any member of a broad class of ascetics in early India, characterized by the practice of extreme austerity and self-mortification.

śrauta An outdoor sacrificial ritual of the Aryas, performed by one, four, or sometimes a great number of priests and accompanied by the hymns of the Ṛigveda.

Śrauta Sūtras Easily memorized aphoristic prose outlines of the performance of the śrauta sacrifices that appeared after 600 B.C.E.

stūpa A burial mound, often said to contain some bodily relic of the Buddha.

śūdras The fourth and lowest varṇa, containing castes whose hereditary work is manual but not grossly defiling.

sūtra ("stitch") Short aphoristic Hindu text that states or summarizes a key doctrine or ritual act in easily memorizable form.

Svetāmbaras The more liberal ("white-clad") party of Jain ascetics.

Tai Ping Rebellion Mid-nineteenth-century movement that combined popular Daoist, folk religious, and Christian elements in an attempt to build a utopian, theocratic state in place of the faltering Qing (Manchu) dynasty. The rebellion was finally put down with Western help after millions of deaths.

Tāntrism A marginal Hindu tradition, taught in scriptures called *tāntras,* that holds the supreme deity to be feminine and insists that liberation *(moksha)* can be won through erotic practices. Influenced Buddhist Vajrayāna.

Tendai Buddhist sect that dominated religious life in Japan throughout the classical period. The founders of the medieval Pure Land, True Pure Land, and Nichiren sects began their religious careers as Tendai monks. Known as *Tiantai* in China.

Theravāda One of the three main early schools of Indian Buddhism, today found primarily in southern Asia. Also called *Hīnayāna Buddhism.*

Tian ("Heaven") Chief deity of the Zhou, to whom only kings (and later, emperors) could sacrifice. Later taken up by Confucianism as an impersonal guardian of the moral order, especially the Mandate of Heaven.

Tiantai See *Tendai.*

Tīrthaṃkaras ("ford finders") Jain saints who have found their way across to the other side of life and hence are liberated from the cycle of birth and death. Jains hold that Mahāvira, the founder of Jainism, was the twenty-fourth and last such ford finder.

trickster A mythic figure whose cunning and playful disobedience brings about changes in the shape of the world. A demiurge who introduces disorder into the cosmos. Often associated with divination.

Tripiṭaka The "Triple Basket" of the Buddhist sūtras, Vinaya, and Abhidharma texts that came to form the core of early Buddhist scripture. Each school of Buddhism developed its own authoritative Tripiṭaka and thus its own Dharma.

universalist ("catholic") schools Buddhist denominations that flourished in the Tan dynasty, especially the Huayan and Tiantai schools. Though each was based on primary allegiance to a particular sūtra (for Tiantai this was the Lotus Sūtra), all tried to find an honored place for all Buddhist texts and practices.

upanishads ("secret teachings") A series of Hindu texts, the first appearing around 600 B.C.E., that focused on mystical knowledge. Of more than 100 written, 13 are held to be revealed scripture.

Vaishṇavas Post-Vedic Hindu monotheists who believe that Vishṇu is the one Lord of the Universe.

vaiśyas The third of the four varṇas and the lowest entitled to study the Veda; the modern varṇa includes merchants and clerical workers.

Vajrayāna One of the three main early schools of Indian Buddhism, today found primarily in Tibet and Mongolia. Also known as *Chenyan* or *Shingon.*

varṇa One of the four broad classes of traditional Hindu society, mentioned in late Vedas and used ever since to provide stratifications for placing the castes in a social hierarchy.

Varuṇa A major deity of the Ṛigvedic pantheon, the sky-dwelling guardian of *ṛita,* overseer of human moral behavior, and patron of kings.

Vedānta ("Veda's End") The upanishads and the teaching regarding Brahman that is essential to them.

Vedas The early religious literature of the Aryas, centered on four collections *(saṃhitās)* of ritual materials: Ṛigveda, Sāmaveda, Yajurveda, and Atharvaveda.

Vinaya The collection of Buddhist regulations that guided behavior in the monasteries.

Vishṇu Vedic deity associated with the sun, germination, growth, and the support of life. Considered the Lord of the Universe by certain believers (Vaishṇavas) in post-Vedic times.

Vṛitra The demon fought and conquered by Indra in the Vedas.

wu-wei ("nonaction") In classical Daoism, the proper way of desireless action characteristic of both the Dao and the sage. Opposed to *wei,* egotistic action typical of ordinary people. If one "acts with nonaction," one achieves naturalness and harmony with the Dao.

Yajurveda One of the four Vedas, consisting of short incantations *(yajuses)* used by the adhvaryus; about half the content is extracted from the Ṛigveda.

yang With *yin,* one of the dual principles or forces underlying all changes in both the natural and human realms, representing open and active power.

yin With *yang,* one of the dual principles or forces underlying all changes in both the natural and human realms, representing hidden and passive power.

yoga In Hinduism, any systematic discipline of meditation directed toward the realization of an arcane religious truth.

yogī A practitioner or master of yoga; a sage or wise man.

yoni In the iconography of Śaivism, the spouted plate, figuratively suggestive of the female organ, that surrounds the liṅgam. The yoni is understood to represent the *śākti* or feminine aspect of Śiva's divine nature.

Zen See *Chan.*

zhunzi Superior man, true gentleman, true aristocrat—the attainable ideal of old Confucianism, conceived of especially as a government bureaucrat with high ideals of selfless service, in virtue less than the sage but similar in quality. One could not be born a *zhunzi* but could aspire to that status through study and conformity to *li.*

Bibliography

INTRODUCTION

Secondary Sources

Baird, Robert D. *Category Formation and the History of Religion.* The Hague, Netherlands: Mouton, 1971. An important study that defines religion as the ultimate human concern.

Barrett, David, ed. *World Christian Encyclopedia: A Comparative Study of Churches and Religions in the Modern World,* AD *1900–2000.* New York: Oxford University Press, 1982. Not limited to Christianity, this work is the most exhaustive demographic and statistical analysis ever done of religions (and unbelief too) around the globe.

Berger, Peter L. *The Sacred Canopy: Elements of a Sociological Theory of Religion.* Garden City, N.Y.: Doubleday, 1967. Religion as the overarching value structure of societies, as discussed by a leading American sociologist of religion.

Blasi, Anthony J., and Andrew J. Weigert. "Towards a Sociology of Religion: An Interpretative Sociology Approach," *Sociological Analysis* 37 (1976): 189–204. Levels of social analysis for the study of religion.

Durkheim, Emile. *The Elementary Forms of the Religious Life,* trans. Joseph Ward Swain. New York: Free Press, 1965. Originally published in France in 1912. Basic work by one of the founders of the sociology of religion.

Eliade, Mircea. *Rites and Symbols of Initiation: The Mysteries of Birth and Rebirth,* trans. Willard R. Trask. New York: Harper & Row, 1965. Symbolic interpretation of the ritual of rebirth as found in many cultures, by a well-known historian of religion.

———, ed. *The Encyclopedia of Religion* (16 vols.). New York: Macmillan, 1987. The first source to consult for the general study of religion.

Geertz, Clifford. "Religion as a Cultural System." In *Anthropological Approaches to the Study of Religion,* ed. M. Banton. London: Tavistock, 1963. Definition of religion as a cultural system of symbols, by a leading cultural anthropologist.

Larson, Gerald James. "Prolegomenon to a Theory of Religion." *Journal of the American Academy of Religion* 46 (1978): 443–463. Religion defined by stressing its analogical affinity to language.

Lessa, William A., and Evon Z. Vogt, eds. *Reader in Comparative Religion: An Anthropological Approach,* 4th ed. New York: Harper & Row, 1979. An excellent collection of essays both classical and recent on the anthropological approach to religious studies.

Melton, J. Gordon. *The Encyclopedia of American Religions,* 2nd ed. Detroit: Gale Research, 1987. A thorough descriptive taxonomy of American religions, listing over 1,300 denominations, sects, and cults and providing basic information on individual groups and the "families" they are related to. Supplementary volumes add hundreds of additional bodies.

Ray, Benjamin C. *African Religions: Symbol, Ritual, and Community.* Englewood Cliffs, N.J.: Prentice-Hall, 1976. Excellent survey of African traditional religions, arranged topically and based on case studies.

Sharpe, Eric J. *Understanding Religion.* New York: St. Martin's Press, 1983. A clear and concise introduction to the field.

Smart, Ninian. *The Phenomenon of Religion.* New York: Herder and Herder, 1973.

———. *The Science of Religion and the Sociology of Knowledge: Some Methodological Questions.* Princeton, N.J.: Princeton University Press, 1973. Two important examinations of methodological problems in the study of religion.

———, and Donald Wiebe. *Concept and Empathy: Essays in the Study of Religion.* New York: New York University Press, 1986. A helpful series of essays on the methodological problems in the study of religion.

Smith, Wilfred Cantwell. *The Meaning and End of Religion.* New York: Macmillan, 1962. Influential criticism of religions and isms as abstractions. Emphasis is on individual faith in relation to cumulative religious traditions.

Streng, Frederick J. "Studying Religion: Possibilities and Limitations of Different Definitions." *Journal of the American Academy of Religion* 40 (1972): 219–237.

———. *Understanding Religious Life,* 3rd ed. Belmont, Calif.: Wadsworth, 1985. Religion emphasized as the ultimate transformation, as seen from the perspective of the history of religion.

Turner, Victor W. *The Ritual Process: Structure and Anti-structure.* Ithaca, N.Y.: Cornell University Press, 1969. Important study of the structure of ritual processes and of the liminal phase of rituals.

Van Gennep, Arnold. *The Rites of Passage,* trans. Monika B. Vizedom and Gabrielle L. Caffee. Chicago: University of Chicago Press, 1976. Originally published in 1909 and still a very useful study.

PART ONE: RELIGIONS OF INDIA

HINDUISM

Primary Sources

Dimock, Edward, trans. *In Praise of Kṛishṇa: Songs from the Bengali.* Chicago: University of Chicago Press, 1981. Originally published in 1967.

Edgerton, Franklin, trans. *The Bhagavad Gītā.* Cambridge, Mass.: Harvard University Press, 1985. Literal and objective, useful for serious studies.

Embree, Ainslee T. *The Hindu Tradition.* New York: Random House, 1972. Brief selections from Hindu writings of all periods.

Doniger, Wendy, trans. *Hindu Myths: A Sourcebook.* New York: Penguin, 1975.

———, trans. *Ṛig Veda: An Anthology.* New York: Penguin, 1982.

———, and Brian K. Smith, trans. *The Laws of Manu.* New York: Penguin, 1992.

Goldman, Robert P., et al., trans. *The Rāmāyana of Vālmīki* (3 vols.). Princeton, N.J.: Princeton University Press, 1984–1992). A continuing translation of the critical edition.

Growse, F. S., trans. *Rāmāyana of Tulasidas.* Columbia, Mo.: South Asia Books, 1978. Originally published in 1877.

Hume, Robert E., trans. *The Thirteen Principal Upanishads,* rev. ed. New York: Oxford University Press, 1971. Originally published in 1931.

Secondary Sources

Adams, Charles J., ed. *Reader's Guide to the Great Religions,* 2nd rev. ed. New York: Free Press, 1977, pp. 106–155. Includes an annotated bibliography to 1977.

Carpenter, James Estlin. *Theism in Medieval India.* Livingston, N.J.: Orient Book Distributors, 1977. Originally published in 1921. Secondary survey, still useful for a general introduction to the field.

Davis, Richard. *Ritual in an Oscillating Universe: Worshiping Śiva in Medieval India.* Princeton, N.J.: Princeton University Press, 1991. Daily worship in a Śaiva temple and its meaning in Śaiva Siddhānta doctrine.

Dowson, John. *A Classical Dictionary of Hindu Mythology.* Columbia, Mo.: South Asia Books, 1987. Originally published in 1879.

Eliade, Mircea. *Yoga: Immortality and Freedom.* New York: Penguin, 1989. Originally published in 1958.

Farquhar, John Nicol. *An Outline of the Religious Literature of India.* Livingston, N.J.: Orient Book Distributors, 1984. Originally published in 1920. Still useful for identifying authors and documents and the traditions to which they belong.

Hiriyanna, M. *Essentials of Indian Philosophy.* Columbia, Mo.: South Asia Books, 1986. Originally published in 1949.

Keith, Arthur Berriedale. *The Religion and Philosophy of the Veda and Upanishads* (2 vols.). Livingston, N.J.: Orient Book Distributors, 1976. Originally published in 1925. A comprehensive manual, with evaluation of earlier interpretations.

Lingat, Robert. *The Classical Law of India.* Berkeley: University of California Press, 1973. Originally published in 1967. General introduction to Hindu codes and concepts.

Mitchell, George. *Hindu Temple: An Introduction to Its Meaning and Forms.* Chicago: University of Chicago Press, 1988. Originally published in 1978.

Pandey, Raj Bali. *Hindu Saṃskāras.* Columbia, Mo.: South Asia Books, 1987. Originally published in 1949. Provides information on the Hindu domestic rituals and their history.

Sivaraman, K. *Śaivism in Philosophical Perspective.* Livingston, N.J.: Orient Book Distributors, 1973. The doctrine of a major Śaivite monotheistic sect.

Whitehead, Henry. *Village Gods of South India.* Columbia, Mo.: South Asia Books, 1986. Originally published in 1921.

Zaehner, Richard C. *Hinduism.* New York: Oxford University Press, 1962. An introduction to the history of Hinduism, stressing selected periods and traditions.

Zimmer, Heinrich. *Myths and Symbols in Indian Art and Civilization.* Princeton, N.J.: Princeton University Press, 1971. Originally published in 1946.

JAINISM

Primary Sources

Ghoshal, Sarat C., ed. *The Sacred Books of the Jainas* (11 vols.). New York: AMS Press, 1917–1940.

Jacobi, Hermann, trans. *The Gaina Sūtras, the Sacred Books of the East,* ed. F. Max Müller. New York: Scribner, 1901, vol. 10. Originally published in 1884. The basic texts.

Secondary Sources

Casa, Carlo della. "Jainism." In *Historia Religionum: Handbook for the History of Religion,* ed. C. Jouco Bleeker and Geo Widengren, vol. 2. Leiden, Netherlands: Brill, 1971. An authoritative presentation by a professor at the University of Turin.

Jain, Muni Uttam Kamal. *Jaina Sects and Schools.* Delhi, India: Concept Publishing Company, 1975. A useful account.

Jaini, Padmanabh S. *The Jaina Path of Purification.* Berkeley: University of California Press, 1979. An excellent introduction that focuses on both the practice of the religion and its history.

Mehta, Mohan Lal. *Outlines of Jaina Philosophy: The Essentials of Jaina Ontology, Epistemology and Ethics.* Bangalore, India: Jain Mission Society, 1954. A careful presentation that contrasts Jainism with other religions and philosophies.

Roy, Ashim Kumar. *A History of the Jainas.* New Delhi: Gitanjali Publishing House, 1984. A useful recent study of Jain history that gives major attention to the different parties in the religion.

Schurbring, Walther. *The Doctrine of the Jainas,* trans. Walter Beurlen. Delhi: Banarsidass, 1962. A scholarly work by a professor at the University of Hamburg.

Stevenson, Mrs. Sinclair. *The Heart of Jainism.* London: Oxford University Press, 1915. A balanced view by a sympathetic Christian observer.

Zimmer, Heinrich. *Philosophies of India,* ed. Joseph Campbell. Chicago: University of Chicago Press, 1969. Originally published in 1951. The chapters on Jainism are especially valuable.

SIKHISM

Primary Source

Singh, Trilochan; Bhai Judh Singh; Kapur Singh; Bawa Harkishen Singh; and Khushwant Singh, eds. *Selections from the Sacred Writings of the Sikhs,* rev. George S. Fraser. London: Allen & Unwin, 1960. A useful collection of the basic documents.

Secondary Sources

Cole, W. Owen. *The Guru in Sikhism.* London: Darton, Longman & Todd, 1982. A careful, definitive study of the role of the succession of Sikh leader-teachers, well written and clear.

———, and Piara Singh Sambhi. *The Sikhs: Their Religious Beliefs and Practices.* London: Routledge & Kegan Paul, 1978. A useful, highly readable presentation by a lecturer at Leeds Polytechnic and the president of the Leeds Gudwara.

Khushwant, K. S. *A History of the Sikhs* (2 vols.). Princeton, N.J.: Princeton University Press, 1963, 1966. A major reference work by an authority in the field.

———. "Sikhism." In *Encyclopaedia Britannica,* 15th ed., vol. 16. A brief, well-organized account.

———. *The Sikhs Today.* Columbia, Mo.: South Asia Books, 1976. A sympathetic treatment of the faith by a member who brings a critical insight into his heritage.

McLeod, W. H. *Early Sikh Tradition: A Study of the Janam-Sakhis.* Oxford: Clarendon Press, 1980. An important and skillful study set in the context of the history of religions.

———. *The Evolution of the Sikh Community: Five Essays.* Oxford: Oxford University Press, 1976. A valuable and illuminating appraisal of the social dimension of Sikhism.

———. *Guru Nanak and the Sikh Religion.* London: Oxford University Press, 1969. A critical delineation of the founder's character and role.

PART TWO: BUDDHISM

Primary Sources

Beyer, Stephan, trans. *The Buddhist Experience: Sources and Interpretations.* Encino, Calif.: Dickinson, 1974. An anthology of texts from a wide variety of Buddhist traditions.

Cowell, E. B.; F. Max Müller; and Takakusa Junjirō, trans. *Buddhist Mahāyāna Texts.* New York: Dover, 1969. A collection that contains three basic texts (sūtras) of the Buddhist Pure Land tradition.

Davids, T. W. Rhys, trans. *Buddhist Sūtras.* New York: Dover, 1969. An old but still useful collection drawn from the *Sutta Pitaka* of the Pali Tripiṭaka. If only one text or set of texts can be read, this collection would be an appropriate choice.

Evans-Wentz, W. Y., trans. *Tibet's Great Yogī Milarepa,* 2nd ed. London: Oxford University Press, 1951. A fascinating hagiography that relates the life of a Tibetan yogī famed for his magic powers and his attainment as a living Buddha.

Freemantle, Francesca, and Chogyam Trungpa, trans. *The Tibetan Book of the Dead.* Berkeley, Calif.: Shambala Press, 1975. A distinctive presentation of the supposed transition from the moment of dying to the point of enlightenment or rebirth.

Hurwitz, Leon, trans. *Sūtra of the Lotus Blossom of the Fine Dharma.* New York: Columbia University Press, 1976. A rich and highly imaginative text important to East Asian Buddhism, particularly the Tiantai (Tendai) school of China and Japan and the Nichiren school and its offshoots in modern Japan.

Khoroche, Peter, trans. *Once the Buddha Was a Monkey: Arya Sura's Jatakamala.* Chicago: University of Chicago Press, 1989. A fine rendition of a highly literary text that recounts 34 stories from the previous lives of the Buddha.

Matics, Marion, trans. *Santideva's Entering the Path of Enlightenment.* New York: Macmillan, 1970. An influential devotional poem that represents the Indian Madhyamika tradition founded by Nāgārjuna.

Reynolds, Frank E., and Mani B. Reynolds, trans. *Three Worlds According to King Ruang*. Berkeley, Calif.: Lancaster & Miller, 1981. A Thai Buddhist treatise on cosmology and ethics that presents an important Theravāda perspective in which the philosophical and mythicosymbolic aspects of the tradition are joined.

Strong, John. *The Legend of King Aśoka: A Study and Translation of the Aśokavadana*. Princeton, N.J.: Princeton University Press, 1983. A superb interpretation and rendition of a popular hagiographic account that deals with Buddhist kingship and lay ideals.

Thurman, Robert, trans. *The Holy Teaching of Vimalakīrti*. College Park: Pennsylvania State University Press, 1976. An early Mahāyāna text that highlights the insight and skill of a lay bodhisattva.

Yampolsky, Philip B., trans. *The Platform Sūtra of the Sixth Patriarch*. New York: Columbia University Press, 1967. A basic text of Chan Buddhism that purports to recount the life and a famous sermon of the Chinese master Hui-neng (638–713).

Secondary Sources

Beyer, Stephan. *The Cult of Tārā: Magic and Ritual in Tibet*. Berkeley: University of California Press, 1973. A difficult book, but still unequaled as a study of Buddhist practice in Tibet.

Collins, Steven. *Selfless Persons: Imagery and Thought in Theravāda Buddhism*. Cambridge: Cambridge University Press, 1982. By far the best available introduction to Theravāda doctrine.

Foucher, Alfred. *The Life of the Buddha According to the Ancient Texts and Monuments of India,* trans. Simone Boas. Middletown, Conn.: Wesleyan University Press, 1963. An excellent reconstruction of the legend of the Buddha at the beginning of the Common Era.

Hardacre, Helen, and Alan Sponburg, eds. *Maitreya, the Future Buddha*. New York: Cambridge University Press, 1988. An intriguing collection of essays on Maitreya in different Buddhist cultures from India to Japan.

Holt, John Clifford. *The Buddha in the Crown: Avalokiteśvara in the Buddhist Tradition of Śrī Lanka*. New York: Oxford University Press, 1991. A very sophisticated account of aspects of Sinhalese Buddhism that involve processes of assimilation and change.

Kasulis, Thomas. *Zen Action/Zen Person*. Honolulu: University of Hawaii Press, 1985. Of the many books on Zen Buddhism, this one is unmatched for clarity and precision.

La Fleur, William. *The Karma of Words: Buddhism and the Literary Arts in Medieval Japan*. Berkeley: University of California Press, 1983. An important study of the pervasiveness of Buddhism in medieval Japanese culture.

Kitagawa, Joseph, and Mark Cummings, eds. *Buddhism in Asian History*. New York: Macmillan, 1989. An excellent, well-organized collection of essays that is appropriate for readers interested in further information on various aspects of Buddhism.

Reynolds, Frank E., et al. "Buddhism." In *Encyclopaedia Britannica,* 15th ed., vol. 15, pp. 263–305. An overview providing an advanced account of various Buddhist schools, doctrines, and literature.

Snellgrove, David, ed. *The Image of the Buddha*. London: Serindia Publications/UNESCO, 1978. A broad-ranging, well-illustrated survey of Buddhist art and iconography that covers all of the major Asian traditions.

Streng, Fredrick. *Emptiness: A Study of Religious Meaning*. Nashville, Tenn.: Abingdon Press, 1967. This study remains the most interesting discussion of the philosophy of Nāgārjuna.

Teiser, Stephen. *The Ghost Festival in Medieval China*. Princeton, N.J.: Princeton University Press, 1988. A comprehensive interpretation of a popular festival that has played a central role in the history of Buddhism in China.

Williams, Paul. *Mahāyāna Buddhism: The Doctrinal Foundations*. London: Routledge & Kegan Paul, 1989. A readable introduction to a very difficult and complicated subject.

PART THREE: RELIGIONS OF CHINA AND JAPAN

CHINA

Primary Sources

Waley, Arthur, trans. *The Analects of Confucius*. New York: Random House, 1938. Extensive introduction and notes emphasizing the historical context of Confucius's thought.

———. *The Way and Its Power*. New York: Grove Press, 1958. Important for its explanatory materials and its emphasis on the mystical elements of Lao-zi's thought.

Watson, Burton, trans. *Chuang-tzu: Basic Writings*. New York: Columbia University Press, 1964. Best-balanced modern translation of this difficult work.

The I Ching or Book of Changes, trans. into German by Richard Wilhelm and into English by Cary F. Baynes. Princeton, N.J.: Princeton University Press, 1967. Extensive introduction and notes. The best attempt so far to render this enigmatic text intelligible to the modern reader.

Wing-tsit Chan, trans. and comp. *A Source Book in Chinese Philosophy*. Princeton, N.J.: Princeton University Press, 1963. A large selection of documents with short but useful introductions. If only one text can be read, it should be this one, but it needs to be balanced with sociological and anthropological materials.

Secondary Sources

Blofeld, John. *Beyond the Gods: Buddhist and Taoist Mysticism*. New York: Dutton, 1974. Engaging account of Buddhist and Daoist piety by an informed traveler in China in the 1930s.

Bredon, Juliet, and Igor Mitrophanow. *The Moon Year*. Shanghai: Kelly & Walsh, 1927. An encyclopedia of folk religion based on the yearly festival calendar.

Chang, Garma C. C. *The Practice of Zen*. New York: Harper & Row, 1959. Despite its title, an insightful and sober account of Chan Buddhism. Valuable for its translations of autobiographies of monks and other religious virtuosi.

Creel, H. G. *The Birth of China*. New York: Ungar, 1937. Popular account of life and attitudes in the Shang and Western Zhou periods. Draws heavily on archaeology.

de Bary, William Theodore, ed. *The Unfolding of Neo-Confucianism*. New York: Columbia University Press, 1975. A collection of scholarly articles emphasizing the religious dimension of Neo-Confucianism. A good balance to the purely philosophical approach.

Fingarette, Herbert. *Confucius: The Secular as Sacred*. New York: Harper & Row, 1972. Sensitive and very readable interpretation of Confucius as a social and religious reformer with insights still useful for modern people.

Levenson, Joseph R. *Confucian China and Its Modern Fate*. Berkeley: University of California Press, 1958. Sociological study of interaction of Confucian elite with political and cultural forces in Chinese history. Extensive discussion of the Confucian attempts and failure to meet the challenge of modernity.

Lifton, Robert Jay. *Revolutionary Immortality: Mao Tse-tung and the Chinese Cultural Revolution*. New York: Random House, 1968. Very readable interpretation of the Cultural Revolution from a psychological viewpoint.

MacInnis, Donald E., comp. *Religious Policy and Practices in Communist China*. New York: Macmillan, 1972. Collection of documents translated from Chinese and eyewitness accounts of religious life in China under Mao.

Overmeyer, Daniel L. *Folk Buddhist Religion*. Cambridge, Mass.: Harvard University Press, 1976. Valuable study of secret societies in Chinese history.

Saso, Michael R. *Taoism and the Rite of Cosmic Renewal*. Pullman: Washington State University Press, 1972. An anthropological account based on extensive fieldwork of contemporary folk Daoism as practiced in Taiwan. A needed corrective to the tendency to view Daoism as a purely philosophical and individual phenomenon.

Taylor, Rodney Leon. *The Cultivation of Sagehood as a Religious Goal in Neo-Confucianism: A Study of Selected Writings of Kao P'an-lung*. Missoula, Mont.: Scholars Press, 1978. Translations of writings showing Neo-Confucian meditation and other religious practices and attitudes.

Wright, Arthur F. *Buddhism in Chinese History*. New York: Atheneum, 1965. A short, popular account of Chinese Buddhism. Especially valuable in evaluating the impact of Buddhism on Neo-Confucianism and later Chinese culture.

Yang, C. K. *Religion in Chinese Society*. Berkeley: University of California Press, 1967. A historical study of traditional Chinese religious values and their social functions. A good one-volume companion to the Wing-tsit Chan collection.

JAPAN

Primary Sources

Aston, W. G., trans. *Nihongi: Chronicles of Japan from the Earliest Times to A.D. 697*. London: Allen & Unwin, 1956. Originally published in 1896. A continuous narrative constructed out of much of the same mythological material as in the Kojiki but with many variant tales and historical asides toward the end.

Phillipi, Donald L., trans. *Kojiki*. Tokyo: Tokyo University Press, 1968. Because of its extensive explanatory notes, this is the best introduction to Shintō mythology. Its nonstandard transliteration of Japanese names attempts to recover archaic forms.

———., trans. *Norito: A New Translation of the Ancient Japanese Ritual Prayers*. Tokyo: Institute for Japanese Culture and Classics, Kokugakuin University, 1959. If only one primary source can be read, it should be this collection of ritual texts, which contains much mythological material.

Tsunoda, Ryusaka; William Theodore de Bary; and Donald Keene, comps. *Sources of Japanese Tradition* (2 vols.). New York: Columbia University Press, 1958. Contains many useful documents (in vol. 2) relating to the Shintō revival in the Tokugawa period and the imperial restoration and ultranationalism of the modern period.

Secondary Sources

Aston, W. G. *Shintō: The Way of the Gods*. London: Longman, 1905. Old but still unsurpassed study of ritual and ethics based primarily on literary evidence.

Blacker, Carmen. *The Catalpa Bow: A Study of Shamanistic Practices in Japan*. London: Allen & Unwin, 1975. A cogent attempt to reconstruct the form and meaning of ancient shamanism through the study of more recent practices, folklore, and literary and archaeological sources.

Buchanan, Daniel C. "Inari, Its Origin, Development, and Nature," *Transactions of the Asiatic Society of Japan,* 2nd series, no. 12 (1935), 1–191. Dated but valuable study of this Shintō cult.

Earhart, H. Byron. *A Religious Study of the Mount Haguro Sect of Shugendo: An Example of Japanese Mountain Religion*. Tokyo: Sophia University Press, 1970. A detailed account of one of the survivors of the ancient *yamabushi* cults.

Hardacre, Helen. *Shintō and the State*. Princeton, N.J.: Princeton University Press, 1987. The best work concerning the important religion-state issues in Japan in the nineteenth and twentieth centuries.

Herbert, Jean. *Shintō: At the Fountainhead of Japan*. London: Allen & Unwin, 1967. A wealth of information valuable mainly as an encyclopedia of Shintō, marred by an apologetic and sometimes theological stance that tries to defend Shintō from "Westernized scholarship."

Hori, Ichirō. *Folk Religion in Japan: Continuity and Change,* ed. Joseph M. Kitagawa and Alan L. Miller. Chicago: University of Chicago Press, 1968. Essays by a leading Japanese scholar showing the enduring power of folk religion and its usefulness in understanding such phenomena as shamanism, the new religions, mountain religion, and Shintō-Buddhist amalgamation.

Kitagawa, Joseph M. *Religion in Japanese History*. New York: Columbia University Press, 1966. The most complete history of all the Japanese religious groups, showing their development and interactions. Especially valuable for the modern period.

McFarland, H. Neill. *The Rush Hour of the Gods: A Study of the New Religious Movements in Japan*. New York: Macmillan, 1967. Despite the title, a valuable and readable introduction to the new religious phenomenon including non-Shintō forms.

Matsumoto, Shigeru. *Motoori Norinaga, 1730–1801*. Cambridge, Mass.: Harvard University Press, 1970. Detailed study of the life and thought of this important "national scholar."

Muraoka, Tsunetsugu. *Studies in Shintō Thought,* trans. Delmer M. Brown and James T. Araki. Tokyo: Ministry of Education, 1964. Good source for modern trends in Shintō scholarship and theology.

Straelen, Henry van. *The Religion of Divine Wisdom: Japan's Most Powerful Movement*. Kyoto, Japan: Veritas Shōin, 1957. A detailed account of Tenrikyō.

Webb, Herschel. *The Japanese Imperial Institution in the Tokugawa Period*. New York: Columbia University Press, 1968. Important study emphasizing the significance of the emperor's religious dimension for an understanding of his function in modern Japanese history.

Index

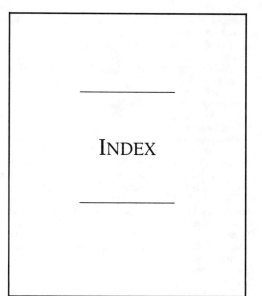